THE PRINCIPLES OF VESTING
IN THE LAW OF SUCCESSION

THE
PRINCIPLES
OF
VESTING
IN THE
LAW OF SUCCESSION

BY

ROBERT CANDLISH HENDERSON, K.C., LL.B.
Professor of Scots Law in the University of Edinburgh

SECOND EDITION

EDINBURGH
W. GREEN & SON LTD.
LAW PUBLISHERS
1938

ISBN 0 414 00832 4

Reprinted
1987
by Martin's of Berwick

PREFACE TO SECOND EDITION

SINCE the publication of the first edition of this book between two and three hundred cases relating to the subjects with which it deals have appeared in the reports. This increase in the volume of decisions has not, however, entailed a corresponding increase in the size of the book ; for, although greater space has been required for the treatment of certain topics, the clarification of points formerly doubtful effected by these decisions has made it possible to abbreviate the discussion of some of the subjects dealt with in other chapters. Thus, while the sections dealing with the law of vesting subject to defeasance run to greater length than was demanded in 1905, the acceptance of Lord Watson's opinion in *Bowman* v. *Bowman* as settling the law in regard to derivative destinations-over has made it unnecessary to retain the detailed examination of the earlier decisions on this point which appeared in the first edition. It is with some hesitation that I have allowed the section of Chapter XVIII. dealing with the rule of *Frog's Creditors* to remain, for the alteration of the law effected by the Trusts Act of 1921 may be thought to render that rule of historical, rather than practical, interest ; but, for the reasons indicated in that section, it seemed better not to omit all reference to a rule which has had so important an influence on the development of the law.

The cases reported down to the end of 1937 are dealt with in the text.

EDINBURGH, *May* 1938.

PREFACE TO FIRST EDITION

THE object of this book is to present a systematic statement of the principles embodied in the numerous decisions on questions of vesting in the law of succession.

Probably in no other department of law is less influence allowed to precedent. A question of vesting is always decided with reference to the character and phraseology of the particular deed submitted for construction ; and it is obvious that in many of the cases which come before the Courts little aid can be derived from previous authorities. But there are at least two purposes served by the existing body of decisions. In some are to be found rules of construction, the fruit of judicial reasoning applied to certain forms of disposition ; and the conveyancer making use of those forms is entitled to assume that they will be construed in accordance with those settled rules. In other cases, again, it was the task of the Court to discover the testator's intention from the inadequate or ambiguous language of his will. Some of these are merely examples of ingenious interpretation, and have no other value. But a large number are useful as revealing the obscurities and imperfections of modes of expression which, on the surface, might seem to be lucid and complete, and as directing attention to some of the contingencies which should be provided for in the framing of testamentary deeds.

I have endeavoured to treat the subject in a practical manner. For this reason, the law of vesting has been considered with reference almost exclusively to trust-dispositions and settlements. As compared with former times, destinations are now seldom employed as a means of testamentary disposition, and are therefore not separately noticed. On the other hand, and for the same reason, some topics in the law of wills, which do not in strictness involve questions of vesting, have been included. The limits of the law of vesting are not very precisely marked ; and these matters were thought to lie near enough the border to justify their inclusion.

The subject has, as every Scots lawyer knows, been treated by Lord M'Laren in his book on " Wills and Succession." In that treatise, however, the doctrine is considered as part of a general review of the law of wills and trusts and within the limits prescribed by that scheme ; and therefore it seemed possible to examine this branch of the law by itself and at more detail without incurring the reproach of having undertaken a subject which had already received final treatment.

To Mr Macmillan and Mr MacRobert, Advocates, and Mr John Smart, Writer to the Signet, who read the proof-sheets, I am indebted for much aid in the way of criticism and suggestion, and it is with pleasure that I avail myself of this opportunity of expressing my gratitude for their assistance.

EDINBURGH, *July* 1905.

TABLE OF CONTENTS

CHAPTER I.

CHAPTER II.

GENERAL RULES.

CHAPTER III.

PERSONAL CONDITIONS—MAJORITY OR MARRIAGE.

CHAPTER IV.

SURVIVORSHIP CLAUSES AND DESTINATIONS-OVER.

CHAPTER V.

CLAUSES OF DEVOLUTION (TO ISSUE, WHOM FAILING SURVIVORS).

CHAPTER VI.

VESTING SUBJECT TO DEFEASANCE.

CHAPTER VII.

ACCRETION 157

CHAPTER VIII.

GIFTS TO PERSONS DESIGNED BY A TERM OF RELATIONSHIP (CHILDREN, ETC.)— GIFTS TO HEIRS.

CHAPTER IX.

GIFTS SUBJECT TO POWERS OF APPOINTMENT.

CHAPTER X.

VESTING AS DEPENDENT ON THE ACTION OF TRUSTEES.

CHAPTER XI.

THE VESTING OF LEGACIES PAYABLE ON THE OCCURRENCE OF A DOUBLE CONTINGENCY

CHAPTER XII.

THE VESTING OF PROVISIONS IN MARRIAGE CONTRACTS AND BONDS OF PROVISION

CHAPTER XIII.

DECLARATIONS AS TO VESTING

CHAPTER XIV.

ACCELERATION OF VESTING OR PAYMENT.

CHAPTER XV.

Repugnant and Ineffectual Conditions.

CHAPTER XVI.

Vesting in the Residuary Legatee or Heir ab intestato

CHAPTER XVII.

The conditio si institutus sine liberis decesserit

CHAPTER XVIII.

The Interest of the Beneficiary : Whether a Liferent or a Fee is Given.

TABLE OF CASES

THE PRINCIPLES OF VESTING

CHAPTER I.

INTRODUCTION.

In an inquiry into the doctrine of vesting, it is material, at the outset, to distinguish the various senses in which the word " vest " may be used. In popular language, the word is employed somewhat loosely as signifying the placing of a person in possession of a subject, or the granting of an authority or privilege. But in the law relating to wills the term has a distinct, though highly technical and refined, meaning. The various definitions which have been given of this technical meaning are, however, of little practical value, and we may best arrive at a comprehension of the legal significance of the term by attending, in the first instance, to the characteristic properties of a vested right.

The meaning of the word " vest."

We may begin by contrasting a vested legacy with a non-vested legacy. Prior to the time at which a legacy vests, the legatee has merely a *spes successionis*, or chance of acquiring a right in the subject ; the legacy is not his property, and he cannot effectually assign or dispose of the subject unless the legacy is, or comes to be, vested in him.[1] On the other hand, when the legacy vests it becomes the property of the legatee, and is at his disposition and will pass to his representatives. In *Haldane's Trs.* v. *Murphy*,[2] Lord Young remarked : " It is perhaps unfortunate that the word ' vest,' and its conjugates, of which we make

The distinction between vested and non-vested legacies.

---

[1] *Trappes* v. *Meredith* (1871), 10 M. 38 ; *Kirkland* v. *Kirkland's Trs.* (1886), 13 R. 798 ; *Reid* v. *Morrison* (1893), 20 R. 510.

[2] (1881), 9 R. 269. The decision in this case was adversely criticised in *Gregory's Trs.* v. *Alison* (1889), 16 R. (H. L.) 10.

such frequent use, are so figurative. But as we use them they have a very real and practical meaning, insomuch that to predicate vesting is to predicate a right of property in the thing vested transmissible by, or through, and in right of the person in whom it is vested. A question of vesting is indeed always a question of capacity to transmit, and, so far as I know, never had or can have any other practical significance." [1]

The technical meaning of " vesting " is vesting in point of interest.

The *jus disponendi*, or power of transmitting the subject, to which attention is directed in this passage, is the peculiar badge of a right of property. [2] Whatever other rights a party may have in a subject, if this element be awanting, he cannot be said to be the absolute proprietor of that subject ; and, on the other hand, if he have the unfettered power of disposal, he has the right of property therein. Now, if a testator directs that a legacy shall be paid to the legatee on his (the testator's) death, a question of vesting can hardly arise, for the legatee acquires at that time all the rights that the testator himself had in the subject. He has the *jus disponendi* and he has the actual possession of the subject ; that is to say, the full right of property. Clearly, then, in this case the legacy vests *a morte testatoris*. But the right of disposal and the right of possession may be, and often are, severed. Thus a legacy may be given subject to a liferent, or with a provision that it shall be payable at a time subsequent to the testator's death. In such cases the legatee does not acquire, at the testator's death, the possession of the subject, but he may have the *jus disponendi* ; and if he have,

---

[1] Cf. Lord Mackenzie's observation in his opinion in *Kilgour* v. *Kilgour* (1845), 7 D. 451 : " The fair meaning of vesting is nothing more than that the subject goes to a man's heirs and assignees " ; and Lord Fullerton's opinion in that case and in *Newton* v. *Thomson* (1849), 11 D. 452, where he speaks of " any vesting, or, in less technical language, any power of disposal." Cf. also Lord Colonsay's opinion in *Carleton* v. *Thompson* (1867), 5 M. (H. L.) 151 ; *Bell* v. *Cheape* (1845), 7 D. 614 ; L. J.-C. Hope's opinion in *Wright* v. *Fraser*

(1843), 6 D. 78 ; and Lord Rutherfurd Clark's opinion in *Grant's Trs.* v. *Ritchie's Exr.* (1886), 13 R. 646, at 652 ; Dig. 36. 2. 5.

[2] " It is the essence of a fee to have power to dispone "—Dirleton's Doubts *voce* " Fee "; Ersk. Inst. II. 2. 1, says, property " is the right of using and disposing of a subject as our own except in so far as we are restrained by law or paction " ; see also *Anstruther* v. *Anstruther* (1836), 14 S. 272, *per* the Consulted Judges at 286.

then the legacy is vested and will pass to his representatives in the event of his death before the time at which the legacy becomes payable. The circumstance that possession is postponed is, in itself, quite immaterial in questions of vesting, for " postponed payment is as consistent with vesting as with not vesting." [1] In its legal acceptation, the word " vest " means vesting in point of interest or title and not in point of possession.[2]

Until a comparatively recent date, it was a general proposition in the law of Scotland, as in the civil law, that an unconditional legacy vested *a morte testatoris*, while a conditional legacy did not vest during the pendency of the condition.[3] For example, if a gift be made simply to A., A. acquires at the testator's death the power of disposing of the subject ; but if the testator makes a gift to A. in the event of his surviving a given time, or attaining majority, it is clear that until A. survive that time or reach majority, he is not the object of the testator's bounty, for the testator has intended that the subject shall be at A.'s disposition only in the event of his fulfilling the condition annexed to the gift. During his minority or prior to the arrival of the time mentioned, A. has merely a *spes successionis* ; but, if he is alive at the time specified or attains majority, the legacy is at once vested.

Vesting depends on whether the gift is or is not conditional.

A certain qualification of the statement that conditions attached to a gift prevent vesting is required, however, in view of the later development of the doctrine of Vesting subject to Defeasance,—a doctrine which may best be explained by means of an example.

Vesting subject to defeasance.

[1] Lord Fullerton in *Clark's Exrs.* v. *Paterson* (1851), 14 D. 141. Cf. also Lord Trayner's opinion in *Wood* v. *Neill's Trs.* (1896), 24 R. 105. In the civil law the distinction between vesting and payment is represented in the terms *dies cedit* and *dies venit*—Dig. 50. 16. 213.

[2] Cf. *Richardson* v. *Power* (1865), 19 C. B., N. S. 780. *In re Coppard* (1887), 35 Ch. D. 350.

[3] Cf. Lord Young's opinion in *Cumming's Trs.* v. *White* (1893), 20 R. 454. In *Forbes* v. *Luckie* (1838),

13 Fac. 324, Lord Corehouse remarked that he knew of no case of vesting with subsequent divestiture. In *Bell* v. *Cheape* (1845), 7 D. 614, it was argued that there was qualified vesting, but apparently the argument was not pressed. Cf. also *Miller* v. *Miller* (1833), 7 W. & S. 1 ; Stair, 3. 8. 22 ; Erskine, 3. 9. 9 : Bell's Principles, § 1883. The civil law apparently treated all conditions as suspensive of vesting—Dig. 35. 1. 41 ; 44. 7. 42.

Let it be supposed that a legacy is given to A. in liferent, and to his issue, and if he have no issue, to B., in fee. In this case two points are, and have always been, clear : first, that if A. have issue, B. takes no benefit, because he is excluded by the prior gift ; and, secondly, that if A. dies without issue, survived by B., the legacy will vest in B. But a third eventuality may occur. A. may die childless, predeceased by B. These were substantially the circumstances of *Taylor* v. *Gilbert's Trs.*,[1] a case which came before the Court of Session and House of Lords in 1878. In this case the Court of Session, applying the general rule that conditional legacies do not vest *pendente conditione*, held that, as B. had predeceased the time at which it could be ascertained whether the gift to him would take effect (A.'s death), the legacy had lapsed. But the House of Lords reversed this decision, and decided that the legacy had vested in B. subject to defeasance or divestiture in the event of A. having issue.

It is clear, therefore, that certain conditions are not incompatible with vesting, and we must seek for the characteristics which differentiate such conditions from those others which prevent vesting. The distinction rests upon a classification of conditions very familiar in other departments of the law, namely, the classification of conditions as suspensive [2] or resolutive.[3] A suspensive condition prevents vesting *pendente conditione* ; whereas a resolutive condition admits of vesting, but renders the right or interest so vested liable to withdrawal in the event of the condition happening.

Personal conditions suspend vesting ; collateral conditions permit vesting subject to defeasance.

Whether any given condition is resolutive or suspensive is to be determined in accordance with what appears to have been the testator's intention in the matter,[4] and there is no technical form of expression distinctive of either kind of

---

[1] 5 R. (H. L.) 217. For earlier cases of vesting subject to defeasance, cf. Ld. Pres. Inglis's dissenting opinion in *Haldane's Trs.* v. *Murphy* (1881), 9 R. 269, where he says that such vesting is no anomaly, and cites the cases of *Stewart* v. *Nicolson* (1859), 22 D. 72 ; *Robertson* v. *Robertson* (1869), 7 M. 1114 (*post*, p. 216) ; and *Balderston* v. *Fulton* (1856), 19 D.

293 (*post*, p. 241). The distinction between resolutive and suspensive conditions was recognised also in class-gifts—*Douglas* v. *Douglas* (1864), 2 M. 1008 (*post*, p. 215) ; and see Chapter VII.

[2] *i.e.* Conditions precedent.

[3] *i.e.* Conditions subsequent.

[4] *Per* Lord Shand in *Haldane's Trs.* v. *Murphy, supra.*

condition. It may be stated, however, as a general rule, that personal conditions suspend vesting, while collateral or extrinsic conditions are merely resolutive.[1] Thus, to recur to an example already given, where the legatee's right is dependent on his survivance of a time or event, or his attainment of majority, vesting is clearly suspended. These conditions enter into the description of the beneficiary, and define the party whom the testator intends to favour. They are personal, for if they happen at all they must happen in the lifetime of the legatee. But, on the other hand, the condition attached to the gift to B. in *Taylor* v. *Gilbert's Trs.* was not personal, for it might happen as well after, as before, B.'s death. At the testator's death,[2] B. stood qualified to take ; and if circumstances remained unchanged, he would take the benefit of the bequest. The possibility of A.'s having issue was a mere contingency ; and although it could not be ascertained before A.'s death on whom the absolute interest would devolve, it became clear whenever A. died without issue that B. had acquired a vested interest at the testator's death, and it was of no moment that he had predeceased A.

The result of the doctrine of vesting subject to defeasance is, then, that certain contingent interests are transmissible by or through the party having such an interest. So long as it remains doubtful whether the contingency will or will not occur, the vesting of the defeasible interest is strictly *sub modo*, and the party in right thereof (B.) cannot in any way injure or affect the right of those called in the event of the contingency happening ; that is, in the case supposed, A.'s issue.[3] If the event happen, B.'s right is carried away and is practically as if it had never vested ; but if the event

---

[1] See L. J.-C. Moncreiff (*dub.*) in *Taylor* v. *Gilbert's Trs.* (1877), 5 R. 49 ; rev. (1878), 5 R. (H. L.) 217. See also *Hickling's Trs.* v. *Garland's Trs.* (1898), 1 F. (H. L.) 7 ; and Lord Young's opinion in *Cumming's Trs.* v. *White* (1893), 20 R. 454. " A condition personal to the legatee suspends vesting. A condition which is not personal, which depends upon the existence of someone yet unborn, is *prima facie* resolutive."—*per* Lord Mackenzie in *Bannatyne's Trs.* v. *Watson's Trs.*, 1914 S. C. 693 at 702 ; and see Lord Skerrington's opinion in *Yule's Trs.* v. *Deans*, 1919 S. C. 570.

[2] As a matter of fact, there were personal conditions which prevented immediate vesting ; but these are immaterial in the general statement of the doctrine. See *post*, p. 130.

[3] *Chambers' Trs.* v. *Smiths* (1878), 5 R. (H. L.) 151.

does not happen, B. is treated as having taken *ab initio* a complete and vested interest.

The conclusion to which these considerations lead is, that a legacy vests when the legatee acquires a right to the subject of the legacy, which is either unconditional or is not qualified by a suspensive condition.[1]

When the legacy is given unconditionally, the vesting is absolute ; when it is qualified by a resolutive condition, the vesting is subject to defeasance.

Such being the meaning of the word " vest " when used in regard to testamentary bequests, the influence and effect upon vesting of certain elements which enter into the composition of all bequests will be readily appreciated.

The terms of the bequest.

It follows, from what has already been said, that the first point to be considered in a question of vesting is the form of the gift :—whether the legacy is expressed in conditional or unconditional terms. A large proportion of the cases in this branch of the law are concerned with the construction to be put upon survivorship clauses and destinations-over. Now, the importance of such ulterior destinations in questions of vesting lies in the fact that they imply the condition that the legatee, to whom the gift is in the first instance given, must, in order to take, be alive at a certain time. And, as it is well settled that that time is *primâ facie* the time of payment, the vesting of legacies to which destinations-over or survivorship clauses are annexed, is suspended when the payment of the legacy is postponed to a period subsequent to the testator's death.[2] Such ulterior destinations are indeed the usual indications of an intention on the part of the testator to suspend vesting. It is important to observe,

Distinction between conditions annexed to the bequest and conditions annexed to directions as to payment.

however, that the effect upon vesting of these and other conditions will depend upon whether they qualify the main purpose of giving, or are designed merely to regulate the time or mode of payment or enjoyment. If the condition be attached to the substance of the bequest, vesting is dependent on the operation of that condition ; but if the

---

[1] " To say that a legacy vests is a short way of stating that the legacy is, or has become, free from any suspensive condition." — *per* Lord Skerrington in *Wylie's Trs.* v. *Bruce,* 1919 S. C. 211 at 239.

[2] See Chapter IV., *post.*

condition affect the payment only of the gift, then, owing to the distinction, already noticed, between the vesting of a gift and its coming into the legatee's possession, the legacy may vest while the condition remains unfulfilled.[1]

Further, gifts which are *ex figura verborum* unconditional are sometimes treated as being in reality conditional. Thus if a legacy be given on the arrival of a specified time or on the occurrence of an event, the nature of the time or event enters into the question of vesting. The civil law drew a distinction between a *dies certus* and a *dies incertus*.[2] A *dies certus* is a time which must inevitably arrive, although it may be uncertain *when* it will arrive. A gift dependent upon a *dies certus* is unconditional, and vests *a morte testatoris*. On the other hand, a *dies incertus* is a time as to which it is uncertain not only when it will arrive but if it will ever arrive at all ; and a gift which is to take effect at a *dies incertus* does not vest until its arrival, according to the maxim, *Dies incertus in testamento conditionem facit*.[3] The distinction between these two kinds of events—events which *must* occur and events which *may* occur—is well illustrated in *Mackintosh* v. *Wood*,[4] where a testatrix, by her will, directed her trustees to pay her son a sum of money on her daughter's death or marriage, and, by a codicil, directed them to pay to him a further sum on her daughter's marriage. The legacy given in the will was held to vest *a morte testatoris* seeing that it was given, at all events, upon the daughter's death (a *dies certus*) ; but the legacy given in the codicil, being dependent on a *dies incertus*, was held to have lapsed, as the son died before the daughter's marriage.

Distinction between a dies certus and a dies incertus.

[1] See *Miller* v. *Finlay's Trs.* (1875), 2 R. (H. L.) 1 ; *post*, p. 58 ; and the cases as to gifts on majority in Chapter III.

[2] Dig. 36. 2. 21 ; 35. 1. 75. and 79.

[3] The maxim *Dies incertus pro conditione habetur* is cited in 1677 in the case of *Belshes* v. *Belshes*, M. 6,327. See also Stair, i. 3. 7. and 8 ; but cf. Lord Skerrington's opinion in *Wylie's Trs.* v. *Bruce*, 1919 S. C. 211 at 240, where, with reference to the Civil Law, his Lordship says : " I venture to think . . . that the texts and the commentaries thereon by the Civilians show that a legacy payable on the death of a person other than the legatee himself was regarded as a conditional one, seeing that the legatee might not be alive when the time for payment arrived," and cites Digest 35. 1. 2 ; 35. 1. 79 ; 31. 12. 1 ; and 36. 2. 4.

[4] (1872), 10 M. 933.

Uncertainty
as to the
amount of
the subject
is not
inconsistent
with vesting.

As to the subject-matter of the gift, it is well settled that an uncertainty as to the amount or value thereof does not affect the vesting of the gift.[1] Thus a residuary bequest vests *a morte testatoris* although the amount of the residue is liable to variation, according to whether the prior legacies lapse or take effect ;[2] and an even more striking example is afforded by class-gifts. If a legacy be given to a person alive at the testator's death in liferent and to his (the liferenter's) children in fee, the gift of the fee is not prevented from vesting by the circumstance that the number of the fiars cannot be fixed until the death of the parent, and the children alive at the testator's death will acquire at once a vested interest in the whole subject, the share of each being liable to be diminished or divested to the extent necessary to give equal shares to any children who may subsequently be born.[3]

The character of the subject appears to exercise comparatively little influence on questions of vesting. In *Hay's Trs.* v. *Hay*,[4] Lord M'Laren observed : "Amongst the elements which influence the decision of a case of vesting, the quality of the estate, as being heritable or moveable, is probably the least important. In the numerous cases of trust conveyance of mixed estate, heritable and moveable, it has been generally assumed that the same principles of construction are applicable to the bequests."

It is in regard to the construction of trust conveyances that questions of vesting arise most commonly in modern practice. Where a testator disposes of his estate by a direct *mortis causa* disposition, and without the creation of a continuing trust, the question of vesting is liable to be affected by the rule of law which prevents the fee of a subject remaining *in pendente*. With regard to heritable destinations it has been laid down that no decision on the vesting of a beneficiary interest under a trust can ever be an authority

---

[1] Lord Fullerton and Lord Jeffrey in *Kilgour* v. *Kilgour* (1845), 7 D. 451.

[2] See Chapter XVI., *post*. So also a gift may vest though it is subject to a power of appointment—see Chapter IX., *post*.

[3] See Chapter VIII., *post*.

[4] (1890), 17 R. 961. There is, however, this distinction, that in heritable property the presumption is for substitution in moveable property for conditional institution. See *post*, p. 54.

:as to the construction of these, as the principles of construction applicable to these different forms of gift are altogether diverse.[1] It is to the consideration of the doctrines of vesting in their application to trust conveyances that the following chapters are mainly devoted.

[1] Cf. Lord M'Laren in *Turner* v. *Gaw* (1894), 21 R. 563.

CHAPTER II.

GENERAL RULES.

SECTION I.

The testator's intention must prevail.

General Rules observed in the Interpretation of Wills.— The leading principle which governs all questions of vesting is that the will must be interpreted in accordance with what appears to have been the testator's intention. In *Carleton* v. *Thomson*,[1] Lord Colonsay said : " When the question arises under a *mortis causa* settlement, whether the benefit given is, or has become, a vested right, the intentions of the testator, in so far as they can be discovered or reasonably inferred from the deed taken as a whole, and from the circumstances, legitimately collected, under which the deed was made, should have effect given to them. It is a *quæstio voluntatis*. That is the cardinal rule and guide." And in an earlier case [2] Lord Justice-Clerk Hope had pointed out that " No rule of interpretation can ever safely be adopted which is not to bend to satisfactory expressions or proof of the testator's intentions on the face of the particular deed which is to be construed."

[1] (1867), 5 M. (H. L.) 151 ; L. R. 1 H. L. Sc. 232.

[2] *Robertson* v. *Richardson* (1843), 5 D. 1117. Cf. Halsbury, L. C., to the same effect in *Bowman* v. *Bowman* (1899), 1 F. (H. L.) 69 ; and L. J.-C. Boyle in *Provan* v. *Provan* (1840), 2 D. 298.

It follows, therefore, from this cardinal rule, that a The testator's intention to be ascertained from the terms of the will. question of vesting is to be determined mainly on a consideration of the terms used by the testator in his deed. The whole provisions of the deed must be taken into account ; and, although the testator may have employed a form of gift which in itself would, according to the canons of vesting, lead to a certain determination of the question of vesting, a different effect may be attributed to the bequest, if this is called for by the indications of intention appearing in, or to be collected from, the context.[1] But the testator's intention is to be gathered from the language of the deed, and the Court will not proceed upon mere conjectures as to that intention. It is a question, in other words, not of what the testator may be supposed to have intended, but of the meaning of that which he has actually written.[2]

Where the will shows clearly what the testator's intention was in regard to vesting, the aid of rules is not required, for the testator has furnished the means of deciding the question. But in the cases which come before the Courts there are comparatively few in which the testator has expressed with absolute clearness his wishes as to vesting,

---

[1] *Bowman* v. *Bowman* (1899), 1 F. (H. L.) 69 ; *Thompson's Trs.* v. *Jamieson* (1900), 2 F. 470. But cf. Lord Brougham's opinion in *Scott* v. *Scott* (1850), 7 Bell's App. 143. In *Turnbull's Trs.* v. *Lord Advocate*, 1918 S. C. (H. L.) 88, it was said that the punctuation of the deed might be taken into account as an aid to its construction.

[2] " It is very often said that the intention of the testator is to be the guide ; but that expression is capable of being misunderstood, and may lead to a speculation as to what the testator may be supposed to have intended to write, whereas the only and proper inquiry is, what is the meaning of that which he has actually written ? " *Per* Lord Wensleydale in *Roddy* v. *Fitzgerald* (1858), 6 H. L. (Clark) 823 at 876. Cf. Lord Moncrieff in *Blair* (1849), 12 D. 97 ; Lord Watson in

Scale v. *Rawlins*, [1892] A. C. 342 ; *Cal. Rly. Co.* v. *N.B. Rly. Co.* (1881), 8 R. (H. L.) 23 ; Lord Wensleydale in *Magistrates of Dundee* v. *Morris* (1858), 3 Macq. 134 ; Ld. Pres. Inglis and Lord Shand in *Royal Infirmary of Edinburgh* v. *Muir's Trs.* (1881), 9 R. 352 ; Lord Jeffrey in *Gordon* v. *Hogg* (1843), 5 D. 840 ; Lord Low in *Bleakley's Trs.* v. *Johnston*, 1907 S. C. 593 ; James, L. J., in *Wilson* v. *O'Leary* (1872), L. R. 7 Ch. 448 ; and Lord Halsbury, L. C., in *Higgins* v. *Dawson* [1902] A. C. 1, at 6. " There are cases where the words used are such that the Court is bound to give an interpretation which in its heart it is perfectly certain is not what the testator would have wished "—*Young's Trs.* v. *Young*, 1927 S. C. (H. L.) 6, *per* Viscount Dunedin, at 9.

and where there is dubiety on the point the general rules are of assistance in the construction of the deed. These rules are not arbitrary or capricious : they are the product of judicial reasoning applied to certain words or forms of bequest ; and, the Courts having come to a conclusion as to the meaning and effect, in the general case, of these forms or words, it is reasonable that that meaning and effect should be attributed to them in the absence of evidence that the testator has used them in a special sense. " In one sense it is true that no decision in this branch of the law can ever be authority for another ; for, as different instruments are being construed, and the sole question is what is the true meaning of each, the decision of the proper construction of the will of A. can never, as authority, rule the construction of the will of B. But none the less the *dicta* of Judges in giving the reasons for holding a certain construction of the will of A. to be the true one may, and often do, act as guide-posts to direct the inquirer for what *indicia* he should look in construing the will of B., and in this sense it is convenient, if not strictly accurate, to speak of the principle of so-and-so as laid down in a case or a series of cases." [1] And a testator employing, without qualification or paraphrase, words or forms of settled meaning in law, must be presumed to have intended that they should have that meaning in his will.[2]

The consideration of the general principles as to the construction of deeds does not fall within the scope of this book, but the following rules of interpretation which have been referred to, or made use of, in questions of vesting may be noticed :—

Words are to be interpreted in their natural sense. (1) In the first place, " the primary duty of a Court of construction, in the interpretation of wills, is to give to each word employed, if it can with propriety receive it, the natural ordinary meaning which it has in the vocabulary of ordinary life, and not to give to words employed in the vocabulary of ordinary life an artificial, secondary, and

---

[1] *Tweeddale's Trs.* v. *Tweeddale* (1905), 8 F. 264, *per* the Lord President (Dunedin), at 273. See also *Ralston* v. *Ralston* (1842), 4 D. 1496, *per* L. J.-C. Hope at 1498 ; and cf. Lord Halsbury's speech in *Bowman* v. *Bowman* (1899), 1 F. (H. L.) 69.

[2] See the cases in notes 4 and 5, *infra*.

technical meaning." [1]   But the will is, as has been said,[2] the dictionary from which the meaning of the terms used is to be ascertained ; and if it appear from the context or from the whole provisions of the deed that the testator has used words in a special sense, that sense will be given to them.[3] Technical terms or forms of gift, which have a fixed legal import, are to be interpreted *primâ facie* in their technical or legal sense ; [4] but the context may displace this meaning, and this would appear to be especially the case where the words are employed in a will made by one who is not a lawyer.[5]

(2) Words are not to be altered or transposed if they are capable, as they stand, of a sensible interpretation.[6] But the rule must be understood with this limitation, that if the whole provisions of the deed make it manifest that a strict adherence to the words would defeat the testator's intention, the words may be sacrificed in order to give effect to that intention.[7] And words obviously miswritten may be corrected.[8]

Words not to be altered.

[1] *Per* Lord Westbury in *Young* v. *Robertson* (1862), 4 Macq. 314 ; Lord Cranworth in *Diggens* v. *Gordon* (1867), 5 M. (H. L.) 75 ; and Lord Chelmsford in *Dickson* v. *Somerville's Trs.* (1867), 5 M. (H. L.) 69 ; Lord Gifford in *Richardson* v. *Stewarts* (1824), 2 Shaw's Apps. 149 ; *O'Reilly* v. *Baroness Sempill* (1855), 2 Macq. 288 ; Lord Halsbury in *Leader* v. *Duffy* (1888), 13 App. Cas. 294. See also Lord Wensleydale's remarks quoted in *Caledonian Rly. Co.* v. *North British Rly. Co.* (1881), 8 R. (H. L.) 23.

[2] Lord Cairns in *Hill* v. *Crook* (1873), L. R. 6 H. L. 265.

[3] *In re Jodrell* (1890), 44 Ch. D. 590 ; affd. *sub nom. Seale-Hayne* v. *Jodrell,* [1891] A. C. 304.

[4] Lord Fitzgerald in *Gordon* v. *Gordon's Trs.* (1882), 9 R. (H. L.) 101 ; *Diggens* v. *Gordon, supra* ; *Ralston* v. *Ferguson* (1860), 22 D. 1442 ; affd. 4 Macq. 397 ; and cases in note 1, *supra.*

[5] Lord Watson, in *Hamilton* v.

Ritchie (1894), 21 R. (H. L.) 35, observed : " I do not say that a testator who writes his own will, and is not a lawyer, is in all cases to be held to have rightly apprehended the meaning of technical words which he may have used on the occasion of his making his will ; but I think it is plain that a testator who uses words which have an intelligible conventional meaning, is not to be held as having used the words with any other meaning, unless the context of the instrument shows that he intended to do so."

[6] Lord Eldon in *Roxburghe Case* (1809), 6 W. & S. App. p. 52, and *Chambers* v. *Brailsford* (1816), 19 Ves. 652.

[7] Knight Bruce, L. J., in *Key* v. *Key* (1853), 4 De G. M. & G. 73 ; *In re Thomson's Trusts* (1870), L. R. 11 Eq. 146 ; *Surtees* v. *Hopkinson* (1867), L. R. 4 Eq. 98 ; *Sweeting* v. *Prideaux* (1876), 2 Ch. D. 413.

[8] *Grant* v. *Dyer* (1813), 2 Dow 73 ; *Bothwells* v. *Earl of Home* (1747),

Again, words are not to be added to the will.[1] It is an apparent, rather than a real, exception to this rule, that the Court may insert words which have been inadvertently omitted. If the will shows that the testator must necessarily have intended that an interest should be given, but there are no words directly giving that interest, the Court may supply the defect.[2] Thus, where a will provided the liferent of a subject to A., and, in the event of his death without leaving lawful issue, to others in fee, it was held that a child surviving A. was entitled to the subject under the implication contained in the form . of the gift-over, although there were no words of direct bequest.[3]

Effect to be
given to all
the words
of a will.

(3) A testator is not to be presumed to have used words superfluously, and therefore a construction which allows to all the words used some effect (whether in the circumstances which occur, or in others which might occur) is, in the first instance, to be preferred to a construction which renders any word meaningless or ineffectual. " We hold it to be a fundamental canon of construction, that, if possible, effect should be given to all the words of the testator. To disregard any of his expressions, when effect can be given to them, is to take a liberty which seems beyond the province and the powers of a Court of law. And the liberty is all the greater the plainer and more stringent the words so ignored are in themselves." [4]

M. 2989 ; *Campbell* v. *Campbell* (1757), M. 2991 (" or " construed " and ")); *Clouston's Trs.* v. *Bulloch* (1889), 16 R. 937 ; *Reid's Trs.* v. *Bucher*, 1929 S. C. 615 ; *In re Dayrell* [1904], 2 Ch. 496.

[1] See Lord Halsbury's opinion in *Muirhead* v. *Muirhead* (1890), 17 R. (H. L.) 45 ; *Paterson* v. *Paterson*, 1935 S. C. (H. L.) 7 ; Kindersley, V. C., in *Lanphier* v. *Buck* (1865), 34 L. J. (Ch.) 650. Contrast *Crawford's Trs.* v. *Fleck*, 1910 S. C. 998, with *Scott's Trs.* v. *Bruce*, 1912 S. C. 105.

[2] *Towns* v. *Wentworth* (1858), 11 Moore P. C. 526 ; *Law's Trs.* v. *Gray*, 1921 S. C. 455, *per* Lord Mackenzie, at 460.

[3] *Douglas* v. *Douglas* (1843), 6 D.

318. Cf. also *Campbell* v. *Campbell* (1852), 15 D. 173 ; *Grant* v. *Grant* (1851), 13 D. 805 ; *Flett's Trs.* v. *Elphinston* (1900), 38 S. L. R. 564 ; *Mearns* v. *Mearns* (1775), M. 13050 ; *Henderson's Trs.* v. *Henderson* (1876), 3 R. 320 ; *Dunlop* v. *M'Crae* (1884), 11 R. 1104 ; *Sword's Trs.* v. *Main* (1902), 4 F. 1005 ; *Spears's Trs.* v. *Spears* (1873), 11 M. 731 ; *Burgh Smeaton* v. *Burgh Smeaton's J. F.* 1907 S. C. 1009 ; *Gibson* v. *Gibson's Trs.* (1893), 1 S. L. T. 61 (Lord Stormonth-Darling).

[4] *Per* the consulted judges in *Boyle* v. *Earl of Glasgow's Trs.* (1858), 20 D. 925, at 941. *Dickson* v. *Somerville's Trs.* (1867), 5 M. (H. L.), 69 ; Lord Low in *Rutherford's Trs.* v.

(4) So far as possible, all the clauses of the deed will be The whole deed to be considered. reconciled ; but if two parts of the will are irreconcilably opposed, that part of the will which occurs last will be preferred.[1] Subordinate clauses are, however, not to be construed in a sense repugnant to the substantive words of gift.[2] Accordingly, while expressions of the testator's motive or wishes contained in the recital or introductory clause may be referred to as aids in the construction of words of bequest which are of doubtful import,[3] they are not permitted to control clear words of gift in the leading part of the deed.[4] And a gift in unambiguous terms is not to be defeated or reduced by subsequent ambiguous expressions.[5] " Where in testamentary writings a provision is once regularly created, it shall not be held to be taken away except by clear words importing or inferring a revocation." [6]

Further, where a deed provides for various contingencies, and the terms of the deed having reference to the con-

Dickie, 1907 S. C. 1280. But this rule must not be pressed too far. In *In re Boden* [1907], 1 Ch. 132 at 143, Moulton, L. J. (afterwards Lord Moulton) observed : " There is no presumption that each word used should change the meaning of the sentence. A word may be inserted for the sake of emphasis or for greater clearness, or descriptively, or because it occurs to the writer as suitable to the idea he is expressing, and this without any thought whether it is or is not absolutely necessary to the expression of his meaning. The objection to an interpretation on the ground that it would make a word or phrase surplusage has weight only when the presence of such word or phrase would be unusual or unaccountable if it were not specially inserted for the purpose of altering the meaning of the sentence. The mere fact that you could omit it without change of meaning has in itself no weight. There is no presumption that human beings use the irreducible minimum of words to effect their purpose." See also Lord Selborne, L. C., in *Giles* v. *Melsom* (1873), L. R. 6. H. L. 24, at 33.

[1] *Constantine* v. *Constantine* (1801), 6 Ves. 100. But this rule will be resorted to only when all other means of construing the deed have failed ; and where substantive words of gift and a direction as to payment are inconsistent, the latter will be disregarded—*In re Bywater* (1881), 18 Ch. D. 17.

[2] *Per* Lord Gifford in *Yeats* v. *Paton* (1880), 8 R. 171, and Ld. Pres. Dunedin in *Smith* v. *M'Coll's Trs.*, 1910 S. C. 1121, at 1127. See the remarks in *Stair* v. *Stair's Trs.* (1827), 2 W. & S. 614, at 623 and 624 as to general and special intent, and L. J.-C. Hope's opinion in *Robson* v. *Shirreff* (1853), 15 D. 297.

[3] As in *Alves* v. *Grant* (1874), 1 R. 969.

[4] *Mackenzie* v. *The Duke of Devonshire* (1896), 23 R. (H. L.) 32.

[5] *Yeats* v. *Paton* (1880), 8 R. 171.

[6] *Scott* v. *Sceales* (1865), 3 M. 1130.

tingency which occurs afford a clear and distinct expression of the testator's intention in these circumstances, the effect of those terms is not to be superseded by inference from obscure or ambiguous expressions referring to the other contingencies which might have, but have not, occurred.[1] In the case in which this rule was stated, the deed under consideration (a bond of provision) provided for the disposal of a sum of money in the various contingencies of the husband's predecease of the wife, or of her predecease of him, with or without issue, these various contingencies all being expressed in one clause. The Court, finding in the clause clear words of gift in favour of the wife in the event which happened (the husband's predecease without issue), proceeded on those words, and disregarded the obscurities of the provisions in the clause for the other eventualities.

Conditions not to be imported into gifts by implication.

(5) " Several independent devises, not grammatically connected, or united by the expression of a common purpose, must be construed separately, and without relation to each other ; although it may be conjectured, from similarity of relationship, or other such circumstances, that the testator had the same intention in regard to both. There must be an apparent design to connect them." [2] These are the words of Mr. Jarman ; and, although this rule has not been formulated in any Scots decision, it has been acted on in various cases. The rule prohibits the importing of conditions from one clause or bequest into a separate clause or gift on the ground of mere conjecture that the testator so intended. There is no general presumption against the vesting of different provisions at different times ; [3] and a variety of expression as between two gifts rather points to a variety of intention. Thus, in *Leitch* v. *Leitch's Trs.*,[4] the truster disponed a heritable

---

[1] *Dill* v. *Earl of Haddington* (1841), 2 Rob. 298 ; *Burnett* v. *Burnett* (1854), 16 D. 780.

[2] Jarman on Wills (7th Ed.), p. 2147. Approved by Chitty, J., in *In re Johnston* (1884), 26 Ch. D. 538.

[3] *Corbet's Trs.* v. *Elliott's Trs.* (1906), 8 F. 610, *per* Lord Kyllachy ;

Jacks's Trs. v. *Jacks*, 1913 S. C. 815, *per* Lord Kinnear.

[4] (1829), 3 W. & S. 366. See also *Halbert* v. *Dickson* (1853), 15 D. 609, at 611 and 616 ; *Rattray's Trs.* v. *Rattray* (1868), 6 M. 476 (stated, *post*, p. 60) ; *Grant* v. *Cowe* (1887), 15 R. 81 ; *Cameron* v. *Young* (1873), 45 S. J. 272, *per* Lord Cowan.

property to trustees in trust to hold for his wife in liferent, and on her death or remarriage for behoof of his brother A., in case he should be alive at the death of the truster and the death or remarriage of the widow ; and, failing A. by death before the truster or the remarriage or death of the widow, for behoof of B. ; and, in case of B.'s death before any of these events, for behoof of C., whom failing for other relatives. A., B., and C. all predeceased the widow, C. leaving a disposition of the property. A minority of the judges thought that the truster had intended to annex to all three gifts the same condition, and that it was implied that C. should survive the widow ; but the majority considered that the difference of expression in regard to A. and B. on the one hand, and C. on the other, indicated that C. was not required to survive the widow, and that the words of gift could not be qualified by inference, and, on appeal, this decision was affirmed in the House of Lords.[1]

(6) Where the words of the will are unambiguous, they cannot be departed from merely because they lead to a result that may be deemed capricious, or even harsh and unreasonable ; but if the words are capable of two constructions, of which one leads to such a result while the other gives a reasonable and probable result, the latter will be adopted.[2] As in most cases of vesting, the question is not as to the meaning of the terms actually used by the testator, but as to the legal inference to be drawn therefrom in regard to a matter on which the will is silent, the results of various constructions, whether reasonable or capricious, would appear to be an element which may legitimately be considered.

Words of bequest not to be varied.

(7) Where a testator leaves more than one testamentary writing (*e.g.* a will and a codicil), these are to be read, so far as possible, as forming one deed.[3] A codicil may revoke a will either expressly or by making provisions incompatible

Will and codicil to be construed as one deed.

---

[1] Note that, the subject being heritable, the subsequent provision was merely a substitution and did not suspend vesting. Cf. *Campbell* v. *Campbell* (1880), 7 R. (H. L.) 100.

[2] Jessel, M. R., in *Selby* v. *Whittaker* (1877), 6 Ch. D. 239 ; *Gordon* v. *Gordon* (1871), L. R. 5 H. L. 254, at 284 ; *Hickling's Trs.* v. *Garland's Trs.* (1898), 1 F. (H. L.) 7 ; *Wilson's Trs.* v. *Wilson* (1901), 3 F. 967 ; *Bowman* v. *Bowman* (1899), 1 F. (H. L.) 69.

[3] Lord Fullerton in *Kilgour* v. *Kilgour* (1845), 7 D. 451 ; *Black* v. *Watson* (1841), 3 D. 522.

with the subsistence of those in the will : but in the latter case the will is to be treated as revoked only so far as is necessary for giving effect to the provisions of the codicil.[1] " If the whole (*i.e.* of the codicil) is inconsistent, a revocation may be inferred ; but if there is only a difference in certain of the bequests—if the latter documents only modify the gifts in the previous ones—in such cases you are, if possible, to adhere to the substance of all the documents, and hold the whole to constitute one will capable of subsisting and being executed together." [2]

Presumption in favour of vesting.

(8) There is a presumption in favour of early vesting ; and therefore, " if two constructions are reasonably possible, that which favours immediate vesting is preferable." [3] " The leaning of the law is towards vesting, unless there be something in the deed to exclude that construction." [4] The result of this presumption is to cast the onus on parties maintaining that a bequest is contingent.

In marriage contracts the terms of the deed may confer on the issue of the marriage a *jus crediti* during the subsistence of the marriage,[5] but in so far as the provisions in favour of issue are proper rights of succession, the presumption is that they vest at the dissolution of the marriage.[6] The terms of the contract may, however, postpone vesting

---

[1] Ld. Pres. Inglis in *Ogilvie's Trs.* (1870), 8 M. 427 ; *Low's Exrs.* v. *Macdonald* (1873), 11 M. 744 ; *Wright's Trs.* v. *Wright* (1889), 16 R. 677 ; *Tweeddale's Trs.* v. *Tweeddale* (1905), 8 F. 264, *per* the Lord President (Dunedin), at 273. But two universal settlements cannot stand together— *Dick's Trs.* v. *Dick*, 1907 S. C. 953, at 960 ; *Rutherford's Trs.* v. *Dickie*, 1907 S. C. 1280.

[2] Lord Truro in *Stoddart* v. *Grant* (1852), 1 Macq. 163 ; *Gordon's Exr.* v. *Macqueen*, 1907 S. C. 373 ; and *Mitchell's Administratrix* v. *Edinburgh Royal Infirmary*, 1928 S. C. 47.

[3] L. J.-C. Macdonald in *Webster's Trs.* v. *Neill* (1900), 2 F. 695. For a criticism of this presumption as a " prejudice " which in many cases tends to defeat the testator's intention, see Lord Sands's opinion in *Wylie's*

Trs. v. *Bruce*, 1919 S. C. 211, at 230.

[4] Lord Colonsay in *Carleton* v. *Thomson* (1867), 5 M. (H. L.) 151 ; Ld. Pres. Inglis in *Jamieson* v. *Allardice* (1872), 10 M. 755 ; Lord Blackburn in *Taylor* v. *Gilbert's Trs.* (1881), 5 R. (H. L.) 217 ; 3 App. Cas. 1287 ; *Finlay's Trs.* v. *Finlay* (1886), 13 R. 1052.

[5] *Walkinshaw* v. *Walkinshaw* (1872), 10 M. 763 ; *Beattie's Tr.* v. *Cooper's Trs.* (1862), 24 D. 519 ; *Booth's Tr.* v. *Booth* (1898), 25 R. 803.

[6] *Grant's Trs.* v. *Anderson's Trs.* (1866), 4 M. 336 ; Lord Deas in *Romanes* v. *Riddell* (1865), 3 M. 348 ; *Wardlaw's Trs.* v. *Wardlaw* (1880), 7 R. 1070 ; Ersk. 3. 8. 43. In *Wardlaw* the question was as to the surviving spouse's property ; *Blackburn's Trs.* v. *Blackburn* (1896), 23 R. 698. Chapter XII., *post*.

till the death of the longer liver of the spouses, or till the majorities of the children.[1] The canons of vesting applicable to wills appear to be applicable to marriage contracts. There is some authority for the proposition that provisions in favour of issue contained in marriage contracts are to be construed more favourably (as regards early vesting) than gifts made by will ; [2] but this view has been criticised by high authorities,[3] and appears to be of doubtful validity. In the recent cases involving the consideration of the vesting of marriage-contract provisions, the deeds have been construed on principles similar to those employed in regard to wills.

In the case of mutual wills, if the deed is capable of being read as simply containing two wills, these will take effect from the deaths of the parties respectively in regard to the separate property of each.[4] Hence the gifts made by the predeceaser may vest at his or her death ; or, on the other hand, vesting may be postponed till the death of the longest liver of the parties.[5] Mutual wills.

(9) There is a presumption against that construction of a will which has the effect of casting the estate in whole, or Presumption against intestacy.

---

[1] As in *Hughes* v. *Edwards* (1892), 19 R. (H. L.) 33.

[2] Lords Cowan (p. 694), Rutherfurd (p. 698), Deas (p. 701), Benholme (p. 704), Curriehill (p. 708) in *Pretty* v. *Newbigging* (1854), 16 D. 667 ; Lords Cowan and Benholme in *Rogerson's Trs.* v. *Rogerson* (1865), 3 M. 684.

[3] Ld. Pres. M'Neill (p. 692), L. J.-C. Hope (p. 677), Lords Handyside (p. 692) and Wood (p. 684) in *Pretty* v. *Newbigging, supra* ; L. J.-C. Hope in *Allardice* v. *Lautour* (1845), 7 D. 362 ; L. J.-C. Inglis in *Rogerson's Trs.* v. *Rogerson, supra.*

[4] *Kay's Trs.* v. *Stalker* (1892), 19 R. 1071 ; *Lang* v. *Lang* (1885), 12 R. 1265 ; *Martin* v. *Ferguson's Trs.* (1892), 19 R. 474, *per* Lord M'Laren. Lord Moncreiff in *Scott's Trs.* v. *Cochrane* (1896), 3 S. L. T. 316. M'Laren on Wills, vol. ii. p. 802. Cf· also *Denyssen* v. *Mostert* (1872), L. R. 4 P. C. 236 ; *Dias* v. *De Liviera* (1879),

5 App. Cas. 123. The question most commonly agitated in regard to such wills is as to the survivor's power to revoke, as to which see *Corrance's Trs.* v. *Glen* (1903), 5 F. 777.

[5] Vesting took place at the death of the first deceaser of the parties in *Nicolson* v. *Ramsay* (1806), M. " Legacy," App. No. 2 (a joint legacy) ; *Kerr* v. *Ure* (1873), 11 M. 780. See also *Scott's Trs.* v. *Scott*, 1919, 1 S. L. T. 78 (Lord Sands). *Nicolson* v. *Ramsay* is referred to in *Wilsone's Trs.* v. *Stirling* (1861), 24 D. 163, at 182, and *Hogg* v. *Campbell* (1863), 1 M. 647. It took place on the death of the survivor in *Berwick's Exr.* (1885), 12 R. 565 (a joint estate in which the survivor had the fee) ; *Lockwood's Trs.* v. *Keith Falconer* (1866), 4 M 1036 (a joint legacy of money) ; *Lawsons* v. *Stewart* (1827) 2 W. & S. 625 (a joint-legacy of money with a destination-over).

in part, into intestacy, because the object of making a will is to exclude the heirs *ab intestato*.[1]   " There is one rule of construction, which to my mind is a golden rule, viz., that when a testator has executed a will in solemn form, you must assume that he did not intend to make it a solemn farce—that he did not intend to die intestate when he has gone through the form of making a will. You ought, if possible, to read the will so as to lead to a testacy, not an intestacy." [2]   This rule, in so far as it is based on the ground that the testator cannot be supposed to have intended to die intestate has, with much force, been criticised as importing an intention to the testator in regard to circumstances which he probably never contemplated,[3] but the rule has been too long and too widely applied to be now shaken by criticism.

Section II.

Vesting takes place commonly either at the testator's death or at the time of payment.

I. *Gifts taking Effect in Possession at the Testator's Death.*—In the general case the time of vesting is either the testator's death or the time of payment appointed, or indicated, by the terms of the will.   " If the term of vesting is not the date of the death of the testator, it is difficult to find any other period of vesting except the period of distribution, if we except some special cases where the testator has either expressly or by implication assigned a term of vesting other than the period of distribution. Such cases have occurred ; but where no other period is suggested, the term of vesting is either (1) the death of the testator, or (2) the period of distribution." [4]

It is obvious that vesting cannot be postponed beyond the term of payment appointed, because, if the legatee is to receive the legacy, his right thereto must be fixed at that

---

[1] Lord Trayner in *Gillies' Trs.* v. *Hodge* (1900), 3 F. 238 ; and see *Lawrence* v. *Stewart*, 1924 S. C. 934 ; *Beveridge's Trs.* v. *Beveridge*, 1930 S. C. 578, *per* the Lord President (Clyde), at 586. Cf. the argument in *Earl of Moray* v. *Stuart* (1782), M. 8103 ; *Halbert* v. *Dickson* (1851), 15 D. 609.

[2] Lord Esher, M. R., in *In re Harrison* (1885), 30 Ch. D. 390.

[3] See Lord Sands's opinion in *Beveridge's Trs.* v. *Beveridge*, 1930 S. C. 578.

[4] Ld. Pres. Inglis in *Marshall* v. *King* (1888), 16 R. 40 ; quoted in *Wylie's Trs.* v. *Bruce*, 1919 S. C. 211.

time. Hence, if the testator directs payment to be made at his death, or if the provisions of the will do not require postponement of payment, vesting will take place *a morte testatoris*. In such cases, as will hereafter appear, even the adjection of conditions to the bequest cannot prevent immediate vesting.

In practice, questions of vesting arise only where payment of the gift or distribution of the estate is postponed. Now, when payment of a gift is suspended, the question of the vesting of the legacy depends on whether the retention of the subject is necessary merely for the convenience of the administration of the estate or for carrying into effect the general scheme of the will, or whether it represents a condition of the legatee's right, so that he must be alive at the time of payment in order to benefit. Hence the decision of the question is liable to be affected by an infinite variety of special features ; for any clause suggesting that the beneficiary is to take a right, so far as is not inconsistent with the other purposes of the will, favours immediate vesting ; whereas, on the other hand, any indication that the subject is to be retained for reasons affecting the beneficiary, and operating independently of the other provisions of the deed, aids the view that a suspension of vesting was intended.

II. *Certain Minor Elements favourable to Vesting* a morte testatoris.—There are certain minor elements favourable to immediate vesting, which may conveniently be noticed at this point.

In the first place, a gift expressed in *de præsenti* and unqualified terms of bequest (*e.g.* " I leave " or " I bequeath "), and without mention of the time at which it is to operate, takes effect *a morte testatoris*, " except in one or the other of these two cases, namely, where to give effect to it from that date would disturb any of the provisions already made in the will, or where the testator has clearly indicated, either by express words or by plain implication, that he did not intend it to operate until a later period." [1]

Where the bequest is made in de præsenti terms.

---

[1] *Per* Lord Watson in *Hamilton* v. *Ritchie* (1894), 21 R. (H. L.), 35. In this case the testator gave a liferent of his heritable property to his widow, and disposed of the fee thus : " I leave to my nephew but . . . in the

Gift of the intermediate interest of the subject.

Again, the gift of interest to the legatee from the testator's death is an element in favour of vesting *a morte testatoris*.[1] Interest is a premium or compensation for forbearance on the part of a creditor to exact the principal : it indicates that the subject is due, and that payment alone is postponed. Conversely, a provision that the interest should be accumulated has been considered in some cases [2] to be adverse to the vesting of the gift during the period of accumulation ; but this provision will not in itself suffice to suspend vesting if the other features of the bequest point to vesting *a morte testatoris*.[3]

Declaration that the gift is in lieu of legitim.

Similarly, where a legacy is given in lieu of legitim, this has been held to support the view that vesting was to take place on the truster's death. " Legal rights vest immediately upon that event (*i.e.* the testator's death), and it is probable that provisions given in lieu of them should be intended to vest at the same time. That affords some presumption." [4] This presumption has been adversely criticised,[5] and it is not easy to perceive on what ground the construction of a bequest should be affected by the incidents of the rights which it is intended to displace. But in a considerable number of cases [6] attention has been directed to declarations excluding legitim as an element to be taken into account.

---

event of my said nephew dying without leaving any lawful heir-male of his body, then and in that event my said lands . . . are to revert back to . . . B." Held that the lands vested *a morte testatoris.* In *Yule's Trs.* v. *Deans,* 1919 S. C. 570 at 573, Lord Skerrington notes that words of substantive bequest are favourable to early vesting, although the period of payment may be postponed.

[1] *Per* Lord Trayner in *Wood* v. *Neill's Trs.* (1896), 24 R. 105 ; *Johns* v. *Munro* (1833), 12 S. 146 ; *Allardice* v. *Lautour* (1845), 7 D. 362. See *post,* p. 37.

[2] In *Robertson* v. *Richardson* (1843), 5 D. 1117, L. J.-C. Hope observed that a direction to accumulate interest was " eminently that purpose which is most apart from, and at variance with, the notion of vested interest " ;

and see also *Hutton's Trs.* v. *Coates* (1868), 6 S. L. R. 146.

[3] *Mowbray's Trs.* v. *Mowbray's Exr.,* 1931 S. C. 595.

[4] *Per* Lord Mackenzie in *Matthew* v. *Scott* (1844), 6 D. 718.

[5] *Vide* L. J.-C. Hope's opinion in *Stewart's Trs.* v. *Stewart's Trs.* (1851), 13 D. 1386.

[6] See Ld. Pres. Boyle in *Clark's Exrs.* v. *Paterson* (1851), 14 D. 141 ; Lord Cowan in *Rogerson's Trs.* v. *Rogersons* (1865), 3 M. 684 ; Lord Neaves in *Muir's Trs.* (1869), 8 M. 53 (" a most important consideration ") ; Lord Gifford in *Elliot* v. *Bowhill* (1873), 11 M. 735 ; Lord Shand in *Young* v. *Stewart* (1875), 13 S. L. R. 5 ; *Angus' Trs.* v. *Angus* (1880), 17 S. L. R. 536 ; Lord Moncreiff in *Wood* v. *Neill's Trs.* (1896), 24 R. 105 ; *Allan's Trs.* v. *Allan,* 1918 S. C. 164, *per* Lord

Again, if a trust be not created by the testator, a pre-Absence of sumption arises that immediate vesting was intended.[1] A trust. continuing trust is the proper and only effectual mode of securing the fulfilment of any conditions attached to a gift. And, further, it must be borne in mind that if no trust be set up, the rule which forbids the fee being *in pendente* will come into operation, and the provisions of the will are liable to be affected by the necessity for finding a lodgement for the fee. In this way, the absence of a trust affords strong ground for saying that a suspension of vesting was not intended ; and if the will merely appoints *executors*, this also, and for the same reason, indicates immediate vesting, because the duty of executors is to distribute, and not to hold.[2]

III. *The Effect on Vesting of the Existence of a Trust.*— But, although the absence of a trust is favourable to immediate vesting, it does not follow that the creation of a trust prevents vesting. There is nothing inconsistent in the legal estate and the *jus crediti* vesting concurrently in the trustees and the beneficiary respectively, and it is settled that the existence of a trust does not in any way affect the vesting of the beneficial interest. In *Carleton* v. *Thomson*,[3] Lord Colonsay stated the law thus : " The general rule of law as to bequests is, that the right of fee given vests *a morte testatoris*. That rule holds although a right of liferent is at the same time given to another, and although that is done through the instrumentality of a trust, and whether the fee be given to an individual *nominatim* or to a class. The postponement of the period of payment till the death of a liferentrix does not suspend the vesting, nor does the interposition of the machinery of a trust for carrying into effect the intentions of the testator. Indeed,

Johnston ; *Wyllie's Trs.* v. *Wyllie's Exr.*, 1926 S. C. 336, *per* L. J.-C. Alness, at 342.

[1] Cf. Lord Medwyn in *Robertson* v. *Richardson* (1843), 5 D. 1117 ; Lord M'Laren in *Hay's Trs.* v. *Hay* (1890), 17 R. 961.

[2] See *Davidson's Exrs.* (1900), 8 S. L. T. 239. As to the distinction between the duties of trustees and executors, cf. *Jamieson* v. *Clark* (1872), 10 M. 399 ; and *Ainslie* v. *Ainslie* (1886), 14 R. 209.

[3] (1867), 5 M. (H. L.) 151 ; L. R. 1 H. L. Sc. 232. Cf. also *Fowke* v. *Duncans* (1770), M. 8092 ; *Nimmo* v. *Murray's Trs.* (1864), 2 M. 1144.

the creation of a trust is a very usual mode of securing the interest of a liferenter, where the right to the fee is nevertheless intended to vest in the person or class of persons for whom it is destined. Although the *jus dominii* may be in trustees, the *jus crediti* is in the beneficiaries as a vested right."

Forms of directions to trustees.

A bequest through the hands of trustees may take the form of a direction to *hold* for the legatee or to *pay* to him. The difference between these modes of expression, taken by themselves and apart from a context, is formal rather than substantial. If the bequest be made unconditionally, the manner in which the testator expresses himself is immaterial. Thus it is settled that directions to trustees to *hold* for A. in liferent, and for B. in fee ; or to *hold* for A. in liferent, and *on his death to hold* the subject for B. in fee ; [1] or to *hold* the subject for A. in liferent, and *on his death to pay* the subject to B.[2] : alike vest the subject in B. *a morte testatoris*.

If, however, conditions are annexed to the bequest, the distinction between these forms of gift becomes more important.

Gifts implied in a direction to trustees to pay.

When the bequest is contained in a direction to trustees to pay, and conditions are annexed to this direction, it is well settled that the conditions are as a general rule to be treated as operative at the time of payment, and that, therefore, vesting is (if the conditions are suspensive) suspended till that time. There being no other words of bequest, it follows that " whatever conditions are adjected to that direction, or whatever qualities are implied in it, necessarily become conditions and qualities of the gift itself." [3]

[1] *Miller* v. *Finlay's Trs.* (1875), 2 R. (H. L.) 1 ; *Mowbray's Trs.* v. *Mowbray's Exr.*, 1931 S. C. 595.

[2] The gift, though made in this form, was held to be vested in *Forbes* v. *Luckie* (1838), 16 S. 374 ; 13 Fac. 324 ; *Maxwell* v. *Wyllie* (1837), 15 S. 1005 ; 12 Fac. 928 ; *Smith* v. *Lauder* (1834), 12 S. 646 ; 9 Fac. 341 ; *Halbert* v. *Dickson* (1853), 15 D. 609 ; *Sterling* v. *Baird's Trs.* (1851), 14 D. 20 ; *Rattray's Trs.* v. *Rattray* (1868), 6 M. 476 ; *Home's Trs.* (1891), 18 R.

1138 ; *Johnston* v. *Johnston* (1868), 7 M. 109 ; *Hay Cunningham's Trs.* v. *Blackwell*, 1909 S. C. 219.

[3] *Per* L. J.-C. Inglis in *Donaldson's Trs.* v. *Richardson* (1860), 22 D. 1527 ; his opinion was sustained on appeal, 4 Macq. 314 (*sub nom. Young* v. *Robertson*). The circumstance that the bequest was contained in a direction to pay was considered to be unfavourable to vesting *a morte testatoris* in *Muirhead* v. *Muirhead* (1890), 17 R. (H. L.) 45 ; *Stodart's Trs.* (1870), 8 M.

In *M'Alpine* v. *Studholme*,[1] where a testatrix gave her estate to trustees in trust for her sisters in liferent, and directed the trustees, on the death of the longest liver of these sisters, to pay certain sums of money " which " (she added) " I hereby leave and bequeath," and to " pay, assign, and dispone " the residue to three nephews and the survivors of them, Lord President Inglis made the following observations in regard to the form of the gifts : " Taking the two clauses together, namely, that which deals with the special legacies and that which disposes of the residue, it is to be noticed that there is an important contrast between them. In the clause which deals with the special legacies there is not only a direction to pay after the death of the longest liver of the liferenters, but the testatrix also uses the words ' which I hereby leave and bequeath,' whereas in the residue clause there are no words of gift, but only a direction to pay. If the matter had stopped there, it might have been a question of some difficulty whether it was not intended to postpone vesting until after the death of the longest liver of the liferenters. I am not sure whether words such as these have by themselves been held to import a postponement of vesting, but it is certainly always a matter of importance that there are no words of gift except an order to pay, and that circumstance is, in the present case, undoubtedly somewhat fortified by the contrast which I have pointed out. But it is very seldom that the single element is present by itself. There are almost always other parts of the deed either fortifying or overcoming it, and this deed is no exception to the general rule."

On the other hand, if the trustees are directed to hold for, and pay to, the legatee, this mode of expression is more favourable to immediate vesting. In this case there are two directions to the trustees, and a question may arise as to which of these directions conditions appearing in the deed are intended to qualify. If the conditions are to be referred to the direction to pay, the vesting of the gift will not

Gifts contained in a direction to trustees to hold and to pay.

---

667 ; *Reeve's Exr.* v. *Reeve's Jud. Factor* (1892), 19 R. 1013 ; *Graham's Trs.* v. *Graham* (1899), 2 F. 232 ; *Ross's Trs.* v. *Ross* (1902), 4 F. 840. Cf. Lord Mure in *Ross's Trs.* (1884),

12 R. 378 ; L. J.-C. Hope in *Bell* v. *Cheape* (1845), 7 D. 614. This is one element in the rule laid down in *Bryson's Trs.* v. *Clark* (1880), 8 R. 142.
¹ (1883), 10 R. 837.

necessarily be suspended ; for it is recognised in our law that conditions which are meant merely to regulate the time at which the legatee is to receive payment, or the manner in which he is to have possession, do not prevent the acquisition by him of a vested interest in the subject of the gift prior to the time of payment. And even if the conditions refer to the direction to hold,—although in this case it would be clear that the conditions were of the essence of the gift,—a question would still remain as to the time at which these conditions were intended to operate.[1] A direction to trustees to hold for a person rather implies that the gift was intended to take effect at the period when the trustees are vested in the estate and enter upon their duties,—that is, in the general case, the death of the testator ; [2] and therefore the conditions might be considered to relate to that time, which would allow of the legacy's vesting *a morte testatoris*. In his dissenting opinion in *Gilbert's Trs.* v. *Crerar*,[3] which was sustained on appeal,[4] Lord Justice-Clerk Moncreiff thus adverted to the distinction between the two forms of directions to trustees : " Now, I do not agree . . . that a bequest to trustees to hold for behoof of a fiar, whether described or named, is the same thing as a direction to pay at a future date. They are two different things. The direction to pay at a future date may infer the same thing as a direction to hold the fee in the meantime ; but a direction to hold the fee *a morte testatoris* for behoof of a certain person, even if not named, if he be designed or indicated, is different from a direction to pay at a future date in this, that the one takes effect *a morte testatoris* and the other only takes effect at an uncertain period." Of course if the time is stated at which the trustees are to begin to hold for the legatee, conditions inserted in the gift are naturally referred to that time ; and hence if trustees are directed to hold for A., with a destination-over or other suspensive condition annexed, from and after a time

---

[1] See *post*, p. 60.

[2] Cf. Lord Neaves in *Alves* v. *Grant* (1874), 1 R. 969. As to the effect of a direction to " hold," see *Waters' Trs.* v. *Waters* (1884), 12 R. 253 ; *Greenlees' Trs.* v. *Greenlees* (1894), 22 R. 136 ; *Ballantyne's Trs.* v. *Kidd* (1898), 25 R. 621 ; *Gillies' Trs.* v. *Hodge* (1900), 3 F. 238 ; *post*, p. 146.

[3] (1877), 5 R. 49.

[4] *Sub nom. Taylor* v. *Gilbert's Trs.* (1878), 5 R. (H. L.) 217.

subsequent to the testator's death, the form of the gift is adverse to vesting in A. before that time or event.[1]

The distinction between a direction to trustees to pay and a direction to hold and pay has been termed " the thinnest of all legal distinctions," [2] and has been criticised by high authorities.[3] But in view of the number of cases in which the form of the gift has been noticed and relied upon as an element in the decision, the distinction cannot safely be ignored by those engaged in the preparation of wills.[4]

The duration of the trust is to be considered in questions of vesting. If trustees are instructed to denude at a time or on an event mentioned, this instruction must be obeyed although there may be other provisions in the deed which cannot receive full effect without the continuance of the trust management ; [5] for the Court has no power to set up a course of management if that is not provided in the deed. And as the retention of the estate by trustees is the only effective mode of securing ulterior rights or rendering the primary legatee's right conditional, it may be assumed that the truster intended that these ulterior interests should vanish, or that the interest of the first legatee should become unconditional, at the time when the trust is to end. Hence destinations-over and survivorship clauses have been held

Ulterior interests evacuated on termination of the trust.

[1] *Melrose* v. *Melrose's Trs.* (1869), 7 M. 1050 ; *Sinclair* v. *Sinclair's Trs.* (1867), 5 S. L. R. 133 ; *Buchanan's Trs.* v. *Buchanan* (1877), 4 R. 754.

[2] By Lord Stormonth-Darling in *Thompson's Trs.* v. *Jamieson* (1900), 2 F. 470.

[2] By Lord Stormonth-Darling in (1884), 12 R. 378, and *Hay's Trs.* v. *Hay* (1890), 17 R. 961 ; Lord Low in *Burgh of Ayr* v. *Shaw* (1904), 12 S. L. T. 126.

[4] Cf. Lord Shand in *Hay's Trs.* v. *Hay, supra.*

[5] Cf. *Hutton's Trs.* v. *Hutton* (1847), 9 D. 639 ; *Ferguson's Trs.* v. *Hamilton* (1862), 4 Macq. 397 ; and *Beveridge* v. *Beveridge's Trs.* (1878), 5 R. 1116 (where, because of the absence of a provision for the continuance of the trust, a person to whom the liferent was given took a fee under the rule of

Frog's Creditors (1735), M. 4262) ; also *Allan's Trs.* v. *Allan* (1872), 11 M. 216 ; *Clouston's Trs.* v. *Bulloch* (1889), 16 R. 937 ; *Mitchell's Trs.* v. *Smith* (1880), 7 R. 1086 ; *Houston* v. *Mitchell* (1877), 5 R. 154 ; *Gibson's Trs.* v. *Ross* (1877), 4 R. 1038 (where the Court declined to continue a trust in order to render effectual declarations that the rights given were to be alimentary, etc.). In *Auld* v. *Anderson* (1876), 4 R. 211, a declaration that the shares should be alimentary was construed as affecting the shares merely while they remained in the trustee's hands, *i.e.*, during the minorities of the legatees. Cf. *Sandys* v. *Bain's Trs.* (1897), 25 R. 261 ; and Lord Young in *Reeve's Exr.* v. *Reeve's Jud. Factor* (1892), 19 R. 1013, as to the distinction between executory and other trusts.

to cease from qualifying the gift at the date when the trustees are directed to make payment.[1] In *Dron's Trs.* v. *Peddie*,[2] for example, trustees were directed to pay, after certain purposes were fulfilled, to A., " in the event of his arriving at a sound state of mind, . . . or, failing that event happening, then to " B. The purposes were satisfied at the time the case was brought, but A. was still alive and of unsound mind. It was urged on his behalf that the trustees were bound to hold the estate until his death, as he might at any time recover, but the Court authorised payment to B., holding that the mental state of A. was to be judged at the time when the truster had ordained payment to be made.

Payment on Dies Certus or after Liferent. IV. *The Effect of Postponement of Payment to a* Dies Certus *or of the Interposition of a Liferent.*—It is a leading principle of the law of vesting, that postponement of the bequest to a time that will certainly arrive does not suspend vesting.[3] Thus, where trustees were directed to pay in a specified year,[4] or on the termination of a lease at a time mentioned,[5] or after the lapse of a period from the testator's death,[6] the legacy was held to vest *a morte testatoris.*

The existence of a liferent,[7] as is pointed out in the passage already quoted from Lord Colonsay's opinion in *Carleton* v. *Thomson*,[8] does not suspend vesting, but the law had been established to this effect long before that case.[9] An annuity has even less force against vesting than a liferent.[10]

---

[1] *Tait* v. *Duncan* (1837), 15 S. 1273 ; 12 Fac. 1162 ; *Campbell* v. *Campbell* (1852), 15 D. 173 ; *Allan* v. *Fleming* (1845), 7 D. 908 ; *Stewart's Trs.* v. *Stewart* (1851), 14 D. 298 ; Cf. *Simpson's Trs.* v. *Simpson* (1889), 17 R. 248.

[2] (1850), 12 D. 825.

[3] Lord M'Laren in *Hay's Trs.* v. *Hay* (1890), 17 R. 961.

[4] *Sellar* v. *Stephen* (1855), 17 D. 975.

[5] *Archibald's Trs.* v. *Archibald* (1882), 9 R. 942.

[6] *Finlay's Trs.* v. *Finlay* (1886), 13 R. 1052 ; *Hood's Exrs.* (1869), 7 M. 774.

[7] Or series of liferents—*M'Alpine* v. *Studholme* (1883), 10 R. 837 ; *Duncan's Trs.* v. *Thomas* (1882), 9 R. 731.

[8] (1867), 5 M. (H. L.) 151 ; L. R. 1 Sc. Apps. 232 (*supra*, p. 23).

[9] *Wallace* v. *Wallace* (1807), M. " Clause," App. 6 ; *Nisbett* v. *M'Dougal*, 27 June 1809, F.C. Lord Corehouse in *Maxwell* v. *Wyllie* (1837), 15 S. 1005 ; 12 Fac. 928, and *Forbes* v. *Luckie* (1838), 16 S. 374 ; 13 Fac. 324 ; Lord Jeffrey in *Calder* v. *Dickson* (1842), 4 D. 1365 ; Lord Medwyn in *Robertson* v. *Richardson* (1843), 5 D. 1117.

[10] *Pursell* v. *Newbigging* (1855), 2 Macq. 273 ; *Alexander's Trs.* v. *Waters* (1870), 8 M. 414 ; *Young* v. *Stewart* (1875), 13 S. L. R. 5. See *post*, p. 62.

The reasoning on which the above rule is founded is that the testator has postponed the fiar's enjoyment of the gift merely in so far as is necessary to admit the liferenter's interest, and not with the intention of qualifying the fiar's title or right. " In regard to interposed interests, such as liferents, the question always is, whether there is any person other than the liferenter himself in whose interest vesting is postponed till the death of the liferenter. If there is not, postponement of the vesting is not necessary, and is not to be presumed. Lastly, where the sole interposed interest is not a liferent so as to exhaust the annual revenue, but only a burden on the annual revenue, the presumption in favour of vesting becomes still stronger." [1] But if qualifications personal to the legatee are annexed—qualifications which would operate if the liferent were cancelled or renounced— vesting is usually postponed. The most common of such qualifications are destinations-over, survivorship clauses, or conditions as to the legatee's majority or marriage. Where none of these appears, the presumption is that vesting is not suspended till the expiry of the liferent.[2]

Where the deed contemplates the termination of the trust management during the lifetime of the person to whom the liferent is given, a strong inference is thereby suggested against any suspension of vesting. Thus in all the opinions in *Carleton* v. *Thomson* stress was laid on the fact that the trustees were empowered to settle the estate on the fiars *when they thought proper*.[3] In *Ross's Trs.*,[4] where a liferent was given to the truster's widow and the fee to his children,

[1] L. J.-C. Moncreiff in *Henderson's Trs.* v. *Henderson* (1876), 3 R. 320.

[2] Lord Colonsay in *Carleton* v. *Thomson* (1867), 5 M. (H. L.) 151 ; L. R. 1 H. L. Sc. 232 ; *Douglas* v. *Douglas* (1864), 2 M. 1008. *Mowbray's Trs.* v. *Mowbray's Exr.*, 1931 S. C. 595. " A suspension of vesting is a thing very difficult to assume as contemplated by a testator, unless for some definite purpose. Almost the only conceivable purpose is to secure some ulterior interest."—*Per* Ld. Pres. Inglis in *Jamieson* v. *Allardice* (1872), 10 M. 755, at 759.

[3] The clause was : " And the residue of my said estate I direct and appoint to be vested in my said trustees for behoof of my said daughter . . . in liferent . . . and her children in fee, to be kept in trust by them, *till they in their discretion shall see proper to settle it in the most safe and secure manner on her and her children.*" See Lord Curriehill's opinion, 3 M. 514, at 520 ; and Lord Colonsay's, 5 M. (H. L.) 151, at 155.

[4] (1884), 12 R. 378.

the feature of the deed which decided the question of vesting was a power bestowed on the trustees of denuding of the estate *at any time after the first term after the truster's death*, on due security being taken for the widow's interest. " It appears to me," said Lord President Inglis, " that the facilities provided by the testator for dividing the residue, even during the survivance of the widow, are conclusive against his intention being to postpone vesting." The very usual provision that the trustees shall make over the estate (in whole or in part) on the liferenter's marrying for a second time is, for this reason, also a circumstance in favour of vesting *a morte testatoris* [1]—but a circumstance of slight importance.

[1] *Richard's Trs.* v. *Roland* (1894), 22 R. 140.

CHAPTER III.

PERSONAL CONDITIONS.—MAJORITY OR MARRIAGE.

I. Gifts on Majority or Marriage. | II. Gifts on Marriage.

I. Gifts on Majority or Marriage.—When the gift to a legatee is dependent upon his or her attainment of majority, or majority or marriage, vesting will not take place before these events, and if the legatee die in minority, or in minority and unmarried, the legacy is not transmitted to his or her representatives. A distinction, however, is drawn between gifts which are conditioned upon these events and gifts in which the legatee's majority or marriage is referred to merely as determining the time of payment. In the first class, the event on which the gift depends being a *dies incertus*, vesting is postponed *pendente conditione* ; in the second class, payment alone being delayed, vesting may take place before the event occurs.[1]

Distinction between gifts on majority and gifts payable on majority.

This distinction was established (after a conflict of authorities [2]) in *Ralston* v. *Ralston* [3] and *Alves' Trs.* v. *Grant*.[4]

---

[1] In the case of *Bells* v. *Mason*, (1749), M. 6332, where a grandfather bound himself to aliment a grandchild till he was sixteen years of age, and to pay him 600 merks " at the term of Whitsunday 1747, which will be the first term after his attaining the age foresaid," the Lord Ordinary (Elchies) held that the sum was payable on a day certain (the said term), but the Court reversed his decision on the ground that the true intention of the grantor was that the obligation should be conditional on the grandchild's attaining sixteen.

[2] In the cases of *Edgar* v. *Edgar* (1665), M. 6325 ; *Oxenfurd* (1671), 2 Br. Sup. 525 ; *Belshes* v. *Belshes* (1677), M. 6327 ; *Elliot* (1687), M. 6342 ; *Bells* v. *Mason*, *supra*, the distinction was not admitted. It was sanctioned in *Kelso* v. *M'Cuby* (1686), M. 6330 and *Burnets* v. *Forbes* (1783), M.

8105 (followed by *Wood* v. *Burnet's Trs*. (1813), Hume's Decs. 271). The distinction, however, was rejected in subsequent cases—*Omey* v. *M'Larty*, (1788), M. 6340 ; *Sempills* v. *Sempill*, (1792), M. 8108 ; and *Home* v. *Home*, (1807), Hume's Decs. 530 (in which the Lord President observed " The case of *Burnets* was ill decided ; so the Judges themselves came afterwards to think "). Cf. also *Arbuthnot* v. *Arbuthnot* (1816), Hume's Decs. 536 ; *Grindlay* v. *The Merchant Company of Edinburgh*, 1 July 1814, F. C. ; *Torrie* v. *Munsie* (1832), 10 S. 597 ; 7 Fac. 462 ; and *M'Kays* v. *Lord Reay* (1790), Bell's Oct. Cases, 394. It holds also in English law—*Leake* v. *Robinson* (1817), 2 Mer. 363 ; *In re Bartholomew* (1849), 1 Mac. & G. 354 ; *Locke* v. *Lamb* (1867), L. R. 4 Eq. 372.

[3] (1842), 4 D. 1496.

[4] (1874), 1 R. 969.

In the latter case, Lord Justice-Clerk Moncreiff stated the law on the point in these terms : " Unquestionably where an uncertain term,—that is to say, a term which may or may not arrive,—is adjected to a testamentary gift or bequest, the presumption is that the legatee's survivance of that term is a condition of his right. It may be otherwise, but not necessarily otherwise, where the term is in words adjected not to the gift itself, but to the payment or enjoyment of it. In the Roman law this distinction was allowed great weight, and Voet in his Commentary lays down the rule thus :—' Conditioni similis est dies incertus : nisi tantum solutionis non obligationis morandæ gratia adjectus sit,' Bk. 28, t. 7, s. 32. In the earlier cases which were quoted to us from the bar, especially in those of *Omey*, *Sempill*, and *Home*, this distinction was controverted, and perhaps with reason. But still it was clearly laid down in *Sempill's* case, and still more clearly in the subsequent case of *Wood*, reported by Hume, p. 271, that these presumptions must yield to the manifest intention of the testator. Indeed, it cannot be doubted that before the uncertain term can operate as a condition of the gift it must be attached or adjected to the gift, and that an uncertain term may be attached to the payment of a gift while the gift itself is intended to take effect and to vest at the testator's death." These remarks were made with reference to a gift in this form : " I hereby nominate and appoint the said A. . . . my residuary legatee, and direct my trustees, upon his attaining the age of twenty-one, to dispone, convey, and make over to him, his heirs and assigns, the whole residue of my means and estate." It was held that the residue vested in A. because of the unqualified initial appointment of him as residuary legatee. There was a further gift to A. in these terms: " I direct my trustees to hold my said heritable estate . . . in trust to convey and make over the same to A. . . . upon his attaining the years of majority, his heirs and assigns for ever." In this gift the provision as to A.'s majority was not so clearly severed from the words of gift, and it was with some difficulty, and only with the aid of other clauses, that the Court came to the conclusion that here also there was immediate vesting in the legatee.

The question whether the reference to the legatee's majority or marriage affects the constitution of the gift or merely the payment thereof, is to be determined on a consideration of the whole provisions of the will,[1] but, as the cases show, with especial reference to the following elements : (*a*) The form of the gift ; (*b*) the destination-over (if there be one) ; and (*c*) the disposal of the intermediate interest, and the power, if any, given to the trustees of making advances out of the capital to the legatee during his minority.

(*a*) *The Form of the Gift.*—Where the condition as to majority is annexed to the words which constitute the gift (*e.g.* "I leave £1000 to A. in the event of his attaining majority " [2]), or where the bequest is contained in a direction to pay on majority,[3] the form of the gift implies that vesting is suspended during minority. Thus in *Graham's Trs.* v. *Graham*, the clause under construction was in this form : " Upon my son William attaining the age of thirty years, I direct my trustees to convey to him " two heritable properties. The son having died under the age of thirty, it was held that he had not acquired a vested interest. " There is no direct gift to William," said Lord Trayner, " nor any words from which a gift can be implied. There is nothing beyond a direction to the trustees to convey to William on his attaining the age of thirty."

But, on the other hand, where there occur words of gift and a direction as to payment, and the conditions as to the attainment of a particular age are annexed to the direction regarding payment, the presumption is that these conditions do not affect the vesting. Thus, in *Burnets* v. *Forbes*,[4] a gift expressed thus : " To A. I leave £500 sterling to be paid when he is sixteen years of age," was held to have vested in the legatee although he died at the age of eleven. In the argument for the successful parties (the pursuers) it was conceded that " in the event which has happened, the bequest would have become void, if it had been devised in this

Form of the Gift.

---

[1] As, for example, in *Hewat* v. *Grant* (1867), 6 M. 47.

[2] Lord M'Laren in *White* v. *Gow* (1899), 2 F. 1170.

[3] *Graham's Trs.* v. *Graham* (1899), 2 F. 232 ; *Brodie* v. *Brodie's Trs.* (1893), 20 R. 795 ; *Fergusson* v. *Smith* (1867), 6 M. 83 ; 40 S. J. 50 (The Jurist gives the opinions) ; *Donald's Trs.* v. *Donald* (1864), 2 M. 922 ; *Arbuthnot* v. *Arbuthnot* (1816), Hume's Decs. 536 ; *Stewart's Trs.* v. *Stewart* (1851), 13 D. 1386.

[4] (1783), M. 8105.

manner : ' To A. when he attains the age of sixteen I leave £500,' " and the Court " moved chiefly by the authority of the Roman law in which the distinction urged by the pursuers seemed clearly established " gave effect to it. Again, in *Ralston* v. *Ralston*,[1] the legacy was in these terms : " To A. . . . and in the event of his death to B. and C. . . . the sum of £500 sterling, with the interest thereof from six months after my death, payable the said interest to their legal guardians, for their behoof ; and the principal sum payable to the said A. on his arriving at majority, or in the event of his decease," to B. and C. on their majorities. The three legatees survived the testator but died in minority. In a competition between their next-of-kin and the residuary legatees, it was held that the legacy had vested *a morte testatoris* in A. " I apprehend," said Lord Justice-Clerk Hope, " the interest of the residuary legatee is excluded by the first direction to pay over to A. . . . A right is given, which, by the survivance of A., passes to those in right of A., in the event of his death,—the postponement of the time of payment being a mere matter of regulation and management for the benefit of A., and according to the pleasure of the truster—but introduced after words which are unqualified, carrying the bequest wholly and completely away from the residue—such as the general direction to pay over to A."

The destination-over.

(*b*) *The Destination-over.*—Where there is a destination-over referring not only to the legatee's death before the testator, but also to his death at any time before his attainment of full age, this circumstance is (at all events in cases where the destination-over is in favour of others than issue of the legatee [2]) almost conclusive against the idea of vesting before that event. Thus, where trustees were instructed to

---

[1] (1842), 4 D. 1496 ; so also *Wilson* v. *Wilson* (1842), 4 D. 1503 ; *Alves' Trs.* v. *Grant* (1874), 1 R. 969 ; *Allardice's Trs.* v. *Ritchie* (1866), 1 S. L. R. 225 ; 38 S. J. 315 ; *Matthew* v. *Scott* (1844), 6 D. 718. Cf. also *Mackinnon's Trs.* v. *MacNeill* (1897), 24 R. 981 ; and *Waters' Trs.* v. *Waters* (1884), 12 R. 253 ; and the cases on gifts to classes.

[2] It is possible, in view of the more recent decisions referred to in Chapter VI., *post*, that, in the case of a destination-over in the event of A. dying under twenty-one in favour of his issue, it might be held that there was vesting in A. subject to defeasance if he died in minority survived by issue. But there is no decision in the reports to this effect.

hold one-half of the residue of an estate for A. " payable on his attaining the . . . age of twenty-five years, but until he attains that age," to " hold the capital in trust and apply . . . the annual interest . . . for his maintenance " (with power to make advances out of the capital to him), " but declaring in the event of the said A. dying without leaving lawful issue of his body before attaining the said age," it should go over to others, it was conceded in the case that vesting was suspended till A.'s majority.   The destination-over, therefore, was considered as outweighing the unqualified initial words of bequest, the gift of interest, and the power in the trustee to make advances—elements which are all favourable to early vesting.   But the decision in the case was for immediate vesting, because by a codicil the testatrix revoked the destination-over and thus removed the sole obstacle to vesting.[1]

The effect of a destination-over is further illustrated by the inference in favour of early vesting drawn in some cases from the absence of any destination-over, or from the fact that the destination-over is expressly referred to some other event than the legatee's attainment of majority.   In *Hewat* v. *Grant*,[2] trustees were instructed to pay the rents of an heritable estate to A., and on his death to convey it to the heirs of his body on his or her attaining majority, " and failing the said A. without leaving lawful issue," to another family.   The fact that the destination-over related to failure of issue as at A.'s death only, and not to failure during the period between that event and their attainment of twenty-one, was considered to aid a construction of the will which gave the issue (although minor) a vested right at A.'s death.

Again, when a testator, in making a gift to a legatee on his majority, provides that the subject of the gift shall go over in the event of the legatee's death or failure, but does not state the time at which that death or failure is to be ascertained, the determination of the question of vesting will depend very much on the construction to be put upon the gift-over.   There is little doubt that, if the gift took

---

[1] *Johnston's Trs.* v. *Johnston* (1891), 18 R. 823. Cf. also *Buchanan's Trs.* v. *Buchanan* (1877), 4 R. 754 ; *M'Alpine* (1883), 10 R. 837, and *Stewart's Trs.* v. *Stewart* (1851), 31 D. 1386. See Chapter IV., *post*.

[2] (1867), 6 M. 47. Cf. *Rogerson's Trs.* v. *Rogerson* (1865), 3 M. 684.

the form of a direction to the trustees to make over the legacy to A. on his majority, whom failing to B., the destination-over would be taken to refer to the case of A. dying in minority ; in this case both the form of the gift and the destination-over would be strongly against vesting in A. before he attained twenty-one.[1]   But it is not altogether clear whether, if the gift were in this form : " I leave to A. the sum of £500, to be paid by my trustees on his majority, and in the event of his death to B.," this destination-over would be referred to the time of payment, A.'s majority, or to the initial gift.   It would appear that in *Ralston* v. *Ralston* [2] (where the gift was held to vest *a morte testatoris*) a destination-over of this kind was considered to qualify the words of gift, and therefore to refer only to the legatee's predecease of the truster.

Construction of destinations-over.
A destination-over in the event of the legatee's death before attaining majority covers the case of the legatee's death in minority before, as well as after, the testator's death.[3]   Where a bequest is made to a person in liferent and to the parties called to the fee on their majorities, and there is a destination-over referring to payment, difficult questions have arisen as to whether the legatees are required to survive the liferenter as well as attain majority.   These cases are discussed in a subsequent chapter.[4]   Where the destination-over is referred in express terms to the legatee's majority, it will not be extended to the period that may elapse between that event and the close of the liferent. Thus, in one case [5] where a gift was made to legatees in the form of a direction to trustees to pay to them at the termination of a liferent and on their attaining majority, it was held that a share had vested in a legatee who had attained majority but died before the liferentrix, because the destination-over was expressed with reference simply

---

[1] Cf. *Greig* v. *Johnston* (1833), 6 W. & S. 406.   See Chapter IV.

[2] (1842), 4 D. 1496.   Cf. also Ld. Pres. Inglis's opinion in *M'Alpine* (1883), 10 R. 837, at 844, and *Peacock's Trs.* v. *Peacock* (1885), 12 R. 878 ; and see *post*, p. 60.

[3] *Aitchison* v. *Allan* (1831), 9 S. 454 ; 6 Fac. 232 ; *Smith* v. *Smith* (1710) and *Denholm* v. *Denholm* (1726), M. 6346.   Cf. also *Dalhousie's Trs.* v. *Young* (1889), 16 R. 681 ; *Sorley* v. *Martin* (1890), 27 S. L. R. 880.

[4] Chapter XI.

[5] *M'Alpine* (1883), 10 R. 837 ; (Lord Deas dissented).   So also *Stewart's Trs.* v. *Stewart* (1875), 13 S. L. R. 5.

to death in minority. In the case of a gift to A. on majority or marriage, the correct form of gift-over is obviously—in the event of A.'s dying unmarried *and* (not *or*) without attaining majority.[1]

(c) *Gift of Interest and Powers of making Advances.*— Gift of the interest during the legatee's minority, and power of advancement. Where the interest of the subject of the legacy is given to the legatee during his minority, a presumption arises that vesting is not postponed by the provisions as to his majority. Great importance was attached to this feature of the gift in *Wood* v. *Burnet's Trs.*[2] and *Ralston* v. *Ralston.*[3] While a destination-over to another in case of the legatee's death under age will rebut the presumption arising from the gift of the interest,[4] the circumstance that the gift appears in the form of a direction to the trustees to convey on the legatee's majority would appear insufficient, according to the later authorities, to do so.[5] Thus, in *White* v. *Gow,*[6] the bequest was in these terms : " I direct my trustees to invest the sum of £1500, and pay the annual interest or produce thereof to my grandniece A. . . . and I provide and declare that during the years of her pupillarity or minority the said interest be paid to her legal guardian, and on the said A. attaining her majority my said trustees shall pay over to her the said sum of £1500 " ; and this was followed by a bequest of the residue of the estate in favour of others. It was held that the sum vested *a morte testatoris,* Lord M'Laren observing that, in his opinion, there was " a very strong presumption where income is given unconditionally

---

[1] *Grant* v. *Dyer* (1813), 2 Dow, 73 ; *Bothwells* v. *Earl of Home* (1747), M. 2989.

[2] (1813), Hume's Decs. 271.

[3] (1842), 4 D. 1496 ; cf. also *Wilson* v. *Wilson* (1842), 4 D. 1503 (where interest was given to legatee's mother); *Fergusson* v. *Smith* (where, however, vesting was postponed by a vesting declaration) (1867), 40 S. J. 50 (the opinion of the Court is given in this report); 6 M. 83 ; *Kennedy* v. *Crawford* (1841), 3 D. 1266 ; 16 Fac. 1367 ; *Allardice's Trs.* v. *Ritchie* (1866), 1 S. L. R. 225 ; 38 S. J. 315 ; and *Stewart's Trs.* v. *Stewart* (1851), 13 D. 1386 (stress laid on absence of gift of interest). See *ante,* p. 22.

[4] *Johnston's Trs.* v. *Johnston* (1891), 18 R. 823.

[5] In the early cases of *Omey* v. *M'Larty* (1788), M. 6340 ; *Home* v. *Home* (1807), Hume's Decs. 530 ; and *Grindlay* v. *The Merchant Co. of Edinburgh,* 1 July 1814, F. C., vesting was suspended despite a gift of intermediate interest ; but in none of the recent cases (viz. *Graham's Trs.* v. *Graham, Brodie* v. *Brodie's Trs.,* and *Donald's Trs.* v. *Donald,* cited *ante,* note 3, p. 33) where vesting was suspended, was there a gift of interest.

[6] (1900), 2 F. 1170.

to the legatee that a direction to pay at majority is to be regarded as merely an administrative direction, for the two rights of income and eventual fee are given to the same person, and in the case supposed no other person is mentioned in the bequest as having any interest." [1]

But, while it is well settled that an order to trustees to pay the interest of the subject to the legatee during his minority is favourable to vesting *a morte testatoris*, it is not clear whether a direction to trustees to pay the interest, or a part thereof, *if they shall consider this proper*, has the same effect.[2] If the legatee's maintenance is provided for by an annuity given out of the general estate, or without reference to the interest of the gift, this provision affords no inference in favour of vesting before the legatee attains majority.[3]

In *Wilson's Trs.* v. *Quick* [4] stress was laid on the fact that the trustees were empowered to make advances out of the capital of the fund to the legatees before their majorities, as indicating the truster's intention that vesting should not be delayed. But a power of this description would seem to be as consistent with non-vesting as with vesting,—indeed, the reason for the power being conferred may be that the testator meant to suspend vesting,—and the latest authorities are in favour of the view that this, in itself, is an element of little or no weight.[5]

If it is provided that any advances made are to bear interest, it has been pointed out [6] that the presumption is against vesting. " No one pays interest on funds belonging to himself. A direction to give children the interest or produce of their prospective shares between the date of the testator's death and the period of division, is held to

---

[1] See to the same effect his Lordship's opinion in *Brodie* v. *Brodie's Trs., infra*.

[2] Cf. *Bogle's Trs.* v. *Cochrane* (1892), 20 R. 108 ; Jarman on Wills (7th Ed.) Vol. II., p. 1389; *Leake* v. *Robinson* (1817), 2 Mer. 363.

[3] *Brodie* v. *Brodie's Trs.* (1893), 20 R. 795 ; *Stewart's Trs.* v. *Stewart* (1851), 13 D. 1386. For English law on this point see Jarman on Wills

(7th Ed.), Vol. II., p. 1382; Theobald on Wills (8th Ed.), p. 657.

[4] (1878), 5 R. 697 ; *Clark's Exrs.* v. *Paterson* (1851), 14 D. 141. Cf. also Lord Low's opinion in the Outer House case of *Cairns* v. *Cairns' Trs.* (1902), 10 S. L. T. 364.

[5] *Fyfe's Trs.* v. *Fyfe* (1890), 17 R. 450 ; Lord Stormonth-Darling in *Brown* v. *Warden* (1905), 12 S. L. T. 670.

[6] *Ross's Trs.* v. *Ross* (1902), 4 F. 840.

tell in favour of vesting, and the direction to the contrary that children should pay interest on an advance seems to me to tell against it." [1]

In *Matthew* v. *Scott* [2] the truster nominated his trustees as tutors and curators to the legatees, and this feature of the will was held to show that the legacy was intended to vest during the legatee's minorities, because the truster had no title to appoint tutors unless the subject was to become the property of the legatees during their years of incapacity. But in the later case of *Stewart's Trs.* v. *Stewart* [3] this circumstance was considered to have no bearing on the question of vesting, and it has not been noticed in subsequent cases.

Nomination of the testator's trustees as tutors to the legatee.

Gifts to a Class on the respective Majorities of the Members.—The rules given above are applicable as well where the bequest is to a class as where it is to an individual. Thus, if trustees are directed to divide a fund among such of the members of a class as attain majority ; or among the members, with a destination-over or survivorship clause referring to the respective majorities of the members, then, for the reasons already given, no member can acquire a vested interest until his majority.[4] But if the gift is made to the members of the class simply on their respectively attaining the age of twenty-one, this mode of expression appears to be open to construction, and the question of

Class gifts.

---

[1] *Per* Lord Trayner.

[2] (1844), 6 D. 718.

[3] (1851), 13 D. 1386.

[4] As in *Buchanan's Trs.* v. *Buchanan* (1877), 4 R. 754 (stated, *post*, p. 198). *Campbell* v. *Reid* (1840), 2 D. 1084 (destination-over) ; *Bogle's Trs.* v. *Cochrane* (1892), 20 R. 108 ; *Stewart's Trs.* v. *Stewart* (1851), 13 D. 1386. See also *Duncan's Trs.* (1877), 4 R. 1093. The words of the will in this case may be quoted. The trustees were directed, on the expiry of two liferents, " to hold the fee of the said sum for behoof of such of the children of A. . . . as shall be then surviving and shall have attained or shall afterwards attain the age of twenty-five years complete, and for behoof of the

issue of any child or children who may have predeceased the cessation of said liferents . . . or who may die before the foresaid age, leaving issue ; and I direct and appoint my trustees to pay and divide said sum to . . . said children or issue upon their respectively attaining the foresaid age of twenty-five years complete," etc. Under this clause the Court had no difficulty in holding that vesting was postponed till the end of the liferents and the attainment by the children of twenty-five. So also in English law— *Bull* v. *Pritchard* (1825), 1 Russ. 213 ; *Dewar* v. *Brooke* (1880), 14 Ch.D. 529 ; *Thomas* v. *Wilberforce* (1862), 31 Beav. 299. As to the ascertainment of the class, see Chapter VIII., *post*.

vesting will depend on whether the reference to the legatees' majorities is to be taken as qualifying the main purpose of giving, or as merely pointing out the times of payment.[1]

The two following cases may be cited as examples of the manner in which such gifts are construed.

In the first of these cases—*Waters' Trs.* v. *Waters* [2]—almost all the elements favourable to early vesting were present. The truster directed his trustees to " hold and divide the whole residue for and among " his children, and, after giving an annuity to his widow, he directed that the surplus income, or such part thereof as the trustees might deem expedient, should be applied for the maintenance of the children " until they respectively attain the age of twenty-five years complete," at which dates the trustees were to make over their respective shares, so far as not required for the annuity, and, on the death of his widow and as the children respectively attained twenty-five, the capital retained to meet the annuity was to be divided. There was a clause substituting issue in the event of any child pre-deceasing the term of payment. On a consideration of these provisions, it was held that a child dying before the widow and without having attained the age of twenty-five had acquired a vested interest.

The Lord Justice-Clerk (Moncreiff) remarked : " I have come to be of opinion quite clearly that the general rule or presumption in favour of vesting *a morte testatoris* is not displaced by this postponement of the period of payment, and that upon this one ground, which appears to me quite sufficient, namely, that the trustees are directed from the first to hold a specific ascertained fund for behoof of the legatees, which is consequently to be set apart for them. . . . Now, it is to be observed that there here occurs the exact element which Lord Cowan desiderated in *Laing* v. *Barclay*,[3] namely, a special provision or interest in favour of the children from the beginning, although there is a postponement of the term of payment of the whole provision until

---

[1] Cf. *Mackintosh* v. *Wood* (1872), 10 M. 933, and *Mackintosh's Trs.* v. *Mackintosh* (1907), 44 S. L. R. 911, 15 S. L. T. 272.

[2] (1884), 12 R. 253. Cf. for dicta *Matthew* v. *Scott* (1844), 6 D. 718 ; but this case was disapproved in *Richardson's Trs.* v. *Cope* (1850), 12 D. 855, and *Stewarts' Trs.* v. *Stewart* (1851) 13 D. 1386.

[3] (1865), 3 M. 1143.

the child should attain the age of twenty-five. The trustees from the first are not only to hold the fund, but to divide it into special shares, and these are to be held for the legatees, each share belonging separately to each." The gift of interest was also relied on by the Court ; and the destination-over to the issue of a predeceasing child was treated as applying to the death of a child before the testator.

In the second case—*Mackinnon's Trs.* v. *MacNeill* [1]—the truster instructed his trustees to pay a sum to a nephew in liferent, and, on the nephew's death, to and among his children " on their respectively attaining the age of twenty-one, payable as such children, after their father's death, respectively attain majority," with interest in the meantime, " the issue of any of the said children who may have predeceased taking the parent's share." It was held that there was vesting in the children, although minors, *a morte testatoris* (the nephew having predeceased the testator). The Court founded on the gift of the intermediate interest, and on the circumstance that the trustees were to pay to the eldest son on his becoming twenty-one, which implied that the objects at that time must have been ascertained.

Gifts to a Class on the Majority of the Youngest Member.— Provisions that the subject of a gift made to a class shall be held until, or paid when, the youngest member attains majority are of frequent occurrence in wills. Where the children are all in minority at the testator's death it might be thought that vesting was necessarily suspended on the principle of *Dies incertus pro conditione habetur* seeing that it is uncertain whether any child will attain majority : [2] but this is not so, for there are cases in which gifts in this form have been held to confer a vested right (either absolute or subject to defeasance) *a morte testatoris*. The motive of the testator in making his gift in this form may have been merely to protect the legatees during their minorities and at the same time to avoid the inconvenience of making the fund payable in portions and at different times. In English law it would seem that the legatees acquire vested interests

---

[1] (1897), 24 R. 981. Cf. *Buchanan's Trs.* v. *Buchanan* (1877), 4 R. 754.

[2] *Allan's Trs.* v. *Allan*, 1918 S. C.

164, *per* Lord Mackenzie and Lord Skerrington.

as they respectively attain twenty-one,[1] but no such rule has been established in our law. The question of vesting depends on the considerations already noted, such as the form of the gift, whether the trustees are directed to hold the fund and pay it over on the majority of the youngest child [2] or, on the other hand, are merely directed to make payment on that event : [3] the presence or absence of a survivorship clause or destination-over applicable to that event : [4] and whether the trustees are instructed to pay the income of the fund or make advances from capital in the interval before the youngest child becomes major.[5]

The difficulties attending the construction of a bequest in this form, where the testator is survived by only one member of the class or where the youngest member dies under age, are discussed in *Maitland's Trs.* v. *MacDiarmid* [6] and the other cases referred to in Chapter IV.

Gifts on
marriage.

II. **Gifts on Marriage.**—There is apparently no decision in Scots law as to the vesting of a gift to a legatee simply on his or her marriage. A bequest of this nature would appear to be analogous to a gift on majority, and governed by the same considerations. Hence, if the legacy is given in the event of the beneficiary's marrying, or if it is implied in a direction to trustees to pay or make over the subject on his or her marriage,[7] vesting would presumably be suspended till that event occurred ; whereas, if direct words of gift are followed by a direction to pay on the beneficiary's marriage, the vesting would, according to the

---

[1] *Leeming* v. *Sherratt* (1842), 2 Hare 14 ; Theobald on Wills (8th Ed.) 661.

[2] *Wilson's Trs.* v. *Quick* (1878), 5 R. 697 ; *Byars' Trs.* v. *Hay* (1887), 14 R. 1034 ; *Ballantyne's Trs.* v. *Kidd* (1898), 25 R. 621 ; *Taylor's Trs.* v. *Cristal's Trs.* (1903), 5 F. 1010.

[3] *Adam's Trs.* v. *Carrick* (1896), 23 R. 828 ; *Ross's Trs.* v. *Ross* (1902), 4 F. 840. See *Allan's Trs.* v. *Allan, supra.*

[4] *Naismith* v. *Boyes* (1899), 1 F. (H. L.) 79 ; *Fyfe's Trs.* v. *Fyfe* (1890), 17 R. 450 ; *Begg's Trs.* v. *Reid* (1899),

1 F. 498. In some of the cases a provision calling the issue or heirs of the legatee in the event of his predecease was treated as not affecting the vesting ; but a different view is now taken of such provisions—see Chapter IV., *post.*

[5] Stress was laid on these features in *Wilson's Trs.* v. *Quick,* and other cases, but it would seem that they could not outweigh a survivorship clause or destination-over.

[6] (1861), 23 D. 732 ; see p. 89, *post.*

[7] *Morgan* v. *Morgan* (1850), 20 L. J. (Ch.) 109.

rules stated in the previous part of this chapter, take place at the testator's death. It must be remarked, however, that in English law a distinction is taken, in this matter, between gifts on marriage and gifts on majority. Thus, in *Atkins* v. *Hiccocks*,[1] where the gift was expressed thus : " I devise to my daughter A. the sum of £200, to be paid her at the time of her marriage—provided she marry with the approbation of my two sons—and my will is that my said daughter shall yearly receive and be paid, until such time as she shall marry, the sum of £12," Hardwicke, L. C., held that the daughter acquired no vested interest, seeing that she died unmarried. The provision for the sons' consent certainly aided this construction ; but this was not the main ground of the judgement, which was based on the general principle of construction applicable to such gifts. Lord Hardwicke thought that a gift on marriage was distinguishable from a gift on majority in this respect, that in the latter case it was known when the legatee, if he lived, would become major, and the payment was postponed merely on account of the legatee's legal incapacity to manage his own affairs, whereas in gifts on marriage the event was in every respect uncertain. He, therefore, held that the maxim *dies incertus pro conditione habetur* applied to the latter case, notwithstanding that the words of gift might be severed from the direction as to payment. It is not certain, however, that this somewhat subtle distinction would be adopted by the Scots Courts. In any case, it would appear that the distinction does not hold in English law where the subject of the gift is residue ; if a residuary bequest is made in outright terms, and thereafter it is directed that it shall be made over on the beneficiary's marriage, the bequest vests *a morte testatoris*.[2]

In *Smith's Trs.* v. *Smith*,[3] a provision as to marriage was treated as a resolutive condition. The testator in that case directed in his holograph will that his widow should have (in addition to an annuity) the household furniture and everything in his house, " provided she remains unmarried,

Vesting subject to defeasance.

[1] (1737), 1 Atk. 500 ; *Elton* v. *Elton* (1747), 3 Atk. 504. Cf. the successful argument in *Burnets* v. *Forbes* (1783), M. 8105.

[2] *Booth* v. *Booth* (1798), 4 Ves. 399 ; *In re Wrey* (1885), 30 Ch. D. 507 ; Jarman on Wills (7th Ed.), p. 1395.

[3] (1883), 10 R. 1144.

but in the event she marries, the annual allowance to be reduced . . . with neither free house nor furniture," and it was held that she had a right of fee in the furniture (and not a liferent), subject to the obligation of surrendering the subjects if she married again. This case, however, is somewhat anomalous.

Gift to a legatee on the marriage of another.

When a bequest is made to a legatee on the marriage of another person, it is probable that a suspension of vesting was intended by the testator. In *Mackintosh* v. *Wood*,[1] a testatrix instructed her trustees to pay £600 to her son in the event of the marriage of her daughter ; and by a codicil she directed them in addition to pay the sum of £400 to him on the marriage or death of her daughter. The son survived the testatrix but predeceased the daughter, who afterwards married. It was held that the legacy of £400 had vested in him, being given in any case on the daughter's death (a *dies certus*), but that the other legacy, being dependent on a *dies incertus* (the daughter's marriage), had lapsed.

Meaning of " unmarried."

Lastly, it may be noticed that the word " unmarried " is of flexible meaning.[2] The usual and primary meaning is " never having been married "[3] ; but it has a secondary meaning, namely, " not having a spouse " at the testator's death, or at the time when the gift is to take effect,[4] and the context may show that it was used in this latter sense.

---

[1] (1872), 10 M. 933.

[2] *Clarke* v. *Colls* (1861), 9 H. L. (Clark) 601.

[3] *Dalrymple* v. *Hall* (1881), 16 Ch. D. 715 ; *In re Sergeant* (1883), 26 Ch. D. 575 ; *Blundell* v. *De Falbe* (1888), 57 L. J. (Ch.) 576 ; *Heywood* v. *Heywood* (1860), 29 Beav. 9 ; *Soutar's Trs.* v. *Spence*, 1937, S.L.T. 207 (Lord Stevenson). Cf. *Kennedy's Trs.* v. *Sharpe* (1895), 23 R. 146 ; *Douglas' Trs.* (1902), 5 F. 69.

[4] *Clarke* v. *Colls*, *supra* ; *Pratt* v. *Matthew* (1856), 8 D. M. & G. 522 ; *In re Chant* [1900], 2 Ch. 345.

CHAPTER IV.

SURVIVORSHIP CLAUSES AND DESTINATIONS-OVER

WHERE a gift is made to an institute and a conditional institute, the effect of this conditional gift-over is to postpone vesting until that time at which it is intended that the institute's right shall vanish if he is not then alive, and that the right of the conditional institute shall emerge.[1]

Such conditional institutions usually appear in the form of a destination-over or survivorship clause (which is the common form where the bequest is to a plurality of persons). These forms are essentially the same, and are subject to the same rule.

I. Survivorship Clauses.—It may be stated as one of the most firmly established canons of vesting, that a survivorship clause has the effect of fixing the vesting of the gift at the time or on the event with reference to which the survivors are to be ascertained. In *Walker* v. *Park*,[2] Lord Cowan observed : " If any general rule can be deduced from the decisions in such cases, it is this, that if there is a survivorship provided for, the effect is to delay the period of vesting till it be seen whether any, and who, the survivors are." And Lord Justice-Clerk Hope remarked, in *Stewart's Trs.* v. *Stewart*,[3] that in most cases a survivorship clause

A survivorship clause fixes vesting at the time to which it relates.

---

[1] Lord Watson in *Bowman* v. *Bowman* (1899), 1 F. (H. L.) 69.

[2] (1859), 21 D. 286.
[3] (1851), 13 D. 1386.

was conclusive against vesting before the event to which it related.

It was further settled, in the very important case of *Young* v. *Robertson*,[1] that words of survivorship are, in the absence of specialties, to be referred to the time of payment or distribution of the gift. That case introduced no new rule into our law,[2] but Lord Westbury's opinion has been accepted as an authoritative exposition of the principle of construction to be applied to such words. The facts of the case were these : The testator gave a liferent of his estate to his wife, and directed his trustees to divide the residue of his estate " after the death of the last liver of me and my said wife, equally . . . among " certain of his grandnephews and grandnieces, " declaring that if any of said residuary legatees shall die without leaving lawful issue before his or her share vest [3] in the party or parties so deceasing, the same shall belong to and be divided . . . among the survivors." Three legatees survived the testator, but died before the widow. The Court of Session decided that the survivors were to be ascertained at the testator's death, and that accordingly shares had vested in these legatees ; but on appeal the House of Lords reversed the judgement, and found that vesting was postponed till the termination of the liferent. The principle of the decision was set forth by Lord Westbury as follows :—" I apprehend it to be a settled rule of construction, that words of survivorship occurring in a settlement (that is, in a will) should be referred to the period appointed by that settlement for the payment or distribution of the subject-matter of the gift. That undoubtedly is the rule now finally established in this country, and it has been ascertained from the authorities which have been cited at the bar that the rule was established in Scotland even before it was finally recognised in this country. The application of that rule would lead to this determination in two cases. If a testator gives a sum of

---

[1] (1862), 4 Macq. 314.

[2] See cases cited on p. 48. And cf. Lord Ordinary Moncreiff's Note in *Provan* v. *Provan* (1840), 2 D. 298 ; and *Johnston* v. *Johnston* (1840), 2 D. 1038 (the reversal does not affect his exposition of the rule as to survivorship).

[3] The effect of these words was simply to show that the testator intended a conditional institution and not a substitution. Cf. argument for Appellants in the case.

money or the residue of his estate to be paid or distributed among a number of persons, and refers to the contingency of any one or more of them dying, and then gives the estate or the money to the survivor, in that simple form of gift which is to take effect immediately on the death of the testator, the period of distribution is the period of death, and accordingly the contingency of death is to be referred to the interval of time between the date of the will and the death of the testator. In such a case, the words are construed to provide for the event of the death of any one of the legatees during the lifetime of the testator.[1] By parity of reasoning, if a testator gives a life estate in a sum of money or in the residue of his estate, and at the expiration of that life estate directs the money to be paid, or the residue to be divided among a number of objects, and then refers to the possibility of some one or more of those persons dying, without specifying the time, and directs in that event the payment or distribution to be made among the survivors, it is understood by the law that he means the contingency to extend over the whole period of time that must elapse before the payment or distribution takes place. The result, therefore, is that in such a gift the survivors are to be ascertained in like manner by a reference to the period of distribution, namely, the expiration of the life estate." [2]

Both branches of the rule are illustrated in *Nolan* v. *Hartley's Trs.*[3] In that case the testatrix by her will directed her trustees " immediately after " her death, and as soon as her estate was realised, to divide it into shares for behoof of her grandsons, with a clause of survivorship similar to that in *Young* v. *Robertson*. The time of division being immediate, vesting was *a morte testatoris*. But by a codicil the testatrix

---

[1] As in *Stiven* v. *Brown's Trs.* (1873), 11 M. 262.

[2] In *Richardson* v. *Power* (1865), 19 C. B. N. S. 780, where the bequest was to a daughter in life and to her sons in tail, and, in default of these, to the testator's son John, and, if John should die without issue before the estates vested in him, to such of the testator's daughters as were then living, it was pointed out that the rule in *Young* v. *Robertson* was stated with reference to a will in which a definite time for payment was appointed; here the " then living " referred to John's death before vesting of his right, whenever that might occur, and not to any fixed time.

[3] (1866), 5 M. 153.

altered the will by providing a liferent of her house to her daughter, and directing payment of the whole on her death to the same parties and under the same terms as set forth in the will. As there was practically no other property except the house, this change in the period of distribution was held to change the time of vesting of the estate from the death of the testatrix to that of the liferentrix.

As the rule which refers words of survivorship to the time of payment is founded on the natural meaning of such words in the vocabulary of ordinary life, it will be set aside only on cogent evidence that the testator has used them in relation to some other period. Of all the provisions which may occur in a will, a survivorship clause is pre-eminently that which is most adverse to vesting before the time at which payment is to be made ; and the cases in which gifts qualified by a clause of this kind have been held to vest before that time are rare.

The rule is exemplified in a large number of cases. These, for the most part, merely establish that, in the application of the rule, it is immaterial what the time of payment appointed by the will may be ; thus, for example, if payment is to be made (as in *Young* v. *Robertson*) at the close of a liferent ; [1] or on the respective majorities of the beneficiaries ; [2] or on the majority of the youngest member of a class : [3] the occurrence of these events (as the case may be) is the time at which the survivors are to be ascertained, and therefore the time of vesting. The cases which contain any qualification of Lord Westbury's statement are discussed in a subsequent section of this chapter.[4]

[1] *Newton* v. *Thomson* (1849), 11 D. 452 ; *Richardson's Tr.* v. *Cope* (1850), 12 D. 855 ; *Roope & Ball* (1872), 9 S. L. R. 341 ; *Marshall* v. *King* (1888), 16 R. 40 ; *Vines* v. *Hillou* (1860), 22 D. 1436 ; *Muirhead* v. *Muirhead* (1890), 17 R. (H. L.) 45 ; *Clelland* v. *Gray* (1839), 1 D. 1031 ; *Smith's Trs.* v. *Graham* (1873), 11 M. 630 ; *Spence* v. *Paterson's Trs.* (1873), 1 R. 46 ; *Seton's Trs.* v. *Seton* (1886), 13 R. 1047. In *Hendry's Trs.* v. *Patrick* (1905), 13 S. L. T. 503, where trustees were directed to pay a legacy to A. and B. and the survivor at the first term after the death of a liferentrix, Lord Dundas held that no right vested in A. seeing that, although she survived the liferentrix, she died before the term.

[2] *Campbell* v. *Reid* (1840), 2 D. 1084 ; *Stewart's Trs.* v. *Stewart* (1851). 13 D. 1386 ; *Buchanan's Trs.* v, *Buchanan* (1877), 4 R. 754.

[3] *Fyfe's Trs.* v. *Fyfe* (1890), 17 R. 450 ; *Walker* v. *Park* (1859), 21 D. 286 ; *Cattanach* v. *Thom's Exrs.* (1858), 20 D. 1206.

[4] *Post*, p. 55.

A condition as to survivorship commonly appears in one or other of these three forms : it may appear as a gift to such of the class or persons as are alive at a time or event mentioned or implied ;[1] or it may be expressed by the addition of the words " or the survivors or survivor " to the names or description of the legatees ;[2] or it may take the form of a devolution clause (that is, a clause providing for the legatee's interest going over to his issue or the survivors (failing issue) in the event of his death).[3] In one case where the settlement was holograph of the testator, the words were " with benefit of survivorship." [4]

Forms of survivorship clauses or words.

II. Destinations-over.

The rule of construction contained in Lord Westbury's statement has been treated as applying as well to destinations-over as to survivorship clauses.[5] So far as the question is as to the vesting in the institute, it is clearly immaterial which form the conditional institution takes.

Destinations-over refer to the time of payment.

The time, then, to which a destination-over refers is *primâ facie* the time appointed for payment.

Hence, if the gift is immediate (payment not being postponed), it will vest *a morte testatoris* ; as, for example, in the case of a simple bequest to A., whom failing to B.[6]

But if the trustees are directed to pay at a period subsequent to the testator's death, the presumption is that vesting is suspended till that period. In the leading case

---

[1] *Wallace* v. *Wallaces* (1807), M. " Clause," App. No. 6 ; *Boyle* v. *Earl of Glasgow's Trs.* (1858), 20 D. 925 ; *Watson* v. *M'Dougall* (1856), 18 D. 971 ; *Dymock's Trs.* v. *Swan* (1873), 45 S. J. 289 ; 10 S. L. R. 263 ; *Naismith* v. *Boyes* (1899), 1 F. (H. L.) 79.

[2] *Newton* v. *Thomson* (1849), 11 D. 452 ; *Cattanach* v. *Thom's Exrs.* (1858), 20 D. 1206 ; *Roope & Ball* (1872), 9 S. L. R. 341 ; *Chancellor* v. *Mossman* (1872), 10 M. 995 ; *Marshall* v. *King* (1888), 16 R. 40.

[3] *Young* v. *Robertson* (1862), 4 Macq. 314 ; *Pearson* v. *Casamaijor* (1839), M'L. & Rob. 685 ; *Robertson* v. *Richardson* (1843), 5 D. 1117 ; *Richardson's Tr.* v. *Cope* (1850), 12 D. 855 ; *Walker* v. *Park* (1859), 21 D. 286 ; *Muirhead* v. *Muirhead* (1890), 17 R. (H. L.) 45 ; *Fyfe's Trs.* v. *Fyfe* (1890), 17 R. 450 ; *Scott* v. *Scott's Trs.* (1881), 18 S. L. R. 436.

[4] *Thornhill* v. *Macpherson* (1841), 3 D. 394.

[5] *Stodart's Trs.* (1870), 8 M. 667 ; Lord Watson in *Bowman* v. *Bowman, supra* ; Lord M'Laren in *Hay's Trs.* v. *Hay* (1890), 17 R. 961.

[6] *Sanderson* v. *Wardrop* (1873), 1 R. 96 ; *Fyffe* v. *Fyffe* (1841), 3 D. 1205.

of *Bryson's Trs.* v. *Clark*,[1] Lord President Inglis formulated the rule as to destinations-over, in terms substantially the same as those used by Lord Westbury. " When nothing is expressed in favour of a beneficiary," he said, " except a direction to trustees to convey to him on the occurrence of a certain event, and not sooner, and failing him, to certain other persons as substitutes or conditional institutes to him, then, if he does not survive the period, he takes no right under the settlement." [2]

In this case the testator directed his trustees to convey an heritable estate, on the death of the survivor of himself and his wife, to A. and the heirs of his body, whom failing to B. A. predeceased the widow, and, in accordance with the principle expressed by the Lord President, it was held that no right had vested in him.

The form which a destination-over commonly takes is " To A. whom failing to B.," or to " A. or B.," the word " or " being construed as equivalent to " whom failing." [3] The word " and " is clearly less appropriate to a conditional institution than " or " for it suggests joint rather than alternative rights. Thus in *Cobban's Exrs.* v. *Cobban* [4] the testator directed that the remainder of his estate should be divided " equally between my brother Peter and his children and my brother George Cobban and his children," and it was held (with some aid from the circumstance that two of Peter's children were expressly excluded) that the children *per capita* participated concurrently with their parents in the bequest. On the other hand, in *Black's Trs.* v. *Nixon*,[5] where a share of residue was bequeathed to a

---

[1] (1880), 8 R. 142. Followed in *Groat* v. *Stewart's Trs.* (1894), 21 R. 961 ; *Forbes* v. *M'Condach's Trs.* (1890), 18 R. 230 ; *Baillie's Trs.* v. *Whiting*, 1910 S. C. 891. Cf. also *Wright* v. *Ogilvie* (1840), 2 D. 1357 ; *M'Lay* v. *Borland* (1876), 3 R. 1124.

[2] In England the law has been stated thus : " A bequest to A., and in case of his death to B., is a gift absolute to A. unless he dies in the testator's lifetime. A bequest to C. for life, and then to A., and in case of his death to B., is a gift absolute to A., unless he dies during C.'s life " (*Home* v.

Pillans, 2 M. & K. 23). But where the gift-over is in contingent terms, as, *e.g.*, in the event of death with or without issue, this is held to mean death at any time (*O'Mahoney* v. *Burdett*, L. R. 7 H. L. 388).

[3] *Bowman* v. *Bowman*, 1 F. (H. L.) 69, *per* Lord Watson and Lord Davey.

[4] 1915 S. C. 82.

[5] 1931 S. C. 590. See also *Mellis's Trs.* v. *Ritchie*, 1909 S. C. 626 ; *Edward* v. *Shiell* (1848), 10 D. 685 ; and *Grant* v. *Gunn's Trs.* (1833), 11 S. 484 ; in which the same construction was adopted.

legatee " and her children," the decision was that the children were conditional institutes, and that accordingly the legatee was entitled to the whole of the share on her survivance of the testator. Lord President Clyde observed : " It was said by Lord Dundas in the case of *Cobban's Exrs.* v. *Cobban*, a case in which the circumstances were, at any rate, comparable to those in the present case, that, unless the context leads necessarily or by natural implication to a different conclusion, ' the word " and " points to a joint right and not to successive rights in the parties named.' A clear case of necessary implication, taking the use of the word ' and ' out of what Lord Dundas thought to be its normal meaning, is provided by the familiar gift ' to A. *and* his heirs.' [1] The meaning must be a gift to A. if he survives, but, if A. predeceases, then to his heirs ; because A. could not share the gift with his own heirs. In like manner a gift to A., B., and C., ' *and* the survivors and survivor of them ' can import nothing but a conditional institution of the survivors or survivor. Even, however, on Lord Dundas's dictum, the true meaning of the word ' and ' in such a clause as we have here may be gathered from the context ; and this is exemplified in the case of *Murray* [2] which does not appear to have been cited in the case in which his Lordship's opinion was delivered." In the most recent case, *Clow's Trs.* v. *Bethune*,[3] the direction being that the residue should be " equally divided between my nephews and nieces and their children," the same construction was adopted as in *Black's Trs.* v. *Nixon*. It was argued that that case was distinguishable because of the use of the word " equally " in Mr Clow's deed which had the effect of bringing it within the authority of *Cobban's Exrs.* v. *Cobban* ; and in the opinions of the Court it was recognised that the use of the word made it more difficult to treat the children as conditional institutes. The decision in *Clow's Trs.* v. *Bethune* was a narrow one, for there was a divergence of opinions on the bench, the Lord Ordinary's interlocutor being reversed, dissenting the Lord Justice-Clerk. The construction which brings in the issue to share along with the parent is not one which would commend

---

[1] See the cases as to this form of gift cited on p. 78, *post*.

[2] (1873), 45 S. J. 574.

[3] 1935 S. C. 754.

itself to most testators, and it would appear that the Court is disposed, if possible, to adopt the other construction.

The distinction between conditional institutions and substitutions.

In considering the influence of destinations on the vesting of the institute's right, the difference in effect of a conditional institution, on the one hand, and a substitution, on the other, must not be overlooked. Conditional institutions always bear reference, either expressly or by implication, to some time or event, and it has been shown in a previous chapter [1] that they cannot be considered as operative after the time at which the trustees are directed to make over the subject, because when the trust terminates there are no means of securing the rights of conditional institutes, and because, also, an order to pay assumes that the recipients are fixed when the order is to be obeyed.

A conditional institution suspends vesting; a substitution does not.

As, therefore, a conditional institution provides, by the creation of an alternative interest, for the disposal of the subject in the event of the institute's death before a given time, it makes the institute's right conditional upon his surviving that time, and therefore in the meantime suspends vesting. A substitution, on the other hand, is designed to regulate the succession to the legatee on his death *at any time*. The substitute is to take whenever the institute's enjoyment terminates, if he dies without evacuating the destination. Hence, as it implies no reference to any point of time, but provides merely for the succession to the subject on the institute's death, whenever that shall occur, it cannot render the institute's right conditional, and is therefore not inconsistent with the vesting of the gift. A substitution always includes a conditional institution, as the lesser right [2]; so that, if the institute dies without acquiring right to the subject, the substitute will take, but the further destination is not thereby sopited. This is no more than a result of the fact that it refers to the institute's death at any time; for a destination which is to operate on the institute's death at any time must include the case of the institute's death before the testator or before the time fixed by the other provisions of the deed as the date of vesting.

The importance of the distinction between conditional institutions and substitutions, in regard to the vesting of

[1] Chapter II. *ante*, p. 27.
[2] *Fogo* v. *Fogo* (1842), 4 D. 1063;

2 Bell's App. 195; *Hutchison* v. *Hutchison* (1872), 11 M. 229.

the institute's right, is illustrated in *Roberton* v. *Davidson*.[1]
In this case the beneficiary under a deed sought acceleration
of the provisions made in his favour, and his claim raised the
question whether these had vested in him. The deed set
out that in the event which happened (namely, the predecease of the wife) the interest should be paid to the
husband and A., and that on the husband's death the
capital should be made over to A., or "to his heirs and
assignees as substitutes." It was held that the provisions
vested in A. on the death of the wife. Lord Fullerton
considered that the words "as substitutes" were sufficient
to put the question of vesting beyond dispute.[2] In *Vines* v.
Hillou[3] Lord Benholme, after holding that a survivorship
clause was not a substitution, said : "The extreme importance of such clauses of survivorship in questions of vesting
entirely depends upon the well-established construction of
these clauses, which in general, delays the period of vesting
just because they have their proper effect as conditional
institutions"; and in *Tristram* v. *M'Haffies*[4] Lord Kinnear
pointed out that a direct conveyance of land to a number
of persons in succession was a substitution, and not merely
a conditional institution, adding : "It follows that the rule
laid down in *Young* v. *Robertson*, 4 Macq. 314, as to the construction of words of survivorship can have no application."

As regards the right of the party called in the second
place, it is familiar law that a conditional institution is
evacuated when the subject vests in the institute, whereas
a substitution remains effectual despite the vesting of the
institute's right. A substitution in a heritable destination
may be defeated by the institute's gratuitous disposition
of the subject, whether by an *inter vivos* deed or by his
general testamentary settlement ;[5] in moveable rights the
destination is evacuated if the institute appropriate the

---

[1] (1846), 9 D. 152.

[2] Cf. also Lord Low's opinion in
Cairns v. *Cairns' Trs.* (1901), 3 F. 545 ;
but the decision does not proceed on
a determination of the question of
vesting.

[3] (1860), 22 D. 1436 ; contrast
Brown's Trs. v. *Smith* (1900) 2 F. 817,
where a survivorship clause in a

direction as to a heritable subject
was held to be a substitution.

[4] (1894), 22 R. 121, at 128. See
also *Houston* v. *Houston's Trs.* (1894),
2 S. L. T. 118 ; affg. 1 S. L. T. 403 ;
and Lord M'Laren's opinion in *Turner*
v. *Gaw* (1894), 21 R. 563.

[5] Ersk. iii. 8. 44 ; *Baine* v. *Craig*
(1845), 7 D. 845.

subject, as, for instance, if he immixes the fund with his own estate, or transfers the investments into his own name.[1] " The genius of the law being against any tying up of moveables, mere possession by the institute without the execution of any deed of evacuation will be sufficient to defeat a substitution." [2]

Conditional institutions presumed in moveable rights; substitutions in heritable.

In determining whether any given destination is a substitution or a conditional institution, the main element is the nature of the subject. There may be a substitution in moveable property [3] and a conditional institution in heritable.[4] But there is a strong presumption in favour of conditional institution where the subject is moveable,[5] and in favour of substitution where it is heritable.[6] In mixed estate—that is, estate partly heritable and partly moveable— a conditional institution is presumed.[7] In *Watson* v. *Giffen*,[8] Lord President Inglis expressed an opinion that in this matter the nature of the subject at the time when the will was made is to be regarded, although it may have been changed prior to the testator's death.

But these presumptions may be displaced by the terms of the deed.

These legal presumptions are of the greater weight because of the absence of any technical form of expression peculiar to either of these kinds of destination. The very common phrase " whom failing," for example, may import either a conditional institution or a substitution, and it takes its meaning from the character of the property.[9] It is true that, as in every question regarding a testamentary

---

[1] *M'Dowall* v. *M'Gill* (1847), 9 D. 1284 ; *Buchanan's Trs.* v. *Dalziel's Trs.* (1868), 6 M. 536 ; *Greig* v. *Johnston* (1833), 6 W. & S. 406 ; *Bell's Exr.* v. *Borthwick* (1897), 24 R. 1120.

[2] *Per* Lord Dunedin in *Robertson* v. *Hay-Boyd*, 1928 S. C. (H. L.) 8, at 13.

[3] *M'Dowall* v. *M'Gill, supra* ; *Dyer* v. *Carruthers* (1874), 1 R. 943 ; *Buchanan's Trs.* v. *Dalziel's Trs., supra* ; *M'Clymont's Exrs.* v. *Osborne* (1895), 22 R. 411 ; *Sutherland* v. *Douglas's Trs.* (1865), 4 M. 105 ; *Logan's Trs.* v. *Ellis* (1890), 17 R. 425. In *Vines* v. *Hillou* (1860), 22 D. 1436, it was decided that a gift-over to survivors was a conditional institution, and not a substitution.

[4] *Marshall* v. *Marshall* (1900), 37 S. L. R. 775.

[5] *Greig* v. *Johnston* (1833), 6 W. & S. 406 (" in the event of the death of . . . A. B. shall *succeed* ") ; *Brown* v. *Coventry* (1792), Bell's Oct. Cases, 310 ; M. 14863 ; *Crumpton's J.F.* v. *Barnardo's Homes*, 1917, S. C. 713.

[6] *Watson* v. *Giffen* (1884), 11 R. 444.

[7] *Paul* v. *Home* (1872), 10 M. 937 ; followed by Lord Kincairney in *M'Lay* v. *Chalmers* (1903), 11 S. L. T. 223 ; *Ramsay* v. *Ramsay* (1839), 14 Fac. 54 ; 1 D. 83.

[8] *Supra.*

[9] Lord President in *Brown* v. *Coventry* (1792), Bell's Oct. Cas. 310.

disposition, the effect to be attributed to a destination is a matter to be determined in accordance with what appears to have been the testator's intention ; but in order to displace these presumptions very clear evidence of a contrary intention in the deed is required.[1] Upon this point the cases afford little instruction. It seems certain, however, that if the destination were expressly limited to the case of the institute's death before he acquired a vested interest, this could be nothing more than a conditional institution, whatever were the nature of the subject ; and, on the other hand, if the will provided that the destination was to take effect on the legatee's death, either before or after vesting, this would necessarily import a substitution even if the subject were moveable. And it may further be suggested that if the legatee's death were spoken of in terms importing a contingency, as, for example, if the subject were given over *in the event of* or *in case of* his death, then, as death is of all things the most certain, this would afford ground, in order to satisfy and give a meaning to those expressions, for construing the provision as referring to his death before some time mentioned or implied in the will ; and, therefore, as no more than a conditional institution.[2] A reference also to the legatee's *predecease*, as it necessarily refers to a time or event, would appear to show that a conditional institution was intended. On the other hand, if the testator state that the party called in the second place is to take in the case of the institute's dying without disposing of the subject, this is favourable to the view that the destination is a substitution [3] and not a conditional institution.

III. Application of the Rule of *Young* v. *Robertson* : Exceptions and Limitations.—The decision in *Young* v. *Robertson* [4] established the rule of construction applicable in

[1] *Greig* v. *Johnston* (1833), 6 W. & S. 406.

[2] Cf. Lord Mackenzie in *Fyffe* v. *Fyffe* (1841), 3 D. 1205 ; and Lord Young in *Peacock's Trs.* v. *Peacock* (1885), 12 R. 878.

[3] Cf. *Bell's Exr.* v. *Borthwick* (1897), 24 R. 1120. As to the effect of the word " revert," see *Buchanan's Trs.* v.

Dalziel's Trs. (1868), 6 M. 536 (especially Lord Deas) ; *Hamilton* v. *Ritchie* (1894), 21 R. 451 ; affd. 21 R. (H. L.) 35 ; *Robertson* v. *Hay-Boyd*, 1927 S. C. 190, 1928 S. C. (H. L.), 8. But cf. *Groat's Trs.* v. *Stewart* (1894), 21 R. 961.

[4] (1862), 4 Macq. 314.

cases where legacies are given to institutes and conditional institutes, without mention of the time or event at which the rights of these parties are to be ascertained. If the testator speaks of the institute's " death," " failure," or " predecease " indefinitely, it becomes necessary to supply a context,[1] and that context is determined in accordance with the principles contained in Lord Westbury's exposition of the law.

The rule merely a presumption, and liable to be displaced. But the rule is merely a presumption,[2] and is therefore liable to be displaced. Where the testator has either expressly or inferentially indicated the time at which the institute's death or failure is to be ascertained, there is no room for the application of the rule. Thus, when the testator speaks of death before " payment," vesting takes place at the date of payment, not in virtue of the presumption, but under the terms of the deed [3]; in such cases the testator has, however, probably expressed what the law, in the absence of any expression, would have presumed.

In *M'Alpine* v. *Studholme*,[4] the testatrix directed her trustees to hold the estate for her sisters in liferent, and " after the death of the longest liver of me and my said sisters . . . to pay, assign, and dispone to " three nephews *nominatim*, " and that on their respectively attaining the age of twenty-one years ; and . . . *if any one or more of my said nephews shall depart this life before he or they shall attain the age of twenty-one years*, then the share or shares of him or them so dying shall go and accresce " to his or their issue, whom failing to the survivors. It was held in this case that a third share had vested in each of two of the nephews who reached majority, but predeceased the liferenters. Had the provision as to predecease been indefinite, or had it been referred to payment, vesting might have been deferred till the expiry of the liferents ;[5] but the clear reference to the legatee's death in minority as the circumstance in which alone the destination-over was to become

[1] Cf. Lord Young in *Peacock's Trs.* v. *Peacock* (1885), 12 R. 878.

[2] Lord Stormonth-Darling in *Webster's Trs.* v. *Neil* (1900), 2 F. 695.

[3] *Muirhead* v. *Muirhead* (1890), 17 R. (H. L.) 45 ; *Reeves' Exr.* v. *Reeves' Jud. Factor* (1892), 19 R. 1013 ; *Vines* v. *Hillou* (1860), 22 D. 1436 ; *Pearson* v. *Casamaijor* (1839), 1 M'L. & Rob. 685 ; *Carter* v. *M'Intosh* (1862), 24 D. 925. As to the meaning of " payment," see Chapter X., *post*.

[4] (1883), 10 R. 837. See also *Sinclair* v. *Sinclair's Trs.* (1867), 5 S. L. R. 133.

[5] Cf. Lord Shand's opinion.

operative, showed that he was intended to take a vested right on attaining majority.[1]

Further, the rule will be displaced by any evidence of a contrary intention appearing in the deed.[2] Thus the truster may gloss the survivorship words or destination-over by the expressions he uses. For example, in *Campbell* v. *Campbell*,[3] the truster directed that a certain heritable property should be made over on his wife's death to A. " *in case of his survivance of me* . . . whom failing, etc.'' There was a further provision for the disposition of the estate in favour of another " in case of the predecease of A." The words first quoted were sufficient to take the case out of the general rule, and it was held that the gift vested *a morte testatoris*. In *Clelland's Trs.* v. *M'Nab*,[4] the truster gave an annuity to his sister and to his wife, and the remainder of the income of his estate to another sister, A. He instructed his trustees, on the death of the longest liver of these three, to make over the estate to A.'s three children *nominatim*, " and the survivor of them . . ., declaring that in the event of any of " them " *predeceasing their mother* and leaving lawful issue,'' his or her share was to go to the issue. Owing to the words italicised, it was decided that vesting in the children took place when their mother died, although one annuitant survived. Similarly, in *Webster's Trs.* v. *Neil*,[5] the bequest was in the form of a direction to pay, on the death or second marriage of the liferentrix, to three persons, " and the survivors and survivor of them . . ., and should the said three . . . all *predecease me*,'' then over to others.

---

[1] For a discussion of the questions that arise where, in cases of complex conditions (as in this case), there is a destination-over, referring merely to payment, or left indefinite, *vide* Chapter XI., *post*.

[2] Thus in *Alston's Trs.* v. *Alston* (1902), 4 F. 654, the force of words of survivorship was overcome by a very special clause in the will.

[3] (1866), 5 M. 206.

[4] (1874), 12 S. L. R. 42.

[5] (1900), 2 F. 695. See, to the same effect, *White* v. *White's Trs.*, 1916 S. C. 435. In two Outer House cases—*Cathcart's Tr.* v. *Ewart* ((1902), 10 S. L. T. 101, and *Duncan's Trs.* v. *Kennedy* (1897), 4 S. L. T. 358— Lord Kyllachy held that a bequest with a survivorship clause annexed vested *a morte testatoris* owing to gifts-over or declarations referring to the legatee's " predeceasing me '' or " surviving me.'' In the former case, where payment was to be made on the death of an annuitant, the fact that the surplus income was to be paid to the beneficiaries yearly was also held to favour early vesting.

Here also vesting was referred by the Court to the truster's death, owing to the words used by the truster in regard to predecease. There are, moreover, several cases where destinations-over were held ineffectual to suspend vesting not because of any distinct statement by the testator, but on account of the general character of the deed. Such cases are all of a very special nature, and afford little instruction in regard to other deeds.[1]

Words of survivorship in subordinate clauses do not suspend vesting

Even in cases where the testator has not stated the term at which the destination-over or survivorship clause is to come into operation, there are certain forms of gift which are not within the rule of *Young* v. *Robertson*. Thus :—

1. Where the words of survivorship do not enter into the description of the beneficiaries in the clause constituting the gift, vesting may take place before the term of payment. In *Miller* v. *Finlay's Trs.*,[2] for example, property was destined in an *inter vivos* deed to a husband and wife in

---

[1] These cases are :—

Allardice v. *Lautour* (1845), 7 D. 362. The decision proceeded on the facts that the deed was a delivered bond of provision, and that interest was provided to the beneficiaries (children) during the father's lifetime in a certain event.

Clark's Trs. v. *Paterson* (1851), 14 D. 141. The Court founded on the word " assignee " and the fact that the trustees were appointed tutors to the beneficiaries.

Marnoch v. *Wilson* (1855), 17 D. 536, where the elements were that there was no trust, and that the words of survivorship occurring in a subordinate clause were insufficient to override clear words of gift without survivorship in the dispositive clause.

These cases are all prior to *Young* v. *Robertson* ; but the effect of words of survivorship in postponing vesting was recognised before that case; and in all the cases cited the decisions proceeded on the view that the specialties of the deeds under consideration prevented the application of the general rule.

In *Angus' Trs.* v. *Angus* (1880), 17

S. L. R. 536 the decision was for vesting *a morte*, as against a clear gift to children alive at a subsequent time ; this decision was based on the conjunction of these elements : (1) that the deed was a marriage contract and not a will ; (2) that interest was given from the father's death ; (3) that the provisions were stated to be in lieu of legitim ; and (4) because of an inference drawn from a power of apportionment retained by the father.

Alston's Trs. v. *Alston* (1902), 4 F. 654, stated *post*, p. 295.

Davidson's Exrs. (1900), 8 S. L. T. 239 (First Division). Gift to a legatee, after the payment of legacies, in " absolute property," whom failing to *nominatim* legatees. The phrase " absolute property " was held to suggest that the legatee " was to have a qualified right to the property at once, which was to become absolute at " the close of liferent. Vesting was held to be *a morte testatoris*, although the legacies were payable on the close of a liferent. There was no trust in this case.

[2] (1875), 2 R. (H. L.) 1.

liferent, and after the determination of the liferents " in trust for the whole lawful children " of the marriage, " declaring that the fee, or principal, of the shares of the children " should be " payable after the determination of the said liferents, and after the whole children who shall have survived " the liferenters, " and who shall be alive shall have attained majority." It was held here that the fee vested at the date of the deed, the rule of *Young* v. *Robertson* being inapplicable, because the condition of survivance was mentioned " not in any clause either giving interests, or defining the conditions upon which interests were given, but in a clause defining the period of time at which interests already given, and given in clear terms, to all the children, should be payable or transferable." [1]

Again, in *Muir's Trs.*[2] the truster gave his wife an annuity of £300, to secure which a sum was to be retained by the trustees. The whole estate was to be divided " equally among my whole children that may be alive at the time of my death." It was declared that the provisions were payable to the children " on their respectively attaining " majority. And in a subsequent part of the deed it was provided that, if any of them died before their shares were payable, these shares should go to their families, and failing families, to the survivors. By a later clause the truster directed that the portion of the estate retained to secure the widow's annuity should be divided at her death " among my said children." The wife survived the truster, and the trustees found it necessary to retain the whole estate for her annuity. It was held here that the survivorship clause did not have the effect of qualifying the plain terms of the initial gift; and that consequently the estate vested in the children in the widow's lifetime. It was considered that the words of survivorship were referable to the times at which the children attained majority. " Where no other part of the deed fixes the vesting, and that requires to be determined by the direction given as to payment and division, a survivorship clause is all-important. The case of *Donaldson's Trs.*,[3] to which reference was made in the

[1] *Per* Lord Selborne.
[2] (1869), 8 M. 53. Cf. also *Marnoch* v. *Wilson* (1855), 17 D. 536.
[3] *i.e. Young* v. *Robertson*.

argument, is of that description. The only direction as to payment and division was ' on the death of the longest liver of the spouses.' The clause in this deed is quite differently expressed, and occurs in the midst of a series of provisions that fix the period of vesting as at the testator's death." [1]

A condition of survivance is not to be annexed by inference.

Further, a clause of survivorship or a destination-over will not be imported into a bequest by implication from other gifts or clauses in the deed. Thus, in *Rattray's Trs.* v. *Rattray*,[2] where the testator appointed his trustees " to make payment of the legacies following at the first term . . . that shall happen after the death of " his wife to the daughters of A. £900, " and failing any of them without leaving children the share of those dying to go to the survivors or survivor ; to B. . . . £100 sterling," the Court (reversing Lord Kinloch's interlocutor) held that the juxta-position of the two gifts did not warrant the inference that the condition of survivance appearing in the first gift affected the right of B. also, and therefore found that his legacy vested *a morte testatoris*. Again, in *Yeats* v. *Paton*,[3] the truster bequeathed sums of money to A. and B., " each payable at the first term . . . after the decease " of his wife ; and after giving his widow an annuity, directed his trustees to pay the residue, " *and any legacy that may have lapsed by the legatees predeceasing* " the widow, to his nephews and nieces. It was held that this last clause was too ambiguous to have the effect of so qualifying the direct bequest to A. and B. in the earlier part of the will as to suspend vesting.

Where the gift is not contained in a direction to pay.

2. The rule of *Young* v. *Robertson* was formulated with reference to a legacy contained in a direction to trustees to pay to the legatees or the survivors, there being no other words of bequest. The distinction between a gift in this form and a direct bequest in *da præsenti* words, or in a direction to trustees to hold for the legatee, has been noticed in a previous chapter, and it was there pointed out that the latter forms of gift were favourable to vesting *a morte testatoris*.[4] In more than one case involving the construction of words of survivorship, stress has been laid on the fact that the only gift to the beneficiaries was contained in a direction to the trustees to make payment as an element

---

[1] *Per* Lord Cowan.

[2] (1868), 6 M. 476. See *ante*, p. 16.

[3] (1880), 8 R. 171.

[4] Chapter II., p. 24 *et seq.*

adverse to vesting before the time of payment,[1] but it has never been decided that this form of gift is essential in order that a survivorship clause shall suspend vesting. If the words of survivorship enter into the description of the legatee, and if the frame of the will require that payment shall be postponed, all the conditions necessary for the application of the principle of *Young* v. *Robertson* would appear to be present ; and it would seem to be a refined and rather unsubstantial distinction to hold the general rule inapplicable merely because the testator had used a direct form of gift and not a direction to his trustees to pay. In the English case of *Hearn* v. *Baker*,[2] this distinction was urged in argument, but Lord Hatherley declined to adopt it, holding that the limitation to survivors deferred vesting, although the gift was made in words of immediate bequest.

3. It does not appear to be necessary for the application of the rule of *Young* v. *Robertson*, that a liferent, or other prior interest, should be given in the subject, for the provision as to survivorship affords, in itself, a sufficient reason for the postponement of the time of payment ; and if the testator defer payment in order to confine his gift to the parties alive at the time at which payment is to be made, vesting is necessarily suspended. Thus, in *Scott* v. *Scott's Trs.*,[3] the truster gave his estate to trustees in trust to hold, and, on the completion of certain contracts in which he was engaged, to divide his estate among his children or the survivors, with a further destination-over to the issue of those who predeceased ; and the Court, on a consideration of these words of gift, held that vesting was suspended until the expiry of the contracts, although there was no liferent or annuity given out of the estate. Similarly in *Fyfe's Trs.* v. *Fyfe*,[4] where trustees were directed to divide the truster's estate among his children on the majority of

Where no previous interest is given.

---

[1] Cf. *Richardson's Trs.* v. *Cope* (1850), 12 D. 855 ; *Stodart's Trs.* (1870), 8 M. 667 ; *Muirhead* v. *Muirhead* (1890), 17 R. (H. L.) 45, *per* Ld. Watson, at 49 ; *Allan's Trs.* v. *Allan* 1918 S. C. 164, *per* Ld. Pres. Strathclyde.

[2] (1856), 2 K. & J. 383. But cf.

Lord M'Laren's Wills and Succession, vol. ii. p. 801. See also *Bogle's Trs.* v. *Cochrane* (1892), 20 R. 108.

[3] (1881), 18 S. L. R. 436. See also the English case of *M'Donald* v. *Bryce* (1853), 16 Beav. 581.

[4] (1890), 17 R. 450.

the youngest, a survivorship clause appearing in the gift was held to postpone vesting till that event, despite the circumstance that the interest in the meantime was given to the children, and that the trustees were empowered to make advances to them out of their shares.

Where the previous interest is an annuity. An annuity which absorbs the whole income of the estate appears to have the same effect on vesting as a liferent. Thus in *Johnston* v. *Johnston*,[1] where trustees were directed to pay an annuity of £25 to the truster's sister, and on her death to her husband, if he survived, and at the first term occurring after six months from the death of the survivor of the annuitants to pay the sum of £500 to their children, with a destination-over, it was held that vesting of the fee was suspended till that event. In this case it was clear that the annual sum given was equivalent to the whole interest of the capital sum, and that the testator had had in view the termination of the annuity as the point of time at which the gift of the fee was to take effect. But, if the annuity does not exhaust the whole income, it may be regarded as merely a burden or charge on the fee, and not as an independent interest necessitating the postponement of the distribution of the subject over which it is given. Thus in *Pursell* v. *Newbigging*,[2] where the truster gave small annuities to several individuals, the annuity of any of these accrescing on his or her death to the survivors, and directed that after the purposes of the trust were executed the residue should pertain and belong to A., whom failing to others, it was held that the residue vested in A., although he died during the currency of two annuities. In this case, Lord Cranworth, L.C., after noticing the case of *Johnston* v. *Johnston*, observed : " It appears to me that, although this doctrine of suspending may be made applicable to the case of an annuity as well as to that of a liferent, it requires much stronger language to satisfy your Lordships that there was an intention to suspend in the case of an annuity than in that of a liferent." So also in *Scott's Trs.* v. *Scott* [3] (where, however, the decision proceeded on the special terms of the

[1] (1840), 2 D. 1038. See also *Muir's Trs.* (1869), 8 M. 53.

[2] (1855), 2 Macq. 273. Cf. also *Henderson's Trs.* v. *Henderson* (1876),

3 R. 320 ; *Buchanan's Trs.* v. *Buchanan* (1877), 4 R. 754 ; *L'Amy* v. *Nicholson* (1850), 13 D. 240.

[3] (1891), 18 R. 1194.

deed [1]), Lord M'Laren remarked, " that in determining the period of distribution there is an important distinction where a general liferent of the estate is given with a destination of the capital at the term of distribution, and the case of an unlimited fee burdened with an annuity."

Again, if a fund is given in general terms to a class, and the trustees are directed to retain a portion of the estate for the security of an annuity, there is a certain presumption that the testator intended that the objects of the gift should be ascertained in regard to the whole fund at one and the same time, namely, at the distribution of the main portion of the fund, and not that the sum retained for the annuity should go to a separate class, as might be the result if the words of survivorship were referred, as to that sum, to the death of the annuitant. There are two terms of payment, the testator's death (or, as the case may be) for the main part of the fund and the annuitant's for the capital retained ; and a strict application of the rule of *Young* v. *Robertson* would lead to the result that there were two periods of vesting. But the Court is averse from this construction and inclines to hold that the survivorship clause or destination-over ceases to operate when the main part of the estate becomes vested. Thus, in *Dickson* v. *Halbert* [2] the residue of the trust estate was made payable at the first term at the end of twelve months from the testator's death, but a portion was to be retained for securing annuities until the annuitants' deaths. There was a survivorship clause which, it was argued, had the effect of suspending the vesting of the sum so retained until all the annuitants were dead ; but it was held that this was not so, as the testator's intention must be taken to be that the rights of the beneficiaries in the whole of the residue should vest at one and the same time, viz., at his death or the first term thereafter.

So, also, in *Wyllie's Trs.* v. *Wyllie's Exr.* [3] where trustees were directed to hold the residue of the estate, and, after setting aside and holding such part as would suffice to yield

---

[1] See this case stated *post*, p. 67.

[2] (1851), 13 D. 674.

[3] 1926 S. C. 336. See also *Young* v. *Stewart* (1875), 13 S. L. R. ; *Fair-grieve* v. *Stirling* (1896), 34 S. L. R. 80 ; Lord Kinloch's opinion in *Carter* v. *M'Intosh* (1862), 24 D. 925.

a certain annuity, to divide the residue among the testator's children, with a gift-over to the issue of such as might die before his or her share should " become payable," it was held that the whole residue, including the part so set aside, vested in the children *a morte testatoris*. Lord Ormidale observed : " The mere provision of an annuity, requiring the temporary retention in the hands of the trustees, whether of the whole or only a portion of the residue, it has been frequently held, does not of itself suspend vesting. Further, there is a presumption against what I may term piecemeal vesting and in favour of vesting at only one period."

This, however, is no more than a presumption, and there is, of course, nothing to prevent a testator directing that the survivors shall be ascertained as the annuities terminate, provided he make this intention sufficiently clear. Thus, in *Pearson* v. *Casamaijor*,[1] the testator, after providing certain annuities, directed that the capital sums set apart for these annuities should be divided among the beneficiaries, and the survivors or survivor, " as and when such capital sums should become tangible " ; and if any died " before the term of payment (one or more, as the case may be)," leaving issue, the issue were to take the deceaser's share. There was a further provision as to the legatees being major. It was held that the survivors were to be determined as each annuity fell in, with regard to the share so disengaged, and that a major legatee, who predeceased an annuitant, took no interest in the sum retained for the security of that annuitant. There were three annuities, and therefore three periods of vesting. Similarly, in *Thornhill* v. *Macpherson*,[2] the provision was that the estate should " be equally divided amongst my children, with benefit of survivorship if any of them shall die . . . before the security of their mother's dowry shall justify a partition " ; and it was held that, although the main part of the estate vested at the truster's death, a sum of £10,000 required for her provision did not vest until her death, she having survived the truster.

---

[1] (1839), M'L. & Rob. 685.

[2] (1841), 3 D. 394. See also *Davidson* v. *Dobbie* (1828), 6 S. 536 ; 3 Fac. 556 (distinguished in *Ramsay* v. *White* (1833), 11 S. 786) ; *Wright* v. *Fraser* (1843), 6 D. 78 ; *Kilgour* v. *Kilgour* (1845), 7 D. 451 ; *Home* v. *Home* (1807), Hume's Decisions, 530.

4. Where the gift to the survivors is contained in a Where the trustees have a discretion as to the time of payment. direction to trustees to pay *when they think proper*, or *when they have realised the estate*, the Court is averse from adopting that construction which would make the ascertainment of the legatees dependent on the trustees actually realising or making payment. Thus, in *Henderson's Trs.* v. *Henderson*,[1] the testator directed his trustees to pay an annuity to his widow, and to divide the surplus income among his three sons, and the lawful issue of any of these on their death. The gift of residue was in these terms : " I direct and appoint my said trustees to divide the residue to my . . . estate equally amongst my said children, *or the survivors of them, at such times and in such manner as my said trustees may think proper.*" The annuity was well within the amount of the total income of the estate, and the remainder of the interest was paid to the children. All the children having predeceased the annuitant, it was held, in a Special Case, that the children's shares had vested in them. " I think the survivorship clause applies," said Lord Justice-Clerk Moncreiff, " and can only apply to the death of the testator, because I think it was in the power of the trustees to make a division at any time after the death of the testator that they thought proper." [2]

This case is an illustration of the general presumption (hereafter discussed [3]), that a testator intends to fix the rights of his beneficiaries at some determinate period, and not to leave to his trustees the control of the selection of the parties who are to take the benefit.

In *Wood* v. *Neill's Trs.*,[4] the truster directed his trustees to make over his estate at the first term occurring twelve months after his death, or as soon thereafter as the estate might be realised, to his children, and provided that the share of any of these dying leaving issue should go to their issue and, failing issue, to the survivors. In this case the Second Division, reversing Lord Kyllachy's interlocutor, held that the estate vested in the children *a morte testatoris*. There were features of the deed which were considered to point to this result, and the decision is therefore somewhat

---

[1] (1876), 3 R. 320.
[2] Cf. also *Maclean's Trs.* v. *Maclean* (1897), 24 R. 988.
[3] Chapter X., *post.*
[4] (1896), 24 R. 105.

special. But the case is noticed in this connexion, because of the opinion expressed by Lord Young in regard to the effect of a postponement of payment for one year. " That," his Lordship observed, " is just the provision found in most wills, that trustees are to pay and divide as soon after the testator's death as the estate can be realised. It cannot well be paid and divided sooner. The law allows executors time for that purpose. The usual rule is that they have six months after the testator's death to realise, and that is also the usual provision in wills. The trustees are usually directed to divide at the first term of Whitsunday or Martinmas, making six months after the testator's death, or as soon thereafter as the same may be realised. But it is a new idea to me that such a clause could postpone vesting. It is a novelty to me that the period allowed for distribution should be supposed to have anything to do with vesting. To postpone the period of distribution for twelve months would not postpone vesting, and neither would the postponement of distribution till the estate can be realised." If this is to be taken as a statement of a general rule that words of survivorship appended to a direction to trustees to pay on the lapse of a year from the truster's death do not postpone vesting till that time, its soundness may be questioned, because that would be equivalent to denying to a testator the power of fixing vesting at that period save by the use of an express declaration as to vesting. If a testator directs payment to be made at a certain time, and then goes on to describe the legatees in terms which, according to the general rule of law, have the effect of confining the gift to those who may be alive at that time, it would seem to be immaterial what the testator's motives may be supposed to have been in fixing one time of payment rather than another.[1]

Where trustees are directed to pay " after " other purposes are satisfied.

5. Again, it should be noticed that the distribution of the estate may be immediate, although the testator has provided that it shall be made only after or when other provisions have been met. The word " after," for instance, may signify not a sequence in point of time, but the order of

---

[1] Cf. *Smellie's Trs.* v. *Glasgow Royal Infirmary* (1905), 13 S. L. T. 450 (Lord Dundas), and *Hendry's Trs.* v. *Patrick* (1905), 13 S. L. T. 503 (Lord Dundas).

priority or preference in the distribution of the estate. In *Scott's Trs.* v. *Scott*,[1] the truster directed his trustees to pay certain legacies six months after his wife's death, and provided that his son should " succeed to whatever may remain of my estate and effects after these payments are made." It was held that the estate vested in the son *a morte testatoris*, although there was a destination-over to other persons, and although he predeceased the truster's widow. In this case the collocation of the words showed that the phrase " after these payments are made " meant merely that the son was to take the estate under deduction of these payments, and not that his enjoyment of the residue was to be postponed until the payments were made.

Similarly, in *Maclean's Trs.* v. *Maclean*,[2] where trustees were instructed to provide certain annuities, and " after the foregoing purposes are served " to divide the residue among the survivors of the testator's children and the family of a child who had predeceased the testator, it was held that the residuary legatees took vested rights at the testator's death. A feature of the deed which contributed to this result was a power given to the trustees to provide for the annuities by the purchase of securities.

It is clear that the word " after " must depend largely for its meaning on the context in which it appears, and it may, and often does, fix the time of distribution.

Again, it would seem that the word " then," in the case of a gift to parties " then alive," should, in the ordinary case, be referred to the last antecedent.[3] Hence, if trustees are directed on the death of a liferenter,[4] or on the majority of the youngest of a class,[5] to make over a subject to the beneficiaries who may be " then alive," the beneficiaries cannot be ascertained before these respective events. In *Wilson's Trs.* v. *Mackenzie*,[6] where the direction to the trustees was to hold a share of the residue for behoof of the testator's son and his wife (if she survived him) in liferent

Construction of the word "then."

---

[1] (1891), 18 R. 1194.

[2] (1897), 24 R. 988.

[3] This is indicated in *Scott* v. *Scott* (1850), 7 Bell's App. 143. Cf. *Archer* v. *Jegon* (1837), 8 Sim. 446 ; Theobald on Wills, p. 666..

[4] *Boyle* v. *Earl of Glasgow's Trs.* (1858), 20 D. 925. Stated *post*, p. 88.

[5] *Naismith* v. *Boyes* (1899), 1 F. (H. L.) 79.

[6] 1924 S. C. 568.

and " thereafter " for behoof of his issue or the survivors,
with a destination-over, it was held (Lord Hunter dissenting)
that this word was the " determining factor in the construction of the clause " and that it was used " for no other
purpose than to mark with emphasis that no right to the
fee is to emerge until both the liferent interests are
spent."

Heritable Destinations.   6. Lastly, the rule of *Young* v. *Robertson* was formulated
with reference to the case of a trust disposition and settle-
ment.[1]

Where a testator disposes of his property, not through
the medium of a trust, but directly in favour of the objects
of his bounty, the application of that rule is controlled by
another rule, namely, that which forbids the fee being held
in suspense.[2] Under this last rule, which applies to both
heritable and moveable property, the vesting of the fee cannot
be postponed in the case of a direct disposition.   Hence,
under a direct conveyance to A. in liferent, and to B., whom
failing to C., in fee, B. takes a vested right at the commence-
ment of the liferent, because otherwise the fee would be
in pendente.[3] A result similar to suspended vesting is
made possible, however, in certain cases, by the fiction of a
fiduciary fee ; and in destinations in which the liferenter is
a fiduciary fiar, the vesting of the beneficiary interest may
be postponed, because for this purpose the constructive fee
serves the same end as a trust.

In the case of a direct conveyance of heritable property,
which is to confer a right of possession on the granter's
death, there is no technical difficulty in treating a clause of
survivorship as a conditional institution, supposing that the
words are sufficiently clear to displace the presumption in
favour of a substitution ; because that construction would
not involve the suspending of the fee.   In *Chancellor* v.
Mossman,[4] where five ladies granted a disposition in favour
of three parties, " or the survivors or survivor of them," it

---

[1] *Per* Lord M'Laren in *Turner* v.
Gaw (1894), 21 R. 563 ; cf. *Main*
v. *Lamb* (1880), 7 R. 688 ; *Foulis* v.
Foulis (1857), 19 D. 362 ; *Fraser* v.
Croft (1898), 25 R. 496 ; *Brown's Trs.*
v. *Smith* (1900), 2 F. 817.

[2] See Chapter XVIII.

[3] Lord M'Laren in *Turner* v. *Gaw*,
supra ; see also *Tristram* v. *M'Haffies*
(1894), 22 R. 121, and *ante*, p. 52 as to
the effect of substitutions.

[4] (1872), 10 M. 995.

was held that this was a conditional institution of such of the grantees as might be alive at the death of the longest liver of the disponers, in the event of any of the grantees predeceasing that event, the Lord President observing, " I think the legal effect and meaning of the clause is to give . . . a joint fee, and conditionally to institute the survivor or survivors, if any one or more of the three should predecease the granters. The words upon which the effect of the clause turns are the words, ' or the survivors or survivor.' If the destination had been to the three ladies ' and the survivor ' of them, it would have been different ; that would have been a joint fee to them, and the longest liver of them ; but the word ' or ' plainly points to this, that the fee is given to those of the three ladies who are in existence at the time when the deed takes effect—that is, at the death of the longest liver of the granters."

IV. Destinations-over to Heirs or Issue.—It is well settled in our law that in a gift to A. " and his heirs " ; [1] or to A. " and his executors " ; [2] or to A., " his heirs, executors, and assignees " ; [3] or to A. " and his heirs and successors " ; [4] or to A. " or his descendants " ; [5] or to A., " whom failing his children," [6] the parties falling under these descriptions are conditional institutes, and take in the event of the legatee named dying before the testator.

This is the general rule in regard to legacies. An exception, however, has been admitted when the gift is in the nature of a provision made by one spouse in favour of the other or by a parent in favour of his child or children.[7]

Provisions to a wife or children.

---

[1] *Grant* v. *Grant's Trs.* (1862), 24 D. 1211 ; Lord Deas in *Findlay* v. *Mackenzie* (1875), 2 R. 909. See also *post*, p. 78.

[2] Ersk. iii. 9. 9. *Findlay* v. *Mackenzie, supra* ; *Scott's Exrs.* v. *Methven's Exrs.* (1890), 17 R. 389 ; and see the cases cited in Chapter VIII., *post*, p. 174.

[3] *Lyon* v. *Gray* (1751), Elchies, *voce* Testament ; *Inglis* v. *Miller* (1760), M. 8084 ; *Boston* v. *Horseburgh* (1781), M. 8099 ; *Earl of Moray* v. *Stuart* (1782), M. 8103 ; *Maxwell* v. *Maxwell* (1864), 3 M. 318 ; *Halliburton* (1884), 11 R. 979 ; *Macleod* v. *Wilson* (1903), 6 F. 213.

[4] *Chalmers* v. *Chalmers* (1827), 5 S. 687.

[5] *Thomson* v. *Cumberland*, 16 Nov. 1814, F. C. ; *Gauden's Trs.* v. *Jamieson* (1902), 10 S. L. T. 326 (Lord Stormonth-Darling).

[6] *Lockwood's Trs.* v. *Keith Falconer* (1866), 4 M. 1036.

[7] In *Findlay* v. *Mackenzie* (1875), 2 R. 909 ; *Baillie's Exr.* v. *Baillie* (1899), 1 F. 974 ; and *Garden's Exr.*

In such cases the words are construed as being merely exegetical of the right given to the party, and not as intended to create a conditional institution ; and accordingly, if the party predeceases the testator, the legacy lapses and cannot be claimed by his heirs. The instances in which this exception has been given effect to are few,[1] and it is difficult to discover any definite criterion by which such provisions may be distinguished from those gifts in which the general rule is applied.[2] In *Findlay* v. *Mackenzie*,[3] Lord Deas thought that the exception was allowed on the ground that a provision in implement of the natural obligation resting on a husband or parent to maintain his wife or child was personal in its nature ; but this explanation fails to account for the decisions in the later cases of *Baillie's Exr.* v. *Baillie* [4] and *Garden's Exr.* v. *More* [5] where the bequest was made by a wife in favour of her husband. But in all of these three cases there occurred the specialty that the gift was expressly conditional on the party's survivance of the donor. The fact that the gift is termed a provision in the deed is not in itself sufficient to bring the case within the exception.[6]

" Derivative " destinations.

While it has long been settled that a " proper " destination-over [7]—that is, one in favour of a named person or of some one described by a term which has no reference to any relationship with the institute or primary legatee— suspends vesting, it was at one time held that the same effect was not to be ascribed to destinations-over in the terms set forth at the beginning of this section. Destinations-over of the latter type have been termed " derivative " destinations,[8] and these were held, for reasons not in all cases the same, to be in no way inconsistent with vesting *a morte testatoris.*

v. *More*, 1913 S. C. 285, the gift was to a spouse. In *Russel* v. *Russel* (1769), M. 6372, the gift was to a child. Cf. *Donald's Trs.* v. *Donald* (1864), 2 M. 922 ; and *Ferguson* v. *Lord Advocate* (1906), 13 S. L. T. 724 (Lord Ardwall). See *post*, p. 287.

[1] Cases in previous note.

[2] The general rule was applied in *Macleod* v. *Wilson* (1903), 6 F. 213 ; *Halliburton* (1884), 11 R. 979 ; *Cleland* v. *Allan* (1891), 18 R. 377 ; *Duncans*

v. *Halkett* (1894), 2 S. L. T. 58 (Outer House, Lord Kincairney). Cf. the very special case of *Birnie* v. *Simpsons' Trs.* (1892), 20 R. 481.

[3] *Supra.*

[4] *Supra.*

[5] *Supra.*

[6] *Macleod* v. *Wilson, supra.*

[7] See Lord M'Laren's opinion in *Hay's Trs.* v. *Hay* (1890), 17 R. 961.

[8] *Ibid.*

Thus, in *Hendry's Trs.* v. *Hendry*,[1] where trustees were directed on the termination of three annuities (as it happened) to sell a property and divide the proceeds among three nephews of the testator, and, " in the event of any or all of their deaths before a division " the share of the deceaser was to go to his children or other next-of-kin, it was held that vesting took place although two of the annuitants survived. " The effect of giving a legacy to A.B. and his next-of-kin " said the Lord President (Inglis), " is simply to give to him and his heirs *in mobilibus*. There is thus no destination-over, no provision to anyone beyond these three persons and their heirs. . . . It, therefore, necessarily vests from the time when the succession opens though the time of payment is postponed." Lord Kinloch added : " The devolution on heirs and successors is not a destination-over in any correct legal sense. It is just the primary destination prolonged. It is the man himself in the person

---

[1] (1872), 10 M. 432. It is difficult to find in the earlier cases any distinct formulation of a principle on which the effect of derivative destinations-over should differ from that of other destinations-over. The cases are not consistent, but throughout the series there may be found traces of an indisposition to treat derivative destinations-over as having any marked effect adverse to vesting in the institute. In *Lawsons* v. *Stewart* (1827), 2 W. & S. 625 a destination-over to " executors or next-of-kin " was held to suspend vesting. On the other hand, in *Marchbanks* v. *Brockie* (1836), 14 S. 521, 11 Fac. 432, a bequest with a destination-over to " heirs " was held (on the phraseology of the deed) to vest *a morte testatoris*, a decision which was disapproved by L. J.-C. Hope in *Robertson* v. *Richardson* (1843), 5 D. 1117, and *Campbell* v. *Campbell* (1852), 15 D. 173, and by Lord Ivory in *Cochrane* v. *Cochrane's Exrs.* (1854), 27 S. J. 25. In *Maxwell* v. *Wyllie* (1837), 15 S. 1005, 12 Fac. 928, a destination-over to " children " was held not to postpone vesting (but

see Lord Shand's observations on this case in *Snell* v. *Morrison* (1877), 4 R. 709), but in *Provan* v. *Provan* (1840), 2 D. 298, and *Johnston* v. *Johnston* (1840), 2 D. 1038, where there was a similar destination-over, vesting was suspended till the date of payment. In *Cochrane* v. *Cochrane's Exrs.* (1854), 17 D. 103, and *Douglas* v. *Douglas* (1864), 2 M. 1008, there was held to be vesting despite destinations-over to " heirs " or " heirs, executors and successors." But in *Stodart's Trs.* (1870), 8 M. 667, where the destination-over was to " heirs and assignees," it was held that such a destination-over was inconsistent with immediate vesting ; and see also *Laing* v. *Barclay* (1865), 3 M. 1143. A bequest with a derivative destination was held not to have vested in *Sloane* v. *Finlayson* (1876), 3 R. 678, and to have vested *a morte testatoris* in *Wilson's Trs.* v. *Quick* (1878), 5 R. 697 ; *Archibald's Trs.* v. *Archibald* (1882), 9 R. 942 ; *Waters' Trs.* v. *Waters* (1884), 12 R. 253 ; and *Ross's Trs.* (1884), 12 R. 378.

of his heir. It was never heard of, so far as I am aware, that a man's right stood suspended in order to operate a contingent fee to his heir-at-law. A disposition to a man and his heirs operates a complete present fee to the disponee."

A similar expression of the rule as to such destinations-over is to be found in the later case of *Jackson* v. *M'Millan*,[1] decided in the Second Division. The bequest there was, on the death of a liferentrix, to the testator's " children, or, if dead, their nearest lawful heirs." A son who predeceased the liferentrix was held to have had a vested right in his share. In the opinion of the Court it is stated that, in order to suspend vesting, the interest of the conditional institute " must be substantially separate, and such as to indicate specific favour on the part of the testator. But a legacy to A. and his heirs, or A. and his children, is not the separate institution of a new and independent object of the testator's bounty, but the expression of a derivative interest favoured by the testator only out of regard to the legatee whose children or heirs are mentioned. They only find a place in the destination through the relation which they bear to the *persona prœdilecta* ; and in cases like the present, in which the gift is only inferred from the direction to divide, the instruction to the trustees to pay to the heirs of the legatee if he predecease the period of division, may be regarded more as the natural result of the legacy having vested than as an indication of the reverse."

Destinations-over to issue : In other cases where the destination-over was confined to children of the institute, a somewhat different reason was found for holding that the destination-over was not inconsistent with vesting *a morte testatoris*. Such a destination-over, it has been said, is no more than what the law would imply under the *Conditio si institutus sine liberis decesserit*, and, therefore, inefficacious to suspend vesting.[2] It will be

---

[1] (1876), 3 R. 627.

[2] *Mackinnon's Trs.* v. *MacNeill* (1897), 24 R. 981. See the opinion of the Lord Ordinary (Moncreiff) in *Provan* v. *Provan* (1840), 2 D. 298, and *Johnston* v. *Johnston* (1840), 2 D. 1038. His decision was reversed, but in *Elliot* v. *Bowhill* (1873), 11 M.

735, L. J.-C. Moncreiff observed that he knew of " no authority adverse to the general views he " (the Lord Ordinary) " expressed on this subject," and reiterated them. But see L. J.-C. Hope's opinion in *Stewart's Trs.* v. *Stewart* (1851), 13 D. 1386. For criticisms of this view, see the

observed that not only is this statement of the rule distinct in principle from that alluded to above, but it is also applicable within a narrower range of cases, for it would apply only in the circumstance in which the *Conditio* is admitted.

Finally, in *Hay's Trs.* v. *Hay*,[1] it was laid down as a general proposition in the law of vesting that derivative destinations were not to be regarded as inconsistent with vesting in the primary legatee. In this case the truster directed his trustees to hold the whole of his estate for his wife in liferent. On her death they were to convey a certain heritable property to A. " and his heirs." A. survived the truster, but predeceased the widow. It was held that he had taken a vested right in the property *a morte testatoris.* " We must endeavour to find," said Lord M'Laren, " some definite criterion to be applied to such cases ; and I think the true criterion is this : that where the legates of the second order are either mentioned by name or by some description independent of the first, then they may be taken to be *personæ delectæ*, and their contingent interest is sufficient to suspend the vesting of the estate. But if the legatees of the second order are described as the children, or issue, or heirs of the institute (there being no ulterior destination), these are to be considered in this question as persons instituted in consequence of their being the natural successors of the institute, and therefore as taking a right which is subordinated to his, and is not intended to interfere with his acquisition of the fullest benefit which it was possible for the truster to give him consistently with the benefits previously given to liferenters or other persons."

This decision was up to the date of the case of *Bowman* v. *Bowman* [2] treated as settling the law and was followed in a series of decisions which it is necessary only to cite.[3]

Side note: Derivative destinations not suspensive of vesting.

Side note: Distinction between derivative and other destinations doubted.

---

opinions of Lord Skerrington and Lord Sands in *Wylie's Trs.* v. *Bruce*, 1919 S. C. 211, at 231 and 237.

[1] 17 R. 961.

[2] (1899), 1 F. (H. L.) 69.

[3] *Richard's Trs.* v. *Roland* (1894), 22 R. 140, *dubitante* Lord Rutherfurd Clark ; *Ross's Trs.* v. *Ross* (1897), 25 R. 65 ; *Ballantyne's Trs.* v. *Kidd* (1898), 25 R. 621 ; *Mellis* v. *Mellis's Tr.* (1898), 25 R. 720 ; *Booth's Trs.* v. *Booth* (1898), 25 R. 606—all before the Second Division ; *Mackinnon's Trs.* v. *MacNeill* (1897), 24 R. 981 (before the First Division). Cf. *Adam's Trs.* v. *Carrick* (1896), 23 R. 828 (doubted in *Ballantyne's Trs.* v. *Kidd, supra,* explained in *Mackinnon's Trs.* v. *MacNeill, supra*).

that case the question of the effect of derivative destinations
came for the first time under the consideration of the House
of Lords, and Lord Watson and Lord Davey took occasion
to discuss the merits of Lord M'Laren's statement in *Hay's
Trs.* v. *Hay.*[1]

In *Bowman* v. *Bowman* [2] the testator conveyed his whole
estate to trustees in trust to provide his widow with the
liferent of his house and with a necessary allowance, and
on her death, or on the dissolution of a partnership, of which
he was a member (whichever of these events should last
happen), to realise and divide the estate into " four equal
shares, and pay one share to each of my children . . ., or to
their respective heirs." On the question arising whether
two children who had survived the truster but predeceased
the widow had taken vested rights in their shares, the First
Division decided in the affirmative, and, on appeal, the
decision was sustained. The judgement of the House of
Lords proceeded on special features of the will which were
considered to render it improbable that the testator's intention was to postpone vesting.[3] But the general rule expressed
in *Hay's Trs.* was disapproved of by Lord Watson and Lord
Davey. Lord Watson considered that destinations-over to
heirs fell, like other destinations-over, within the rule of
Young v. *Robertson.*[4] " I fail to see," he said, " why a
gift-over in favour of the heirs of an instituted child should
be otherwise construed or have any different effect than a
gift-over in favour of another relative or of a stranger
nominatim. In every such case the question as to when the
gift-over becomes operative depends upon the same considerations. . . . It appears to me to be in vain to contend
that the provision of the trust settlement which your Lordships have to construe in this appeal is, in substance, anything other than a clause of survivorship. The direction to
the trustees is to divide the whole estate, and to pay the
shares to each of certain children named, and, in the event
of their previous failure, to their respective heirs, who are
the conditional institutes. The testator has not expressly
or, so far as I can see, by plain implication, specified the
time at which the failure of the *nominatim* institutes is to be

[1] 17 R. 961.
[2] (1899) 1 F. (H. L.) 69.
[3] As to these see *post*, p. 248.
[4] (1862), 4 Macq. 314.

ascertained for the purposes of and with reference to that alternative gift, and the time must therefore be determined according to the reasonable construction which the law supplies. I cannot avoid the conclusion that the words to be construed in the present case, if they are not differentiated by the single exceptional feature which they present, are within the rule of legal construction laid down by the members of this House in *Young* v. *Robertson* ; and that, if not so differentiated, they disclose the testator's intention to be that the failure of his children named was a contingency which might occur at any time before the arrival of the period appointed by him for the division and distribution of his trust-estate." Lord Davey agreed with Lord Watson, remarking, in regard to the passage already quoted from Lord M'Laren's opinion in *Hay's Trs.* v. *Hay* [1] : " I find great difficulty in concurring in this reasoning of the learned judge, or in seeing why a different construction as regards the time of vesting should be given to a conditional limitation in favour of persons unnamed, but described as heirs, issue, or the like of the first legatee, and to one in favour of named persons, or persons described by some description independent of the first legatee, *e.g.*, of the other legatees or their children. I cannot, therefore, assent to the proposition laid down by Lord M'Laren as a general rule of construction or criterion to be applied in such cases. But I think the circumstance that the gift-over is not in favour of some *persona delecta* by name may be taken into consideration, together with other circumstances appearing on the will which affect the construction." [2]

The views of Lord Watson and Lord Davey were not shared by all the members of the House,[3] and the actual decision was in favour of vesting *a morte testatoris*. Hence, there was for a considerable period some hesitation in regard to the effect of the case. In *Parlane's Trs.* v. *Parlane* [4] and *Forrests' Trs.* v. *Mitchell's Trs.*[5] the First Division accepted the observations of Lord Watson and Lord Davey as in

[1] *Ante*, p. 73.
[2] In *Dawson* v. *Smart* (1903), 5 F. (H. L.) 24, Lord Davey repeated his views.
[3] See Lord Shand's speech. The Lord Chancellor's (Halsbury) judgement proceeded on the special terms of the testator's deed.
[4] (1902), 4 F. 805.
[5] (1904), 6 F. 616.

effect over-ruling *Hay's Trs.* v. *Hay*, and there were a number of decisions in the Outer House to the same effect.[1] On the other hand, in *Matheson's Trs.* v. *Matheson's Trs.*,[2] *Taylor's Tr.* v. *Christal's Tr.*[3] and *Ogle's Tr.* v. *Ogle*,[4] the Second Division held that destinations-over to issue or children did not prevent the bequest vesting in the primary legatee, Lord Moncreiff observing in the first of these cases that he was not prepared to hold that the earlier authorities had been overruled by *Bowman*.

In consequence of this divergence of judicial opinion, the question was in *Wylie's Trs.* v. *Bruce*[5] remitted to the whole Court. In that case the testator directed his trustees on the death of his widow (as it happened) to dispone a house to his cousin " or his heirs in heritage." The cousin survived the testator, but predeceased his widow. It was held (without any dissent) that no right had vested in the cousin. In his opinion,[6] Lord Dundas said : " It is, I consider, the settled law of Scotland that a destination to heirs is quite as good a conditional institution as one in favour of a named person, whether a relative or a stranger, and will, as a rule, be suspensive of vesting. If the question were open, there would be ample room for argument upon both sides, as is sufficiently evident by the varying currents of decision in the reported cases, but I think it is not open. It is needless to review the authorities ; they are adequately set out in the able minutes of debate lodged for the parties. For a long time the current was strong, though not entirely uniform, in favour of the view clearly enunciated by Lord M'Laren in *Hay's Trs.* that, if legatees of the second order were described as the children, or issue, or heirs, of the institute, there being no ulterior destination, these were to be considered

[1] *Moncreiff* (1900), 8 S. L. T. 281 (Lord Kincairney) ; *Gauden's Trs.* v. *Jamieson* (1902), 10 S. L. T. 326 (Lord Stormonth-Darling); *Cairns* v. *Cairn's Trs.* (1902), 10 S. L. T. 364 (Lord Low ; *Bowman*, however, being distinguished here) ; *Corstorphine's Trs.* v. *Corstorphine* (1903), 11 S. L. T. 294 (Lord Kincairney) ; *Hendry's Trs.* v. *Patrick* (1905), 13 S. L. T. 503 (Lord Dundas) ; *Anderson* v. *Cunningham's Trs.* (1907), 14 S. L. T. 589 (Lord Ardwall) ; *Cordiner* v. *Duffus*, 1909, 2 S. L. T. 164 (Lord Guthrie) ; and *Highet's Trs.* v. *Hamilton*, 1912, 1 S. L. T. 474. See also *Thompson's Trs.* v. *Jamieson* (1900), 2 F. 470.

[2] (1900), 2 F. 556.

[3] (1903), 5 F. 1010.

[4] (1904), 6 F. 359.

[5] 1919 S. C. 211.

[6] Concurred in by Lords Guthrie, Ormidale, Hunter, and Anderson.

as having been instituted because they were his natural successors, and therefore as taking a right merely subordinate to that of the institute and not such as to interfere with full vesting in his person. But this tide of authority was, I think, stemmed and turned by the judgement of the House of Lords in *Bowman's Trs.*"

This decision has been treated as conclusively settling the law [1] and it may now be accepted that a destination-over in favour of the institute's heirs suspends vesting in the institute.

But the rule formulated in *Hay's Trs.* went beyond destinations-over to heirs, for Lord M'Laren in his opinion in that case grouped with " heirs," " children," and " issue " [2]; and in *Bowman*, while Lord Watson deals only with destinations-over to heirs, Lord Davey speaks of a conditional limitation " in favour of persons " described as heirs, issue, or the like, of the first legatee."

It is not surprising, therefore, that in *Parlane's Trs.* v. *Parlane* [3] and *Forrest's Trs.* v. *Mitchell's Trs.* [4] the rule of *Bowman* was regarded as covering all such derivative destinations-over. In these two cases there was a bequest to legatees with a destination-over, in the event of any legatee predeceasing the date of payment, in favour of his issue ; and it was held that this had the effect of suspending vesting until that date. But the only question before the Court was whether vesting took place *a morte testatoris* or was suspended till the date of payment, and certain decisions in favour of vesting subject to defeasance in such circumstances were not brought to the notice of the Court. [5] In the more recent cases these decisions have been followed. The result is, therefore, that a marked distinction obtains between the effect of a destination-over to heirs and that of a destination-over to children or issue. The former suspends vesting in the institute ; in the latter there is vesting in him subject, however, to defeasance in the event

---

[1] See *Montgomerie Fleming's Trs.* v. *Carre*, 1922 S. C. 688 ; *Mackenzie's Trs.* v. *Georgeson*, 1923 S. C. 517.

[2] See also his Lordship's opinion in the case of *Bowman*, 25 R. 811.

[3] (1902), 4 F. 805.

[4] (1904), 6 F. 616.

[5] See *Allan's Trs.* v. *Allan*, 1918 S. C. 164 ; and cf. Lord M'Laren's opinion in *Forrest's Trs.* v. *Mitchell's Trs., ante.*

of his predeceasing and leaving issue.   In order that all
the instances of vesting subject to defeasance may be
considered together, the discussion of these cases has been
reserved for the chapter dealing with that subject.[1]

The rule being that a destination-over to the heirs of the
legatee has the effect in the general case of suspending
vesting in the legatee when the time of payment of the
legacy is postponed, it remains to consider how far that
rule is affected by variations in the expression of the
destination-over.   In some cases the bequest has been made
to A. *and* his heirs.   As the cases noticed on a previous
page [2] show, the word " and " points, in the ordinary case,
rather to a joint right than to successive rights.   But, where
the secondary legatees are called as " heirs " of the primary
legatee, there can be no question of their taking jointly
with the primary legatee, for their ascertainment is necessarily
dependent on the latter's death.[3]   It has accordingly been
held in a series of cases that there is no substantial difference
between a destination to " A. and his heirs "[4] and one to
" A. or his heirs," and that both are governed by the
decisions following *Bowman* v. *Bowman*.[5]

Destinations-over to heirs and assignees.   An argument against the suspensive force of a destination-over to heirs has been based in some cases on the use,
in connection with that term, of the word " assignees."   The
meaning of the latter word is authoritatively settled in *Bell*

----

[1] See *Gibson's Trs.* v. *Gibson*, 1925
S. C. 477, and other cases cited in
Chapter VI., sec. 3.

[2] See p. 50, *ante*.

[3] *M'Lachlan's Trs.* v. *Harvey*, 1909
S. C. 201, *per* Lord Low, at 205.

[4] This was the form of the destination in *Montgomerie Flemings Trs.* v.
Carre, 1922 S. C. 688 ; *Mackenzie's
Trs.* v. *Georgeson*, 1923 S. C. 517 ;
and the Outer House cases of *Gauden's
Trs.* v. *Jameson* (1902), 10 S. L. T.
326 (the bequest was to legatees " and
their descendants ") ; *Corstorphine's
Trs.* v. *Corstorphine* (1903), 11 S. L. T.
294 ; *Hendry's Trs.* v. *Patrick* (1905)
13 S. L. T. 503 ; and *Anderson* v.

Cunningham's Trs. (1907), 14 S. L. T.
589.

[5] See *Wylie's Trs.* v. *Bruce*, 1919
S. C. 211, *per* the Lord President
(Strathclyde), at 234, Lord Dundas, at
225, Lord Sands, at 232, and Lord
Cullen, at 241 ; and see also the cases
in note 4, *supra*. See also the observations of Lord Adam in *Hay's Trs.* v.
Hay (1890), 17 R. 961, of Lord
M'Laren in the case of *Bowman* in the
Court of Session (1898), 25 R. 811 ;
and of Lord Low in *M'Lachlan's Trs.*
v. *Harvey*, 1909 S. C. 201. For a
bequest to legatees " and their
respective children," see *Gibson's Trs.*
v. *Gibson*, 1925 S. C. 477.

v. *Cheape*.[1] In that case a testatrix conveyed her estate to trustees, to pay the income thereof to A., and to make over the estate to A.'s issue in fee, and, in the event of there being no issue, to B., " her heirs, executors, or assignees." A. died without issue, predeceased by B., who left a settlement. It was conceded that no right had vested in B.,[2] and the question in the case was whether the legacy fell to the trustees under her settlement or to her next-of-kin. The Court, consisting of all the judges, preferred the latter. It was treated as settled law that the term " assignees " meant those to whom the legatee should assign the subject in the event of her acquiring a vested right.[3] Heirs and executors were fixed and designated by law and not by the act of the institute, and therefore they might take as conditional institutes ; but assignees could have no existence but for the act and deed of the cedent, and their right was wholly derivative and dependent on the legatee's acquisition of a vested interest. They could not, therefore, be conditional institutes. In several of the opinions it was admitted that the term might have been construed as equivalent to " nominees," had the will disclosed an intention that the legatee should have the power of disposing of the subject irrespective of the situation of her own interest ; and in more recent cases, where such indications of intention have appeared in the will, the assignees of parties in whom no right vested have been held entitled to the legacy.[4]

A very good example of the terms of a deed calling for a departure from the rule of *Bell* v. *Cheape* is afforded by the case of *Barr* v. *Parnie* [5] in the Outer House, where the gift was to A. in liferent and to her issue in fee, and failing issue to her " heirs and assignees." Here Lord Kyllachy held that the legacy was carried by A.'s will, on the ground

" Assignees " construed as " nominees."

---

[1] (1845), 7 D. 614. See also *Graham* v. *Hope* (1807), M. " Legacy," App. No. 3 ; *Maxwell* v. *Maxwell* (1864), 3 M. 318.

[2] See *post*, p. 135.

[3] A person may of course assign the subject of a legacy in anticipation ; and if the subject come to be vested in him thereafter, it will be carried by the assignation. " It is not necessary to assignability that a right should

have vested at the date of the assignment."—Lord Kinloch in *Carter* v. *M'Intosh* (1862), 24 D. 925.

[4] See *Manson* v. *Hutcheon* (1874), 1 R. 371 ; *Scott's Exrs.* v. *Methven's Exrs.* (1890), 17 R. 389 ; *Montgomery's Trs.* v. *Montgomery* (1895), 22 R. 824. *Post*, p. 174.

[5] (1903), 11 S. L. T., 426. This case was referred to in *Wilson's Trs.* v. *Mackenzie*, 1924 S. C. 568.

that, as the fee was not given to A., the testator could have used the word in no other sense than that of nominees or appointees. His Lordship treated the case as equivalent to a bequest to one in liferent and to the nominees of another in fee. In an earlier case (not reported) [1] involving the construction of the word " assignees," his Lordship observed : " The case of *Bell* v. *Cheape* was quoted as an authority—the contention being that according to that decision a destination to ' assignees ' always means assignees *after vesting*, and that a destination to the assignees of a person who never had a vested fee was necessarily inept and nugatory. I cannot, however, so read the decision in *Bell* v. *Cheape* or the more recent decisions in which that case has been followed. These cases, no doubt, decide this, that, where a destination to assignees *admits* of being read as a destination to assignees after vesting, it will be so read ; but none of these cases, I think, decided what is a quite different proposition, that where it is impossible so to read a destination to ' assignees,' the destination must be blotted out of the deed and held *pro non scripto*."

Effect on vesting of the word " assignees."

Such, then, being the meaning of the term, what is its effect, when appearing in conjunction with the words " heirs " or " executors," on the question of vesting ? This has been the subject of discussion in a number of cases. In *Clark's*

---

[1] The case is *Miller* v. *Miller's Trs.*, decided in 1892. The circumstances were these :—The testator directed his trustees " to retain and set aside the sum of £15,000, and invest it on heritable or other good security, and to pay the interests, dividends, and annual profits thereof to my said daughter during her life, and at her death to divide the sum so retained among- her children in such shares and proportions as she may appoint by any writing under her hand, which failing equally share and share alike, if more than one, and if only one, then the whole to be paid to such child ; and failing a child or children, or in the event of there being a child or children, and of such child or children predeceasing her, then the said sum so retained and set aside shall be paid or assigned and disponed to her heirs and assignees whomsoever." By a later clause the daughter's liferent was declared to be alimentary and not assignable by her. The daughter died without issue, leaving a will disposing of her estate. Lord Kyllachy held that the fee of the sum vested in her subject (*a*) to the burden of her own alimentary liferent, and (*b*) to defeasance in the event of her having children who survived her. But his Lordship went on to say that, if the daughter had merely a liferent, he would be disposed to hold that she had a power of disposal under the destination to her heirs and assignees, and gave his reasons for this in the passage quoted in the text.

Exrs. v. *Paterson*,[1] where trustees were directed, on the youngest of the testator's children attaining eighteen, to convey the residue of the estate to them, " their heirs and assignees," with a survivorship clause in the event of any child dying " intestate " before receiving payment, it was held that the gift vested *a morte testatoris*, largely because of the power given to the children to assign and test. Of this feature of the deed Lord Fullerton observed : " There may be cases in which a destination to heirs and assignees, and a power of testing, are not conclusive in favour of vesting ; but these must be cases in which the words of the deed cannot be reconciled to vesting. If it can be made out that the words of the deed are conclusive against vesting, a power to test will not overrule them ; but the weakness of this case is, that there is nothing whatever in the deed against vesting. . . . I apprehend that when a legacy is so granted that the legatee has the power of testing upon it, or assigning it, to all intents and purposes, that legacy vests, unless there is the strongest evidence of an intention that it shall not vest." [2]

In a more recent case in which the subject was discussed,[3] the gift was expressed as a direction to trustees, on the termination of a liferent and in the event (which happened) of the liferenter dying without issue, to pay a legacy to A. " and his heirs or assignees " ; and it was held that the term " assignees," together with certain very special features of the will, fixed vesting at the testator's death. The effect of the word is fully discussed in Lord Stormonth-Darling's opinion. His Lordship, after pointing out that the reason why a gift-over to heirs suspends vesting is that the testator may be assumed to have desired that in the event of the legatee's predecease the legacy should go to his heirs rather than to his creditors or voluntary disponees, added : " If, however, the testator makes the gift, not to the heirs of the institute, but to his heirs or assignees, he declares unequivocally that he has no preference in the matter. The

---

[1] (1851), 14 D. 141.
[2] Quoted with approval by Lord Lee in *Kippen's Trs.* (1889), 16 R. 668. See *Roberton* v. *Davidson* (1846), 9 D. 152 ; *Alves' Trs.* v. *Grant* (1874),

1 R. 969. Cf. *Douglas's Trs.* (1902), 5 F. 69.
[3] *Thompson's Trs.* v. *Jamieson* (1900), 2 F. 470. *Post*, p. 93.

use of the word ' assignees ' may be ineffectual in law to create a substantive right in their favour, but it is surely not on that account to be read out of the will altogether. To do so would be contrary to fundamental principles of construction. The word ' assignees ' must, I think, be accepted, like every other word in the instrument, as an index of the testator's state of mind ; and if so, it entirely displaces the theory on which a gift to heirs may be supported as creating a proper destination-over. For that reason I demur altogether to reading a destination to ' heirs or assignees ' as if it were a destination merely to ' heirs,' and I arrive at the conclusion that it was not intended by this testator to create any right in competition with the right of the institute. Lord Fullerton, in the case of *Bell* v. *Cheape*, quoted the destination there (which was to Miss Macintosh, her ' heirs, executors, or assignees '), and added, ' These last expressions are often used as expressing merely the full and complete right of the disponee or legatee—his perfect right to transmit, by testate or intestate succession, the right when vested in him.' That is exactly the sense in which I think they are used here." Lord Young treated the words " heirs or assignees " as being superfluous and merely emphasising the absolute nature of the legatee's right. Lord Low thought that, as the word "assignees" would be inoperative unless A. took a vested right, " the use of that word must be regarded as an indication of the testator's intention that A. should take a right which he could assign, and that the previous calling of heirs was not to prevent such a right vesting in him."

Criticism of the argument for vesting from the use of the word " assignees."

The contention that the addition of the word " assignees " neutralises the effect of the destination to heirs has been criticised as not " very intelligible." [1]   The arguments based

[1] " It was argued that when a destination to assignees was added to a destination to heirs, the effect was that vesting was not postponed, but that the effect of the destination to heirs was neutralised, and that the mention of assignees indicated the testator's understanding that he had conferred a right vesting at his death. I am unable to accept that argument. I do not find it very intelligible, and I think it presses too far the somewhat artificial meaning which decisions have put on the word assignees. It may be that the word is meaningless and would not itself prevent vesting ; but I am unable to follow the argument that it destroys and nullifies the effect of the destination to heirs."—Lord Kincairney in *Corstorphine's Trs.* v. *Corstorphine* (1903), 11 S. L. T. 294.

on the use of the word appear to rest on the not wholly consistent grounds (a) that the word is a tautological description of the legatee's interest ; and (b) that, in order to give effect to the word, the legatee must be held to have been in a situation validly to assign the subject. It would appear also to be somewhat doubtful whether the expressions of opinion quoted are, in reality, consistent with *Beïl* v. *Cheape*, because if " assignees " means, as that case decides, the parties to whom the legatee shall assign in the event of his acquiring a vested interest, it would seem to be of the nature of a *petitio principii* to found an argument on it as to the time of vesting. The addition of the word " assignees " would be of value in determining the *quality* of the estate taken by the legatee,—as showing that he was to have a fee and not a liferent merely, supposing that question to arise,[1]— but it could not under that decision logically support any inference as to the *time* at which the legatee was to have the power of assigning ; that is as to the time of his acquiring a vested right. This view appears to be fortified by the opinion of Lord President Inglis in *Findlay* v. *Mackenzie*,[2] in which, speaking of a destination to " heirs and assignees," he says : " One suggestion has been made, in the way of construing these words and taking off the presumption which arises from the meaning which they usually bear, which I cannot adopt, namely, that the addition of the words ' and assignees ' rather takes off from the effect of naming heirs. But there is nothing inconsistent in a conveyance to a person and his heirs if he predeceases, and his assignees if he does not predecease, and assigns his right. And so it has happened that, in a great number of cases where the right of the heirs has been sustained, the words ' and assignees ' were adjected, and a competition arose between the assignees to whom the legatee had assigned his right before it vested, and the heir-at-law, and in all these the heir-at-law was preferred, simply because the party who had assigned had no power to do so. But that only shows that the addition of the word ' assignees ' does not militate against the right of the heir, failing the original disponee." In the

---

[1] Cf. *Rattray's Trs.* v. *Rattray* (1899), 1 F. 510 where the use of this word was held to show that a liferentrix was truly fiar. [2] (1875), 2 R. 909.

case of *Halliburton* [1] also the Lord President, in reference to a destination-over in these terms said : " The word assignee does not affect the question."

In accordance with these views it was decided in *Montgomerie-Fleming's Trs.* v. *Carre* [2] that the vesting of a bequest to a legatee " and his heirs and assignees " was, by force of this destination-over, suspended until the date of payment. It would appear, therefore, that in the present state of the authorities a destination-over to heirs and assignees has the same effect as a simple destination-over to heirs except, possibly, that it may be more susceptible to the influence of other features of the deed favourable to early vesting.

V. Whether Words of Survivorship or Destinations-over may be referred to a Time intermediate between the Testator's Death and the Period of Distribution.— In the normal case the point of time at which a legacy vests is either the death of the testator or the date of payment of the legacy or distribution of the fund [3] ; and it has been seen that words of survivorship are presumed to refer to the date of distribution and to suspend vesting till that date. This rule is applicable where the import of the words of survivorship is to limit the benefit of the bequest to such of the legatees as may be alive at the time to which they refer ; and in this case the legacy will fail if all the legatees die before that time. But there is another sense in which such words may be used. They may signify survivorship *inter se*, in which case, while all the legatees alive at the time of payment will participate in the bequest, yet, if all die before that time, the longest liver will, on his survivance of the other legatees, acquire a vested interest in the whole of the subject of the bequest. Under this construction there will be no failure of the legacy unless all the beneficiaries predecease the testator. Which of these meanings is to be attributed to such words becomes a question of importance where all the legatees die before the time of payment or distribution.

Questions of a similar nature arise in cases where the survivorship is in the deed referred to a contingent event, and that event does not occur ; and in regard also to

[1] (1884), 11 R. 979.   [2] 1922 S. C. 688.   [3] See *ante*, p. 20.

destinations-over, where the institute predeceases, and it becomes necessary to determine whether the conditional institute thereupon takes a vested interest owing to the disappearance of the prior right.[1]

As the authorities stand, it is difficult to discover any definite criterion for determining in which of the above senses words of survivorship are to be interpreted. But in all the cases in which the construction of survivorship *inter se* has been adopted, the destination has been to the " survivor " of the legatees ; and it would seem to be impossible to adopt it where that word is used in the plural.

To legatees " or the survivors."

The first case in which this construction was noticed is *Newton* v. *Thomson*.[2] In that case the trustees were directed to hold the estate for the testator's sister in liferent, and on her death to make payment to two nieces, " *or the survivor of them*," in fee. Both nieces survived the testator. Thereafter one died in the lifetime of the liferentrix. As the other legatee survived the liferentrix, the case decides only that, under such a bequest, where a legatee dies before the period of distribution, his or her share passes to the legatee surviving that period. But, in the opinions delivered, the further point was discussed, whether, if both of the legatees had predeceased the liferentrix, the fund would have vested in the longer liver of the two. Lord Fullerton suggested that the provision as to survivorship might be considered as designed simply to regulate the claims of the beneficiaries *inter se*, and therefore as purified when only one claimant remained. In this view, the circumstances to which the condition referred having disappeared, it was to be treated as having become inoperative. On the other hand, Lord Mackenzie rejected this view. He regarded survivance of the liferentrix as a condition of any interest in the gift vesting ; and, if no one fulfilled that condition, then the estate would pass into residue, or, it might be, intestacy.

In the case of *Ferguson's Trs.* v. *Readman's Exrs.*[3] Lord Fullerton's view was adopted by the Second Division. In

---

[1] See page 92, *post*.

[2] (1849), 11 D. 452. See for comments on this case, *Boyle* v. *Earl of Glasgow's Trs.* (1858), 20 D. 925, *post*, p. 88.

[3] (1903), 10 S. L. T. 697. See also *Downie's Trs.* v. *Cullen* (1882), 9 R. 749, and *Fraser* v. *Fraser's Trs.* (1883), 11 R. 196, stated *post*, p. 147.

this case the testator directed his trustees, on the death of a liferenter, to divide the estate and make over a share to B. and C., " *and the survivor of them*." The liferenter, B. and C. survived the testator, and thereafter B. died. At the date when the case was brought into court, the liferenter and C. were alive. It was decided that C. acquired a vested right in the whole share on the death of B.[1] In this case, as in *Newton* v. *Thomson*, it will be observed that the gift was in the form of a direction to trustees to convey at the termination of the liferent.

So also in *Gardner* v. *Hamblin*,[2] where (in an *inter-vivos* deed) certain stock was given, on a contingency which occurred, to three brothers " or the survivor," it was held that the stock vested in the longest liver of the three, although he died in the lifetime of the liferenter, on whose death the gift was to take effect ; and in *Macfarlane's Trs.* v. *Macfarlane's Curator Bonis* [3] a similar result was reached. In this case the testamentary trustees were directed to hand over a sum to other trustees who were to hold it for the testator's brother in liferent, and on his death the capital was to go equally to another brother and sister, A. and B., declaring that, should either predecease the liferenter, the survivor should take the whole. A. and B. both died before the liferenter, B. being the survivor. It was held that the sum had vested in B., Lord Blackburn observing : " I think that the construction of such a destination is settled, and that, during the lifetime of the liferenter, no right vests in any of the persons entitled to share in the fee until there is only one survivor of them left, when the right to the whole fee vests immediately in that survivor whether he predecease the liferenter or not."

Gifts to legatees, and, if they predecease, to their issue, whom failing to survivors.

The form in which the element of survivorship appeared in the above cases—viz., a bequest to legatees *nominatim* and the survivor—is probably that which is most favourable to the construction adopted ; for, as observed in *Boyle* v.

---

[1] Lord Moncreiff dissented, holding that there was vesting *a morte testatoris*. See, however, his Lordship's opinion in *Begg's Trs.* v. *Reid* (1899), 1 F. 498, and in *Webster's Trs.* v. *Neil* (1900), 2 F. 695.

[2] (1900), 2 F. 679. Lord Adam dissented, and Lord Kinnear was absent. Treated as a special case in *Highet's J. F.* v. *Hamilton* 1912, 1 S. L. T. 474 (Lord Ormidale) ; and followed in *Aitken's Trs.* v. *Aitken's Trs.*, 1930, S. L. T. 509 (Lord Moncrieff).

[3] 1934 S. C. 476.

Earl of Glasgow's Trs.[1] " the survivorship " is " not stated as a condition of the party's own right, but merely as a possible ground of another party's preference." But the same interpretation was applied in *Lindsay's Trs.* v. *Sinclair* [2] to a bequest to legatees with a gift-over to the issue of a predeceasing legatee and to the survivor of the legatees. There trustees were directed to convey certain heritable properties after the death of the truster's wife, to whom the liferent of the property was given, to his two sons, A. and B., " declaring that if either of my said sons shall predecease my said spouse without lawful issue, then my trustees shall denude and convey the said several subjects to my surviving son; but should such predeceasing son leave lawful issue, then such issue shall come in their father's room and stead, and my said trustees shall denude and convey the father's share to such issue." A. died ; then B. died—both were unmarried ; and lastly the testator's widow. It was held that the properties had not fallen into intestacy, but had vested in B. on his brother's death.

The difficulty as to this construction is that the issue of the legatees were called as well as the survivor ; and there would seem to be no reason for denying effect to this gift-over. This difficulty was not felt in *Lindsay's Trs.* ; for, as the law then stood, such destinations-over were not adverse to the vesting of the bequest. But on this point the law has undergone a change,[3] and the authority of the decision is in consequence seriously impaired. From the anxious manner in which Lord President Inglis, in his opinion, directed attention to the fact that a destination-over to issue did not affect the vesting of the gift, it may be inferred that he would not have reached the same conclusion if the rule now adopted as to such destinations-over had then been fully established. Hence it would seem that, where the provision as to survivorship appears in the form of a clause calling issue, and failing issue, the survivor, the

---

[1] (1858) 20 D. 925, at 942.

[2] (1885), 12 R. 964., cf. *Smith* v. *Wighton's Trs.* (1874), 1 R. 358.

[3] *Ante*, p. 73 ; and see Lord Dundas's opinion in *Wylie's Trs.* v. *Bruce*, 1919 S. C. 211, at 227, and Lord Mackenzie's opinion in *Bannatyne's Trs.* v. *Watson's Trs.* 1914 S. C. 693. Lord Shand, in *Lindsay's Trs.* v. *Sinclair*, thought the destination-over to issue had the effect of rendering the legatee's right subject to defeasance in the event (which had not occurred) of his predeceasing leaving issue (see the cases cited, *post*, p. 149).

vesting should remain suspended until the time appointed for payment, although the number of the legatees be reduced to one. Further, when the legatees are described as the children of a person who is in life and the survivor of them, it would be difficult to hold that vesting could take place in that person's lifetime, in view of the possibility that the class might be augmented by further members of it coming into existence.

In regard to clauses in this form, there are decisions in England to the effect that the words of survivorship are to be referred to the happening of the contingency (namely, the death of a legatee without issue) and not to the period of distribution ; [1] but the authority of *Young* v. *Robertson* [2] is against the adoption of this view in our law. In that case (which has already been stated) [3] there was a liferent with a gift of the fee to the truster's grand-nephews and grand-nieces, subject to a devolution clause in favour of issue, whom failing the survivors. In the lifetime of the liferentrix, A. (a grand-nephew) died without issue, and thereafter B. (also a grand-nephew), leaving issue. It was held that B.'s son was entitled to his father's share under the devolution clause, but that he did not participate in A.'s share because his father, *although he survived* A., was never entitled, seeing that he predeceased the liferentrix.

Gifts to such of the legatees as may be alive at a specified time.

Where the gift is in the form of a direction to trustees to convey or pay to such persons as may be alive at a given time, it would be difficult to hold that the testator's intention was other than to suspend vesting in any circumstances until that time. Thus, in *Boyle* v. *The Earl of Glasgow's Trs.*,[4] there was a gift of the interest of the fund to the truster's daughter and her husband in liferent ; and on the expiry of these liferents the trustees were directed to make over the capital to " the child or children then existing of the marriage . . . if one, to that one solely ; and if more, to be divided equally among them." There was only one child of the marriage, a daughter. She survived her father, but predeceased her mother. It was held that the gift had not vested in her. Lord Fullerton's opinion [5] was pressed in

[1] *Crowder* v. *Stone* (1827), 3 Russ. 217 ; *Ive* v. *King* (1852), 16 Beav. 46.

[2] See Lord Stormonth - Darling's opinion in *Macfarlane's Trs.* v. *Macfarlane* (1906), 8 F. 787.

[3] *Ante*, p. 46.

[4] (1858), 20 D. 925.

[5] In *Newton* v. *Thomson, ante,* p. 85.

the argument, but the Court observed that the words used in the deed were not favourable to the application of Lord Fullerton's reasoning. The clause was, in the words of Lord Wood,[1] " so worded as not only to import a provision of survivorship among the children, which would suspend the vesting as long as it was undetermined which of the children as *inter se* were the survivors or the only survivor, but a provision by which it is made a *condition* of the children having any right in the fee of the trust property, that one or more of them shall have survived the longest liver of the liferenters."

In all the above cases the time to which the survivorship was referable was a *dies certus* ; but in the following cases the words of survivorship depended on a contingent event, and the Court was required to construe the bequest, that event not having happened. In *Maitland's Trs.* v. *MacDiarmid*,[2] the testator directed his trustees to " hold the residue . . . for behoof of my children " : and declared, first, that it was to be made over to them on the majority of the youngest ; and, secondly, that if any of them died before that event leaving issue, the issue should take his or her share, and failing issue the survivors. Two sons survived the testator, and thereafter both died in minority. It was held that the residue had vested in the younger son on the death of his brother. The term " youngest " referred to the period of division,[3] but being a relative term—for " the youngest must have that inherent property of greater youthfulness than another at the period of division "—had no meaning when the class was reduced to one member. Hence it followed that in the circumstances which had occurred the clause was inapplicable, and the absolute gift contained in the prior clause took effect in favour of the surviving child. In his opinion the Lord Justice-Clerk [4] points out that the clause would have been of no effect in the following cases also : (1) had all the testator's children been major at his death ; (2) had he been survived by only one child ; and (3) had he been

Gifts to a class on a contingent event which does not occur.

---

[1] At p. 936.
[2] (1861), 23 D. 732. Referred to in *Duncan's Trs.* (1877), 4 R. 1093.

And see also *Peacock's Trs.* v. *Peacock* (1885), 12 R. 878.
[3] See *post*, p. 200.   [4] Inglis.

survived by more than one child, and had all died save
one who at the time when he became sole survivor was
major.

Again, in *Mackie* v. *Gladstone*,[1] trustees were instructed
to make over the residue of the estate to the truster's two
sons " when the younger of them shall attain twenty-five
years of age." It was declared that, if either of them died
before the succession opened to him leaving issue, his
share should fall to his issue ; and, if the predeceaser
did not leave issue, then his share was to " be paid,
assigned, and disponed to the survivor." The younger son
having died in minority, it was held, on the principle of
Maitland's Trs., that the whole residue had vested on his
death in the elder son, although he was still under the age
of twenty-five.

In *Purves's Exr.* v. *Purves*,[2] the testatrix bequeathed
legacies of money to four nephews and four nieces ; and to
one of the nieces, Christina, she also gave the residue of her
estate. The testatrix further provided that the estate was
not to be divided until Christina attained the age of twenty-
one ; and, in case any niece should die unmarried before
Christina attained twenty-one, her share was to be divided
among the surviving nieces ; and, if any nephew so predeceased, his share was to be divided among the surviving
nephews. All the nieces were unmarried at the date of
the case. Christina died in minority. It was held that the
bequests did not vest during her lifetime, but that on her
death the suspensive condition vanished and all the gifts at
once vested. Christina's share was held to be carried to the
other nieces under the declaration as to predecease. The
Lord Ordinary (Kincairney) observed : " The next question
is whether the suspension of vesting has ceased by the death
of Christina ; and I am of opinion that it has. The testatrix's
words refer not to a date, but an event. That event cannot
happen. The words express a suspensive condition which
has become impossible, and I am of opinion that they
must—in accordance with an elementary rule in the construction of wills—be held *pro non scripto*, and therefore as
deleted from the deed at the date of her death." As an
alternative construction his Lordship suggested that the

---

[1] (1876), 13 S. L. R. 368.   [2] (1898), 25 R. 1084.

condition might be read as if to the words referring to Christina's attaining twenty-one there were added the words " if she survived," in which case, as the testatrix must have contemplated Christina's death, the event on which the survivorship clause and destination-over depended had happened.

In *Robert's Trs.* v. *Roberts*,[1] where the testator directed his trustees to divide the estate among his sons on the majority of the youngest, it was held that on the death of the youngest under age the other sons thereupon acquired vested interests ; but in this case all the surviving sons had attained majority.

Lastly, in *Lawrie's Trs.* v. *Lawrie* [2] the testator directed his trustees to hold the residue of his estate for behoof of his children, payable on the youngest attaining twenty-five, with a declaration that in the event of any of them dying before " the said period of division " leaving issue, such issue should take the share to which their parent would have been entitled if in life, and that, if any died without leaving issue, his share should fall to the survivors and survivor jointly with the issue of predeceasers. It was declared that the period of vesting should be at the date when the youngest child attained the age of twenty-five. One of the two children having died, the survivor, who was aged twenty-three, claimed that, in accordance with the decision in *Maitland's Trs.* v. *M'Diarmid*, the residue had vested in him. But the Court rejected this claim. No doubt was cast on the decision in *Maitland's Trs.*, but it was held to be distinguishable mainly because of the presence in the will of the express declaration as to the date of vesting.

It is hardly necessary to remark that in all of these cases there was no ulterior destination applicable to the contingency of the failure of all the legatees before the period of payment. Such a destination would not be compatible with vesting at any earlier period. This is shown by the decision in *Begg's Trs.* v. *Reid*.[3] The circumstances of that case were that the testator made a gift of a share of his estate to each of three families, " and the survivors " of the members of each family, on the death of his wife and on

No intermediate vesting where there is a gift-over on failure of all the legatees.

the youngest attaining the age of twenty-five : and declared that " in the event of any part of the foresaid shares of my means and estate provided to any family not having been paid over to such family, and of the members thereof and their issue all failing by death," the same should pass to the other families. It was held that there could be no vesting until the youngest of each family attained twenty-five. Lord Moncreiff noticed the case of *Maitland's Trs.* v. *MacDiarmid*, and remarked that the ulterior destination contained in the clause quoted was sufficient to exclude the authority of that case, even if otherwise it had been applicable.[1]

Vesting in heirs called as conditional institutes.

Another case in which a question as to vesting at an intermediate date may arise is that in which a bequest is made to a person whom failing his heirs. As we have seen, the effect of such a destination is to suspend vesting in the primary legatee until the date of payment of the legacy, for the reason that the destination-over on his failure is considered to import a condition that he must survive that date in order to become entitled to the legacy : it remains to consider the position of the heirs called as conditional institutes.

It is clear that there can be no vesting in these heirs till the death of the *propositus*, for not until then can his heirs be ascertained ; and it is also settled that, if the *propositus* predecease the testator, the heirs are to be ascertained on the death of the latter. In *Maxwell* v. *Maxwell* [2] a bequest was made to A., " his heirs, executors and assignees." The Intestate Moveable Succession Act of 1855 having been passed after the making of the will and also after the death of A., but before the death of the testatrix, it was held that the heirs as ascertained in terms of that statute, and not the heirs as at A.'s death, were entitled to the bequest.

But it may be that the primary legatee survives the testator and dies before the date of payment of the legacy, and it has been questioned whether in that case the heirs should not be treated as taking a vested right on the death of the legatee, irrespective of whether they do or do not

---

[1.] *Cattanach* v. *Thom's Exrs.* (1858), 20 D. 1206, may also be referred to as bearing on this point.

[2] (1864), 3 M. 318 ; see also *Ewart* v. *Cottom* (1870), 9 M. 232, and, as to the testator's heirs, *Nimmo* v. *Murray's Trs.* (1864), 2 M. 1144.

survive the date of payment of the legacy. A person's heirs are as a general rule ascertained at his death.[1] This being so, why, it may be asked, should not the heirs at once acquire a vested right if there is nothing in the deed expressly prescribing that they must survive till the legacy becomes payable or that vesting is only then to take place ?

This question first came into prominence in the whole Court case of *Thompson's Trs.* v. *Jamieson*.[2] In that case the trust disposition and settlement provided that on the death of a liferentrix without issue a sum of money should be made over to " Robert Nisbet, junior, and his heirs or assignees." The liferentrix died without issue predeceased by Robert Nisbet. On a consideration of the whole of the provisions of the deed, the majority of the Court came to the conclusion that vesting took place *a morte testatoris* in Robert Nisbet ; but the members of the Court who thought that it was suspended took occasion to discuss the position in that case of his heirs.

Lord M'Laren (with whom Lord Pearson concurred [3]) was of opinion that, while the conditional institution of Robert Nisbet's heirs suspended vesting during the joint continuance of his life and that of the liferentrix, there was nothing to prevent vesting in his heirs on his death. " Robert Nisbet," he said, " died in Mrs Thompson's life-time, and it appears to me that the effect of his death was to free the destination from the suspensive condition with which it had been affected. The death of Robert was equivalent in legal effect to striking his name out of the destination, which then became in legal effect a provision in favour of Mrs Thompson in liferent and her child or children in fee, whom failing, to the heirs of Robert. This is, in form and substance, a destination to a class of ascertained and existing persons subject to the contingency of the birth of issue to Mrs Thompson. The right of Robert's heirs was then only affected by a resolutive condition ; and it follows, in my opinion, that the provision vested in Robert's heirs, subject to defeasance in the event of Mrs Thompson leaving issue."

---

[1] See *post*, p. 225.
[2] (1900), 2 F. 470.
[3] Had he found it necessary to decide the point, Lord Kincairney also would have concurred (see p. 489 of the report.). In *Aitken's Trs.* v. *Aitken*, 1930, S.L.T., 509, Lord Moncrieff preferred Lord M'Laren's construction.

On the other hand, Lord Kyllachy, with the concurrence of Lord Adam and Lord Kinnear, was of opinion that under the frame of the bequest vesting was postponed till the death of the liferentrix and that no right could vest in anyone prior to that event. If this was so, his Lordship pointed out that, if the heirs of Robert Nisbet were to be ascertained at his death, then, if all of these predeceased the liferentrix, the legacy would fall into residue or become intestate succession, and added, " I am not able to hold that a designative bequest to the heirs or next of kin either of the truster himself, or of a legatee or other third person, can possibly be read otherwise than as applying to persons who exist and possess the described character at the period of vesting—that is, the period when the gift takes effect. It is therefore the period presumably in the testator's mind as the period at which the class shall be ascertained.[1] At all events, it is quite certain that in no case which has yet occurred has an institution or conditional institution of a class of heirs been read as applicable to any other period. That may be affirmed even where the bequest is conceived in favour, *e.g.* of the heirs or next-of-kin of the testator himself. For, although it is doubtless true that such bequests have always been held to operate in favour of the heirs or next-of-kin at the testator's death, it is at the same time equally true that in all such cases the testator's death has been also the period of vesting. . . . The point, however, is not left—at least in the kind of case here in question—to merely negative inference. For we have here to deal with a bequest, not to the heirs of the testator, but to the heirs of a legatee ; and it has been expressly determined in two cases—one in each Division of the Court—that where vesting is postponed to the period of distribution, such bequest operates in favour of the persons who stand at that period in the described relation to the legatee. I refer to the cases of *Maxwell* [2] and *Stodart's Trs.* [3] I am not aware that the authority of these cases has been questioned : nor can I

---

[1] This passage was approved in *G.'s Trs.* v. *G.*, 1937 S. C. 141.

[2] (1864), 3 M. 318. In this case the bequest was to A., " his heirs, executors, and assignees." A. predeceased the testator. It was held that his heirs were to be ascertained on the death of the testator.

[3] (1870), 8 M. 667. In this case trustees were directed to hold for A.

assent to the view that there is any legal anomaly in ascertaining the heirs of a deceased person otherwise than at the time of his death. *Prima facie* it may be true that a person's heirs are the persons who are entitled to serve or to confirm to his estate at the time of his death. But alike in heritable and in moveable succession there might formerly have been, and I suppose may still be, service or confirmation long after a person's death, expede by persons who did not exist at that date, and who, if they had existed, would have been excluded by nearer heirs. In truth, however, the question in cases like the present is not at all a technical question, but a question simply of the intention of the testator. And assuming that vesting was here postponed till the death of the liferentrix, I see no sufficient reason for rejecting the claim of the third parties who were at the date of vesting, and still are, the heirs in mobilibus of Robert Nisbet." In a later part of his opinion, Lord Kyllachy pointed out that the result of Lord M'Laren's view would be that, where at the death of the testator a number of persons were instituted in succession who all predeceased the period of distribution, the assignee of the last person instituted might take in preference to the assignees of the first.

It will be observed that the question in this case was complicated by the fact that the issue of the liferentrix were called in the first instance, and, therefore, any vesting which might take place in Robert Nisbet or his heirs during the subsistence of the liferent could only be subject to defeasance in the event of issue being born to the liferentrix. The indisposition of the Court to extend the doctrine of vesting subject to defeasance [1] had a part in influencing the decision ; but in subsequent cases of simple bequests, with a postponed period of payment, to a person whom failing his heirs, these opinions have been frequently referred to.

Lord M'Laren's view accords with a dictum of Lord

---

in liferent, and on his death to make over the subject to B. or his heirs. B. survived the testator but died before A. The heirs of B. entitled to the bequest were held to be the heirs as at A.'s death. But the only question raised in the case was whether the bequest had or had not vested in B., and Lord Cowan pointed out that the question had not been raised whether B.'s heirs were to be ascertained at his death or at that of A.

[1] See *Lees's Trs.* v. *Lees*, 1927 S. C. 886, and other cases cited, p. 135, *post*.

Davey in *Bowman* v. *Bowman*,[1] but otherwise the trend of authority is in favour of the postponement of vesting in the heirs till the date of payment. In two Outer House cases Lord Kyllachy's view was applied ;[2] and in 1918 the question was considered in the whole Court case of *Wylie's Trs.* v. *Bruce.*[3] There the testator directed his trustees to hold his house and a sum of money for his widow in liferent, and on her death to make over both to his cousin " or his heirs in heritage." The cousin died before the widow survived by his eldest son, who also, however, predeceased the widow ; and this gave rise to the question whether under the destination-over the right had vested in that son or whether, on the other hand, vesting took place only on the widow's death in the younger son who survived the widow and was at the date of her death the cousin's heir in heritage. It was the unanimous decision of the Court that the heir was to be ascertained at the date of the widow's death, and, accordingly, that the younger son was entitled to the subjects bequeathed. The argument for the elder son was based on the ground that a man's heirs fell to be ascertained at his death and that there was nothing to prevent vesting in him as the heir at that date. Now, in the case of a bequest by a testator to his own heirs " it would require very special words to overcome the presumption that they are to be sought for as at his own death and at no other period " ;[4] but in the case of a destination-over to a legatee's heirs, "the question must always be one of intention, to be ascertained from the language employed, whether the heirs of a legatee, who are called as conditional institutes and whose right is not one of succession to him, are the legatee's heirs at his death or at some other period ; and the destination must be read just as if it were in favour not of persons described as so-and-so's heirs, but of a named third party. It stands to reason, and the cases illustrate, that, in this sense, a man may have one heir at his death and another

---

[1] 1 F. (H. L.) 69, at 77. It is also apparently in accordance with English law—see Theobald on Wills (8th Ed.), p. 379.

[2] *Highet's J.F.* v. *Hamilton*, 1912, 1 S. L. T. 474 (Lord Ormidale) ; *Anderson* v. *Cunningham's Trs.* (1906), 14 S. L. T. 588 (Lord Ardwall). Cf. also *Baillie's Trs.* v. *Whiting*, 1910 S. C. 891, as to a heritable destination.

[3] 1919 S. C. 211.

[4] *Per* Lord Dundas, at p. 226 ; see the cases as to such bequests, p. 225, *post.*

at some later period ; the question is at what date did the testator intend the heir to be looked for whom he called as an independent conditional institute to the legatee." [1] " A.," said Lord Sands,[2] " can only have one heir to his property passing *ab intestato* at his death, and no other person can ever occupy that position, just as A. can have only one eldest son at the date of his death, and no other person can ever occupy that position. But to deduce therefrom that this person must necessarily be treated as the person designated as ' heir ' or ' eldest son ' in a settlement by a third party directing a conveyance at some future date to A.'s ' heir ' or ' eldest son ' appears to me to beg the question, At what date, on a fair construction of the settlement, is the ' heir ' or the ' eldest son ' to be sought ? " [3]

The term employed in this case was " heirs in heritage," but in the opinions delivered (although in some of them stress was laid on the use of the plural term " heirs "), the case was treated as raising the general question as to the construction of a conditional institution of the heirs of a legatee. Accordingly, it was followed in *Wilson's Trs.* v. *Mackenzie* [4] where the direction to the trustees was to hold a share of the trust estate for a son of the testator and his (the son's) wife in liferent, and " thereafter " for behoof of his issue and the survivors whom failing his (the son's) " nearest lawful heirs and assignees in fee." It was held that the son's heirs were to be ascertained at the termination of the liferent of the son's widow ; and, therefore, that no right vested in a child of the son who survived him but predeceased the liferentrix.

There would appear to be support in the English authorities for a third construction, namely, that the heirs of the legatee are to be ascertained at the death of the legatee, but that only such of these as survive the date of vesting are entitled to the bequest ; but this construction has never been adopted in our Courts.[5]

---

[1] *Per* Lord Dundas, at p. 226 ; see also Lord Skerrington's opinion at p. 238.

[2] At p. 233.

[3] Cf. also *G.'s Trs.* v. *G.*, 1937 S. C. 141.

[4] 1924 S. C. 568 ; see also *Wright's Trs.* v. *Wright* (1894), 21 R. 568.

[5] For a further discussion of this construction see *post*, p. 229.

Gifts-over
to issue.

In the opinion of Lord Dundas in *Wylie's Trs.* v. *Bruce* [1]
reference is made to another class of case in which the
question of intermediate vesting has been raised, viz., where
a legacy is to be paid to the legatee at a future date with a
provision that if he predecease his children or issue shall
take the legacy.   The decisions in regard to such bequests—
which were considered by Lord Dundas to have no "feasible
application or useful analogy" to destinations-over to heirs
—are noticed in a subsequent chapter.[2]

Heritable
Destinations.

In all of the above cases the heirs were called as
conditional institutes.   Where, as in the case of heritable
destinations they are called as substitutes, the destination
must be construed in the light of the rules of feudal conveyancing.   In *Baillie's Trs.* v. *Whiting* [3] the testator,
Sir William Baillie, directed his trustees to dispone a heritable estate on the death of the liferentrix to his nephew,
"whom failing to the heirs of his body, whom failing to my
own heirs-male and the heirs of their body, whom failing
to my own nearest heirs whomsoever, excluding heirs-
portioners."   The testator's heir-at-law at his death was the
nephew, but he predeceased the liferentrix without issue ;
and his brother who survived him also predeceased her,
leaving a son (Sir Gawaine G. S. Baillie).   It was held that
no right vested in the heirs till the death of the liferentrix.
The Lord President pointed out that the purpose in the
testator's deed dealing with the estate contained "a
direction in very specific terms as to the conveyance which
the trustees are to make, and the conveyance which they
are to make is to be a conveyance containing the destination
contained in that purpose.   If that is so, that, of course,
ends the question, because it is trite law that, taking this
as a destination of Scottish heritage, the expression 'whom
failing' means that it is necessary to invoke the destination
in order to ascertain who is to take after the party first
called.   After all, the meaning of a destination, if you go

[1] 1919 S. C. 211.

[2] See *Martin* v. *Holgate* (1866),
L. R. 1 H. L. 175, and the Scottish
cases in which that case was canvassed.

[3] 1910 S. C. 891 ; see also *Smith's
Trs.* v. *Smith's Trs.* (1905), 7 F. 815,

and *ante*, p. 8 ; and contrast
M'Donald's Trs. v. *M'Donald*, 1907
S. C. 65 (stated *post*, p. 227), where
the destination was read as a conditional institution.

back to early law, is very simple. It is simply the agreed-on rule by which you are to discover who is the person who is entitled to demand an entry of the superior when the fee is no longer full owing to the death of the last vassal ; and, although this seems to have been forgotten in a great many of the discussions that have taken place upon the matter, it is almost the A B C of conveyancing. Accordingly, there are hundreds of estates in Scotland where one particular series of heirs having been exhausted the estate has then reverted, under the standing destination, to another series of heirs and nobody ever dreamt that those heirs should be sought for at any time except that at which the succession opened. Treating this, then, as a destination of heritage, I suppose no Scottish conveyancer could have any doubt whatever that Sir Gawaine, being the person who answers the description of heir-male of the late Sir William at the opening of the succession is the person who must take." No one maintained in this case that the right vested on the death of the nephew in his brother, but the reasons given for the decision make it plain that this contention could not be entertained.[1]

VI. Survivorship Words in Liferent Gifts.—In a gift of a liferent to parties and the survivors, the words of survivorship refer to the death of a liferenter *at any time.* Thus in *Fergus & Others* [2] the testator gave his estate in trust for his widow in liferent, and, after her death, for his three children " and the survivors and survivor of them, equally, share and share alike, also in liferent," and for their issue *per stirpes* in fee. All the children survived the widow (who died some time after the testator), and thereafter one died leaving issue. The issue claimed the one-third liferented by their mother, free from the burden of any further liferent ; the remaining children, on the other hand, maintained that they were entitled to the liferent of the whole estate. The question was thus sharply raised whether the survivorship

Gift to survivors construed as referring to death at any time.

---

[1] This case is referred to in the opinions of Lord Dundas and Lord Skerrington in *Wylie's Trs.* v. *Bruce, ante,* and of Lord Ormidale in *Cripps's Trs.* v. *Cripps,* 1926 S. C. 188 at 203.

[2] (1872), 10 M. 968. The question was raised by assignees of the surviving children.

words were satisfied by survivance of the widow, or whether they operated on the termination at any time of any of the liferents. The Court adopted the latter construction, and admitted the claim of the remaining children.

This decision is supported by that of the House of Lords in *Richardson* v. *Macdougall*.[1] The will under consideration in that case had been construed in *Young* v. *Robertson*,[2] where it was held that the survivorship clause prevented vesting in the legatees—grand-nephews and grand-nieces—until the end of the widow's liferent. But by a codicil the testator directed the trustees to hold the shares of grand-nieces for them " and their respective husbands " in liferent, and for their issue in fee ; " whom failing to the survivors of them and my grand-nephews . . . equally in liferent, and their issue also equally in fee." A grand-niece died childless before the widow. It was held that her husband (who survived the widow) was entitled to the share in liferent, and that on his death it went over to the grand-nephews and grand-nieces *then* alive, and to their issue in fee. " To bestow a liferent," said Lord Benholme, " or a share of a liferent, upon a party or parties who do not survive the time when that liferent is to commence, is simply absurd."

A further point was also decided, namely, that in a gift to

Conjunct liferents. A. and B. in liferent, B. will take the whole liferent in the event of A. predeceasing the time at which the liferent is to open. A similar construction prevailed in *Reid's Trs.* v. *Reid*,[3] where the liferent was described as " conjunct." There the estate was given to the trustees in trust for the testator's widow in liferent, and " after her death " the estate was to be paid to the testator's son, or, if the trustees thought fit, held for him and his wife in conjunct liferent, and for their issue in fee. On the expiry of the widow's liferent, the trustees had not paid over the estate, and the son had died leaving a widow. It was decided that the right of the son's widow was not conditioned on the son's survivance of his mother, and that she took the liferent of the whole.

Liferenter's repudiation of her liferent. If, however, in the case of a liferent given to two parties and to the survivor, one of the liferents is terminated by

[1] (1868), 6 M. (H. L.) 18.   Cf. *Dennistoun* v. *Dalgleish* (1838), 1 D. 69.   [2] (1862), 4 Macq. 314 ; *ante*, p. 46.   [3] (1879), 6 R. 916.

the legatee's repudiation of the gift, the forfeited share may not pass to the other liferenter. Thus, where a liferent was given to two parties " equally between them while both should be in life and to the survivor," and one claimed legitim, it was held that the forfeited share went to the parties injured by the claim for legitim. The decision proceeded on the terms of the gift and on the principle of equitable compensation.[1]

The result of the rule as to survivorship in regard to liferents is further illustrated in the cases, such as *Ward* v. *Lang*,[2] which involve the question whether, and in what circumstances, " survivors " may be construed as equivalent to " others."

---

[1] *Breadalbane's Trs.* v. *Pringle* (1841), 3 D. 357. See also *Rose's Trs.* v. *Rose*, 1916 S.C. 827.

[2] *Post*, p. 116.

CHAPTER V

CLAUSES OF DEVOLUTION (TO ISSUE, WHOM FAILING SURVIVORS).

I. Whether Issue take Parent's Original Share only.

II. Whether Conditions affecting Parent also affect (by Implication) the Issue.

III. Whether Accrescing Shares are subject to Conditions affecting the Legatee's Original Share.

IV. When " Survivors " may be read as " Others."

General rule is that issue do not take accrescing shares.

I. Clauses substituting Issue for Parents. Whether Issue take Accrescing Shares.—In a clause of devolution, the issue of the predeceasing legatee may be substituted for their parent either explicitly or by implication. The testator may provide for the contingencies of the legatee's predecease, either with or without issue, by giving his share, in the one event, to issue, and, in the other, to the survivors of the legatees ; [1] or he may simply declare that, if the legatee shall predecease without leaving issue, his portion shall pass to the survivors, in which case the issue are called by a plain implication.[2] These forms do not, in substance, differ ; [3] and they are subject to the same general rule (which is very firmly established in a series of cases), namely, that the issue take their parent's original share only, and are

---

[1] As in *Earl of Lauderdale* v. *Royle* (1830), 8 S. 771 ; 5 Fac. 603 ; *Greig* v. *Malcolm* (where children were entitled under a destination-over to executors) (1835), 13 S. 607; 10 Fac. 395; *Vines* v. *Hillou* (1860), 22 D. 1436 ; *M'Nish* v. *Donald's Trs.* (1879), 7 R. 96 ; *Henderson* v. *Hendersons* (1890), 17 R. 293 ; *Cumming's Trs.* v. *White* (1893), 20 R. 454 ; *Still's Trs.* v. *Hall* (1899), 36 S. L. R. 390 ; *Baxter's Trs.* v.

Bell (1900), 8 S. L. T. 176 (Lord Kincairney) ; *Crichton's Trs.* v. *Bell* (1900), 8 S. L. T. 177.

[2] *Clelland* v. *Gray* (1839), 1 D. 1031 ; *Walker* v. *Park* (1859), 21 D. 286 ; *Young* v. *Robertson* (1862), 4 Macq. 337 ; *Graham's Trs.* v. *Graham* (1868), 6 M. 820.

[3] *Per* Lord Mackenzie in *Clelland* v. *Gray, supra.*

not entitled to participate in any shares which may accresce through the death of other legatees without children.

Thus, in the *Earl of Lauderdale* v. *Royle*,[1] the testator gave the liferent of his estate to his widow, and directed his trustees on her death to divide the whole remainder into five portions, and to pay one portion to each of his widow and his four natural children, declaring that " in case of any of the said four natural children dying before receiving their share of the said effects hereby settled on them, the same shall be paid to their children, if they shall leave any ; and failing thereof, it shall be divided equally amongst the said surviving natural children." All the legatees survived the testator. Thereafter two children died leaving issue ; then a daughter died without issue ; and lastly the widow died survived by the remaining daughter. It was held that the issue took their parent's shares, but were not entitled to participate in the portion of the other predeceasing daughter, which went to the daughter in life at the widow's death. Under the terms of the will, the shares of those predeceasing without leaving children went to " survivors " ; and it was not permissible to qualify this word by the *Conditio si sine liberis*, because that condition proceeds on the presumption that the testator has overlooked the claims of issue, whereas the clause in this case, by introducing them in regard to the parent's original share, negatived any idea that they had been inadvertently omitted in regard to the other portions.[2]

The same principle was applied by the House of Lords, in *Young* v. *Robertson*,[3] to a will in which the issue were called by implication. The facts of the case have been stated in connexion with the first question which arose on the will, namely, as to the time of vesting. The Court having decided that vesting was suspended until the death of the truster's widow, another case (which also went to the House of Lords) was brought to determine whether, under the clause which provided that the shares of legatees who predeceased without leaving issue should belong to the survivors, these shares were to be distributed among the

---

[1] *Supra.*
[2] See Lord Corehouse's opinion in *Greig* v. *Malcolm* (1835), 13 S. 607 ; 10 Fac. 395 ; and Chapter XVII., *post.*

[3] (1862), 4 Macq. 337 ; stated *supra*, p. 46. See *Macfarlane's Trs.* v. *Macfarlane* (1908), 8 F. 787.

surviving legatees and the issue of predeceasing legatees, or whether they fell to be divided among the surviving legatees alone. The House of Lords (affirming the decision of the Court of Session) rejected the claim of the issue to participate in these shares. on the ground that the will gave them to the survivors.

In *Henderson* v. *Hendersons*,[1] Lord President Inglis said : " I can see no distinction in principle between the case in which the *conditio* is expressed and that in which it is implied. The principle in both cases is simply this, whether the *conditio* is implied or expressed, that the share of the predeceasing parent goes to his or her issue,—that is, the original share of the parent,—and not any further provision that may come to the parent by the lapse of a legacy to some predeceasing legatee in virtue of any other provision in the deed." This principle has been held to be applicable to cases in which the subject of the gift was an annuity and not a share of capital.[2]

The order in which the legatees predecease is, as already observed,[3] immaterial. " Survivors " or " surviving " refer to the period at which the general fund vests ; and although the parent of the issue may survive the legatee who predeceases without issue, if he afterwards himself predecease, he is not considered a survivor, and his issue are not admitted to participate in the portion of the childless predeceaser.[4] Nor are the rights of the issue any higher in regard to shares that lapse by the death of a legatee without issue before the testator, than in regard to shares of legatees surviving the testator but dying before the time of distribution and vesting.[5]

---

[1] (1890), 17 R. 293. As to the *conditio*, see *Crosbie's Trs.* v. *Crosbie*, 1927 S. C. 159, and other cases discussed in Chapter XVII.

[2] *Drybrough's Tr.* v. *Drybrough's Tr.*, 1912 S. C. 939. See *Burnett* v. *Burnett's Trs.* (1894), 21 R. 1040, for a case in which a widow substituted to the share of income bequeathed to her husband was held entitled to an accrescing share of that income.

[3] *Ante*, p. 88.

[4] This was the case in *Young* v.

Robertson (1862), 4 Macq. 337 ; *Clelland* v. *Gray* (1839), 1 D. 1031 ; *Cumming's Trs.* v. *White* (1893), 20 R. 454 ; and *Macfarlane's Trs.* v. *Macfarlane* (1908), 8 F. 787. Lord Rutherfurd Clark notices the point in *Groat* v. *Stewart's Trs.* (1894), 21 R. 961.

[5] *Bowman* v. *Richter* (1900), 2 F. 624, where the First Division reversed Lord Kyllachy's interlocutor, which proceeded on this distinction. This was a case in regard to the *conditio*.

The rule will of course be displaced if the testator declares that the issue are to take their parent's share, as well accrescing as original, or provides that the share of a legatee who predeceases shall go over to the survivors and the issue of those who may have died, or otherwise indicates that he intends the share of issue to be enlarged by accretion. But it requires clear and unmistakable evidence of such an intention to effect this purpose. Thus, in *M'Nish* v. *Donald's Trs.*,[1] where it was provided that issue should " be entitled to the share of their mother as if she had been in life," and in *Cumming's Trs.* v. *White*,[2] where the provision was that children should " be entitled to succeed to their parent's share . . . in the same manner and as fully as if such parent had survived," it was submitted in argument that these expressions were sufficient to set aside the rule, but without success.[3]

On the other hand, if there is a destination-over in the event of all the legatees dying without issue, this may have the effect of entitling the issue of predeceasers to a larger share than that given in the first instance to their parents. Thus, in *Neville* v. *Shepherd*,[4] the residue was given to the truster's daughter and her husband in liferent, and thereafter to her " whole children . . . or last survivor of said children." In a subsequent part of the will it was provided that " in the event of its happening that all of my said grandchildren predeceased the terms of payment . . . without leaving lawful issue," the residue should go over to certain nephews and nieces. Four of the truster's grandchildren died between the date of the will and the time of payment (namely, the first term after the death of the daughter), which was also the time of vesting, all without children. A fifth died leaving issue ; and one survived the period of vesting. The issue were preferred to a half (and not to a one-sixth share), largely because of the clause last quoted.

---

[1] (1879), 7 R. 96.

[2] (1893), 20 R. 454 ; and see also *Henderson* v. *Hendersons* (1890), 17 R. 293.

[3] See observations as to these expressions in *Beveridge's Trs.* v. *Beveridge*, 1930 S. C. 578, *per* Ld. Pres. Clyde, at 585 and Lord Sands,

at 589, and *Miller's Trs.* v. *Brown*, 1933 S. C. 669, *per* Ld. Pres. Clyde, at 679.

[4] (1895), 23 R. 351. Cf. also *Cattanach* v. *Thom's Exrs.* (1858), 20 D. 1206, and *Bell* v. *Grieve* (1840), 2 D. 880.

From this clause it was clear that the testator did not intend
the bequest to pass out of the line of his direct descendants
so long as there were any in existence ; hence, had no
grandchildren survived to take, the residue must have gone
to any great-grandchildren who were alive at the daughter's
death, and if there were only one great grandchild, he or
she would have taken the whole ; from which it was to be
inferred that the testator's general intention was not to limit
the issue to the original shares of their parents.   This decision
was followed in *Craik's Trs.* v. *Anderson.*[1]

Rule displaced
where intestacy
would result.
    There is another instance in which the rule of *Young* v.
Robertson is displaced, viz., where the result of its application
would be to produce intestacy.   This exception was admitted
for the first time in *Beveridge's Trs.* v. *Beveridge.*[2]   In that
case the testator instructed his trustees at a certain period
after the death of himself and his wife to pay over two-fifths
of the residue of his estate to a named nephew, and to pay
over the remaining three-fifths to five other nephews and
nieces.   There was a declaration that, if any of them predeceased leaving issue, the issue should succeed to the share
his or her parent would have been entitled to had he or she
been in life, and that, if any predeceased without issue, his
or her share was to go to the survivors.   All of the nephews
and nieces died before the testator's widow, and only two
of them (nephews) left issue.   In these circumstances, if,
as the Lord President observed, " the competition in the
present case had been between the survivors or survivor of
the testator's named nephews and nieces and the issue of
predeceasers, I should have entertained no doubt that we
were bound to prefer the survivors or survivor."   But there
being no surviving nephew or niece, the result of confining
the issue of the two nephews to their parents' original shares
would have been that the remaining portion of the residue
would have lapsed into intestacy :   and, so strong was the
law's abhorrence of intestacy held to be, that the Court felt
justified in finding that the shares of the childless nephews
and nieces were divisible between the two families of the
nephews *per stirpes*.

    In the cases hitherto considered, one of the features of

[1] 1932 S. C. 61.   [2] 1930 S. C. 578.

the deed was that the share of the legatee dying without issue was expressly destined to the survivors or to other legatees ; and it was with reference to a bequest in this form that the rule of *Young* v. *Robertson* was formulated. But the bequest may take the form of a gift to a class or number of legatees, with a provision that the issue of predeceasers shall take their parent's share, but without any provision in regard to the shares of those who predecease without issue ; and in the case of such bequests there was for long some uncertainty as to the extent of the benefit conferred on the issue, although the weight of authority was in favour of the view that the rule of *Young* v. *Robertson* did not apply. *Where there is no institution of survivors, issue may participate in accrescing shares.*

Thus, in *Laing* v. *Barclay*,[1] where the testator bequeathed the proceeds realised by the sale of certain heritable property, at the expiry of a liferent, to his children, and declared that " in the event of any of my children predeceasing the said term of division leaving lawful issue, it is my desire that such issue shall represent and be entitled to the proportion which would have been payable to their parent," issue were preferred to the shares that accresced owing to the death of certain of the children without issue. The cases of *Clelland* v. *Gray* and *Young* v. *Robertson* were distinguished on the ground that it was impossible to apply the principle therein established, " where there is no clause of survivorship, and where, as in the present deed, there is an express declaration of the extent of interest to be taken by the issue of predeceasing children." [2] With reference to the terms of the clause substituting issue, Lord Cowan remarked : " I cannot read these words as importing anything else than that the issue are to stand in the place of their parent, and be entitled to take whatever he would have taken had he survived the term of division. Had the parent survived, all his brothers having predeceased childless, he would have been entitled to the whole as survivor. Such is the construction to which, as already said, the clause

---

[1] (1865), 3 M. 1143. Followed in *M'Meekan's Trs.* v. *M'Clelland*, 1918, 1 S. L. T. 193 (Lord Hunter). The interlocutor in the early case of *Johnston* v. *Johnston* (1840), 2 D. 1038, is in accordance with *Laing* v. *Barclay*.

[2] *Per* Lord Cowan. This case was distinguished by Lord Kincairney in *Baxter's Trs.* v. *Bell* (1900), 8 S. L. T. 176, as proceeding on the absence of a survivorship clause.

must be subjected, for ' the children ' cannot but mean children alive, and capable of taking, at the time of division."

This case was followed in *M'Culloch's Trs.*[1] The facts of this last case, however, are very special. The testator instructed his trustees to pay the residue to " my brothers and sisters who may survive me, jointly with the lawful issue of any of them who may have predeceased me leaving issue, the division being *per stirpes*." He further provided that one sister, A., should take in liferent only, the fee of her share being held for her children, " whom failing for behoof of my brothers and sisters who may be surviving at the date of her decease, jointly with the lawful issue of such of them as may have predeceased leaving issue, the division being *per stirpes*." By a codicil he cancelled " all share that my brother B. would have been entitled to," and gave " that share " to his children. A. died without issue ; and on the question arising whether the children of B. were entitled to a portion of her share, it was held that they were. The main ground of the decision was that in the codicil the children were called to the whole interest withdrawn from their parent. It will also be observed that the bequest was in the nature of a direct bequest ; and further, it may be noticed (although this element was not founded on in the opinions delivered) that the gift was to the children " jointly " with the other parties. As the characteristic incident of a joint tenancy is the benefit of survivorship among the parties, it might be assumed from the use of the word that the children were expressly called to partake in accrescing shares.

In the following year, in *White's Trs.* v. *Chrystal's Trs.*,[2] the decision in *M'Culloch's Trs.* was treated as exceptional, and the issue of the predeceasing legatee were held to be entitled only to the parent's original share although there was no gift-over to the survivors.[2] The ground of decision as explained by Lord Trayner [3] was that the rule of *Young* v. *Robertson* applied even where there was no clause of

---

[1] (1892), 19 R. 777.

[2] (1893), 20 R. 460.

[3] In *Cumming's Trs.* v. *White* (1893), 20 R. 454, at 460. In *White's Trs.* v. *Chrystal's Trs.* (which con-cerned the same parties), Lord Trayner referred to his opinion in *Cumming's Trs.* v. *White* as explaining the grounds of the decision.

survivorship " unless there be some clear indication of the testator's intention that a different rule is to be followed."

Such being the state of the authorities, when the question again arose in 1933 in *Miller's Trs.* v. *Brown* [1] the First Division found it necessary to remit the case to a Court of Seven Judges. The circumstances were that the testator directed his trustees on the death of his wife to divide one half of the residue of his estate equally among his children ; [2] and declared that the provisions to the children should not vest until payment, and should any of the children " predecease my said wife, leaving lawful issue, such issue shall be entitled to the share that would have fallen to their parent by survivance." [2] Of the seven children who were alive at the testator's death, two only survived his widow. Two of the predeceasing children left families and the other three died without issue. The question of the right of the grandchildren to participate in the shares which would have fallen to the three childless children had they survived was thus sharply raised under the terms of a will which contained no specialties affecting the decision. After a full discussion of the authorities and of the considerations bearing on the question, it was held that the residue was divisible into four shares falling to the children and grandchildren equally, *per stirpes*. [3] The opinions of the majority of the Court make it plain that in the general case, if there is no clause disposing otherwise of the shares of legatees who predecease without leaving issue, the issue who are called to take in room of their parent in the event of his predecease will not be excluded from participating in these shares.

II. Clauses substituting Issue for Parents. Whether Conditions affecting the Parent's Right affect also, by Implication, the Children's Rights.—In an earlier chapter there was occasion to inquire whether, in the case of a bequest at a postponed date to A. or his heirs, vesting in the general case took place on A.'s predecease in his heirs or whether there was a suspension of vesting until the

Vesting in issue and predeceasers.

---

[1] 1933 S. C. 669.

[2] There were provisions as to the sons' shares being payable at twenty-five and as to part of the daughters' shares being held for them in liferent and their issue in fee.

[3] The Lord President and Lord Blackburn dissented.

arrival of the date of payment.[1] A somewhat similar question may arise in regard to issue under the form of bequest now under consideration, should the parent predecease the period at which he would acquire a vested right.

The leading authority on this point is the case of *Martin* v. *Holgate* [2] decided by the House of Lords in 1866. The testator there directed his trustees to pay the annual proceeds of the residue of his estate to his wife ; and after her death to divide the residue among such of four nephews and two nieces as should be living at the widow's death, " but if any or either of them should then be dead, leaving issue, then it is my will and meaning that such issue shall be entitled to their father's or mother's share, but in equal proportions." One of the nephews survived the testator but predeceased the widow leaving a daughter *who also predeceased the widow*. In these circumstances the question arose whether this daughter was entitled to the share which her father would have taken had he survived the widow. Admittedly the condition of survivorship excluded vesting in the nephews and nieces until the death of the widow, but it was held that this condition did not attach to their issue, and that accordingly the share of the predeceasing nephew vested on his death in his daughter. The Lord Chancellor (Cranworth) said : " When we speak of a person having died leaving a child or children, we mean leaving a child or children at his death. If, therefore, the language here had been, if any of them should, at the death of my wife, have died leaving issue, it would have meant if any should at or before that time have died leaving issue at his own death, and, if that be so, it is hard to say that any difference is to arise from the circumstance that the words are not ' shall then have died leaving issue,' but ' shall then be dead leaving issue.' Such a distinction would savour of technical sublety barely intelligible to ordinary minds."

Lord Chelmsford said : " The word ' issue ' must here be read ' children,' and this gift to the children is not a substitutional, but an original gift. It is not to nephews and nieces absolutely, and in the event of their dying in the lifetime of the tenant for life, then to their children ; but to such of the nephews and nieces as shall be living at

---

[1] *Ante,* p. 92.　　　　[2] L. R. 1 H. L. 175.

the death of the tenant of life, and to the children of such of them as shall then be dead leaving children. The shares which the children are to take could never have vested in their parents, because it is only in the event of the parents not having become entitled to them that they are given to the children. This distinction between original and substitutional gifts may furnish some aid to the construction of the will. Where a gift is substitutional, it may much more easily be presumed that a contingency on which the original gift depends is intended to be applied to the gift which comes in its place, than in the case of two original and independent gifts."

Lord Westbury spoke of the gift to the issue as " an independent bequest," and pointed out that an intention to make this bequest contingent could not be assumed from the fact that the bequest to the parent was contingent.

The question decided in *Martin* v. *Holgate* had been frequently raised in England prior to 1866 and had been the subject of conflicting decisions in a series of cases in the lower courts. It is the more remarkable, therefore, that it did not come before the Scots Courts till the year 1907, although Lord M'Laren had called attention to the importance of the decision in his work on Wills and Succession.[1] His Lordship observes that " the *ratio* of the ultimate decision," *i.e.* of the House of Lords, " appears to be applicable to destinations in trust settlements in the Scotch form," [1] and in *Addie's Trs.* v. *Jackson* [2] Lord Kinnear says, " There can be no question as to the binding authority of that decision (*Martin* v. *Holgate*), and this Court must necessarily follow it." On the other hand, the decision has more recently been described as contrary to what had been the understanding of Scottish law and as arriving at " a result which cannot be regarded otherwise than as unreasonable and improbable " ; [3] and the fact that in only one of the cases [4] in which it has been necessary to canvass the decision in *Martin* v. *Holgate* has the same result been reached serves

---

[1] Wills and Succession (3rd Ed.), p. 704.

[2] 1913 S. C. 681.

[3] *Per* Lord Sands in *Robertson's Trs.* v. *Mitchell*, 1930 S. C. 970 at 977.

[4] *Campbell's Trs.* v. *Dick*, 1915 S. C. 100, stated *post*, p. 114.

to indicate the disfavour with which it is regarded by the Scots Courts.[1]

In the first of the Scots cases—*Banks' Trs.* v. *Banks' Trs.*[2]—the trustees were directed to divide the residue of the testator's estate on the death of his widow, among his children, with the declaration in the case of provisions to children under these presents, that " if any child shall die, either before or after me, leaving lawful issue, and without having acquired a vested interest in such provision, such issue shall be entitled to the share or shares, *original and accruing*, which their parent would have taken by survivance " and that the share of any child dying without leaving issue should be divided among the surviving children and the issue of predeceasers. The point of distinction from *Martin* v. *Holgate* was found in the words italicised in the above quotation. The rights of issue, it was said, were intended to be the same in regard to both original and accruing shares ; and, as there was difficulty in holding that the accruing shares could vest in the issue on the parent's predecease, the vesting of the original as well as the accruing shares must be postponed to the period of distribution. Hence no right was held to have vested in a granddaughter on her father's predecease during the lifetime of the testator's widow.

In the subsequent cases of *Addie's Trs.* v. *Jackson*,[3] *Todd's Trs.* v. *Todd's Exr.*,[4] and *Robertson's Trs.* v. *Mitchell* [5] a more general ground of distinction was advanced.

In the first of these cases the testator directed his trustees to hold a share of the residue of his estate for his son in liferent and his issue in fee ; and, if (as happened) the son died without issue, then the capital was to fall to the testator's other children and the survivors of them, " the issue of any of them predeceasing being entitled equally among them, if more than one, to their deceased parent's share." Here issue of a predeceasing child who also predeceased the liferenter were held not to be entitled

---

[1] The cases are reviewed in *Robertson's Trs.* v. *Mitchell, supra.*

[2] 1907 S. C. 125. *Martin* v. *Holgate* was referred to on another point in *Macfarlane's Trs.* v. *Macfarlane* (1906), 8 F. 787.

[3] 1913 S. C. 681. Decided by the Extra Division.

[4] 1922 S. C. 1. Decided by the Second Division.

[5] 1930 S. C. 970. Decided by the First Division.

to share in the residue. With reference to the decision in *Martin* v. *Holgate*, Lord Kinnear referred to the passage from the Lord Chancellor's speech quoted on page 110, as stating the ground on which the House of Lords had proceeded, and pointed out that there was no reference in the deed with which the Court was dealing to the parent's *leaving* issue : " there is here," he added, " but one reference to one period at which the gift is to take effect in favour of any of the legatees. There is no reference at all to the death of parents as determining the period at which the right of their children is to come into operation." Both Lord Kinnear and Lord Mackenzie [1] further pointed out that the bequest to the issue was substitutional and that in *Martin* v. *Holgate* the House of Lords was careful to show that the bequest there was original.[2] In *Todd's Trs.* v. *Todd's Exrs.* and *Robertson's Trs.* v. *Mitchell* it was again ruled that the principle of *Martin* v. *Holgate* does not apply where the gift to the issue is substitutional.[3]

This being so, it is somewhat unfortunate that the criteria for differentiating an original from a substitutional gift are not more distinct. The form of bequest which is substitutional is illustrated in *Addie's Trs.* v. *Jackson* [4] and the two more recent cases in which it was followed. In

[1] Lord Johnston founded on the fact that, as the issue of the liferenter were called in the first instance, there could only be vesting subject to defeasance, and that the terms of the bequest excluded such vesting. As to this see *Lees's Trs.* v. *Lees*, 1927 S. C. 886, and other cases cited in Chapter VI.

[2] The distinction between original and substitutional gifts has been put thus : " A gift to issue is substitutional when the share which the issue are to take is by a prior clause expressed to be given to the parent of such issue ; and a gift to issue is an original gift when the share which the issue are to take is not by a prior clause expressed to be given to the parent " (*per* Kindersley, V.-C., in *Lanphier* v. *Buck* (1865), 2 Dr. & Sm. 484, at 494). In *Martin* v. *Holgate* the bequest was original : but, if the bequest had been to the widow for life and after her death to the testator's nephews and nieces, but if any one of these died before her then to the issue of the predeceaser, the issue taking the parent's share, that would have been a substitutional bequest (see *Lanphier* v. *Buck*, *supra*).

[3] See also Lord Dundas's opinions in *Dixon's Trs.* v. *Duneher*, 1918 S. C. 90, and *Wylie's Trs.* v. *Bruce*, 1919 S. C. 211 at 227. In English law the principle of *Martin* v. *Holgate* is now applied whether the bequest is original or substitutional. See Jarman on Wills (7th Ed.), p. 1304, and Theobald on Wills (8th Ed.), p. 762.

[4] The terms of the bequest in *Addie's Trs.* v. *Jackson* have been given in the text. In *Todd's Trs.* v. *Todd's Exrs.* the bequest was on the death of a liferenter to four sons *nominatim* and the survivors,

contrast with these the type of an original bequest is to be found in *Banks' Trs.* v. *Banks' Trs.*[1] (because, apart from the reference to accruing shares, the case would have been held to be ruled by *Martin* v. *Holgate*) and *Campbell's Trs.* v. *Dick.*[2] In the latter case the trustees were directed on the marriage or death of three of the testatrix's daughters to divide her estate among " the whole of [her] sons and daughters that may then be in life, share and share alike, and failing any of them by death to any child or children they may respectively have left, also in equal portions." This bequest was held to be indistinguishable from that in *Martin* v. *Holgate*. In the case, therefore, of children predeceasing the liferentrixes, it was held that their issue acquired vested interest on their survivance of their parents and was not conditioned on their being still in life at the death of the last liferenter. In this decision—the only one in Scotland in which this result has been reached—the bequest to the issue was regarded as an independent bequest, a construction which was questioned by the Lord President in *Robertson's Trs.* v. *Mitchell*.

Application of personal conditions.

It would seem to be clear that personal conditions—such as conditions as to the legatee's age—attached to the gift to the institute ought not to be extended merely by implication to the issue called as conditional institutes in the event of their parent's predeceasing.[3] Thus, in *Cattanach's Trs.* v. *Cattanach*,[4] where the shares of residue were given to sons " to vest in them on their respectively attaining thirty years of age complete, and not sooner, the issue of any of them dying before that age being entitled . . . to their parent's share," it was held that on

" declaring always that the children of a predeceasing parent shall in every such case take equally amongst them the share which would have fallen to his father had he been in life at the time." In *Robertson's Trs.* v. *Mitchell* the bequest was on the death of the testator's widow to his children, equally, then alive, " declaring that the issue of any of my said children who may have predeceased leaving issue shall be entitled to take equally among them the portion of said preference shares and said sums . . . which would have been payable to their deceased parent if he or she had survived."

[1] The terms of the bequest in this case are given on p. 112, *supra*.

[2] 1915 S. C. 100.

[3] *White's Trs.* v. *White* (1896), 23 R. 836.

[4] (1901), 4 F. 205.

the death of a son under that age his share thereupon vested in his child (who was in pupillarity). Vesting was not suspended till the date at which her father would have attained, or she would attain, thirty.

III. Whether Accrescing Shares are subject to the Conditions adjected to the Original Share.—The general rule upon this point appears to be that the conditions or limitations annexed to the gift made in the first instance to the legatee do not attach to portions to which the legatee becomes entitled by accretion, unless the deed expressly indicate that this was intended. Thus in *Mylne* v. *Campbell* [1] the residue of the estate was given to the truster's children. The trustees were directed to hold the daughters' shares for them in liferent and for their children in fee ; " but if no children, then in that case her share shall revert and be divided, share and share alike, among my other children." A daughter died unmarried, and survived by a brother and two sisters. The brother received his share ; but the question was raised whether the sisters took merely a liferent or whether they took a fee. The Lord Ordinary, observing that the restrictions as to the daughters' shares were not to be imported by implication into the accrescing portions, decided that the daughters took these portions in fee.[2] There appears to be no other case on the point in the reports, but the principle of this decision is supported by a large body of authority in English law.[3] In *Downie's Trs.* v. *Cullen*,[4] Lord President Inglis remarked that the words

Conditions annexed to the original gift not presumed to qualify accrescing shares.

---

[1] (1882), 19 S. L. R. 679. Outer House, Lord M'Laren.

[2] In *Paris's Trs.* (1870), 8 S. L. R. 184, a contrary decision was pronounced ; but the decision proceeded on the very special terms of the deed under consideration. It may be noted that in English law it is held that a clause of accruer does not carry shares which have previously accrued. Thus, if A. has under the terms of a bequest an original share and a second share accrues to him under a clause of accruer on the death of another beneficiary, then on A.'s death this clause would carry his original share

but not the second share which accrued to him. " This doctrine, though it has been much disapproved of, is now well established "—Jarman on Wills (7th Ed.), p. 2050 : see Lord Gifford's opinion in *M'Nish* v. *Donald's Trs.* (1879), 7 R. 96, at 100.

[3] *Gibbons* v. *Langdon*, 6 Sim. 260 ; *Ranelagh* v. *Ranelagh*, 4 Beav. 419 ; *Ware* v. *Watson*, 7 D. M. & G. 248.

[4] (1882), 9 R. 749. Of this case it is sufficient to say, in this connexion, that sums of money were given to the testator's daughters in liferent and their issue in fee. If a daughter remained unmarried, power was given

" accresce and belong " in themselves suggested that the accrescing shares were to be taken in fee ; and this presumption appears to be especially strong where the gift-over is to a class, of which some of the members take their original shares absolutely while others take them under restriction, and is made without discrimination between these members ; because it is difficult to hold that the same words are to bear two meanings, so as to carry in regard to certain members of the class an unrestricted, and, in regard to others, a restricted, interest.[1]

All difficulty on this point may be prevented by an express provision that accrescing shares shall be subject to the same terms and shall be dealt with in the same manner as the original shares.[2]

IV. Clause calling Survivors. Whether " Survivors " or " Survivor " may be construed as " Others " or " Other."— The circumstances in which the question of the meaning of the word " surviving " is usually raised may be indicated by a reference to the facts of a leading case, *Ward* v. *Lang*,[3] in which the law on the point was very fully discussed in the opinion of the Court. The testator gave the residue of his estate to his seven children respectively in liferent and to their issue in fee ; " declaring that, in the event of any of my children dying without leaving lawful issue, his or her share of the liferent . . . shall thereafter be divisible and payable equally among my *surviving* children and their issue in liferent and fee respectively." Three daughters, A., B., and C., died leaving issue ; then D. died without issue ; then E. died leaving issue ; and lastly F.

to her to dispose of a portion of her share by will, and the remaining part was to accresce to her brother and her surviving sisters, under the same conditions as affected the original gift. All the daughters remained spinsters ; and all having died, it was held that the original portion of the longest liver of the daughters, and the shares that had accresced to her, were carried by her will. The decision proceeded largely on the special terms of the deed ; but the principle underlying the decision appears to be that the restriction on

the power of testing was merely for the purpose of securing the interest of the survivors under the provision for accretion ; and as there could be no devolution on survivors when only one daughter remained in existence, the restriction disappeared with the disappearance of the purpose for which it was designed.

[1] Cf. *Downie's Trs.* v. *Cullen, supra.*

[2] As, for example, in *Forrest's Trs.* v. *Rae* (1884), 12 R. 389.

[3] (1893), 20 R. 949.

died without issue, survived by G. and her issue. A case was brought to decide as to the disposal of the shares liferented by the children who died without issue, D. and F. The children of A., B., C., and E. claimed to be entitled to participate in both shares, on the ground, *inter alia*, that " surviving " was to be construed as " other." But the Court negatived these claims, holding that the share of D. fell at his death to the children then alive (E., F., and G.) in liferent and to their issue in fee, and that F.'s share (including the portion of D.'s that had fallen to her) went wholly to G. and her issue.

It was pointed out in the opinion of the Court that, if the words of the declaration were to be construed literally, there could be no question as to their meaning. " The words of survivorship must be referred to the event upon which the devolution to survivors is to take place, and the accrescing shares must be given in liferent to those of the testator's children who may survive the predeceasing liferenter, and in fee to the issue of such surviving children." In some cases a wider interpretation than the literal one had been given to the word " surviving " ; but the mere facts that the literal meaning might be regarded as capricious, inasmuch as it made the rights of the grandchildren in the fee depend on the accident of their parents' survivance of another liferenter, or that it might in certain circumstances lead to intestacy would not justify a departure from that meaning. There were English cases in which the wider interpretation had been adopted, but in order " to bring into operation the rule of construction which was followed in those cases, it is necessary in the first place to find from the indications of the will, apart from the clause immediately under construction, some reason for holding that the literal language of that clause is inadequate to express the full meaning of the testator, and then to find in the will some clear indication of an intention to do something different from what a literal interpretation of the clause would infer." [1]

[1] This sentence was quoted by Lord Shaw in *Curle's Trs.* v. *Millar*, 1922 S. C. (H. L.) 15 at 20. See also *Gilmour* v. *MacPhillamy* [1930], A. C. 712, where it is said : " In order to justify a departure from the natural and ordinary meaning of any word or phrase there must be found in the instrument containing it a context which necessitates or justifies such departure. It is not enough that the natural and ordinary meaning may

" Survivors "
to be read in
primary sense.
This decision is in accordance with the earlier cases of *Forrest's Trs.* v. *Rae*[1] and *Hairsten's J. F.* v. *Duncan*,[2] and was itself followed in *Monteith* v. *Belfrage*[3] and *Swan's Trs.* v. *Swan*.[4] As appears from these cases, the weight of authority is in favour of a strict and literal interpretation of the words " survivors " and " surviving " ; but this interpretation may be displaced by their context. There are three reported cases in Scotland in which a wider meaning was given to these words ; and from the decisions in these cases guidance may be obtained as to the nature of the context which has been held sufficient to influence the interpretation of the terms.

Construed
liberally in
order to avoid
intestacy.
The first of these cases is *Ramsay's Trs.* v. *Ramsay*,[5] where the word " survivors " was construed " others " in order to prevent intestacy. In that case the trustees were directed to make over the estate, on the death of the testator's widow, to his brothers and sisters in liferent " and the issue of their bodies respectively, whom failing to the issue of the survivor or survivors in fee." Four of the brothers and sisters predeceased the widow, three leaving issue. The fifth survived the widow, but died unmarried. Here, if the words of gift were read in their literal sense, the share liferented by the fifth fell into intestacy, as there remained no surviving brothers or sisters. But the Court read " survivors " in the sense of " others," and gave the fee to the issue of the predeceasers. The judgement was rested on the testator's presumed intention not to die intestate in regard to any portion of his estate.[6] But it

---

produce results which to some minds appear capricious or fail to accord with a logical scheme of disposition."

[1] (1884), 12 R. 389.

[2] (1891), 18 R. 1158. This is a marked example of the strict interpretation ; because in a clause subsequent to that providing for the devolution of the shares to the issue of survivors, it was declared that, if a liferenter so desired, the trustees should invest his or her share in heritable security, taking the title for her in liferent and her issue in fee, " whom failing, to my said *other* daughters," etc.

[3] (1894), 21 R. 615.

[4] 1912 S. C. 273.

[5] (1876), 4 R. 243. This case is referred to in *Smith's Trs.* v. *Smith's Trs.* (1905), 7 F. 815, where in a destination in favour of the heirs of the bodies of the survivors of a family the word " survivors " was read as " others," as it was a contradiction in terms to speak of the heirs of the body of the survivors at the time of the opening of the succession.

[6] The case was distinguished on this ground in *Forrest's Trs.* v. *Rae*, *ante*.

may be doubted whether, in view of more recent authorities, the avoidance of intestacy would now be held sufficient, without aid from the context, to warrant a modification of the literal meaning of the term.[1]

In *Paterson's Trs.* v. *Brand* [2] the wider interpretation of the word was held to be justified owing to the presence in the deed of a destination-over. Where the gift-over to the survivors is followed by a destination-over in the event of *all* the liferenters dying without issue, the reference in the destination-over to this one contingency alone indicates that the testator considered that the bequest would be operative in all other contingencies ; and, therefore, if there should happen to be issue in existence, whether their parent was or was not a survivor, the destination-over would be excluded and the issue would take under the bequest. This being so, the terms of the destination-over afford a clear inference that it was not the testator's intention to confine his favour to such of the issue only as are descended from a surviving parent. " In the condition attached to the gift-over, there may, according to the particular terms of the conditions and of the settlement generally, be found positive evidence of the testator's true intention strong enough to shew that the word ' survivors ' in the survivorship clause is wrongly used, and that ' others ' is meant." [3]

In the case last cited the testator gave a sum of money to his two nephews equally between them ; and if " both or either . . . should hereafter predecease me leaving issue, such issue shall take the share that would have fallen to their parent if in life, and in default of such issue the same shall fall . . . to the survivor . . . and the issue of the survivor, *whom all failing* the same shall fall into and form part of the residue of my estate." Both brothers predeceased the testator ; the nephew who died first left issue ; the other died childless. It was held [4] that the issue took the whole

Effect of Gift-over.

---

[1] See Lord Kinnear's opinion in *Ward* v. *Lang*, *ante* ; Ld. Pres. Clyde's opinion in *Curle's Trs.* v. *Millar*, 1920 S. C. 607 ; *King* v. *Frost* (1890) 15 App. Cas. 548 ; *Inderwick* v. *Tatchell* [1903], A. C. 120 ; *Harrison* v. *Harrison* [1901], 2 Ch. 136, at 143. But the case was referred to in *Beveridge's Trs.* v.

Beveridge, 1930 S. C. 578, as an authority for a construction which avoided intestacy.

[2] (1893), 21 R. 253.

[3] *Curle's Trs.* v. *Millar*, 1920 S. C. 607, *per* Ld. Pres. Clyde, at 617.

[4] Dissenting Lord Rutherfurd Clark. The effect of such a destination-over

gift, because the destination-over assumed the failure of issue of both of the brothers.

And for the same reason, where a testator gave his estate to trustees in trust for his two sons in liferent, and if either died leaving issue, for the issue in fee, with a declaration that " in the event of the first deceaser of my said two sons dying without lawful issue, his share shall be held . . . for the use and behoof of the survivor of my said two sons, or his issue as aforesaid," the Court adopted a liberal interpretation of the word " survivor." What happened was that the first deceaser left issue, but the survivor died childless. It was held that the issue took the whole estate. The feature of the deed which supported this construction was a gift-over to charities " in the event of both (of the sons) dying without lawful issue, or failing such issue." " A bequest to B. on the death of A.," said Lord Justice-Clerk Moncreiff, " implies a liferent to A., and this bequest to these charities, failing the issue of the two sons, implies a bequest to that issue." [1]

The case of *Aberdein*, it has been said,[2] is one rather of implied gift than of construction of the word " survivor " ; and in it, as in *Paterson's Trs.* v. *Brand*, the question was not between the issue of the different legatees, but between the issue and the parties who were called under the destination-over, but the influence of the destination-over in the two cases would appear to be essentially the same.[3]

Stirpital construction.

In *Ramsay's Trs.* v. *Ramsay* and *Paterson's Trs.* v. *Brand* the construction adopted was to treat the words " surviving " and " survivor " as equivalent to " other." But an alternative construction was suggested in *Waite* v. *Littlewood*.[4] In

was referred to by Lord Shand in *Forrest's Trs.* v. *Rae*, *supra*. In England this exception is recognised : *Badger* v. *Gregory*, L. R. 8 Eq. 78 ; *Wake* v. *Varah* (1876), 2 Ch. D. 348 ; *Waite* v. *Littlewood* (1872), L. R. 8 Ch. 70 ; *Lucena* v. *Lucena* (1876), 7 Ch. D. 255, were cited by the Lord Ordinary (Stormonth-Darling) in *Paterson's Trs.* v. *Brand*.

[1] *Aberdein's Trs.* v. *Aberdein* (1870), 8 M. 750.

[2] *Per* Ld. Pres. Clyde in *Curle's Trs.* v. *Millar*, 1920 S. C. 607 at 616.

[3] See the opinions in *Wake* v. *Varah* (1876), 2 Ch. D. 348 ; Lord Wrenbury's opinion in *Curle's Trs.* v. *Millar*, 1922 S. C. (H. L.) 15 at 23 ; and Ld. Pres. Clyde's opinion in *Leiper's Trs.* v. *Forret*, 1930 S. C. 892 at 897.

[4] (1872), L. R. 8 Ch. 70. See also *Lucena* v. *Lucena* (1876), 7 Ch. D. 255 ; *In re Bilham* [1901], 2 Ch. 169 ; *Powell* v. *Hellicar* [1919], 1 Ch. 138. For an adverse criticism see *O'Brien* v. *O'Brien* [1896], 2 Ir. Rep. 459. It is possible to find in Lord Medwyn's opinion in *Thornhill* v. *Macpherson* (1841), 3 D. 394, at 407, and Lord MacKenzie's opinion in *Clelland* v.

that case Lord Selborne said that he did not assent to the view that the question was whether the term " survivor " was to be read as " other." His Lordship thought that a strong *onus probandi* was cast on anyone who would do such violence to the language ; and he suggested that the meaning might to some extent be conserved by construing it as meaning those who survived either in person or figuratively in their *stirpes*. The result of this construction is that the share of the predeceaser goes, not to all the legatees called along with him (as is the case if the word be held to mean " other "), but to those legatees (if any) who survive him and to the issue then alive of predeceasing legatees, to the exclusion of parties claiming in right of deceased legatees who are not represented by issue at that date.

This construction was adopted and applied by the House of Lords in *Curle's Trs.* v. *Millar*.[1] In that case the testator was survived by three children : Mrs Lamont, who died in 1909 leaving issue ; Robert, who died in 1916 unmarried ; and Mrs Millar, who survived him and had issue. The question which arose on Robert's death was whether the share of the testator's estate liferented by him passed to Mrs Millar and her issue to the exclusion of Mrs Lamont's issue, or whether the latter were entitled to one half of that share. In the judgement of the House of Lords the claim of Mrs Lamont's issue was sustained on the ground that from the terms of the will the words of survivorship must have been intended to include stirpital survivorship. The testator directed his trustees to hold his estate for his three children equally in liferent and for their issue respectively in fee, " and in the event of my son or daughters or any of them dying without leaving lawful issue or of such issue all dying before majority or marriage, I direct my trustees to hold and retain the fee or capital of the said shares for behoof of the survivors of my said son and daughters equally among them share and share alike if more than one, and in the event of only one surviving for his or her behoof *in the same way as is hereinbefore provided with regard to the shares originally*

Gray (1839), 1 D. 1031, sentences which suggest that the possibility of some such construction as that favoured in *Waite* v. *Littlewood* was present to their minds.

[1] 1922 S. C. (H. L.) 15.

taken by the said survivors or survivor in their own right."
Great importance was attached to the words italicised. No
shares, it was pointed out, were taken in fee by the children
of the testator " in their own right " ; " if, therefore, the
words ' survivors ' or ' survivor ' occurring in this clause
be read in their ordinary meaning, it necessarily follows that
the only interest in a share accruing to one or more of them
on the death of a brother or sister is a life interest, leaving
the capital of that share undisposed of, which is probably the
very last thing the settler aimed at or desired. But if the
word ' survivor ' be read, as it may be read, as meaning an
individual surviving in person or figuratively in *stirps*, the
paramount intention of the settler would be effectuated." [1]
" There was no share originally taken in fee by a child in
his or her own right. The share was given in settlement
and the child was but a liferenter. The survivor, therefore,
who is here spoken of as taking in his own right, is not the
child to the exclusion of his or her issue, but the *stirps* of
which the child as a liferenter and the issue as absolute
owners in reversion were the beneficiaries, taking, ' as is
hereinbefore provided.' From this it is plain that the word
' survivors ' and the words ' his or her ' cannot mean
children to the exclusion of issue, but must mean the *stirps*
in which the child is parent of the issue. The words are
' for behoof of the survivors ' or ' for his or her behoof '
in the same way ' as is hereinbefore provided.' That which
had been ' hereinbefore provided ' was not a gift to the
child to the exclusion of the issue, but a gift to the child as
liferenter and then to the issue as absolute owners. Both,
however, are included under the expression ' for behoof of
the survivors ' or ' for his or her behoof,' for, if they are
not so included, there are no words expressive of the behoof
of the issue." [2] Lord Wrenbury also directed attention to
a destination-over " failing any survivor of my said son and
daughters or issue of any of them " as further supporting
the stirpital construction.

The decision in this case was distinguished in *Leiper's
Trs.* v. *Forret*,[3] where the estate was settled on the testator's
nephews and nieces in liferent and their issue in fee " and

[1] *Per* Lord Atkinson at p. 18.   [3] 1930 S. C. 892. See also *Gilmour*
[2] *Per* Lord Wrenbury at p. 22.   v. *MacPhillamy* [1930], A. C. 712.

failing any one or more of them without issue, who shall survive and obtain a vested interest as aftermentioned for behoof of the survivors equally or the survivor in liferent and their respective issue in fee." The terms of the destination-over were not the same as those in *Curle's Trs.* v. *Millar,* and there was no ultimate gift-over : in these circumstances the Court were unable to find anything in the context which would justify a departure from the natural meaning of the terms.

CHAPTER VI.

VESTING SUBJECT TO DEFEASANCE.

Nature of doctrine.

THERE was occasion in the introductory chapter to notice the doctrine of vesting subject to defeasance, and it was there shown that it depended upon the distinction between suspensive and resolutive conditions, and further, that personal conditions belonged to the first category and postponed vesting, while collateral conditions were not inconsistent with vesting, and had the effect merely of rendering the legatee's right defeasible in the event of the condition coming into effect.[1] Resting as the doctrine does on this general classification of conditions, it would seem to be susceptible of wide application. But it has not been received with universal approbation in the Scottish Courts. By some it has been criticised as a contradiction in terms,[2] and termed an " excrescence upon the Scottish law of vesting " : [3] by others it has been commended as " a useful working principle," [4] a principle " not in any way exceptional

---

[1] See p. 3, ante.

[2] " I confess frankly that I think it might have been a better world if it could have been contrived that there should have been no decisions whatever on vesting since the date of *Carleton* v. *Thomson* and *Young* v. *Robertson*. But unfortunately that is not the state of matters, and I cannot go back on the long series of decisions that have been given on this subject, affirmed as they have been by the House of Lords ; and accordingly I have got to apply the doctrine of vesting subject to defeasance—a doctrine which I think was said by Lord Rutherfurd Clark, and I agree with him, to be a contradiction in terms."—Ld. Pres. Dunedin in *Searcy's Trs.* v. *Allbuary*, 1907 S. C. 823.

[3] *Ibid.*, per Lord M'Laren.

[4] *Allan's Trs.* v. *Allan*, 1918 S. C. 164, per Lord Mackenzie ; and see also *Young's Exr.* v. *Gray's Hospital*, 1917 S. C. 707, per Lord Skerrington.

in the law of Scotland " and " of a deep-rooted and wide-spreading character." [1] In consequence no doubt of this divergence of opinion there may be traced in some of the decisions a certain reluctance to accept developments of the doctrine to the extent which logic might seem to demand.

It seems to be correct to say that the law as to the vesting of legacies was worked out in Scotland for the greater part of its history without any recognition of the distinction between suspensive and resolutive conditions in the matter of testamentary bequests, and there are certainly cases in the older reports in which vesting was held to be suspended where the theory of defeasible vesting would now be applied. [2] But it is not difficult to discover early instances of, or analogies to, that theory in cognate departments of the law. In a case [3] which occurred so long ago as 1765, there is an elaborate discussion of principles very similar to those on which the doctrine of vesting subject to defeasance is based. The deed under consideration in that case was a destination of heritable property. The estate was settled upon A., and the heirs male of his body ; whom failing, on the heir male of the body of B. ; whom failing, on C. and the heirs male of his body. A. made up his title, possessed the estate, and died without issue. At his death B. was alive, but had then no children, and C. served heir and was infeft. After he had possessed for some years, a son was born to B. It was held that C. was bound to denude in favour of this heir on his birth. As B. had sold part of the estate, it was necessary to consider somewhat minutely the nature of his right prior to the emergence of the nearer heir, and after an examination of the various theories on which the rights of the heir expectant and the possible nearer heir might be reconciled, the Court adopted the view that the service and infeftment of the former was " a conveyance of the estate *sub conditione*, to be purified in case a nearer heir exist not, and to be void *a principio* if a nearer heir exist." In consequence, the heir expectant, although

Early instances of vesting subject to defeasance.

In destinations of heritage.

[1] *Yule's Trs.* v. *Deans*, 1919 S. C. 570, *per* Lord Skerrington.

[2] See the cases cited in note 3, p. 3 ; and *Donald's Trs.* v. *Donald* (1864), 2 M. 922.

[3] *M'Kinnon* v. *M'Donald*, M. 5279, 5290, 6566, 14,938 ; 5 Br. Supp. 848 and 904. Aff. 2 Pat. 252. See Stair, iii. 5. 50.

he was entitled to uplift the rents and do ordinary acts of administration, could not prejudice the possible preferable right. The sale was sustained, however, in this case largely on the ground that it had been necessary to relieve the subject of debt and to preserve it, and the opinions suggest that but for this specialty the judgement would have been otherwise. The decision in this case was no doubt compelled by the rule of law which required that the fee should not be left in abeyance, but the circumstances are almost identical in other respects with those in which the modern doctrine of defeasible vesting has been applied. Similarly, in the case of an entail, the nearest heir at the death of the heir in possession will take, although there is the possibility that another may be born who is called before him in the destination ; but if this nearer heir come into existence, the right will be resolved.[1] This doctrine was adopted in order to give effect to the will of the settler of the property, and it is held that where the devolution of the property depends not upon the will of any person, but upon the regulation of the law, there is no room for its application. Hence in the case of intestacy the nearest heir at the opening of the succession takes absolutely, and his right is not affected by the birth of one who, had he been alive at that time, would have excluded him.[2]

In entails.

In modern times heritable destinations are less common than formerly, their place being largely taken by trust deeds, and, as regards these, various cases may be instanced of vesting subject to defeasance prior to the case of *Taylor* v. *Gilbert's Trs.*[3] and the subsequent decisions in which the doctrine has been articulately developed. The case of a residuary bequest appears to be in point.[4] Suppose a testator to make a gift which is to vest on the fulfilment of a condition or on the happening of a contingent event, and to give the residue of the estate in outright terms ; then, in the event of the condition not being satisfied or the event not happening, the portion so given away as a special legacy

In residuary bequests.

---

[1] *Stewart* v. *Nicholson* (1859), 22 D. 72. Cf. Ld. Pres. Inglis's opinion in *Haldane's Trs.* v. *Murphy* (1881), 9 R. 269.

[2] *Grant* v. *Grant's Trs.* (1859), 22 D. 53. *Bell's Prin.* § 1642.

[3] (1881), 5 R. (H. L.) 217 ; 3 App. Cas. 1287.

[4] Chapter XVI., *post*, p. 346. And see as to intestacy, *post*, p. 349.

will be held to have vested in the residuary legatee, as part of the residue, although he may have died before the time at which it could be ascertained whether the gift would or would not take effect in favour of the legatee to whom in the first instance it was destined. The theory here appears to be no other than that the residuary legatee takes a vested right subject to defeasance if the condition be satisfied or the contingency occur. And so, also, where a fund is given *In gifts subject to a power of appointment.* to a class subject to a power of apportionment, the fund vests equally in the members of the class, although each member is liable to be excluded, or to have his share reduced, by the exercise of the power.[1] Again, in the ordinary case of a bequest to a class of children which is liable to be *In gifts to a class liable to enlargement.* enlarged, the children alive at the time of vesting take an interest in the whole subject of the bequest under the condition that their shares will be diminished to the extent required to admit to equal rights other children who may be born prior to the period appointed for the distribution of the subject.[2] A further instance of defeasance is to be found in cases where a fund is given to all the members of a family other than the one who may succeed to a heritable property, under which form of gift all the members have vested rights until the date at which it is ascertained which of the members is thereby excluded, the clause of forfeiture *In gifts to a class with a clause of forfeiture.* or exclusion operating merely to carry away the share of the member so succeeding as at that date.[3]

These instances serve to demonstrate that defeasible vesting was not wholly unknown in our earlier law. The modern development of the principle which has brought within its application cases to which it was never previously applied in our Courts may be said to begin with the decision of the House of Lords in *Taylor* v. *Gilbert's Trs.*,[4] a decision which was probably influenced by the principles of English Law. Since that case the principle has been applied in a large number of instances and in circumstances not always precisely the same. With the exception of one or two rather special cases to be noticed at the conclusion of this chapter [5]

---

[1] *Post*, Chapter IX., p. 232. And cf. also *Chamber's Trs.* v. *Smiths* (1878), 5 R. (H. L.) 151, stated *post*, p. 337.

[2] *Post*, Chapter VIII., p. 192.

[3] *Post*, Chapter VIII., p. 215.

[4] (1881), 5 R. (H. L.) 217 ; 3 App. Cas. 1287, stated *post*, p. 130.

[5] See *post*, p. 155.

the decisions fall into three classes represented respectively by *Taylor* v. *Gilbert's Trs., Lindsay's Trs.* v. *Lindsay*,[1] and *Snell's Trs.* v. *Morrison*.[2] These cases may conveniently be introduced by the following general exposition of the grounds of decision taken from Lord Kinnear's opinion in *Johnston's Trs.* v. *Dewar* [3] : " The only doctrine, so far as I understand it, that has received effect in a description of vesting subject to defeasance is this, that when a gift is made in such terms that it would take effect absolutely at the death of the testator but for the single contingency of the possible birth of issue to a particular person, that is a possibility which interferes so little for practical purposes with the primary legatee treating the legacy as his own, subject to his being divested by the single event, that it must be presumed that the testator intended that he should so treat it. In the leading case [4] it is pointed out that it is for the benefit of the object of the testator's bounty that he should be able to deal with his expectant interests as if they were vested in him subject to being divested upon the happening of the subsequent event, rather than that he should be prevented from dealing with them at all on the ground that they are kept in suspense. It must be presumed that the testator intended to give that benefit in a case in which the contingency which should exclude the primary legatee is so simple as that of the birth of children to one particular person. . . . The condition upon which that doctrine has been applied has always been that there is no other contingency but that very simple one, and that it is the possibility of issue without any further destination on their failure that raises the presumption." [5]

One general limitation of the principle may be noticed.

[1] (1880), 8 R. 281, stated *post*, p. 141.

[2] (1877), 4 R. 709, stated *post*, p. 149.

[3] 1911 S. C. 722. This passage is quoted in *Bannatyne's Trs.* v. *Watson's Trs.*, 1914 S. C. 693.

[4] *I.e. Taylor* v. *Gilbert's Trs.*

[5] For similar statements see the opinions of Lord M'Laren and Lord Kyllachy in *Thompson's Trs.* v. *Jamieson* (1900), 2 F. 470 ; of Lord M'Laren in *Gardner* v. *Hamblin* (1900), 2 F. 679 ; and of Lord Sands in *Lees's Trs.* v. *Lees*, 1927 S. C. 886. In *Coulson's Trs.* v. *Coulson's Trs.*, 1911 S. C. 881, Lord Dundas treated Lord Kinnear's statement as " intended rather to describe the circumstances of previous cases which had actually occurred than to limit absolutely the application of the doctrine or rule of vesting subject to defeasance for all time to cases where the contemplated contingency is the possibility of the birth of issue to a particular person " ; and the decision in *Yule's Trs.* v. *Deans*, 1919

With the exception of the cases noted in the preceding pages vesting subject to defeasance has not been applied to heritable destinations. In *Studd* v. *Cook*[1] Lord Watson observed : " The vesting and divestiture of a proper feudal fee as distinguished from a heritable *jus crediti*, is, I humbly conceive, alien to the principles of the law of Scotland," and this statement was accepted as authoritative and followed in *Young's Exr.* v. *Gray's Hospital*[2] and *Cripps' Trs.* v. *Cripps*.[3]

There is always, indeed, much difficulty in applying the doctrine of defeasible vesting in cases where trustees are not appointed to hold the subjects during the pendency of a condition affecting the right of the primary institute or legatee. In the two following cases[4] the Court was compelled to apply the doctrine in order to give effect to the terms of badly drawn deeds. In *Martin's Trs.* v. *Milliken*[5] the testator assigned and disponed his whole estate to his sister in liferent and to A., as to one half, and to the children of the liferentrix, as to the other half, in fee, and, failing such children, to A. in fee. It was then provided that, failing A. and the said children by death before the liferentrix, the heirs of the testator should take. The liferentrix died without issue predeceased by A. It was held that the fee vested in A. at the testator's death subject to partial defeasance if the liferentrix had children, a result very similar to that which obtains in the case of class-gifts. The ultimate destination to the testator's heirs was treated, and is referred to in the interlocutor of the Court, as a substitution which was evacuated by a settlement left by A.[6]

In *M'Lay* v. *Borland*[7]—a case which has been described as a very peculiar one from which no general principle can be deduced[8]—the testator conveyed all his property to his

---

S. C. 570, *post*, p. 156, cannot be brought within the scope of this statement.

[1] (1883), 10 R. (H. L.) 53, at 63.

[2] 1917, S. C. 707.

[3] 1926, S. C. 188 ; see also *Turner* v. *Gaw* (1894), 21 R. 563.

[4] These cases were founded on by the parties who were successful in

Taylor v. *Gilbert's Trs.*, see Lord Ormidale's opinion, at 5 R. 53.

[5] (1864), 3 M. 326.

[6] See p. 52, *ante*, as to the effect on vesting of a substitution.

[7] (1876), 3 R. 1124. Lord Deas dissented.

[8] *Per* Lord Low in *Turner* v. *Gaw*, *supra*.

son, if in life, whom failing to his three daughters and the survivor in liferent ; and after the death of the survivor to a grandson and the heirs of his body, " whom failing by predecease without lawful issue," to a nephew and his heirs in fee. Nothing was known of the testator's son and the case was disposed of on the footing that he had predeceased the testator. The grandson died before the termination of the liferents without issue. In these circumstances, as it was necessary that the fee should vest in someone, it was held that it had vested in the nephew subject to defeasance depending on two resolutive conditions, one depending on the life of the testator's son and the other on the grandson or his issue surviving the liferenters. This decision was followed by Lord Ormidale in the Outer House case of *Christie's Trs.* v. *Lawson's Exr.*[1]

I. Gifts to A. in Liferent and his or her Issue in Fee, whom failing to B.—In *Taylor* v. *Gilbert's Trs.*[2] the truster instructed his trustees to hold and apply the residue in the following proportions : one-third for behoof of each of two nieces, A. and B., in liferent and of their issue in fee ; and the remaining third for four nieces, C., D., E., and F., in liferent and for their issue equally *per stirpes* in fee. He provided that if either of A. or B. should die without issue, the share of the one so predeceasing should go to the survivor in liferent and to her issue in fee. Then he declared that if both died " unmarried, or without leaving lawful children, or in the event of such children existing but afterwards deceasing before attaining the years of majority or being married," then their shares should fall to the other four nieces and their children " respectively in liferent and fee, and equally among them *per stirpes*, as is provided with respect to their own shares of my estate." A. had no issue ; B. had a pupil son, who predeceased her. The shares thus fell to the four nieces and their children. One of these four nieces had had a son, G., who survived the testator and attained majority, but predeceased A. and B. It was held that a portion of the shares liferented by A. and B. had vested in him. The fact that the gift was dependent on their dying without leaving issue did not suspend the vesting

Gift to A. in liferent and to his issue, whom failing B. in fee.

---

[1] 1919 1 S. L. T. 106.   [2] (1878) 5 R. (H. L.), 217, 3 App. Cas. 1287.

till it could be ascertained that this condition was purified
(that is, till their deaths), but merely rendered the right
liable to divestiture during their lives ; and as the event
which entailed divestiture—the birth or survivance of issue—
had not occurred, G.'s right became absolute. On the other
hand, it was provided that the children of the four nieces
must attain majority ; and, as this was a suspensive condition, the vesting could not take place before the son
reached majority. The result was that his share vested in
him at twenty-one, and was carried by his will.

The application of the principle is (as Lord Kinnear The applica-
points out in the passage quoted above from his opinion in tion of the rule.
Johnston's Trs. v. *Dewar* [1]) limited to cases where there is
no existing object between a claimant and his right, but
merely the possibility of a prior beneficiary becoming entitled
to the bequest. In such cases there is no one to challenge
the legatee's right, but only the chance that a preferable
legatee may emerge. And the effect of the doctrine extends
no further than this, that that possibility is not to be treated
as a condition suspensive of the vesting of the gift in
the existing beneficiary. Whether, and at what time, the
legacy will vest in him, depends entirely upon the terms in
which the gift in his favour is made. If the terms are such
as would be sufficient, if the gift were made to him directly
and without mention of the issue of the liferenter, to confer
a vested interest at the testator's death or at a time anterior
to the liferenter's death, there will be vesting in him subject
to defeasance ; whereas, on the other hand, if the terms in
which the legatee is called are in themselves such as to
defer vesting till the end of the liferent, vesting subject to
defeasance is excluded.

The conditions under which vesting will take place are Statement of
set forth in the following passage taken from Lord President of the appli-
Inglis's opinion in *Steel's Trs.* v. *Steel* : [2]—" Where a fund rule.
is settled on daughters of the testator for their liferent use
allenarly and their children, if any, in fee, whom failing to
another person or other persons in absolute property, with
no further destination, the vesting of the fee in the last-
named person or persons will depend on these considerations :
whether the person so called to the succession, if only one,

---

[1] *Ante*, p. 128.   [2] (1888), 16 R. 204.

was a known and existing individual at the death of the testator, or, if more than one, whether the persons so called were all of them known and existing at that date ; or if the destination is to a class called by description, whether the individuals who constitute the class are ascertained at that date, or whether he or they cannot be known or ascertained till the death of the liferenter or the occurrence of some other event. If the person or persons are not known, or the individuals who are to constitute the class are not ascertained at that date, the fee will not vest until the occurrence of the event which will determine who are the persons called, or the individuals composing the class are ascertained. But when the person or persons called are known, or the individuals composing the class are ascertained, at the death of the testator, then the fee will vest in them *a morte testatoris*, subject to defeasance in whole or in part in the event of the liferenters or any of them leaving issue."

In the case considered by the Lord President, the liferentrix is a daughter, but the rule has been applied where the relationship was more distant,[1] and it would seem, in point of principle, immaterial whether the liferenter is a relative or a stranger. It may be the result of the rule that the liferenter is himself the party in whom the right of fee vests subject to defeasance, as, for example, where he is the testator's heir or next-of-kin, and the fee is given to him in liferent and to his issue in fee, whom failing to the testator's heir or next-of-kin ; in which case the fee will, under the ultimate destination, vest in the liferenter, subject to defeasance if issue be born.[2] This, however, is no obstacle to the admission of the rule, for there is no anomaly in

The liferenter may also be fiar.

---

[1] As in *Cumming's Trs.* v. *Anderson*, (1895), 23 R. 94, where the liferentrix was the truster's niece. Lord M'Laren expressed the opinion that the doctrine applies if the gift is to any other favoured person in liferent, or, at all events, to any other favoured person to whom the testator stood *in loco parentis* ; and further, that the Lord President's statement did not limit the application of the principle to the cases mentioned in it.

[2] Cf. the opinions of the minority in *Haldane's Trs.* v. *Murphy* (1881), 9 R. 269, approved by the House of Lords in *Gregory's Trs.* v. *Alison* (1889), 16 R. (H. L.) 10 ; 14 App. Cas. 125 ; *G.'s Trs.* v. *G.*, 1937 S. C. 141, stated *post*, p. 138 ; *Miller's J. F.* v. *Miller's Trs.* (O. H., Lord Pearson) (1903), 11 S. L. T. 308 ; *Barron's Trs.* v. *Barron's Trs.* (O. H., Lord Pearson) (1897), 5 S. L. T. 100.

distinct rights of liferent and fee vesting concurrently in the same party. It is also immaterial that more than one liferent is given.[1] In *Taylor* v. *Gilbert's Trs.*,[2] considerable stress was laid by Lord Justice-Clerk Moncrieff on the fact that the gift to the parties called in default of issue was made in the form of a direction to trustees to hold for them, but it is now settled that cases where the gift to them is implied in a direction to convey at the termination of the liferent are also within the rule.[3]

The essential conditions of the adoption of the principle, as set forth in the opinion of the Lord President, are that the parties are known and existing and that there is no further destination.

In *Corbett's Trs.* v. *Pollock*[4] the doctrine was excluded, because the parties were not ascertainable until the expiry of the liferent. In that case the trustees were instructed to hold the residue of the estate for three children (A., B., and C.) in liferent, and on the death of the longest liver of them to divide it equally, in fee, among the issue respectively of the liferenters ; but if any liferenter died without issue, his one-third was to go to the issue of the other liferenters and two other children (D. and E.), or in the event of the death of these last two children leaving issue, their issue. It was held that the share of a liferenter who died without issue did not vest until the death of the longest liver of the liferenters, because until then it could not be known whether (a) D. or E. or their issue would be entitled, and (b) whether the last liferenter would leave issue to participate in the share.

Again, it was for the same reason that vesting subject to defeasance was rejected in *Haldane's Trs.* v. *Murphy.*[5] In that case the testatrix instructed her trustees to pay the income of her estate to A. and B. (in terms which forbade

The rule applies although the gift is implied in a direction to pay.

The rule excluded where the parties are not ascertained.

Gift to testator's heirs or next-of-kin.

---

[1] As in *Taylor* v. *Gilbert's Trs.*, *Cumming's Trs.* v. *Anderson, supra*. and *G.'s Trs.* v. *G.*, *supra*. See *Jamieson* v. *Thornhill's Exr.* (1896), 4 S. L. T. 95, where Lord Low held that the rule was excluded, owing to the possibility that the liferent might, by the terms of the will, be raised into a fee.

[2] (1877), 5 R. 49.

[3] As in *Cumming's Trs.* v. *Anderson, supra* ; and *Corbet's Trs.* v. *Elliott's Trs.* (1906), 8 F. 610 ; and *Thomson's Trs.* v. *Pringle* (O. H., Lord Pearson) (1901), 9 S. L. T. 11.

[4] (1901), 3 F. 963.

[5] (1881), 9 R. 269.

accretion), and on their death to convey one-half of the
residue of her estate to the issue of each, and if they should
die without leaving issue, or if there were issue but they
should die before attaining the age of twenty-two, then to
make over the estate to the testatrix's "nearest heirs in
moveables whomsoever." The liferenters both survived the
testatrix, and died without issue. The question in the case
was whether a portion of the residue had vested in them as
among the testatrix's heirs, subject to defeasance if they had
issue who became qualified to take. A minority of the
judges, consisting of Lord President Inglis, Lord Mure, and
Lord Shand, thought that the heirs were to be ascertained
at the death of the testatrix, and that the liferenters had
also had a right of fee which in the circumstances became
absolute. But the majority of the Court ruled that the
heirs were to be selected at the period of payment, and that
therefore the liferenters were excluded from the fee, and
that there was no vesting subject to defeasance. The
divergence of these views was due not to any doubt as to the
soundness of the rule established in *Taylor* v. *Gilbert's Trs.*,
but solely because of the difference of opinion as to the time
at which the heirs were to be ascertained, and the reasoning
of the opinions both of the majority and of the minority is
quite consistent with the authority of that case.[1]

That the opinion of the minority of the Court was correct
became apparent in the subsequent case of *Gregory's Trs.* v.
Alison,[2] in which the House of Lords reviewed and practically
overruled the decision. There by a marriage contract the
parties appointed trustees, and each conveyed his or her
estate to the other in liferent and to the children of the
marriage in fee. It was declared that if there were no
issue or if they predeceased the survivor of the spouses, the
parties might dispose of their proper shares of the estate,
and, failing such disposal, the estate was to be divided on the
death of the survivor, the separate shares of the parties
going to their respective nearest of kin. The husband died
without disposing of his share. He was survived by a son,
who predeceased the widow, leaving a child, who also predeceased her. It was decided that the husband's nearest of

---

[1] *Per* Ld. Pres. Inglis in *Steel's Trs.*
v. *Steel* (1888), 16 R. 204.

[2] (1889), 16 R. (H. L.) 10 ; see also
G.'s Trs. v. *G.*, 1937, S. C. 141.

kin were to be ascertained at his death ; that they took subject to defeasance if there were issue of the marriage alive at the death of the widow ; and that, as the son was not only the primary legatee, but also the nearest of kin, he had taken an absolute vested interest.

When the gift in default of issue of the liferenter is qualified by a personal condition, as, for example, a provision as to the legatee's majority, *Taylor* v. *Gilbert's Trs.*[1] decides that the gift will vest on the fulfilment of that condition.

Suspensive conditions attached to the gift.

Again, the bequest must be given to the parties " in absolute ownership, with no further destination," phrases which are apparently synonymous.[2] Hence, if a survivorship clause be annexed, there can (unless the survivorship intended is survivorship *inter se* [3]) be no vesting before the termination of the liferent, because the gift in that case falls within the authority of *Young* v. *Robertson*,[4] which refers such clauses to the time of payment.[5] Similarly, a destination-over to *personæ designatæ* [6] or to heirs [7] will also exclude vesting, unless on the special features of the deed it is shewn to refer to the testator's death or to some time anterior to the close of the liferent.[8] The question whether, in the case of a destination-over to heirs, vesting may take place in the heirs of the legatee on his death prior to that of the liferenter subject to defeasance in the event of the latter leaving issue has been discussed in an earlier chapter.[9]

In the case of destinations-over and survivorship clauses the qualification affecting the legatee's right is of a suspensive nature, so that, apart from the bequest to the liferenter's issue, the legatee would not acquire a vested interest till the termination of the liferent. But the qualification may be resolutive in its effect. Thus, where the bequest in default

Resolutive conditions attached to the gift.

[1] *Ante*, p. 130.
[2] *Per* Lord Trayner in *White's Trs.* v. *Chrystal's Trs.* (1893), 20 R. 460.
[3] As in *Gardner* v. *Hamblin* (1900), 2 F. 679, and see p. 84, *ante*.
[4] (1862), 4 Macq. 314.
[5] *Cumming's Trs.* v. *White* (1893), 20 R. 454 ; *Steel's Trs.* v. *Steel* (1888), 16 R. 204 ; *Bannatyne's Trs.* v. *Watson's Trs.* 1914, S. C. 693.
[6] See *Wright's Trs.* v. *Wright* (1894),

21 R. 568 ; *Johnston's Trs.* v. *Dewar*, 1911 S. C. 722.
[7] *Mackenzie's Trs.* v. *Georgeson*, 1923 S. C. 517. In *Turner* v. *Gaw* (1894), 21 R. 563, the destination-over was to the heirs of the body of the legatee.
[8] As in *M'Dougall's Trs.* v. *M'Dougall's Trs.* (1902), 39 S. L. R. 375.
[9] Chapter IV., *ante*, p. 95.

of issue of the liferenter is to a class which is capable of enlargement, the interest of the existing members is subject to defeasance to the extent required to allow of *postnati* participating in the bequest. In this case the defeasance is merely partial ; and, if members of the class who are qualified to take are in existence, the fact that other members may come into existence will not postpone vesting. As in the case of direct gifts to a class,[1] the right will vest in the members of the class in existence for the benefit of themselves and of other members who may be born. That this is so is established by the decisions in the cases of *Houston* v. *Houston's Trs.*,[2] *Corbet's Trs.* v. *Elliott's Trs.*[3] and *Searcy's Trs.* v. *Allbuary.*[4] In the first of these the testator bequeathed his estate to his children equally in liferent and to their issue in fee ; and, if any child died without issue, his or her share was to pass to the other children in liferent and to their issue in fee. Of the testator's two children, one, Mrs Reid, had at the date of the case no issue ; the other, Mrs Cassels, had two sons. It was held that the share of the estate liferented by Mrs Reid was vested in her nephews subject to (a) total defeasance if she left issue, and (b) partial defeasance in favour of any further children who might be born to Mrs Cassels.

So also in *Corbet's Trs.* v. *Elliott's Trs.* the bequest, if the liferenter died without issue, was *inter alios* to the children of the testator's brother James. This brother survived the testator for sixteen years, but the fact that " membership of the class," *i.e.* of his children, " might fluctuate between the death of the truster and the period of division " did not exclude vesting *a morte testatoris* subject to defeasance if the liferenter left issue. This decision was approved and followed by the First Division in *Searcy's Trs.* v. *Allbuary, supra,* where the bequest failing issue of the liferenter was to the families of John Searcy and William Brown. The Session papers shew that the latter survived the testator for six years, and John Searcy for sixteen years.

But it may be that the legatee's right is liable to total

Bequests subject to two resolutive conditions.

---

[1] See p. 192.
[2] (1894), 2 S. L. T. 118 ; 1 S. L. T. 403.
[3] (1906), 8 F. 610.
[4] 1907 S. C. 823.

defeasance, not only in the case of the liferenter having issue, but on some other contingency also. Thus the bequest may be to A. in liferent and to her issue in fee, whom failing to B., and, if he predecease leaving issue, to his issue. It is now accepted that in itself the calling of the issue of a legatee on his predecease does not suspend vesting in the legatee, but merely divests him in the event of his predecease survived by issue.[1] In strict logic, therefore, there would seem to be no reason why, in the case put, B. should not take a vested right (subject to defeasance) on the testator's death ; for as neither of the two conditions is *per se* inconsistent with vesting their conjunction might be thought to have no different effect. In the case of *Bannatyne's Trs.* v. *Watson's Trs.*[2] an opinion was expressed by Lord Mackenzie that " there is no reason in principle why a fee should not vest subject to divestiture upon one or more than one contingency." But the application of the doctrine of vesting in a case of this kind was rejected by the First Division in *Lees's Trs.* v. *Lees.*[3] In that case trustees were directed to hold a share of the testator's estate for each daughter in liferent and her issue in fee, and, failing such issue the share was to pass (as the Court construed the clause) to the sons, the issue of the other daughters, and the issue of any son predeceasing the period of division. A daughter having died without issue, it was held that no right in the share vested in the parties called in that event until her death. Lord Sands observed : " The peculiarity in this case is that it is a double contingency—the contingency of an intervening family and the contingency of a family of the predeceaser. As I have already said, the intervening family would not have prevented vesting subject to defeasance nor would the subsequent family—that is the family of the son—have prevented vesting subject to defeasance according to recent authority ; but then the specialty in this case is that there are two contingencies. . . . It (the doctrine of vesting subject to defeasance) has

---

[1] See p. 149.

[2] 1914 S. C. 693.

[3] 1927 S. C. 886 ; and see *M'Donald's Trs.* v. *Gordon,* 1909 2 S. L. T. 321 (Lord Skerrington). Cf. Lord Kyllachy's opinion in *Corbet's* *Trs.* v. *Elliott's Trs.* (1906), 8 F. 610 ; and see *M'Lay* v. *Borland, ante, p.* 129 ; and *Turner* v. *Gaw* (1894), 21 R. 563, where the destination-over was to the " heirs of the body " of the legatee.

not been held to operate where there was a contingency and then a bequest subject to another contingency." The case was held to be ruled by the decisions in *White's Trs.* v. *Chrystal's Trs.*[1] and *Turner* v. *Gaw.*[2]

The contention that vesting subject to defeasance was excluded where the bequest was dependent on more than one contingency was again considered in *G.'s Trs.* v. *G.*[3] The trust in this case was for behoof of the testator's elder daughter in liferent and the heirs of her body in fee ; if she died without leaving such heirs, for the younger daughter in liferent and the heirs of her body in fee ; and, if both died without heirs of their bodies, for the testator's " own nearest heirs." These heirs were ascertainable at the testator's death and were his two daughters.[4] It was held that there was vesting in them subject to defeasance if either had issue. Their right was liable to be defeated if either were survived by issue, but this was deemed to be no obstacle to the immediate vesting of the right, and it was pointed out that in *Gregory's Trs.* v. *Alison*[5] there was a double contingency, viz. (*a*) the possible emergence of issue and (*b*) the exercise of a power of disposal. The effect of the decision in *G.'s Trs.* v. *G.* is, it would appear, to weaken or restrict the authority of *Lees's Trs.* v. *Lees* ; for, while in the earlier case vesting in the " other children " called in the ultimate destination was excluded because of the possible existence of their issue, in the later vesting took place in the heirs of the testator despite the possible existence of their issue.

Effect of the various forms of gift.

The question as to the event on which the legatee called in the second place is to be divested, must be determined on a consideration of the terms in which the prior beneficiary is called. The divesting of the ulterior right, it is thought, depends upon, and is simultaneous with, the vesting of the prior right. If the gift be, as in *Steel's Trs.* v. *Steel*,[6] to A. and to her issue, and failing issue, to B. in fee, B.'s right would be defeated by the birth of issue, whether the

---

[1] (1893), 20 R. 460.

[2] (1894), 21 R. 563.

[3] 1937 S. C. 141.

[4] It was held that these were beyond the age of child-bearing—see Chapter XIV.

[5] *Ante*, p. 134. See also *Coulson's Trs.* v. *Coulson's Trs.* 1911 S. C. 881, stated *post*, p. 155.

[6] *Ante*, p. 131.

issue do or do not survive the liferenter ; for it is well settled that, in the general case, the expression " failing issue " means " in the event of there being no issue," and whenever issue come into existence they acquire a vested interest.[1] By parity of reasoning, if the gift were to A. in liferent, and if she leaves issue to such issue, and, failing her leaving issue, to B. in fee, it would appear that B.'s right is defeasible not by the birth of issue, but by the existence of issue at the death of the liferenter ; because where a bequest is made to the issue of a person in the event of his dying leaving issue, it is a condition of the gift taking effect in favour of issue that there are issue alive at their parent's death.[2] Similarly, if the gift were to issue, in terms which suspended the vesting of their interest until their respective majorities, there would be no defeasance of the ulterior gifts unless a child became major. In the two last cases there would (if the above views are correct) be a vested right in the ulterior beneficiary, although there were issue of the liferenter alive, provided these had not fulfilled the qualification annexed to the bequest in their favour. Unless the children, in the one case, survive their parent, or, in the other, attain twenty-one, they are not the objects of the testator's bounty ; and as regards the gift they are to all intents and purposes non-existent. Hence, there being no object interposed between the party called in the second place and the bequest, it seems to follow in principle that he should have a vested right unless and until there emerge parties answering the description contained in the prior gift. Thus, in *Taylor* v. *Gilbert's Trs.*[3] the bequest was to devolve on the fiars favoured in the second place in the event of the liferenters dying without leaving issue who should attain majority, so that there could be no vesting in the issue unless they attained majority and survived their parent ; but, nevertheless, the gift was held to vest in the ulterior legatees during the currency of the liferent, and although there actually was a child born to the liferenter who died in minority.[4] So also in *Gregory's Trs.* v. *Alison* [5]

[1] See *post*, p. 207.

[2] See *post*, p. 210.

[3] (1878), 5 R. (H. L.) 217 ; 3 App. Cas. 1287.

[4] Lord Gordon's opinion in the House of Lords and the Session Papers shew that the report in 5 R. 49 is in this point incorrect.

[5] (1889), 16 R. (H. L.) 10, stated *ante*, p. 134.

the next-of-kin acquired a vested interest although there was a child alive who would exclude them if he survived his mother, and it was a mere coincidence that this child happened also to be sole next-of-kin. In his opinion,[1] Lord Shand observes : "The existence of the liferent was no good reason against vesting, and no other reason could be suggested to suspend vesting. It seems to me that the existence for a time of a son, and afterwards of a grandson, neither of whom took an indefeasible right, did not suspend vesting either in the next-of-kin of the testator at his death, or postpone vesting till the death of the liferenter."

The bearing of these decisions was apparently overlooked in *White's Trs.* v. *Chrystal's Trs.*[2] where Lord Trayner observed that as "the issue who were first called as fiars had no vested right until the death of the liferentrix, the fiars next called could not have a vested right at an earlier date." But this reasoning fails to take account of the purpose of the ulterior gift, namely, to catch the funds in the event of the prior gift not coming into effect, and it has been held to be unsound.[3]

Development of the principle.

In *Cumming's Trs.* v. *Anderson*,[4] Lord M'Laren observed that the Lord President's statement in *Steel's Trs.* v. *Steel* was not to be considered as necessarily limiting the application of the principle to the cases there summarised ; and the opinion of the Court in *Ross's Trs.* v. *Ross*[5] appears to favour a certain development of the principle. In that case the truster instructed his trustees to hold the estate for his widow in liferent, and on her death to pay one-third to A., one-third to B., and one-third to the truster's brothers, etc. In the event of either of A. or B. predeceasing the widow, his share was to go to the brothers. A. and B. predeceased. In the circumstances of the case it was immaterial whether the shares of A. and B. vested only on their deaths in the truster's brothers, or whether vesting took place *a morte testatoris*, subject to defeasance if the two legatees survived the widow. But Lord Moncreiff (who

---

[1] (1887), 14 R. 368.

[2] (1893), 20 R. 460. In *Turner* v. *Gaw* (1894), 21 R. 563, Lord Low proceeded on the same reasoning but, while his decision was affirmed in the Inner House, the Court explicitly refrained from adopting it.

[3] *G.'s Trs.* v. *G.*, 1937 S. C. 141.

[4] (1895), 23 R. 94.

[5] (1897), 25 R. 65.

delivered the opinion of the Court) expressed the opinion that there was immediate vesting subject to defeasance if A. and B. survived the widow.

In *Hickling's Trs.* v. *Garland's Trs.*,[1] a gift of a sum to the truster's daughter in liferent and on her death leaving issue to her issue in fee, was held to vest in all the issue (whether they did or did not survive their mother), subject to defeasance if no child was alive at her death. As there were children then alive, it was held that the sum fell to be divided among these children and the representatives of the other children who had predeceased.

Gift to a liferenter and to his issue if he leaves issue.

II. Gift to A., with Direction to Trustees to hold for him in Liferent and his Issue in Fee.

—This class of cases differs from the preceding category, in that here the doctrine of vesting subject to defeasance is invoked in favour of the institute or legatee called in the first instance. The *species facti* to which the rule applies and the reasons on which it is based, may most conveniently be treated with reference to the leading case of *Lindsay's Trs.* v. *Lindsay.*[2] The testator gave a sum of money to his daughter in these terms : " I leave and bequeath to A. the sum of £1000." In a subsequent part of the will there occurred this clause : " I direct that the legacy . . . shall be held by the trustees . . . and shall be settled or placed so as validly and effectually to provide to herself a liferent only thereof, and to the lawful issue of her body equally among them the fee thereof." The daughter survived her father, and died without having married. There thus occurred a state of circumstances not explicitly provided for in the will, because, while the testator gave the fee to his daughter's children, he failed to declare whose was to be the fee in the event of no children being born. It was held that the daughter was the fiar. The initial words of gift were, taken by themselves, sufficient to vest a fee in her, and the subsequent clause in no way revoked this gift, but merely added a provision in favour of issue. The event on which the fee was to be withdrawn from the daughter was the

To A., with a subsequent direction to trustees to hold for him in liferent and his issue in fee.

---

[1] (1898), 1 F. (H. L.) 7. Lord Watson and Lord Herschell dissented. More fully stated, *post*, p. 211.

[2] (1880), 8 R. 281.

birth of issue (or the survivance of her by issue), and as that event had not happened, the fee remained with her by force of the original gift. Until the daughter's death it could not be known, indeed, whether the bequest which had vested in her had vested absolutely in fee or only in liferent. But when she died unmarried, it became apparent that her interest was that of an absolute fiar.

A similar construction prevailed in *Dalglish's Trs.* v. *Bannerman's Exrs.*,[1] where the testator directed his trustees to " divide " the residue among his sons and daughters, and then by a codicil directed the trustees to invest the daughters' shares " upon heritable security, taking the rights thereto conceived in favour of such daughters for their liferent use allenarly, and to the child or children of their bodies . . . in fee." An attempt was made in argument in this case to distinguish *Lindsay's Trs.* on the ground that here the direction to hold for the daughters in liferent occurred, not in the will, but in a codicil, so that it was to be presumed that the testator had intended to revoke the prior gift ; but the Court rejected this distinction.

Statements of the principle.

The principle on which the Court in such cases is enabled to construe the gift as a gift of the fee, has been stated in varying terms. In *Dalglish's Trs.* v. *Bannerman*,[2] the provision in favour of the issue was considered as being nothing more than a burden on the daughter's right of fee ; so that when it was ascertained that issue had failed, the burden fell off, leaving an absolute right in the daughter. On the other hand, in *Logan's Trs.* v. *Ellis*,[3] the case was treated as an instance of vesting subject to defeasance, the event on which the fee was defeasible being the birth of issue. These modes of stating the law, however, appear to be variations in expression rather than in substance. As the effect of the rule under consideration is to construe the bequest as equivalent to a gift to A. in liferent and her issue in fee,

[1] (1889), 16 R. 559.

[2] *Supra*. Cf. Lord Young in *Lindsay's Trs.* v. *Lindsay* (1880), 8 R. 281.

[3] (1890), 17 R. 425. See also these cases : *Cheyne & Stuart* (1889), 26 S. L. R. 391 ; *Stewart's Trs.* v. *Stewart* (1896), 23 R. 416 ; *Laing's Trs.* v. *Hamilton* (1899), 36 S. L. R. 701 ; *Mackay's Trs.* v. *Mackay's Trs.* (1897), 24 R. 904 ; *Dunlop's Trs.* v. *Sprot's Exr.* (1899), 1 F. 722 ; *Downie's Trs.* v. *Cullen* (1882), 9 R. 749. Cf. also *Greenlees' Trs.* v. *Greenlees* (1894), 22 R. 136.

whom failing to A.,[1] it becomes apparent that there is no real distinction between this class of cases and *Taylor* v. *Gilbert's Trs.*[2]

The principle thus established is, as is pointed out in the case of *Donaldson's Trs.* v. *Donaldson*,[3] common both to the law of England and to the law of Scotland. In that case the House of Lords approved of, and applied, the law as stated by Lord Davey in *Hancock* v. *Watson* [4] and by Lord Dunedin in *Tweeddale's Trs.* v. *Tweeddale*.[5] In the former case Lord Davey formulated the principle in these terms : " It is settled law that if you find an absolute gift to a legatee in the first instance, and trusts are engrafted or imposed on that absolute interest which fail, either from lapse or invalidity or any other reason, then the absolute gift takes effect so far as the trusts have failed to the exclusion of the residuary legatee or next-of-kin as the case may be." In *Tweeddale's Trs.* v. *Tweeddale* the principle was canvassed by a Court of Seven Judges and was stated by Lord Dunedin thus : " When in the beginning of an instrument you find words which purport to bestow a certain gift or interest, and then subsequently find further provisions or declarations which obviously deal with the gift or interest of the same donee, then the further expression of the donor's will must have been inserted by him for one of two purposes, either (1) to enlarge or abridge the gift from what, had the original words remained unadded to, it would have been, or might have seemed on a certain construction of the words to be ; or (2), leaving the gift the same, to adhibit further conditions or directions as to the way in which the gift is to be enjoyed. Let me inter-polate that it does not seem to me that these propositions are affected by the point whether there is or is not what I may call a warning expression in the first clause that there is more on the same subject to come. The final proposition I take to be this : That where the subsequent declaration does not in terms purport to affect the first purpose, *i.e.* to enlarge or abridge the gift itself, then on the well-known

---

[1] Cf. Lord Gifford in *Lindsay's Trs.* v. *Lindsay, supra*, and *Aitken's Trs.* v. *Aitken*, 1921 S. C. 807, *per* Ld. Pres. Clyde.

[2] (1880), 5 R. (H. L.) 217.
[3] 1916 S. C. (H. L.) 55.
[4] [1902], A. C. 14.
[5] (1905), 8 F. 264, at 273.

view of allowing continued effect to *all* the testator has said, that construction will *in dubio* be preferred which assigns it to the second rather than to the first category."

Whether issue to take must survive liferenter.

Where this principle of construction applies the fee will remain with the liferentrix if she dies without issue. But it may be that there are issue who, however, all predecease her ; and the question arises whether her right is divested when issue come into existence or only if she is survived by issue. It might be thought that this should depend on the terms in which the issue are called. Thus in a gift to A. in liferent and her issue in fee, the fee vests in the children as they come into existence, and therefore the fee would be withdrawn from A. on the birth of the first child ; if, however, the issue were described as surviving at the end of the liferent, it is thought there could be no defeasance unless issue outlived the liferentrix. In other words, the event on which defeasance depends would, in this view, be ascertained by determining when the issue were meant to take a vested right. It appears to be incorrect to consider the issue as taking by way of succession to their mother. They are institutes under the testator's deed. But the weight of authority is in favour of the view that the liferenter is divested only if there are issue in existence at her death. In *Lindsay's Trs.* v. *Lindsay* [1] Lord President Inglis observed : " Even if there are children, theirs is only a contingent right ; and if they predecease their mother, the bequest takes effect . . . according to its own absolute terms."

An initial gift necessary.

The conditions of the application of the principle are these:

1. There must in the first instance be a bequest capable, in itself, of carrying the fee if the direction to the trustees to hold for the issue does not take effect ; there must, in the words of Lord Davey, be " an absolute gift to a legatee in the first instance." In a leading authority—*Muir's Trs.* v. *Muir's Trs.*[2]—the only gift to the legatee was contained in these words : " I direct and appoint my trustees to hold and retain the whole residue . . . for behoof of my children, and to divide the same amongst them . . . the shares

---

[1] (1880), 8 R. 281 ; and see Lord Low's opinion in *Fyfe's Trs.* v. *Duthie*, 1908 S. C. 520, and *Gilbertson's Trs.* (1893), 1 S. L. T. 354.

[2] (1895), 22 R. 553.

. . . respectively being to be set aside, and held, and invested, and otherwise dealt with as after mentioned." There followed a declaration that the shares were to be held for the children in liferent and for their issue in fee. It was held that no right of fee had vested in a son who died without issue, because the words quoted were insufficient to vest an absolute interest in him. In delivering the opinion of the Court, Lord M'Laren said : " If a testator begins by making an unqualified division of his estate or residue amongst children, and then by a subsequent clause empowers his trustees to retain the shares of one or more of them, and to pay the income to the child or children for life, and the fee or capital to their issue, it may very well be that the power is only given to the trustees for the protection of the immediate beneficiaries. Accordingly, if one of these should die without issue, and leaving a will, it may be held that the original gift was not displaced, but its effect only suspended during the lifetime of the beneficiary, and for his or her protection. . . . It is, however, essential to the proper application of this principle of construction, that there should be an independent unqualified gift to the immediate beneficiary capable of taking effect when the special trust fails or is exhausted." In the gift in question this condition was not satisfied, because there was in the first instance no absolute bequest to the legatee, the conditions limiting his interest being attached from the outset.

With reference to the condition laid down in Lord M'Laren's statement, Lord Skerrington observed in *Nicol's Trs.* v. *Farquhar* : [1] " By an ' initial gift ' I mean a gift expressed in words which plainly and unambiguously confer an absolute right of fee upon a legatee. A clause conceived in terms which are not clear or which are susceptible of two meanings, though it may ultimately be construed as an absolute gift of the fee, falls within a different category, because its meaning and effect have to be cleared up by inferences drawn from other parts of the will." In the case of bequests which fall within the latter category the whole provisions of the deed, and, more especially, those

What words amount to a gift in fee.

[1] 1918 S. C. 358 ; *Donaldson's Trs.* v. *Donaldson*, 1916 S. C. (H. L.) 55, *per* Lord Parker, at 64 ; *Mackay's Trs.* v. *Mackay's Trs.* (1897), 24 R. 904, *per* Lord M'Laren.

which relate to the particular bequest must be taken into account in determining what interest is conferred on the legatee. Subject to this general qualification, it may be said that, if the gift is made at the outset in the shape of a simple and unconditional bequest,[1] or, if the legacy is to be " paid " or " made over " to the legatee,[2] or if it is referred to as " belonging " to the legatee,[3] this points clearly to the legatee being entitled to the fee if he or she dies without issue. A direction to " hold for behoof of " the legatee, if nothing more is said, imports a bequest of the fee,[4] but this expression is susceptible in a marked degree to the influence of the context, and in the cases in which the effect of this direction has been considered the decision has generally been founded on the provisions accompanying it.[5] Where the direction is to " hold and apply for behoof of " the legatee, these words " are in themselves strongly indicative of a provision in fee." [6] Again, if the testator's estate is to be distributed among his children (no discrimination being made between sons and daughters), and there is added a direction that the daughters' shares are to be held for them in liferent and their issue in fee, then, as the original bequest to the daughters rests on the same words as express the gift to the sons, it would be hard to hold, if the sons take in fee, that there was no initial gift of fee in favour of the daughters, although it may be that the subse-

---

[1] As in *Lindsay's Trs.* v. *Lindsay*, *supra*, and *Dunlop's Trs.* v. *Sprot's Exr.* (1899), 1 F. 722 (where the words were " I hereby leave and bequeath to," etc.).

[2] As in *Tweeddale's Trs.* v. *Tweeddale*, *supra*; *Stewart's Trs.* v. *Stewart* (1896), 23 R. 416; *Mackay's Trs.* v. *Mackay's Trs.*, *supra*; Ld. Pres. Dunedin in *MacGregor's Trs.* v. *MacGregor*, 1909 S. C. 362.

[3] *Milne's Trs.* v. *Milne's Ex.*, 1937 S. C. 149.

[4] As in *Murray's Trs.* v. *Murray* 1919 S. C. 552. See observations in *Greenlees' Trs.* v. *Greenlees* (1894), 22 R. 136, at 139; *Ballantyne's Trs.* v. *Kidd* (1898), 25 R. 621; *Peden's Trs.* v. *Peden* (1903), 5 F. 1014; *Anderson's Trs.* v. *Anderson*, 7 F. 224.

[5] *Donaldson's Trs.* v. *Donaldson*, 1916 S. C. (H. L.) 55 at 68; *Aitken's Trs.* v. *Aitken*, 1921 S. C. 807; *Milne's Trs.* v. *Milne's Exr.*, 1937 S. C. 149, where Lord Moncrieff says: " A direction ' to hold,' if used in a context, will take the colour of the context in which it is used." See also *Nicol's Trs.* v. *Farquhar*, *supra*; *Gillies' Trs.* v. *Hodge* (1900), 3 F. 238; and *Smith's Trs.* v. *Clark*, 1920 S. C. 161, *per* Lord Dundas.

[6] *Per* Ld. Pres. Clyde in *Aitken's Trs.* v. *Aitken*, 1921 S. C. 807—a case " near the border-line." Contrast *Young's Trs.* v. *Young* (1901), 3 F. 616, *Neilson's Trs.* v. *Neilson*, 1909 2 S. L. T. 282, and *Smith's Trs.* v. *Clark*, *supra*.

quent provisions have the effect of reducing the right which the daughters otherwise would have taken.[1] Moreover, if after the bequest to the legatee in liferent and his or her issue there appears a gift-over in the event of the legatee's predeceasing the testator, this is a feature which supports the construction which would lodge the fee in the legatee in the event of his or her surviving the testator and dying without issue ; for the restriction of the gift-over to the case of predecease of the testator indicates that he had supposed that in other contingencies the fee was disposed of under the terms of the bequest.[2] The force of this consideration would, however, vary with the nature of the bequest ; it is most forcible in the case of a residuary bequest where the alternative is resulting intestacy, for the presumption against that result would give it support which would be wanting in the case of a legacy.

2. Further, the application of the principle is excluded when the deed contains a destination to other parties capable of taking effect, failing issue, on the termination of the liferent.[3] In such cases the fee is disposed of under the testator's directions. Where, however, these directions are found to be inoperative in the circumstances which have occurred—as, for example, if there is a gift-over to survivors and there are no survivors at the critical time—the fee may be held to be vested in the liferentrix. Thus, in *Fraser* v. *Fraser's Trs.*,[4] the testator burdened his lands with provisions in favour of his daughters, and declared that they

There must be no disposal of the fee failing issue.

Rule not excluded where provisions as to the fee failing issue become inoperative.

---

[1] *Mackay's Trs.* v. *Mackay's Trs.* (1897), 24 R. 904 ; *Milne's Trs.* v. *Milne's Exr.*, *supra*, *per* Ld. Pres. Normand ; *Watson's Trs.* v. *Watson*, 1913 S. C. 1133 ; *Cowan's Trs.* v. *Jardine*, 1913 S. C. 927 ; *Baird's Trs.* v. *Jackson* (1903), 5 F. 472 ; *Laing* v. *Hamilton* (1899), 30 S. L. R. 701.

[2] *Aitken's Trs.* v. *Aitken*, *supra*, *Tweeddale's Trs.* v. *Tweeddale*, 8 F. 264, *per* Lord Low ; In the following cases in which the principle was applied there was a destination-over : — *Dalglish's Trs.* v. *Bannerman ; Stewart's Trs.* v. *Stewart; Laing's Trs.* v. *Hamilton*, *supra* ; and *Cheyne & Stuart* (1889), 26 S. L. R. 391. In *Logan's Trs.* v. *Ellis*, *supra*, the principle was applied,

the gift-over being treated as a *substitution*—cf. Lord Shand's opinion.

[3] Cf. *Muir's Trs.* v. *Muir's Trs.*, *supra*, where there was a destination-over which was construed as referring to the daughter's death. See also *Baird's Trs.* v. *Jackson*, *supra; Barr* v. *Parnie* (1903), 11 S. L. T. 426.

[4] (1883), 11 R. 196. So also *Downie's Trs.* v. *Cullen* (1882), 9 R. 749. In both of these there were special terms in the deed which indicated an intention to give the daughters the fullest benefit consistent with the other purposes of the deed. See also *Fulton's Trs.* v. *Fulton* (1901), 8 S. L. T. 465 (Lord Stormonth-Darling).

were to have the interest only of these provisions, and were not to have power to call up the capital. On the death of any daughter her provision was to go to her issue, and if she had no issue, it was to devolve on her brothers and sisters then alive. A daughter survived all the other members of the family, and died without issue. It was decided that the fee had vested in her, subject to defeasance in the event (a) of her having children, or (b) of her dying survived by her brothers and sisters. On the death of the other members of the family the gift-over became inapplicable, and thereafter the bequest remained as a bequest to the daughter and her issue.

Nor by a power to settle on a contingency which does not occur.

3. Again, the distinction must be observed between these cases in which the testator in his will calls parties in default of issue of the favoured individual, and those other cases in which the parties are mentioned as the objects of a settlement to be made by the trustees in a specified contingency. Thus, in *Mackay's Trs.* v. *Mackay's Trs.*,[1] the truster directed that (as it happened) on his widow's death the trustees should divide the estate among his children. The daughters' shares were to be held by the trustees for their liferent use while they remained unmarried. If the daughters married, the trustees were to take care that the shares were settled so that the *jus mariti* and the *jus administrationis* were excluded ; and so also that if the daughters died without issue, they should have power to dispose of one half of the shares by will, and that the other half should go to the other children of the truster. A daughter died a spinster and leaving a will. It was held that the fee of her whole share had vested in this daughter. If our interpretation of the judgement is correct, this decision proceeded on the view that under the terms of the will the gift to the other children and the provision as to the daughter's power of testing depended on the trustees making a settlement in these terms, which settlement could be made only on the daughter's marriage. As, therefore, the daughter never married, the settlement could not be executed, and the gift remained as one to the daughter, to be held for her behoof in liferent by the trustees.[2]

---

[1] (1897), 24 R. 904.

[2] That this is the correct reading of the decision appears (it is submitted)

from the remark in the opinion of the Court that the clause as to the daughter's power of testing and as to

4. Lastly, the principle is inapplicable in a case such as *Turnbull's Trs.* v. *Turnbull's Trs.*[1] In that case the trustees were empowered to reduce the legatee's interest to a liferent, and to suspend the vesting, and to settle the share on his issue in such shares as he should appoint, and failing appointment on the issue equally. The testator under the will had declared that the legatee's share should vest on his majority. Prior to the son's attaining majority, the trustees restricted the legatee's interest. Thereafter the son died after attaining majority without issue. The share was held to fall into intestacy. In this case the rule was inapplicable, because the testator's express purpose was not merely to burden the fee, but to give his trustees a discretionary power to reduce the legatee's right.

Where trustees have a power to restrict the legatee's interest.

III. Cases in which a Fee is given subject to the Condition that if the Legatee predecease leaving Issue, the Issue shall take.—The view that in cases of this nature a defeasible fee is conferred on the beneficiary, was first adopted in Lord Shand's elaborate opinion in *Snell's Trs.* v. *Morrison.*[2] In this case the trustees were instructed, on the death of the truster's widow, to hold a part of the residue for behoof of his daughter and her husband in liferent and of their children in fee. This gift was qualified by a declaration " that in case of any grandchild having died without having received payment of his or her share leaving lawful issue, such share shall fall to such issue, if more than one, equally among them." Some of the grandchildren survived their parents and the testator's widow ; others predeceased these without leaving issue. Lord Shand held that the fee had vested in all the grandchildren, subject to defeasance if they predeceased survived by issue. The ground of this decision is explained in the following sentences of his Lordship's opinion : " If the natural meaning be given to the words

the gift-over had only an indirect bearing on the question, " as we are here concerned with the case of a daughter who died unmarried," and that, if the fee was not in the daughter, it was not disposed of. Cf. also *Bradford* v. *Young* (1884), 11 R. 1135.

[1] (1900), 2 F. 1183 ; see also *Chambers' Trs.* v. *Smiths* (1878), 5 R. (H. L.) 151, and cases cited, post, p. 337.

[2] (1877), 4 R. 709. In *Hutton's Trs.* v. *Coates* ((1868), 6 S. L. R. 146) the Lord Ordinary (Ormidale) treated a clause of this kind as suspensive of vesting ; and so also in *Sloane* v. *Finlayson* (1876), 3 R. 678.

actually used, and no more, namely, that in the case of any particular grandchild dying before the term of payment leaving issue, the issue of such child shall take, this does not affect the case of children predeceasing the term of payment but dying without issue, and the representatives of such children, either legally or by force of deeds of conveyance, would take the shares of such children, and there would be no intestacy. . . . I am of opinion that by the earlier clauses of the deed the testator gave a right of fee to each of the children . . . in life at his death, subject to the annuity and liferents ; the term of payment being therefore postponed, that the right so given was not an absolute fee, but was a right which might be defeated in one event, but in one event only, viz., the death of the grandchild before the term of payment, leaving issue. That event did not occur in the case of any of the children ; and I therefore hold that the right of fee, although for a time defeasible in the case of each child, in the result became absolute." It should be observed that the gift in this case was in the form of a direction to pay at the termination of the liferents. This principle of construction was sanctioned and applied by the First Division in *Dalhousie's Trs.* v. *Young,*[1] where the facts were not materially different from those in *Snell* v. *Morrison.*

The principle expounded and applied in these cases was, however, rather lost sight of for many years. The view which was then in the ascendant was that a gift-over to issue was no more than a " derivative " destination which had no effect in qualifying the right of the institute. Under a bequest to A. and if he predeceased leaving issue to his issue, A., it was held, took an absolute right *a morte testatoris.*[2]

The effect of *Bowman* v. *Bowman* on this doctrine.

But, as we have seen, the whole doctrine of derivative destinations was overthrown by the opinions of Lord Watson and Lord Davey in *Bowman* v. *Bowman.*[3] The destination-over in that case was to the legatee's heirs, but in the course

---

[1] (1889), 16 R. 681. See also *Byar's Trs.* v. *Hay* (1887), 14 R. 1034, and Lord Shand's opinion in *Lindsay's Trs.* v. *Sinclair* (1885), 12 R. 964. In *Richard's Trs.* v. *Roland* (1894), 22 R. 140, the Second Division referred to the principle, but as the features of the case pointed to vesting *a morte,* did not apply it. See the English cases, *Gray* v. *Garman,* 2 Hare, 268 ; *In re Wilmott's Trust* (1869), L. R. 7 Eq. 532 ; *Salisbury* v. *Patty,* 3 Hare, 86.

[2] *Ante,* p. 70.

[3] (1899), 1 F. (H. L.) 69.

of his opinion Lord Davey observed that he had difficulty in seeing " why a different construction as regards the time of vesting should be given to a conditional limitation in favour of persons unnamed, but described as heirs, issue, or the like of the first legatee, and to one in favour of named persons, or persons described by some description independent of the first legatee, *e.g.* of the other legatees or of their children." [1]

Accordingly in two cases [2] before the First Division which occurred shortly after *Bowman* v. *Bowman* that decision was regarded as having the effect of assimilating not only a destination-over to heirs, but also a destination-over to issue, to one in favour of strangers. In both cases the facts were such as to allow of the application of the principle of *Snell's Trs.* v. *Morrison* ; but the decision was that a clause calling the issue of the legatee in the event of his predeceasing leaving issue excluded vesting even in the case where the legatee died without issue. The principle of defeasible vesting was not, however, distinctly brought under the attention of the Court. It is true that in one of these cases [3] Lord M'Laren adverted to the doctrine only to hold with regret that it was ruled out by *Bowman*, but no argument for the application of the doctrine was advanced, and neither *Snell's Trs.* nor *Dalhousie's Trs.* was cited in the course of the debate.

The first re-assertion of the doctrine after the date of *Bowman* is to be found in Lord Kyllachy's decision in the Outer House case of *Wylie's Trs.* v. *Wylie*.[4] In that case the facts were that spouses by their marriage contract provided that the income of their estate should be paid to them, and that on the death of the survivor the capital should be payable to the children of the intended marriage, " declaring that if any child of the said intended marriage shall have predeceased the said term of payment, leaving lawful

---

[1] But see his Lordship's opinion in *Dawson* v. *Smart* (1903), 5 F. (H. L.) 24, at 27, where, after referring to *Bowman* v. *Bowman*, he observes that, there being a destination-over to issue, the legatee's right was " liable to be defeated by her death in her father's lifetime leaving issue."

[2] *Parlane's Trs.* v. *Parlane* (1902), 4 F. 805 ; *Forrest's Trs.* v. *Mitchell's Trs.* (1904), 6 F. 616.

[3] *Forrest's Trs.* v. *Mitchell's Trs.*, *supra.*

[4] (1902), 8 F. 617.

issue, such lawful issue shall succeed to the share of such child predeceasing." A son (Napier Wylie) predeceased the wife (who was the survivor of the spouses), leaving issue and having assigned his share. Lord Kyllachy held that the son had taken a vested interest subject to defeasance if he predeceased leaving issue, and as that contingency had occurred, he had been divested and the share belonged to his child. His Lordship pointed out that *Hay's Trs.* v. *Hay* [1] had been overruled by *Bowman*, and that in any case absolute vesting on the death of the granter was excluded by the express reference to the time of payment. He added : " Up to a recent date, and according, I think, to a preponderance of authority going back for a long period, the result would have been suspension of vesting—suspension which would in this case have operated to defeat Napier Wylie's right even if he had died without issue. One does not wonder that such a result was always reached with reluctance, but it was, as I have said, the result reached in, I think I may say, many cases going back for a long period. Fortunately, however, this Court, with the approval of the House of Lords, has of late years found the means of re-dressing this anomaly, and of doing so without unnecessarily postponing vesting, and without, on the other hand, sacrificing the interests of issue if they existed. For it has now, I think, to be taken as an established rule of con-struction that a contingency depending merely upon the existence or survivance of issue falls to be read as a resolutive and not as a suspensive condition. In other words, in a case like the present there is no suspension of vesting, but vesting subject to defeasance—defeasance in the event of the primary legatee leaving issue. This general doctrine was expressly affirmed by at least five of the judges in the recent case of *Thompson's Trs.* v. *Jamieson*,[2] and was in effect, I think, affirmed by the whole Court. I may add that it had previously been recognised, if not formulated, in various cases. Particularly it was recognised, and formed an alternative ground of judgement in Lord Rutherfurd Clark's opinion in the case of *Byar's Trs.*,[3]—a case which I rather think has been a good deal misunderstood."

[1] (1890), 17 R. 961.   [3] (1887), 14 R. 1034.
[2] (1900), 2 F. 470.

The purport of this passage is apparently to assimilate gifts in this form to cases such as *Taylor* v. *Gilbert's Trs.*[1] It is not altogether obvious, however, that the conditions of the two modes of gift are precisely the same. In *Taylor* v. *Gilbert's Trs.* the contingency was not personal to the legatee : it was the existence or non-existence of issue of another person ; but in *Snell's Trs.* v. *Morrison* the contingency was to some extent personal, for it depended upon the legatee's survivance or non-survivance of a certain time.

The decision in *Wylie's Trs.* was followed in a series of cases before the Second Division [2] and in *Allan's Trs.* v. *Allan*,[3] on a full review of the previous decisions, by the First Division. It may, therefore, be accepted as firmly established that, while a destination-over to heirs suspends vesting, a destination-over to children or issue merely renders the vesting of the institute's right defeasible in the event of his predeceasing and leaving issue.

This difference in the operation as regards vesting of the two forms of destination-over is justified by these considerations. It can rarely happen that a person dies without heirs, and, therefore, where a will provides that, in the event of the legatee's predecease, his heirs shall take the legacy, there is a complete and exhaustive disposition of the legacy in that event in favour of others—the heirs ; and accordingly in no circumstances can the legacy be subject to disposal by the legatee as part of his estate, if he fail to survive. On the other hand, a legatee may or may not have issue ; and in the case of a bequest to him with a declaration that, if he predecease leaving issue, the issue shall take in his room and place, there is no provision for the case of the legatee's failure except in the case of his leaving issue ; if he predeceases without leaving issue the will is silent as to the destination of the legacy and there is nothing to deprive the legatee of his right.

It is immaterial whether the bequest takes the form of

[1] *Ante*, p. 130.
[2] *Cairns' Trs.* v. *Cairns*, 1907 S. C. 117 ; *M'Donald's Trs.* v. *M'Donald*, 1907 S. C. 65 ; *Penny's Trs.* v. *Adam*, 1908 S. C. 662 ; *Gibson's Trs.* v. *Gibson*, 1925 S. C. 477.
[3] 1918 S. C. 164.

a legacy to A. " whom failing his issue " [1] or contains a clause such as that in *Wylie's Trs.* v. *Wylie*; and the principle has been applied where the bequest was to A. " and his children," " and " being read as equivalent to " whom failing." [2]

There is another question which may arise under this form of bequest. Supposing the legatee to die before the time of payment leaving issue, does the legacy vest in the issue on his death, or is vesting in them suspended till the time of payment ? This question was noticed in *Cairns' Trs.* v. *Cairns* [3] and *Penny's Trs.* v. *Adam*,[4] but the circumstances of these cases did not call for its decision, and Lord Kyllachy and Lord Stormonth-Darling reserved their opinion on the point. In the Outer House case of *Davidson's Trs.* v. *Davidson* [5] before Lord Skerrington the question was sharply raised. The bequest there was to certain legatees *nominatim* on the expiry of a liferent " the provisions of any of them dying and leaving issue to be divided equally among his or her issue." All the legatees predeceased the liferentrix and all left issue, but some of the issue predeceased the liferentrix. His lordship held that the issue acquired an absolute vested right on the death of the parent ; there was nothing in the terms of the bequest to require that the issue should survive the liferentrix, and his Lordship could find " no good reason for reading into the will a condition which the testator has not expressed." A contrary decision was, however, pronounced by Lord Guthrie in *M'Kune's Trs.* v. *M'Kerrow*,[6] where the bequest was to A. and the heirs of his body, and the question must, therefore, be regarded as still an open one in Scots Law. The decisions as to the date of vesting in the heirs under a bequest to A. or his heirs have been noticed in an earlier chapter,[7] and these decisions tend to support Lord Guthrie's view ; but it cannot be said that decisions regarding destinations which have the effect of suspending vesting are direct authorities as to destinations which allow of vesting subject to defeasance for the considerations applicable to the cases are not the same.

[1] *Nisbet's J. F.* v. *Nisbet*, 1911 2 S. L. T. 171 (Lord Cullen).

[2] *Gibson's Trs.* v. *Gibson*, *supra*.

[3] *Supra*.

[4] *Supra*.

[5] 1909 2 S. L. T. 20. See also *Fraser's Trs.* v. *Fraser*, 1913 1 S. L. T. 254.

[6] (1908), 16 S. L. T. 18.

[7] *Ante*, pp. 92 and 109.

The decision in *Coulson's Trs.* v. *Coulson's Trs.*[1] represents a certain extension of the doctrine under consideration. In that case the testator directed his trustees, on the expiry of a liferent given to his widow, to divide the residue among his children. As regards his sons he made the following provision for the case of their predeceasing the time of payment : If a son left issue, these were to take his share ; if he did not leave issue, but was survived by a widow, another disposition of the share was made. It was held that the son's shares vested subject to defeasance if a son who predeceased the widow either (*a*) left issue, or (*b*) left no issue, but was survived by a widow. It will be noticed that there were here two alternative contingencies. But there was no general provision for the case of the son's predecease without leaving issue ; had there been such a provision, the doctrine, it is conceived, could not have been applied.

IV. Extensions of the Doctrine.—The discussion of this subject may be concluded by directing attention to an *obiter dictum* by Lord Watson in *Gregory's Trs.* v. *Alison*,[2] which indicates a possible, and the decision in *Yule's Trs.* v. *Deans*[3] which is an example of an actual, extension of the principle. In the first of these cases there was a provision in favour of the issue of the marriage, and if they predeceased the longest liver of the spouses, to the husband's next-of-kin. The child of the marriage did so predecease. Lord President Inglis, in stating his opinion that the next-of-kin were to be selected on the death of the survivor of the spouses, observed that the vesting of the gift to the issue was suspended till the same event.[4] But the House of Lords came to the conclusion that this judgement was erroneous, and that the next-of-kin were to be ascertained at the husband's death, and that, therefore, the child took in his capacity of next-of-kin. Hence it was not necessary to examine minutely the nature of the gift to issue. But Lord Watson, who delivered the opinion of the Court, intimated that, supposing the next-of-kin were to be fixed as at the death of the longest liver of the spouses, and that,

Extensions of the Doctrine.

[1] 1911 S. C. 881.
[2] (1889), 16 R. (H. L.) 10.
[3] 1919 S. C. 570.
[4] (1887), 14 R. 368.

therefore, the right of the child depended on the terms of that gift, then the child would have taken a vested interest liable to defeasance in the case, which happened, of his dying before that event.

In *Yule's Trs.* v. *Deans* the testator instructed his trustees to expend the income of his estate in maintaining his son in an asylum, and to make over the estate to him if he recovered the use of his mental faculties. If he did not recover, bequests were made to certain persons and institutions in simple and unconditional terms. It was held that, as no conditions were attached to these bequests, they vested in the legatees subject to defeasance if the son recovered. No precedent for this decision was cited, but the Court rejected the argument that conditional vesting was not to be applied unless a precedent could be found.[1]

---

[1] See also the cases of *Martin's Trs.* v. *Milliken* (1864), 3 M. 326, *ante*, p. 129 ; *M'Lay* v. *Borland* (1876), 3 R. 1124, *ante*, p. 129 ; and *Coulson's Trs.* v. *Coulson's Trs.*, 1911 S. C. 881, *ante*, p. 155.

CHAPTER VII.

ACCRETION.

WHERE a bequest is made to several persons *nominatim* or to a class, the question may arise, whether their interest is joint (so that the portion of any dying before the period of vesting will accresce to the survivors) or several (in which case the death of one will not enlarge the interest of the survivors). If words of survivorship are used which apply to the contingency which occurs, the effect of the bequest is clear ; but, in the absence of an express provision of this kind, there may be difficulty in regard to what is to happen to the portion of the predeceasing legatee. The general rule upon the point is, that if the subject be given to the parties without words of severance,[1] or " jointly," [2] or, according to Mr Bell,[3] " jointly and severally," the *jus accrescendi* obtains ; but if, on the contrary, the bequest be to the parties " equally," or " share and share alike," or with similar words of severance, the portion of a predeceaser will not be carried to the others. In this last case the parties, though called in the same sentence, are " separate as to the matter, because their portions are severed and expressed " ; [4] and the bequest is, in substance, merely an abbreviation of that form of gift in which the legatees are called in a series of sentences, each containing a separate and distinct gift to an individual legatee.[5]

---

[1] Stair, iii. 8. 27, *q.v.*, for an exposition of the possible cases in which the question may arise.

[2] Bell's Prin. 1882 ; Ld. Pres. Inglis in *Buchanan's Trs.* (1883), 20 S. L. R. 666.

[3] *Supra*.

[4] Stair, *supra*.

[5] Lord M'Laren observes in *Menzies' Factor* v. *Menzies* (1898), 1 F. 128 (and the observation was approved in *Roberts' Trs.* v. *Roberts* (1903), 5 F. 541) : " If a testator gives £5000 to five persons by name, adding the words ' share and share alike,' according to the ordinary use of language, it is the same thing as if he said, ' I give £1000 to A., and £1000 to B.,' and so on, the only difference being that in the case supposed the testator

As an example of a joint bequest the case of *Andrew's Exrs.* v. *Andrew's Trs.*[1] may be cited. The testatrix directed her trustees to hold the residue of her estate for behoof of her "sisters A. and B. and (*per stirpes*) their children absolutely." There was nothing in the deed to suspend the vesting. A. predeceased the testatrix. It was held that B. was entitled to the whole of the residue on the ground that the bequest contained no words of severance. This bequest was contrasted with another bequest in the deed to these sisters and others "equally between" them, in which case the words quoted would have prevented the share of a predeceaser from passing to the others.

The circumstances under which the *jus accrescendi* is excluded are set forth in the following passage from the Lord President's opinion in *Paxton's Trs.* v. *Cowie*[2] :—

Effect of words of severance.

"There is a rule of construction," he said, "settled by a series of decisions, beginning in the last century,[3] and coming down to the case of *Buchanan's Trs.*[4] in 1883, to the effect that when a legacy is given to a plurality of persons, named or sufficiently described for identification,[5] 'equally among them,' or 'in equal shares,'[6] or 'share and share alike,'[7] or in any other language of the same import,

---

begins by using words descriptive of the entire sum which he means to bequeath, and then adds words explaining that he does not intend a joint bequest, but a series of separate bequests." See also *Young's Trs.* v. *Young*, 1927 S. C. (H. L.) 6, *per* Lord Wrenbury, at p. 14.

[1] 1925 S. C. 844. See also *Wright's Exrs.* v. *Robertson* (1855), 27 S. J. 341, and *Napier's Trs.* v. *Napier*, 1908 S. C. 1160.

[2] (1886), 13 R. 1191. The decision is that of a Court of seven judges.

[3] See *Paterson* v. *Paterson* (1741), M. 8070; *Rose* v. *Roses* (1782), M. 8101.

[4] (1883), 20 S. L. R. 666.

[5] See below, p. 163.

[6] As in *Rose* v. *Roses* (1782), M. 8101; *Wilson's Trs.* v. *Wilson's Trs.* (1894), 22 R. 62; *Paul* v. *Home* (1872), 10 M. 937.

[7] As in *Torrie* v. *Munsie* (1832), 10 S. 597; 7 Fac. 462; *Bowman* v. *Richter* (1900), 2 F. 624; *Farquharson* v. *Kelly* (1900), 2 F. 863. Cf. also *Tulloch* v. *Welsh* (1838), 1 D. 94; and *Barber* v. *Findlater* (1835), 13 S. 422; 10 Fac. 246. In *Paterson* v. *Paterson* (1741), M. 8070, the words were "equally and proportionately"; in *Flett's Trs.* v. *Elphinstone* (1900), 38 S.L. R. 564 (Lord Kincairney), there was a direction to "divide . . . into equal shares"; in *Stirling's Trs.* v. *Stirling* (1898), 1 F. 215, the direction was to "divide equally among them." For the law in England see Jarman on Wills (7th Ed.), vol. iii., p. 1768; the words "respective shares" (*Ive* v. *King*, 16 Beav. 46; *Heathe* v. *Heathe*, 2 Atk. 121), "participate" (*Robertson* v. *Fraser*, L. R. 6 Ch. 696), and "between them" (*Att.-Gen.* v. *Fletcher*, L. R. 13 Eq.

each is entitled to his own share and no more, and there is no room for accretion in the event of the predecease of one or more of the legatees. The rule is applicable whether the gift is in liferent [1] or in fee [2] to the whole equally, and whether the subject of the bequest be residue,[3] or a sum of fixed amount,[4] or corporeal moveables.[5] The application of this rule may, of course, be controlled or avoided by the use of other expressions by the testator importing that there shall be accretion in the event of the predecease of one or more of the legatees." In the case in which these words were used, the testator directed his trustees to divide his estate into two halves and to deal with one half in this way ; " £200 to my late wife's sister A. ; in the event of her predeceasing me, said sum to be paid to my sister B., the remaining portion to be equally divided between my late wife's sisters C. and D., my late wife's brother E., and my late wife's niece F." E. predeceased the testator. It was held that his share did not accresce to C., D., and F., but fell to the testator's heirs *ab intestato*.

While the actual decision in the case is of little value as a precedent,[6] the statement of the law is of high authority. It has been accepted as authoritative in a series of cases, including *Cochrane's Trs.* v. *Cochrane*,[7] decided by a Court

128), were treated as words of severance. In *Robertson* v. *Fraser* (*cit.*) Lord Hatherley, L. C., said : " I cannot doubt, having regard to the authorities respecting the effect of such words as ' amongst ' and ' respectively,' that anything which in the slightest degree indicates an intention to divide the property must be held to abrogate the idea of a joint tenancy and to create a tenancy in common."

[1] As in *Haldane's Trs.* v. *Murphy* (1881), 9 R. 269 ; *Napier's Trs.* v. *Napier*, 1908 S. C. 1160 ; *Scott* v. *Scott* (1843), 5 D. 520 ; *Stobie's Trs.* (1888), 15 R. 340 ; *Buchanan's Trs.* (1883), 20 S. L. R. 666 ; *Stevenson* v. *Macintyre* (1826), 4 S. 776.

[2] As in *Paxton's Trs.* v. *Cowie*, *infra*.

[3] As in *Wilson's Trs.* v. *Wilson's Trs.*, *supra* ; *Torrie* v. *Munsie*, *supra* ;

Rose v. *Roses*, *supra* ; *Crawford's Trs.* v. *Crawford* (1886), 23 S. L. R. 787 ; Lord M'Laren in *Macfarlane's Trs.* v. *Oliver* (1882), 9 R. 1138.

[4] Cf. *Menzies' Factor* v. *Menzies* (1898), 1 F. 128.

[5] *Wauchope* (1882), 10 R. 441 ; (" plate and pictures ") ; *Graham's Trs.* v. *Graham* (1899), 2 F. 232 ; (" the stock and crop on farms ") ; *Paterson* v. *Paterson* (1741), M. 8070 (" household plenishing and made work ").

[6] *Young's Trs.* v. *Young*, 1927 S. C. (H. L.) 6, *per* Lord Shaw.

[7] 1914 S. C. 403. It was argued in this case that the words " in the proportions following," were less unfavourable to accretion than " share and share alike." The terms of the Settlement were somewhat special.

of seven judges, and *Young's Trs.* v. *Young* [1] in the House of Lords.

The general principle being thus clearly established, it is unnecessary to refer to the cases cited in the notes, save in so far as they supply a commentary on the exceptions therein noticed, or afford examples of the influence of the context upon particular words of severance.

Like other matters depending upon the construction of wills, it is a *quæstio voluntatis* whether legacies do or do not accresce, and even words such as " equally " or " share and share alike " are not so strong but that they will yield to satisfactory manifestations in the will of the testator's intention to confer a joint right.

Indications that testator intended accretion.

Thus in one case [2] the income of the estate was given to three of the testator's daughters in liferent " equally among them, share and share alike, *and that during all the days of their lives respectively*," and the fee was to be made over to their issue *per capita*. As the fiars, and the shares to be taken by each, could be ascertained only on the death of the last of the liferenters (seeing that the gift was *per capita*), it was considered that the testator must have had in view that the estate should be held as a *unum quid* by the trustees, and that the whole interest in the meantime should be absorbed by the liferents. Accordingly, the share of a liferenter was found to accresce on his death to the survivors. [3]

In *Bartholomew's Trs.* v. *Bartholomew* [4] the testator directed that the interest of the residue should be " equally divided " among his unmarried daughters, and that the capital should be divided in the event of their subsequent marriage or death. Five of the six daughters who were unmarried at the testator's death having married, it was

---

[1] *Supra.*

[2] *Barber* v. *Findlater* (1835), 13 S. 422 ; 10 Fac. 246, followed in *Ritchie's Trs.* v. *M'Donald*, 1915 S. C. 501.

[3] In *Paul* v. *Home* (1872), 10 M. 937, Lord Neaves remarked that it was easier to presume that accretion was intended in the case of liferents than in the case of gifts in fee ; but *contra* L. J.-C. Moncreiff in *Fergus & Others* (1872), 10 M. 968.

[4] (1904), 6 F. 322. In *Mackenzie* v. *Dickson* (1840), 2 D. 833, where an annuity was created a real burden on an estate in favour of children " equally amongst them during their respective lives " ; it was decided that the annuity did not suffer abatement on the death of each child, but that the full sum was payable so long as any child survived.

held that the remaining daughter was entitled to the whole interest, Lord M'Laren observing : " This is the equivalent of a bequest of a series of half-yearly payments and the members of the class who are entitled to the benefit of it must be determined at the period at which each half-yearly payment falls due."

Again, if provision be made for accretion or non-accretion on the termination of a liferent in a specified contingency, an inference may be drawn from that provision in the case of the liferent terminating on another, and unforeseen, contingency. Thus, in *Tulloch* v. *Welsh*,[1] an estate was given to A. and B. " in liferent during all the days of their lives," the interest to be paid to them " share and share alike." " On *their decease*," C. was to have the liferent of the whole, and the fee was to belong to her issue. It was further provided that if A. predeceased B., C. was to be entitled to a half of the interest. A. did die before B., but C. was then dead. It was held that B. took the whole interest. The elements which weighed with the Court were : (*a*) that the expression of non-accretion in case of A. being survived by C. implied that otherwise and in other contingencies there should be accretion ; and (*b*) the words " on *their* decease " (as indicating a joint interest).

On the other hand, a contrary inference was drawn in *Hunter's Trs.* v. *Dunn*.[2] There the trustees held the residue for the testator's three daughters " and the survivors and survivor of them equally " in liferent, and for their issue in fee ; " declaring that in the event of any of my said daughters predeceasing me leaving issue, such issue shall succeed to the share . . . their parent would have been entitled to had she survived." All the daughters survived the testator, but one thereafter died without issue. The liferent enjoyed by her was held to lapse ; the declaration quoted operated to exclude the claims of the surviving sisters, because it testified to the testator's intention not to allow accretion in the contingency he had contemplated (a daughter's death survived by issue), although the one-third of the interest

Marginal note: Inference from provisions for accretion or non-accretion in a specified event.

[1] (1838), 1 D. 94. Cf. the English case of *In re Hobson* [1912], 1 Ch. 626 (Parker, J.).

[2] (1904), 6 F. 318. It should be

noted that the words " survivors and survivors " were referred to the testator's death.

was then set free. And the Court, not without difficulty, inferred therefrom a similar intention in the event which had happened.

In these cases the bequest was of the income of the funds, and the rule as to such bequests was stated by Lord M'Laren in *Napier's Trs.* v. *Napier*[1] in these terms : " A bequest to a plurality of persons for life is in law a joint bequest unless (1) there are words of severance such as ' in equal shares,' or (2) the bequest is capable of being construed as a family provision under which the issue of each liferenter takes the parent's original share."

No distinction between residuary and other gifts.

Where the bequest is of the fee, a distinction was in several cases drawn between gifts of residue and legacies. Influenced by the presumption which always exists against intestacy, the Courts declined to admit the rule in gifts of the former class.[2] But this distinction is now disapproved, and the principle of *Paxton's* case is applied even where the necessary result is intestacy.[3]

Class-gifts.

There is, however, one category of cases which is clearly outside the rule of that case. Accretion obtains in class-gifts, although words such as " equally " or " share and share alike " are used. A gift of this nature vests the subject in its entirety or not at all ; it cannot be partially vested and partially non-vested. The testator bestows the gift upon those members of the class, and those only, whatever their number, who acquire vested interests in the subject.[4] If at the time of vesting fixed by the provisions of the will there is only one member of the class in existence, or qualified to take, he acquires a vested right in the whole, subject to a partial defeasance to the extent necessary to give equal shares to other members who may come to have vested rights also ; and if there are no other members who become entitled to participate, he remains fiar of the whole. Hence, while the gift may lapse by a total failure of the class, there cannot be a partial lapse.

---

[1] 1908 S. C. 1160. See Lord Moncreiff's opinion in *Johnston* (1899), 1 F. 720.

[2] *Robertson* v. *M'Vean* (1819), Hume's Dec. 273 (disapproved in *Paxton's Trs.* v. *Cowie*) ; *Bannerman* v. *Bannerman* (O. H.) (1844), 6 D. 1173 (Lord Wood).

[3] As in *Paxton's Trs.* v. *Cowie* ; *Torrie* v. *Munsie* (1832), 10 S. 597 ; 7 Fac. 462 ; *Wilson's Trs.* v. *Wilson's Trs.* (1894), 22 R. 62.

[4] See Chapter VIII.

In *Muir's Trs.* v. *Muir*,[1] a truster directed his trustees to hold and administer the residue of his estate for behoof of, and equally among, the children of his son, and to accumulate the interest until the children respectively attained the age of twenty-five, or, in the case of daughters, married. The shares of the sons were made payable at that age ; and, on the daughters attaining that age or marrying, their shares were to be ascertained and set apart and were to be held for them in liferent and for their issue in fee. It was held that the share of a daughter who died under that age and unmarried passed to the other children. The Lord President pointed out that the exception as to class-gifts was recognised in his statement in *Paxton's* case. " Now, the first condition," he said, " for the application of that rule is, that the persons to whom the legacy is left must either be named or sufficiently described for identification. It cannot, therefore, apply to a class of persons of unascertained number, and therefore I think that *Paxton's* case has no application to the present."

It was observed in *Roberts' Trs.* v. *Roberts*,[2] that by the words " named or sufficiently described for identification," the Lord President must have meant, not that the parties are capable of identification (a condition of the validity of any legacy), but that they are individually named or identified. In the case cited, the truster directed his trustees as follows : " Upon the youngest of my sons now born or that may be born to me reaching the age of twenty-one years, to convey and make over to them, equally among them, all mill property," and so on. Of the truster's three sons, the youngest died in minority after his father. It was held that the whole of the property vested on his death in his two surviving brothers. The argument in favour of accretion in this case was strengthened by the words " or that may be born," for they showed that the testator was moved not by favour for existing individuals, but by the desire to provide for his sons collectively. There was a direction in a subsequent codicil as to certain rights that the eldest son was to have in his " third share " on attaining twenty-five, but this was held to be merely demonstrative

[1] (1889), 16 R. 954.
[2] (1903), 5 F. 541. Cf. *Brown* v.
Warden (1905), 12 S. L. T. 670 (Lord Stormonth-Darling).

and of little importance as compared with the description
of the legatees as " sons " in the words of gift.[1]

In *Bartholomew's Trs.* v. *Bartholomew*,[2] Lord M'Laren
commented thus upon *Paxton's Trs.* v. *Cowie* : " In the case
of *Paxton's Trs.* the late Lord President stated that, to make
the rule against accretion applicable, the beneficiaries must
be ' named or sufficiently described for identification,' which
I take to mean that there must be such a description as
will separately define the members of the class. This might
be by the use of such words as ' to my eldest daughter ' or
' to my second and third daughters '—words which, if not
identical with, are at least equivalent to, a designation by
name. But it is quite settled that where the bequest is to
the members of a family as a whole, the bequest vests in the
surviving members of the family at the period of distribution."

Menzies' Factor v. *Menzies* [3] represents the furthest point
to which the exception in favour of class-gifts has been
carried. In this case the testatrix made a bequest of £2000
to " the grandchildren of my brother A., who are (here
followed their names), equally among them, share and share
alike." The Court held, with difficulty, that the portion of
one of these grandchildren who died before the testatrix,
accresced to the survivors. The elements which led to this
result, and without which the decision would have been
otherwise, were the parenthetical manner in which the names
were given, and a reference in a subsequent clause to the
" legacy bequeathed to the grandchildren of A."

In these cases the fact that the bequest was in favour
of a class was held to exclude the rule of *Paxton's Trs.*, but
in *MacGregor's Trs.* v. *MacGregor*,[4] although the beneficiaries
undoubtedly formed a class, it was considered that there
was no room for accretion on account of the scheme of the
bequest. The testator instructed his trustees to hold the

---

[1] Cf. *Burnett* v. *Burnett* (1854), 16
D. 780 (noticed in *Carleton* v. *Thomson*
(1867), 5 M. (H. L.) 151 ; L. R. 1 Sc.
App. 232). In this case vesting
depended on the majorities of the
children, and the share of one dying
in minority fell to the others who
reached majority ; and compare also
Moir's Trs. (1871), 9 M. 848.

[2] (1904), 6 F. 322 ; stated *ante*
p. 160.

[3] (1898), 1 F. 128. This case and
Menzies' Factor v. *Menzies, supra*, were
distinguished in *M'Laren* v. *M'Alpine*,
1907 S. C. 1192.

[4] 1909 S. C. 362.

residue of his estate for such of his children as should survive him " equally, share and share alike," and to pay the shares of sons as the same became available for distribution, but to hold the shares " original and accrescing " of daughters for them in liferent and their issue in fee. A daughter (Miss Effie MacGregor) died unmarried two years after the testator's death. It was held that, notwithstanding the use of the word " accrescing," the share liferented by her did not accresce to the other children, but fell into intestacy. The ground of judgement was thus explained by the Lord President (Dunedin) : " I am bound to say it is impossible to hold that there is accretion to the other residuary legatees, because here the dividing of the estate into shares was an operation which necessarily took place at the death of the testator, and which did take place, and effectually took place, as to the share of Miss Effie MacGregor, which share was separated from the others, and perfectly properly held for the purpose of providing her with her alimentary liferent allenarly during the period she survived her father ; and when she dies I do not see how it ever can come back again to have an operation performed which has already been performed once and for all. It therefore seems to me perfectly different from the class of case that was quoted to us, viz., *Roberts' Trs.*,[1] where the question was whether severalty should prevent a gift taking effect in favour of a family as a whole as that family existed at the testator's death. Here the family at testator's death is distinctly described by the testator to be the family surviving at his death. Then the separation of the provision is to take place and did take place, and I do not think you can ever go back and do it again." This decision would appear to be in harmony with the result arrived at in *Wilson's Trs.* v. *Wilson's Trs.*[2] (where the whole residue was to be held for the children in liferent and for their respective issue in fee), but it is not so easy to reconcile it with the decision in *Muir's Trs.* v. *Muir.*[3] There is, however, one respect in which the two cases are distinguishable. In *MacGregor* the Lord President laid great

---

[1] *Ante*, p. 163.
[2] (1894), 22 R. 62. So also *Fulton's Trs.* v. *Fulton* (1880), 7 R. 566 ; but contrast *Roper* (1871), 43 S. J. 546.

[3] (1894), 22 R. 62. This case was not cited in *MacGregor's Trs.* v. *MacGregor.*

stress on the fact that a division of the estate had taken place and that the question of accretion arose in regard to a share which had been severed and set apart.[1] In *Muir's Trs.*, on the other hand, all the grandchildren were in minority at the date of the case [2] and no division could have taken place. In his opinion the Lord President (Inglis) said, " the fund to be divided is the residue " and " the share which would have fallen to " the daughter, " had she attained the age of twenty-five or been married, just forms part of the residue which is undivided."

The characteristics of a class-gift. In the cases in which the beneficiaries are called, not by name, but under a term of relationship, there is little difficulty in treating the bequest as a class-gift. In England the question as to what gifts are class-gifts has been the subject of numerous and refined distinctions, from which the law of Scotland is free. The characteristics of a class-gift appear to be that the legatees are united or connected by some common tie or quality, and that the terms of the gift are such as to indicate that the testator had regard to the body as a whole rather than to the constituent members individually ; [3] and these seem to be the tests applied in the Scots cases.

The legatees must be called as a class. The fact that the beneficiaries *de facto* form a class is not sufficient, if they are not called as a class, to admit the *jus accrescendi*. Thus, in *Crawford's Trs.* v. *Crawford*,[4] the testator directed that on the death of his wife his whole property should " be divided into seven equal portions or shares, of which one share should be given to each of his three sons (who were named) and two shares to each of his two younger children " (who were also named). It was held that the shares of those who died before their mother did not pass to the child alive at her death, but fell into intestacy.

This also holds although the relationship be expressed in the deed. In *Blair's Exrs.* v. *Taylor*,[5] the gift was to A., B.,

---

[1] But in the special case it is stated : " No interim division of the testator's estate has yet been made."

[2] This appears from the papers in the case.

[3] See Lord Macnaghten's and Lord Davey's speeches in *Kingsbury* v. *Walter* [1901] A. C. 187. Cf. Lord

Selborne's speech in *Pearks* v. *Mosely* (1880), 5 App. Cas. 714.

[4] (1886), 23 S. L. R. 787. This is implied in *Menzies' Factor* v. *Menzies*, *supra*.

[5] (1876), 3 R. 362, this is also implied in *Menzies' Factor* v. *Menzies*.

C., etc., " my brothers and sisters, equally among them, share and share alike." These persons being the whole of the testator's brothers and sisters, it was held that the share of one predeceasing the testator accresced to the survivors. But this decision was held to be inconsistent with *Paxton's Trs.* in *Farquharson* v. *Kelly*,[1] and accordingly it is to be assumed that in such cases the Courts will not now admit accretion. In the case last cited the deed under construction was a mutual will between spouses, in which the husband gave his estate to A., B., C., D., " my lawful children, equally among them, share and share alike," and the wife also gave her estate to these four persons by name (not, however, describing the relationship). It was held that there was no accretion in regard to the estate given by the wife. But here the construction was aided, possibly, by the circumstance that one of the beneficiaries was an illegitimate child of the testatrix.

So also, where [2] a testator (who had three sons) made a gift to " A. and B., my sons," it was held that the portion of a son dying before the time of vesting fell into residue.

The effect of admitting the *jus accrescendi* in the cases hitherto discussed, was to carry the shares of legatees who died before the time of vesting to the other legatees by virtue of an implied right of survivorship. When the legatee has once acquired a vested interest in the subject of the gift, it would seem that there is no room for the application of that doctrine, because if a testator gives a subject and does not make provision for its disposal on the death of the legatee, it ought to pass as part of the legatee's estate if he survive the time of vesting. In *Carleton* v. *Thomson*,[3] where this point was discussed at some length, a plea to the effect that the portions which vested in certain members of the class at the truster's death passed by accretion on their death before the period of payment to the members alive at that time, was repelled, and the opinion of Lord Colonsay is adverse to the view that accretion may take place in regard to vested shares.

Whether accretion may take place after vesting.

---

[1] (1900), 2 F. 863. Cf. also *Bowman* v. *Richter* (1900), 2 F. 624 ; where the gift was to " my nephews and nieces," the names following.

[2] *Graham's Trs.* v. *Graham* (1899), 2 F. 232.

[3] (1867), 5 M. (H. L.) 151 ; L. R. 1 Sc. App. 232.

In *Paul* v. *Home*,[1] the point was considered with reference to an estate which was partly moveable and partly heritable. There the testatrix by a codicil disponed to " A. and B. equally between them, and in case of the death of either without heirs of his or her body, to the survivor of them, my whole real and personal estate and effects whatsoever." Both A. and B. survived the testatrix, and thereafter A. died survived by B. B. claimed A.'s share, on the ground that there was a substitution in favour of the survivor, or, alternatively, that it accresced to him. Both pleas were repelled, and the share was held to go to A.'s heirs. The argument for accretion was treated as having little substance. Lord Justice-Clerk Moncreiff observed : " The other question is, whether the right conferred subsequently by the codicil is a conjunct right of such a nature that the right of the predeceasing disponee accrued to the survivor, or, on the other hand, as is contended for the other parties, that it was only on the predecease of the testatrix by one or other of the disponees that the conditional institution was to take effect. There is no proper case of accretion here. Conjunct fiars take *pro indiviso*—that is the rule of law as stated by Lord Stair. There is a distinction in that respect between the law of England and the Scotch feudal law, which is clearly pointed out by Craig (ii. 27. 7). The general rule of Scotch law, as I have said, is that conjunct fiars take *pro indiviso* ; that is unquestionable. Cases in regard to accretion have only occurred in connection with moveable property."

Bequest to trustees

Lastly, the case of *Mellis's Trs.* v. *Legge's Exr.*[2] may be noted. Here the testator appointed three individuals his trustees, and instructed them to divide the residue of his estate among themselves. One of these predeceased the truster. It was held that, as the testator's intention apparently was to give the estate to these persons in recompense for their undertaking the duties of trustees, the deceaser's share did not pass to his representatives or to the testator's heirs *ab intestato*, but went to the two acting trustees.

[1] (1872), 10 M. 937. Cf. *Johnston*   [2] (1898), 25 R. 954.
(1899), 1 F. 720.

CHAPTER VIII.

I. Definitions of Class-Names.—When a testator describes
the objects of his bounty by a class-name or term of relationship, that term or name is to be understood in the
sense in which the testator is found to have employed it ;
and this sense is to be discovered, in the first place, from the
whole provisions of the will read and considered in the light
of the circumstances with reference to which it was made.
If the will, so read, affords no guidance as to the construction
of the term, the Court will attach to it its primary meaning in
ordinary language. Many of the terms of relationship are
capable of more than one meaning, and, where a word has
more than one meaning, there is usually a strict or primary
meaning ; and the decisions of the Courts upon the construction of any word are useful as showing what that primary
meaning is. Beyond this point, there appears to be no
general rule binding the Court in its attempt to interpret

the testator's words.[1]   In a question as to the meaning of a
term of relationship, the decisions of the English Courts are
of value, and are frequently appealed to.   Accordingly,
some of the English cases are referred to in this section ;
but the mass of authority in England is so great that
considerations of space have made it impossible to do
more than notice some of the more important or recent
cases.

"Children" does not include grand-children.

Children primarily means offspring in the first degree
—sons and daughters, to the exclusion of more remote
descendants.[2]   This primary meaning may, however, be
displaced by a context showing that the testator intended
to include grandchildren.

In *Rhind's Trs.* v. *Leith*,[3] Lord Cowan, dealing with a
claim that under a bequest to " children" grandchildren
(whose parents had predeceased) might be included along
with children, observed :   " In a certain class of cases the
term ' children ' has sometimes been construed to include
grandchildren ;   but this has never been held in circumstances similar or analogous to the present.   Under the
presumed condition,[4] when applicable, grandchildren have
taken as coming in place of their parents ;   but there is no
instance of the term ' children ' being construed to embrace
grandchildren as well as the immediate issue.   They may

---

[1] See *Seale Hayne* v. *Jodrell*, [1891]
A. C. 304 ;   affirming *In re Jodrell*
(1890), 44 Ch. D. 590.

[2] *Wishart* v. *Grant* (1763), M. 2310 ;
Halliday (1869), 8 M. 112 ;   *Rhind's
Trs.* v. *Leith* (1866), 5 M. 104 ;   Lord
Macnaghten in *Hughes* v. *Edwardes*
(1892), 19 R. (H. L.) 33 ;   *Adam's Trs.*
v. *Carrick* (1896), 23 R. 828 ;   *Adam's
Exr.* v. *Maxwell*, 1921 S. C. 418, *per*
L. J.-C. Scott-Dickson, at 431 ;
M'Donald's Trs. v. *Gordon*, 1909 2
S. L. T. 321 ;   *Bowen* v. *Lewis* (1884), 9
App. Cas. 890 ;   *In re Atkinson* [1918],
2 Ch. 138.   In *Ranken* (1870), 8 M.
878, trustees were directed to dispone
a heritable property to A. in liferent
allenarly and to her children in fee,
and, failing such children, to B. in
liferent (the word " allenarly " being

omitted) and her children in fee, whom
all failing to the testator's heirs whatsoever.   A. died unmarried and B.
(who survived her) died without
leaving children, but survived by two
grandchildren.   It was held that on
the death of B. the property passed to
her eldest grandchild.   The question
was complicated by the circumstance
that under the rules of conveyancing
B. was fiar, and the opinions leave it
rather uncertain whether, as matter of
construction, the Court would have
been prepared to treat the word
" children," as used in the destination, as including grandchildren.

[3] (1865), 5 M. 104.

[4] *I.e.*, the *conditio si institutus sine
liberis decesserit.*

have been held entitled to take as coming in place of their parents *ex presumpta voluntate*, but not as direct legatees."

Again, it is a well-established rule, that where a gift is made to persons described by a term of relationship, persons of illegitimate descent are not included.[1] A gift to " children " is a gift to legitimate children, and, in the absence of clear evidence, afforded by the deed or the surrounding circumstances of a different intention on the part of the testator, natural children do not fall within the description. Thus, in *Dorin* v. *Dorin*,[2] where a gift was made by the testator to " my wife " A., with a power of appointment " amongst our children," and failing appointment the subject was to be divided among " my children by her," it was held that illegitimate children of the testator and A. were not objects of the gift. The will was made by the testator after his marriage with A. He had at the time when the will was made two illegitimate children by her, and he never had legitimate issue. The illegitimate children were excluded, because, supposing that the testator had meant to make the gift to lawful children who might subsequently be born, he would have used no other terms than those he had used, and because there was nothing on the face of the will or in the circumstances of the case to necessitate a departure from the strict interpretation of the words.

Legitimate relations alone included under a bequest to relations.

But there is no law to prevent a bequest to illegitimate children (at least if they are born before the testator's death), and where the terms of the will or the circumstances with reference to which it was made lead clearly to the conclusion that the testator intended to include illegitimate children, that intention will be carried into effect. The authority in Scots law as to this question is curiously scant. Writing in 1894, Lord M'Laren remarks that in no case has a claim " been put forward in our Courts on behalf of illegitimate children to the benefit of a designative bequest." [3] Since that date six cases on this point have been reported, but

Circumstances in which illegitimate children included.

---

[1] *Cairnie* v. *Cairnie's Trs.* (1837), 16 S. I. ; 13 Fac. 1 ; *M'Donald's Trs.* v. *Gordon*, 1909 2 S. L. T. 321 (O. H. Lord Skerrington).

[2] (1875), L. R. 7 H. L. 568.

[3] Wills and Succession (3rd Ed.), vol. i., p. 694.

none of these has reached the Inner House.[1] These cases all recognise that cogent evidence of a contrary intention on the part of the testator is required in order to displace the general rule which confines the term " children " to lawful children, but beyond this they lay down no general principle of construction.

In England, on the other hand, there is a large body of case law on this topic. The decisions are said in Jarman on Wills [2] to be " not in a satisfactory state," and have been criticised as in many cases proceeding " on baseless legal presumptions, arbitrary rules and false notions of morality which have never been adopted in Scotland." [3]

But even in English law there are, according to the decision of the House of Lords in *Hill* v. *Crook*,[4] two exceptions to the rule that lawful children only are entitled under a bequest in favour of " children." The facts of that case were, briefly, that the testator gave a subject to trustees in trust to pay the rents to his daughter, whom he described as the wife of A., independently of her present or any future husband, and on her death for her child or children. The testator's daughter was living with A. as his wife, and had children by him at the date of the will, but she was not, as the testator knew, his lawful wife. In these circumstances, and looking to the fact that the daughter was described in the will as the wife of A., it was held that the testator must have intended in making the gift to benefit the issue of that union. They were, therefore, found entitled to the subject. In his opinion Lord Cairns observed that there were two classes of cases in which illegitimate children would take under a gift to " children." " One class of cases," he said,

---

[1] *Robb* v. *Cables* (1893), 30 S. L. R. 969 (Lord Kincairney); *Sharp's Trs.* v. *Sharp* (1894), 2 S. L. T. 124 (Lord Kincairney); *Turnbull* v. *Govanlock* (1895), 3 S. L. T. 163 (Lord Stormonth-Darling); *Allan* v. *Adamson* (1902), 9 S. L. T. 404 (Lord Kincairney); *Gentle's Trs.* v. *Bunting* (1908), 16 S. L. T. 437 (Lord Skerrington); *M'Donald's Trs.* v. *Gordon*, 1909 2 S. L. T. 321 (Lord Skerrington); *Purdie's Trs.* v. *Doolan*, 1929 S. L. T. 273 (Lord Murray).

[2] (7th Ed.), vol. iii., p. 1755, where the development of the English law in this matter is traced.

[3] *Per* Lord Kincairney in *Allan* v. *Adamson, supra*. In *Robb* v. *Cables, supra*, the same judge described the English rules as " technical and conventional," and observed that they could not be safely followed in Scotland.

[4] (1873), L. R. 6 H. L. 265.

" is where it is impossible from the circumstances of the parties that any legitimate children could take under the bequest." As illustrating this exception, Lord Cairns instanced the case of a gift to the children of a person dead at the date of the will, who had left illegitimate but no lawful children.[1] The second class of cases was : " Where there is upon the face of the will itself, and upon a just and proper construction and interpretation of the words used in it, an expression of the intention of the testator to use the term ' children ' not merely according to its *primâ facie* meaning of legitimate children, but according to a meaning which will apply to, and which will include, illegitimate children " ; and it was within this class that the case of *Hill* v. *Crook* fell. These two classes are the only exceptions to the general rule recognised in English law.[2]

In England, it appears to have been doubted at one time whether a gift to illegitimate children not in existence at the date of the will was not *contra bonos mores*, and therefore void, but it is now settled that a gift to illegitimate children who are born before the testator's death is good, seeing that the will does not take effect until the death of the testator.[3] On the other hand, a gift to illegitimate children to be born after the testator's death cannot receive effect.[4]

Gift to illegitimate children nascituris.

Cousins.—*Primâ facie*, the word " cousin " means cousin-german.[5] " Second cousins " does not include first cousins once removed where there are second cousins alive at the testator's death,[6] but where there were no second cousins in existence at the date of the will and at the testator's death, first cousins once removed have been held to be pointed out

Cousin.

---

[1] In *In re Taylor* [1925], Ch. 739, Eve, J., held that this exception applied only where the testator was aware that the children were illegitimate.

[2] *In re Bleckly* [1920], 1 Ch. 450 *per* Lord Sterndale, M. R., at 461 ; *In re Pearce* [1914], 1 Ch. 254 ; *Dorin* v. *Dorin* (1875), L. R. 7 H. L. 568.

[3] *Occleston* v. *Fullalove* (1873), L. R. 9 Ch. 147 ; *In re Hastie's Trusts* (1887), 35 Ch. D. 728. But if the issue are described with reference to their paternity (as, *e.g.*, the children

of A. a male) or to all and every my children (the testator being a male), and not to their reputed paternity, then, as there is no legal criterion of paternity save marriage, the gift is held not to be good. *In re Bolton* (1886), 31 Ch. D. 542.

[4] Theobald on Wills (8th Ed.), 325 ; *Crook* v. *Hill* (1876), 3, Ch. D. 773.

[5] *Copland's Exrs.* v. *Milne*, 1908 S. C. 426 ; *Stoddart* v. *Nelson* (1855), 6 D. M. & G. 68.

[6] *In re Parker* (1880), 15 Ch. D. 528 ; 17 Ch. D. 262.

by that term.[1] But the term " second cousins " is often used in popular language to denominate first cousins once removed, and the Court will yield to evidence that the testator has so used the term. Thus, in *Drylie's Factor* v. *Robertson*,[2] where a testatrix gave a legacy to A., describing him as her second cousin, whereas he was in reality a first cousin once removed, and then provided annuities to her second cousins, it was held that first cousins once removed were entitled to these annuities ; for the inaccurate use of the term in regard to A. showed that the testatrix used it in a loose sense.

Descendants.

Descendants is a comprehensive term, and means children, grandchildren, great-grandchildren, and so on.[3]

" Executors," " Representatives."

Executors, Representatives.—Where a gift is made to " executors " or " representatives," the question arises whether these terms denote executors-nominate or testamentary representatives, or whether, on the other hand, they point out the parties entitled under the rules of intestate succession. In *Bell* v. *Cheape*,[4] it was decided that under a bequest to A., " her heirs, executors, or assignees," the trustees under A.'s will were not brought in as conditional institutes on her predecease, but that the subject went to her heirs *in mobilibus*. That decision has been regarded in subsequent cases as governing the construction of words of similar import. But, in themselves, the terms " executors " and " representatives " are of flexible meaning, and the sense to be attributed to them would seem to depend upon the context, and particularly on the meaning and influence of any term with which they may be conjoined, on the nature of the deed, and on whether the gift is to the testator's own representatives or executors, or to those of a legatee in the event of his dying before the time of vesting.

Meaning of " Representatives."

In English law it is ruled that " representatives " means primarily executors or administrators appointed by the party whose representatives are spoken of, and not his legal successors.[5] In Scots law the word has no very definite

---

[1] *In re Bonner* (1881), 19 Ch. D. 201.

[2] (1882), 9 R. 1178.

[3] *In re Flower* (1890), 62 L. T. 216 ; *Ralph* v. *Carrick* (1879), 11 Ch. D. 873.

[4] (1845), 7 D. 614 See *ante*, p. 79.

[5] *In re Crawford's Trusts* (1854), 2 Drewry, 230. But it was pointed out in this case that if the subject is to be made over on the testator's death, the word is considered to mean next-of-

significance. In *Manson* v. *Hutcheon*,[1] Lord President Inglis observed : " It is used in many senses. It means, among other things, all kinds of executors—executors-nominate, executors-dative, executor-creditor. An assignee is the representative of the cedent ; a mandatary is the representative of the mandant. All kinds of heirs are representatives in different degrees and manners. The true meaning in every case depends upon the particular terms of the deed in which it is used."

In the early case of *Stewart* v. *Stewarts*,[2] where a bequest was made to a party, " or in the event of his death to his personal representatives," it was held, the legatee having died before the time of vesting, that the legacy fell to his heirs *in mobilius*, and not to his executor-nominate. *(Construed as heirs in moveables.)*

But, on the other hand, a different construction was put on the word in *Manson* v. *Hutcheon*.[3] In this case a husband by marriage contract disponed his moveable estate to himself and his wife in conjunct fee and liferent, and to the children of the marriage in fee, and, failing children, it was provided that the estate should on the death of the longest liver be divided equally between " the representatives of each of them." There were no children of the marriage. The wife survived, and died leaving a will in favour of A. In a competition between A. and the wife's heirs *in mobilibus* as to the share of the estate destined to the wife's representatives, it was held that it went to A. Great weight was attached to the fact that the shares of the estate were given to the representatives of both parties ; and, as the husband was fiar, it followed that in regard to his share representatives meant the persons to whom he might assign it, and, this being the sense of the term when used in the deed as to the one half of the estate, the same meaning was naturally to be attributed to it when used in regard to the other half. *Stewart* v. *Stewarts* was distinguished on the ground that there the terms appeared in a will, and described those *(Construed as testamentary assignees.)*

kin, because the legatee does not know of the legacy during the testator's life, and cannot exercise his judgment as to its disposal ; and it is improbable, therefore, that the testator should have intended to put it at his disposal before the will comes into operation.

[1] (1874), 1 R. 371. Cf. also Lord Corehouse's opinion in *Mann* v. *Thomas* (1830), 8 S. 468 ; 5 Fac. 376.
[2] (1802), M. " Clause " App., No. 4.
[3] *Supra.*

called as conditional institutes on a legatee's failure, whereas here it was used in a marriage contract, and in a direct gift to those representing the granter.[1]

"Executors" construed as next-of-kin.

The earliest case upon the meaning of the word " executors " is *Lawsons* v. *Stewarts*,[2] in which a gift was made by will to a party " his executors or next-of-kin." In this case the next-of-kin were preferred. The terms executors and next-of-kin were considered to be synonymous, and the meaning of the composite phrase was fixed by the more definite expression " next-of-kin." The same construction has been put on destinations-over to " heirs, executors, or assignees," [3] heirs, executors and successors whomsoever," [4] and " heirs and executors." [5]

Construed as executors-nominate.

On the other hand, in *Scott's Exrs.* v. *Methven's Exrs.*[6] where the term was not conjoined with any expression pointing to the law of succession, the destination-over to executors was held to carry the subject to the executors-nominate. In that case a legacy was bequeathed to a party, and in the event of his predeceasing the testator, to his " executors and representatives whomsoever." The legatee predeceased the testator, and in a question as to the parties entitled to the subject under the gift-over, the legatee's executors-nominate were preferred to his next-of-kin. Lord Kyllachy said : " Apart from authority, I see no reason for denying to those words their full generality, or for limiting them so as to exclude executors-nominate, or assignees general or special. There is no reason in point of principle why a right not yet vested, or even a *spes successionis*, may not be assigned by anticipation. Neither is there, so far as I know, any reason why a testator should not, if he is so minded, make a conditional institution in favour of the testamentary assignees or heirs-designate of a particular individual. The question only is, whether an intention to this effect is sufficiently

[1] See *Haldane's Trs.* v. *Sharp's Trs.* (1890), 17 R. 385, *per* Lord Lee and Lord Kyllachy.

[2] (1827), 2 W. & S. 625. In any case the term " executors " does not denote those who might happen to be appointed executors, as, for example, creditors ; it means those having by law right to the executry funds (*Max-*

well v. *Maxwell* (1864), 3 M. 318 ; *Blair* v. *Blair* (1849), 12 D. 97 ; 21 S. J. 612) or executors-nominate.

[3] *Bell* v. *Cheape* (1845), 7 D. 614.

[4] *Lady Kinnaird's Trs.* v. *Ogilvy*, 1911 S. C. 1136.

[5] *Mackenzie's Trs.* v. *Georgeson*, 1923 S. C. 517.

[6] (1890), 17 R. 389.

clear, and, apart from authority, I repeat that the expression
' executors and representatives whomsoever ' appears to me
to be wide enough to cover every description of representatives, or, in other words, to include every title, general or
special, by which property is capable of being transmitted."
In this case both expressions were flexible, and the Court
was enabled to put that construction on the whole phrase
which gave effect to what appeared to be the testator's
meaning. In the opinion of Lord Kyllachy, importance
was attached to the circumstance that the gift-over was to
take effect only in the event of the legatee's predeceasing
the testator, so that the word necessarily bore reference to
the legatee's death before acquiring a vested interest.[1]

Again, in *Montgomery's Trs.* v. *Montgomery*,[2] a similar
expression was construed as indicating parties taking under
a voluntary disposition. By a marriage contract, funds
were given to trustees for behoof of the spouses and the
survivor in liferent, and for the children of the marriage
who should be alive at the death of the survivor of the
spouses in fee, and failing such issue for the spouses'
"assignees, executors, or nearest of kin." The wife died
first, survived by children, who all predeceased the husband.
The primary objects of the contract having failed, the
question arose whether the wife's share of the funds fell to
the universal legatory under her will, or devolved upon her
legal representatives. The former was preferred. *Lawsons*
v. *Stewarts* was distinguished on two grounds. In the first
place, the wife here was the fiar, for it was only in the event
of children being alive at the death of the survivor that the
property was to pass away from her ; and in the event which
happened, she remained undivested. This, therefore, was a
gift by a proprietor to his own executors and assignees.
Now, where such terms are used to describe those who are
to take in right of a legatee in case of his predecease, it is
not unnatural to presume that the testator intended to
benefit a fixed class, and not those to whom the legatee
might happen to assign the subject[3] ; but where the
provision is in favour of the testator's own executors or

----

[1] But see note 5, *ante*, p. 174.

[2] (1895), 22 R. 824.

[3] See the opinion of Lord President Strathclyde in *Lady Kinnaird's Trs.* v. *Ogilvy, supra.*

assignees, there is no such presumption, for it may well be that in employing these terms the testator meant merely to reserve the power of nominating the persons to take under this description. " It is difficult to conceive," said Lord M'Laren, " a more clear and more comprehensive declaration of the reservation by the granter of his right of fee on certain events than a declaration that failing other purposes the property shall pass to himself,[1] his assignees, executors, and next-of-kin. . . . Considering the source from which this money came, and that the purposes of the marriage contract are just the ordinary purposes of a provision to the wife and to the children, it is most natural to suppose that the funds settled by each spouse should return to himself or herself if there were no longer any marriage purposes to be fulfilled. There is no reason to suppose that anything different was intended than that if all the children predeceased the termination of the trust, so that there were no longer objects of the marriage trust, all the right of the settler in the estate was reserved." [2]   A further ground of decision was that the word " assignee " suggested that the power of voluntary disposition was meant to be given, and this was thought to distinguish the phrase under construction from that in *Lawsons* v. *Stewarts*, where the term with which "executors " was conjoined was " next-of-kin." [3]

These grounds of decision were criticised by Lord Skerrington in *Battye's Tr.* v. *Battye* [4] as being inconsistent with the judgement of Lord President Inglis in *Brown's Trs.* v. *Brown*.[5] In the latter case, where the circumstances were similar to those in *Montgomery's Trs.*, a provision in a marriage contract to the wife's " heirs or assignees " was held to be a conditional institution under which the heirs took, not as on intestacy, but by operation of the destination. This construction was considered by Lord Skerrington to be preferable to that adopted in *Montgomery's Trs.*

---

[1] There was, in fact, no express provision to the lady herself, but this was held to be the effect of the clause.

[2] See also *Murray's Trs.* v. *Murray* (1901), 3 F. 820, at 827.

[3] But see *Bell* v. *Cheape, ante.*

[4] 1917 S. C. 385.

[5] (1890), 17 R. 1174.

Family.—The word " family " is of wide and indefinite meaning, and is used as signifying the persons living in a household and under one head, or those of the same blood, or deriving from a common stock, or descendants generally, or merely children. Hence the meaning in any particular case will depend very much on the connection in which it is used. The question which has been agitated in the Scots cases is whether it primarily means descendants or only children. In *Irvine* v. *Irvine*,[1] where there was a destination-over to the families of legatees in the event of their pre-deceasing, grandchildren whose parents were dead were admitted along with his children to the share of a pre-deceasing legatee, and it was said that *primâ facie* " family " must be considered to include descendants generally. But in a more recent case [2] this decision was distinguished as proceeding on the principle of an implied institution of issue, and it is now settled that the word is to be construed, in the absence of evidence that the testator attributed to it a wider signification, as meaning children to the exclusion of remoter descendants.[3] In English Law also the primary meaning is children,[4] save in the case of a devise of real property, where it is interpreted as designating the heir at law.[5]

Heirs.—This word is interpreted according to the nature of the subject-matter of the gift. If that be heritable, the

" Family " primarily means children.

Heirs.

[1] (1873), 11 M. 892. Followed, owing to special circumstances, in *Macdonald's Trs.* v. *Macdonald* (1900), 8 S. L. T. 226 (Lord Low).

[2] *Low's Trs.* v. *Whitworth* (1892), 19 R. 431.

[3] *Greig's Trs.* v. *Simpson*, 1918 S. C. 321 ; *Searcy's Trs.* v. *Allbuary*, 1907 S. C. 823, *per* Lord Johnston; *Cattanach's Trs.* v. *Cattanach* (1901), 4 F. 205, *per* Lord Trayner ; *Low's Trs.* v. *Whitworth, supra* ; *Phillip's Trs.* v. *Davies*, 1910 2 S. L. T. 161 (Lord Skerrington). Cf. also *Fyffe* v. *Fyffe* (1841), 3 D. 1205. The circumstances of these cases did not admit of the application of the *conditio si institutus sine liberis decesserit.*

[4] *Pigg* v. *Clarke* (1876), 3 Ch. D. 672 ; *Barnes* v. *Patch* (1803), 8 Ves. 603.

[5] *Wright* v. *Atkyns*, 1823, Turn. & Russ. 143 ; *Lucas* v. *Goldsmid* (1861), 29 Beav. 657. The following points are also settled in English Law :—(1) A gift by a testator to his family does not include his wife (*In re Hutchinson & Tenant* (1878), L.R. 8 Ch. D. 540); (2) a power to appoint in favour of a married woman and her family would not, in general, include her husband as an object of the power (*Macleroth* v. *Bacon* (1799), 5 Ves. 159) ; (3) a gift to the family of a person does not include that person (*Barnes* v. *Patch, supra*). In *Williams* v. *Williams* (1851), 1 Sim. N. S. 358, the word " family " was construed as meaning the descendants in every degree of the person whose family was spoken of.

term designates the heir-at-law ; if moveable, the heirs *in mobilibus*.[1] If the subject consist in part of heritage and in part of moveables, the heritable portion falls to the heir in heritage, the moveable to the heirs *in mobilibus*.[2] Whether the destination is to the heirs of the testator or to the heirs of a legatee, the heir-at-law claiming the heritable portion is not entitled to participate in the moveables unless he chooses, as he is entitled to do, to exercise his right of collation.[3]

Under a gift to a person's heirs, his widow is not included.[4]

The word " heirs " has in some cases been construed in the limited sense of " heirs of the body " ;[5] but in the absence of a clear context the Court will not so limit the meaning.[6]

" Heirs of the body " means descendants of the person whose heirs of the body are spoken of who are alive at his death. They cannot, therefore, be ascertained during his lifetime, and consequently under a gift to the heirs of the body of A., vesting is suspended till A.'s death ;[7] but in some cases, on a construction of the context, the term has been interpreted as meaning simply children.[8]

" Heirs *in mobilibus* " means heirs *ab intestato*, and does not include an executor-nominate.[9]

" Nearest heirs " does not apply only to those heirs who are nearest in blood ; it includes all those who are entitled to succeed under the law of intestate succession.[10]

[1] Ersk. iii. 8. sec. 47 ; *Bowie* v. *Bowie*, 23 Feb. 1809, F. C. ; *Blair* v. *Blair* (1849), 12 D. 97 ; 21 S. J. 612 ; *Nimmo* v. *Murray's Trs.* (1864), 2 M. 1144 ; *Brown's Trs.* v. *Brown* (1890), 17 R. 1174 ; *Grant's Trs.* v. *Slimon*, 1925 S. C. 261 ; *Kirsop* v. *M'Culloch* (1881), 19 S. L. R. 216 (O. H.).

[2] *Blair* v. *Blair*, *supra* ; Ld. Pres. Inglis in *Brown's Trs.* v. *Brown*, *supra*. See also *Angus* v. *Angus* (1825), 4 S. 279 ; 1 Fac. 106 ; *Burrell* v. *Burrell* (1825), 4 S. 317 ; 1 Fac. 129 ; *Cathcarts* (1830), 8 S. 803 ; 5 Fac. 620 ; *Mitchell's Trs.* v. *Waddell* (1872), 11 M. 206, where the question of conversion was involved.

[3] *Grant's Trs.* v. *Slimon*, *supra*.

[4] *Inglis* v. *Inglis* (1869), 7 M. 435.

[5] *Craw's Trs.* v. *Craw* (1899), 1 F. 572 ; *Hunter* v. *Nisbit* (1839), 2 D. 16 ; *Anderson* v. *Anderson* (1829), 7 S. 743 ; 4 Fac. 1010.

[6] *Thorburn* v. *Thorburn* (1858), 20 D. 829.

[7] *Gollan's Trs.* v. *Booth* (1901), 3 F. 1035 ; *Campbell's Trs.* v. *Campbell* (1891), 18 R. 992.

[8] *Matthew* v. *Scott* (1844), 6 D. 718 ; Lord Rutherfurd in *Baillie* v. *Seton* (1853), 16 D. 216.

[9] *Haldane's Trs.* v. *Sharp* (1890), 17 R. 385.

[10] *Nimmo* v. *Murray's Trs.* (1864), 2 M. 1144 ; *Smith's Trs.* v. *Macpherson*, 1926 S. C. 983.

Issue.—This word is open to construction and may be Issue.
read as meaning " children," [1] or as including grandchildren
or remote descendants,[2] according to its context; but
it is now a settled rule that " if there is nothing said
to show that it is used with a limited significance as
applicable to direct children only, then the term includes
grandchildren." [3] As illustrating the exception to the
rule those cases may be referred to in which the term
occurred in conjunction with the word " children " so as to
imply that the two words were treated as synonymous ; [4]
and, if the word " father," " mother," or " parent " is
used in relation to " issue," this will support the narrower
interpretation of the term but is not necessarily conclusive.
In *Bannerman* v. *Bannerman's Trs.*,[5] where trustees were
directed to pay to " the issue of each of my said children the
fee of the respective shares of my estate directed to be
liferented by their parents respectively," Lord Ardwall held
that, in respect of the use of the word " parent," this bequest
was one in favour of children alone. On the other hand, in
Stewart's Trs. v. *Whitelaw* [6] it was held that any inference
which might be drawn from the use of the words " father "
and " mother " was overcome by the circumstance that the
bequest was to the issue *per stirpes.*

It is stated in Jarman on Wills [7] that " under a gift
to issue, descendants of every degree are, as a general rule,
entitled *per capita* as tenants in common or joint tenants
according as there are or are not words of severance, children
taking concurrently with their parent." Thus, where a
bequest was made to legatees, and, in case of their decease,
to their issue share and share alike, and a legatee died
leaving, *inter alios*, a daughter who had children, it was held

---

[1] As in *Young's Trs.* v. *M'Nab*
(1883), 10 R. 1165 ; *M'Murdo's Trs.*
v. *M'Murdo* (1897), 24 R. 458 ;
Cattanach's Trs. v. *Cattanach* (1901),
4 F. 205.

[2] As in *Bowie's Trs.* v. *Black* (1899),
36 S. L. R. 475 ; *Turner's Trs.* v.
Turner (1897), 24 R. 619 ; *Macdonald*
v. *Hall* (1893), 20 R. (H. L.) 88 ;
Dalziel v. *Dalziel's Trs.* (1905), 7 F.
545 ; *Stewart's Trs.* v. *Whitelaw*, 1926

S. C. 701. Cf. *Glendinning* v. *Walker*
(1825), 4 S. 241 ; 1 Fac. 46.

[3] *Per* Lord Adam in *Bowie's Trs.* v.
Black, supra.

[4] As in *M'Murdo's Trs.* v. *M'Murdo*
and *Cattanach's Trs.* v. *Cattanach,*
supra. The latter case was referred
to with approval in *Dalziel's Trs.* v.
Dalziel, supra.

[5] (1906), 13 S. L. T. 754.

[6] *Supra.*   [7] Vol. iii., p. 1564.

that these grandchildren were entitled to share in the legacy along with their parent and the other children of the legatee.[1] This question has received little attention in Scotland, but such authority as there is is hostile to this construction. In *Young's Trs.* v. *M'Nab* [2] the terms of the deed were deemed sufficient to exclude this construction, but Lord Shand observed : " I think it is a very improbable thing in itself that in a bequest to ' the issue ' of a person named there is thereby called to share equally in that bequest not only the children but the grandchildren, each taking *per capita* ; and, if there were no specialities in the deed, I should be against such a construction " ; and in *Black's Trs.* v. *Nixon* [3] the Lord President said : " A gift to the issue of A. (whose son together with that son's son survives the testator) is read to mean a gift to the son, not a gift to the son and the grandson equally between them." On the other hand, if the objects of a power of apportionment are described as " issue," there would seem to be nothing incongruous if the donee of the power were to exercise it by conferring benefits on children and their children concurrently.

" Nephews " and " nieces."   *" Nephews " and " Nieces."*—These terms include *primâ facie* nephews and nieces of the half blood (whether consanguinean or uterine) as well as those of the full blood.[4]

Primarily, the term would seem not to include grandnephews or grandnieces,[5] but these may be admitted if the terms of the will show that the testator so intended,[6] or if there are no nephews or nieces.[7] In English law the term has been held, in cases where the testator has no nephews or nieces of his own, to denote nephews or nieces by affinity.[8]

[1] See *Freeman* v. *Parsley* (1797), 3 Ves. 421 ; *Cancellor* v. *Cancellor* (1862), 2 Dr. and S. 194 ; *Weldon* v. *Hoyland* (1862), 4 De. G. F. & J. 564. In the first of these cases the Lord Chancellor (Loughborough) said that he suspected this construction did not accord with the testator's intention, but added : " I do not know what enables me to control it."

[2] (1883), 10 R. 1165, at 1172.

[3] 1931 S. C. 590. Cf. also *M'Meekan's Trs.* v. *M'Clelland* (1918), 56 S. L. R. 280 ; 1918, 1. S. L. T. 193 (Lord Hunter).

[4] *Norris* v. *Norris* (1839), 2 D. 220 ; *Clow's Trs.* v. *Bethune*, 1935 S. C. 754 ; *Jeans's Trs.* v. *Walker*, 1933 S. L. T. 500 (Lord Fleming). See *Grieves* v. *Rawley* (1852), 10 Ha. 63 ; *In re Cozens* [1903], 1 Ch. 138.

[5] *Crook* v. *Whitley* (1857), 26 L. J. (Ch.) 350.

[6] *Still's Trs.* v. *Hall* (1899), 36 S. L. R. 390.

[7] *In re Fish* [1894], 2 Ch. 83.

[8] *Grant* v. *Grant* (1870), L. R. 5 C. P. 727 ; *Sherratt* v. *Montford* (1873), L. R. 8 Ch. 928.

Next-of-Kin.—According to the common law, this term was synonymous with heirs *in mobilibus,* but since the passing of the Intestate Moveable Succession Act (18 & 19 Vic. c. 23), this has ceased to be so. The word " heirs " embraces a wider class than next-of-kin, and this distinction is preserved in the provisions of the statute, because the office of executor is conferred, in the first instance, exclusively on the heirs under the older law. Accordingly, under a bequest to next-of-kin, the heirs at common law are denoted to the exclusion of those whose right to participate in the event of intestacy is created by the statute.[1] Thus it has been decided that a brother of the testator will take the whole subject given by the will to next-of-kin, to the exclusion of the children of a brother who has predeceased the testator.[2] If the term is used with qualifying expressions, the meaning will largely depend on the force of these expressions. A bequest to the " nearest of kin according to law," [3] or to " nearest heirs and next-of-kin whomsoever in accordance with law," [4] has been held not to be equivalent to one to heirs, as the added expressions denoted merely that " next-of-kin " was used in its legal significance. On the other hand, the qualifying expressions may serve to shew that the testator intended to invoke the rules of intestate succession. Thus bequests to " my next-of-kin who would have been entitled to succeed to my moveable estate had I died intestate," [5] and to " my next-of-kin according to the law of moveable succession in Scotland," [6] were construed as denoting the heirs *in mobilibus.* Again, in *Connell* v. *Grierson,*[7] a destination in an entail to the entailer's " nearest of kindred " was held, in view of the nature of the subject and the purposes of the deed, to mean the heir-at-law, so that the great-great-grandson of the entailer's brother was preferred to the granddaughter of his sister.

---

[1] *Gregory's Trs.* v. *Alison* (1889), 16 R. (H. L.) 10 ; *Young's Trs.* v. *Janes* (1880), 8 R. 242 ; *Fulton's Trs.* v. *Fulton* (1901), O. H., 8 S. L. T. 465 ; *Tait's Trs.* v. *Neill* (1903), 6 F. 138. Cf. also *Webster* v. *Shiress* (1878), 6 R. 102 ; *Muir* (1876), 4 R. 74.

[2] *Young's Trs.* v. *Janes, supra.*

[3] *Murray's Factor* v. *Melrose,* 1910 S. C. 924.

[4] *Steedman's Trs.* v. *Steedman,* 1916 S. C. 857.

[5] *Tronsons* v. *Tronsons* (1884), 12 R. 155.

[6] *Rutherford's Trs.* v. *Dickie,* 1907 S. C. 1280.

[7] (1867), 5 M. 379.

In *Young's Trs.* v. *Janes*, Lord President Inglis, and, in *Gregory's Trs.* v. *Alison* Lord Watson, reserved their opinion on the question whether in a gift to next-of-kin the legatees were to be determined in accordance with the rules of intestate succession as to the line and order of preference. In the English case of *Withy* v. *Mangles*,[1] where the bequest was to such persons as should be A.'s next-of-kin at her death and A. died survived by her father, her mother, and a child it was decided that the term had no technical meaning but signified merely those who were nearest in proximity of blood, and that all three, being related in the same degree to A., were included. But this point has been foreclosed in a manner contrary to the English authority, by the decision of the Second Division in *Honeyman's Tr.* v. *Donaldson*. In that case a party by her marriage contract conveyed moveable property to trustees, directing them to make it over on her death to her next-of-kin. Her nearest relations at her death were her mother and a paternal uncle and aunt. The Court were of opinion that the words "next-of-kin" were *voces signatæ* in Scots Law, and meant those to whom the succession was given on intestacy by the common law and that accordingly the mother was not entitled to take under the destination.[3]

Relations.—In the case of a bequest to "relations," the Courts, in order to avoid holding the bequest void from uncertainty, construe the term as designating those who would be entitled to succeed to the intestate succession of the party whose relations are spoken of ;[4] and it would appear from the decisions in *Williamson* v. *Gardiner* and *Cunningham's Trs.* v. *Cunningham*, that these take in the

---

[1] (1843) 10 Cl. & F. 215. See also *Elmsley* v. *Young* (1835), 2 M. & K. 780 ; *Halton* v. *Foster* (1868), L. R. 3 Ch. 505.

[2] (1900), 2 F. 539.

[3] See also to the same effect *Andrew's Trs.* v. *Andrew*, 1918 2 S. L. T. 12 (Lord Hunter). In *Johnston's Trs.* v. *Dewar*, 1911 S. C. 722 (where however the question was merely as to the date at which next-of-kin were to be ascertained) Lord

Kinnear observed : "The mere word 'nearest of kin' to my mind conveys no significance whatever except that of propinquity of blood at whatever time it is necessary to look for the persons who answer the description."

[4] *Williamson* v. *Gardiner* (1865), M. 66 ; *Cunningham's Trs.* v. *Cunningham* (1891), 18 R. 380 ; *Johnston's Tr.* v. *Johnston* (1891), 18 R. 823 ; 20 1 46 . Cf. *Seale Hayne* v. *Jodrell* [1891], A. C. 304.

proportions to which they would be entitled were the distribution of the subject regulated by the rules of intestate succession, so that representatives taking in virtue of the Intestate Moveable Succession Act [1] receive merely that portion which would have fallen to their parent had he survived.[2]

But the terms of the will may show that this construction of the word would defeat the testator's intention. Thus, in *Scott* v. *Scott*,[3] a testator who was survived by a brother-german and his family, the children of a deceased brother-german, and the children of a deceased sister uterine, gave his estate, after the trust purposes had been fulfilled, to his " nearest relations then alive." The trust purposes could not be fulfilled until the death of the brother-german, and accordingly he was not included in the bequest to the nearest relations. In the will a special legacy was given to the sister uterine, she being described simply as the testator's sister, and legacies were also given to her children, who were described as nephews and nieces. In consideration of these features of the deed, it was held that the children of the half-sister were entitled to participate along with the nephews and nieces related to the testator by the full blood. The decision proceeded entirely upon these specialties, and it is intimated in Lord Cranworth's opinion that the words " nearest relations," if not affected by the context, must receive the meaning of heirs *ab intestato*. All the nephews and nieces stood in the same degree of relationship to the testator, and in a subsequent case [4] it was observed that, " had the half blood been nearer by one degree than the full blood, upon the principle of the decision it would have excluded the full blood altogether."

Where a gift is made in the form of a direction to

Where a power of selection is given.

---

[1] 18 & 19 Vic. c. 23.

[2] In the Outer House case of *Stewart's Trs.* v. *Stewart*, 1917, 2 S. L. T. 267, Lord Cullen observed : " I think that the term ' relatives,' used without any aid to its construction afforded by the context of an instrument in which it occurs, would probably fall to be construed as including only those related by blood "; but the decision was that, owing to specialties in the deed, relations by affinity were included.

[3] (1855), 2 Macq. 281.

[4] *Per* Lord Benholme in *Nimmo* v. *Murray's Trs.* (1864), 2 M. 1144. In the case of *Scott* the Lord Ordinary (Rutherfurd) observed : " Nearest relations depends, properly speaking, not upon blood, but upon degree (14 D. 1057).

trustees to select the legatees from among the testator's relations, there is not the same necessity for confining the meaning of the term, and it has been held to include as objects of the power all who were in any way related to him.

In *Brown* [1] a power was given to trustees to divide residue " among my poorest friends and relations," and this phrase was held to comprehend relatives, both on the father's side and the mother's " without distinction of degree." In *M'Cormack* v. *Barber*,[2] a similar power to apportion an estate between " relations " was read as referring to all who could trace any relationship, however remote, to the testator, whether that relationship was on the father's or on the mother's side ; the case being distinguished from one where there was no power of disposal, as also from the case of a gift to " nearest relations."

In a case in the Outer House,[3] " nearest relatives entitled to succeed to my moveable estate " was held to mean heirs *ab intestato*, and not next-of-kin.

Bequest to trustees, tutors, executors.

Trustees, Executors, Tutors.—Where a legacy is given to one who is nominated by the testator as trustee, executor, or tutor, there is a presumption that the legacy is given only in the case of his accepting the office, whether it is or is not stated in the will that the gift is in recompense for his services. Thus, in *Mellis's Trs.* v. *Legge's Exr.*,[4] the testator appointed three persons to be his trustees, and directed them to pay the interest of his estate to his sisters, and on the death of the longest liver of these to divide the residue of his estate among themselves, declaring that if any of " my said trustees " should die before the residue became payable,

Presumption that the legacy is annexed to the office.

their shares should pass to their heirs, executors, and successors. One of the three persons having predeceased the testator, it was held that no portion of the estate was transmitted to his heirs, the Court being of opinion that the

---

[1] (1762), M. 2318. Cf. *Wharrie* (1760), M. 6599 ; *Murray* v. *Fleming* (1729), M. 4075 ; *Snodgrass* (1806), M. " Service," App. No. 1. The cases are reviewed in *Hill* v. *Burns* (1826), 2 W. & S. 80, and *Crichton* v. *Grierson* (1828), 3 W. & S. 329. Cf. also *In re Deakin* [1894], 3 Ch. 565.

[2] (1861), 23 D. 398.

[3] *Thomson's Trs.* v. *Thomson* (1903), 11 S. L. T. 67 (Lord Low).

[4] (1898), 25 R. 954. Cf. *Bryce* v. *Aitken* (1827), 5 S. 817.

legacy was given in consideration of the trustees assuming office, and that the gift-over was to operate only in the case of a legatee becoming a trustee and dying before the period of payment.[1]

The presumption is recognised in English Law.[2] A gift to parties " as executors " is qualified by the condition that they accept office.[3] And in a case [4] where the truster, after appointing A. and B. his executors, provided in a later part of the will legacies to " the said A." and " the said B.," it was held that these legacies lapsed, seeing that A. and B. did not become executors.

But the deed may disclose that the gift was made for personal reasons, in which case the legatee will take the legacy although he does not accept the office to which he was nominated by the truster. Of this kind of case *Henderson* v. *Stuart* [5] would appear to be a clear instance, but for the fact that the decision was pronounced by the narrowest possible majority. The testator requested his trustees to accept " each of them a sum of £500 sterling, as a mark of my friendship for them, and the further sum of £105, as a recompense for their trouble in the management of my affairs, and as a further testimony of my affection for them." One of the persons nominated survived the truster but declined to act. On his death his representatives claimed the legacy of £500, admitting that no further sum was due to them, and the Court by a majority sustained the claim. As the legacy was given, as it expressly bore, from motives of friendship, the divergence of opinion in the case is a striking testimony to the strength of the general presumption.

On the same ground it has been held in England that where the legatee is described by a term of relationship, the legacy is not conditional on his assumption of the office. In *Dix* v. *Reed*,[6] legacies were given to two parties on

---

[1] Lord Trayner dissented.

[2] Sir Richard Arden, M.R., in *Harrison* v. *Rowley* (1798), 4 Ves. 212, said : " Nothing is so clear as that if a legacy is given to a man as executor, whether expressed to be for care and pains or not, he must, in order to entitle himself to the legacy, clothe himself with the character of executor."

[3] *Abbot* v. *Massie* (1796), 3 Ves. 147.

[4] *Calvert* v. *Sebbon* (1841), 4 Beav. 222.

[5] (1825), 4 S. 306 ; 1 Fac. 122. See *Stackpoole* v. *Howell* (1807), 13 Ves. 417.

[6] (1823), 1 Sim. & St. 237.

condition of their becoming executors, and in a later clause of the will there occurred these words, " unto my cousin A. the sum of £50, whom I appoint as joint executor." Here it was found (not without difficulty) that A. took the gift although he refused the executorship, the ground of judgement being that the words of the will afforded an inference that it was given because of the relationship between the testator and A. And so, where a testator bequeathed a sum to his " friend and partner A.," and appointed him one of his executors, it was held that the bequest was A.'s, although he did not become executor.[1]

But the circumstance that the legacies given to a number of trustees differ in amount or in the nature of the subjects given, has been deemed insufficient to displace the presumption that they were given by way of recompense for trouble in the administration of the estate.[2] And in the early Scots case of *Scrimzeour* v. *Wedderburn*,[3] a legacy was considered to be forfeited because the legatee did not accept the office of tutor to the testator's children, to which he was nominated in the will, although he was related to the testator, and although three tutors were appointed, but he alone was given a legacy.

II. Ascertainment of the Objects of the Gift.—When a testator makes a bequest to his own children, little difficulty can arise in regard to the ascertainment of the class, because all the objects of the gift must be in existence at (or shortly after) the time when the will comes into operation ; but in the case of a gift to children of a living person, the question assumes importance, because the number of the class is liable to variation so long as that person remains in life.

" A bequest to the children of a living person may admit of several constructions. It may mean merely the children at the date of the will, or it may mean children at the date of the testator's death, or the distribution or disengagement of the fund ; or it may mean the children born and to be born at any time during the parent's life.

---

[1] *Cockerell* v. *Barber* (1826), 2 Russ. Ch. Cas. 585.

[2] *In re Appleton* (1885), 29 Ch. D. 893.

[3] (1675), M. 6357. See also *Leckie* v. *Renny* (1748), M. 6347.

It will depend on the context and whole frame of the deed which of these meanings is to receive effect in any particular case." [1]

The general rule of construction, however, is that the members of the class are to be fixed not later than the time when the subject of the gift falls to be paid or distributed.[2] This may not be the natural mode of interpreting the term " children " ; but the rule is supported by the consideration that, as the directions in the will as to the distribution of the subject cannot be carried out unless the parties and the shares to be taken by each are determined, the testator must have intended the objects of his gift to be fixed at that time. The rule may of course be set aside by the expression of a contrary intention in the will. Thus the testator may so express himself as to limit the gift to members of the class alive at the date when the will was made, but very special language is required for this purpose ; [3] and, conversely, he may make it clear that he intended that all children born at any time should participate.[4]

The general rule yields the following results when applied to bequests in these forms :—

(a) *When the Gift is to take effect in Possession at the Testator's Death.*—An immediate bequest comprehends those children, and those only, in existence at the testator's death. " When the bequest is to take effect at the death of the testator, and when there have been children at the date of the deed,[5] the fair and reasonable presumption is that those children alone are entitled to take who are able to take when the distribution of the estate is to be made, and the succession opens." [6] Thus, in *Pearson* v. *Corrie*,[7] where the residue of an estate was bequeathed to the lawful heirs

Where payment is immediate.

---

[1] *Per* Lord Neaves in *Biggar's Trs.* v. *Biggar* (1858), 21 D. 4. The rules in English Law as to the ascertainment of the class are summarised in the opinion of Astbury, J., in *In re Chartres* [1927], 1 Ch. 466.

[2] *Wood* v. *Wood* (1861), 23 D. 338 ; *Ross* v. *Dunlop* (1878), 5 R. 833. This rule applies not only in gifts to children, but in gifts to all persons called under a term of relationship, *e.g.* nephews and nieces. The rule is

the same in English Law—*In re Knapp's Settlement* [1895], 1 Ch. 91.

[3] Lord Ivory in *Biggar's Trs.* v. *Biggar, supra.*

[4] Ld. Pres. Inglis in *Ross* v. *Dunlop, supra.*

[5] The meaning of this qualification is not clear.

[6] *Per* Lord Cowan in *Wood* v. *Wood* (1861), 23 D. 338.

[7] (1825), 4 S. 119.

(which was interpreted as *children*) of the testator's sister, it was held that the children alive at the testator's death were entitled to immediate payment, although their mother was still in life.

Some doubt as to this rule of construction was expressed in *Biggar's Trs.* v. *Biggar*.[1] In that case the testator provided that in the event which happened (the predecease of his wife) his estate should go to the children of A., his son, whom failing to A. The Lord President (Colonsay) and Lord Ivory adopted the view of the Lord Ordinary (Neaves), that the children favoured were those alive at the testator's death, and that they were entitled to immediate payment. In addition to the weight of the general rule, they founded on the specialties of the deed, namely, the absence of any direction to the trustees to hold, or to deal with, the interest ; and above all, the conditional institution of the father to his own children, which, if the gift was to all the children he might have, postponed his succession till his own death. Lord Curriehill preferred to leave open the question whether after-born children would share, but decided that caution as security for subsequent claims was not required, and that in any event their claims would resolve into personal actions against the recipients of the fund. Lord Deas was in favour of caution being found.[2]

But this doubt must be considered as removed by *Stopford Blair's Exrs.* v. *Heron Maxwell's Trs.*,[3] where the testator bequeathed sums of money to his daughter's children in these terms : " I bequeath to each of her children by this her present marriage a thousand pounds each." Certain children were born after the testator's death. On the question being raised whether these were comprehended, the Court held that the bequest was confined to the children alive at the testator's death.

A feature of the will which was favourable to the construction adopted in this case was that distinct legacies were given to each of the members of the class. When a testator gives a gross sum which is to be divided among a class, that sum may be set apart and the distribution of

---

[1] (1858), 21 D. 4.
[2] But in *Ross* v. *Dunlop, supra,*

Lord Deas said he had modified his opinion as to caution.
[3] (1872), 10 M. 760.

the general estate may be proceeded with, although the class to which the sum is given is capable of enlargement ; but where distinct legacies are bestowed on each of the members, the total sum to be withdrawn from the general estate for the purpose of the gifts depends upon the number of the legatees. In such cases the distribution of the general estate cannot be completely carried out until the number of the class is fixed ; and so it has been held in England that, in order not to hinder the division of the estate, the members of a class to whom the legacies are given must be ascertained and fixed at the testator's death, and this although the term of payment of the legacies is deferred to a later date.[1]

In this as in other questions regarding the ascertainment of a class of children, a child *in utero* is treated as already born.[2] In England it is settled that, if there are no children in existence at the testator's death, all the children born subsequently will be admitted.[3]

The general rule will be displaced if it appears from the terms of the will that children subsequently born were intended to participate. But it must be clear that the words refer to birth after the testator's death, and not merely to the period elapsing between the date of the will and the testator's death. In *Hayward's Exrs.* v. *Young*,[4] the testator directed that the residue of his funds should be divided " among the children *lawfully begotten, or who shall be lawfully begotten,* of my cousins (naming three), share and share alike, on each of them attaining the age of twenty-one years," and appointed executors. At the testator's death the cousins had children who were all in minority ; after his death another child was born. It was held that this last child was excluded. The considerations which influenced the Court, were, that one division of the fund was intended, and that, as trustees were not appointed, the division was meant to be immediate.

---

[1] *Ringrose* v. *Branham* (1794), 2 Cox 384 ; *Mann* v. *Thompson* (1854), Kay, 638 ; *Rogers* v. *Mutch* (1878), 10 Ch. D. 25. In the last of these cases the bequest was one of £100 to each of the children of M. At the date of the testator's death M. was alive, but had no children. *Held* that any child which M. might thereafter have could not take under the bequest.

[2] *Grant* v. *Fyffe*, 22nd May 1810, F. C. ; see *Elliott* v. *Joicey*, 1935 S. C. (H. L.) 57.

[3] *Weld* v. *Bradbury* (1715), 2 Vern. 705.

[4] (1895), 22 R. 757.

It is difficult to reconcile this decision with the general principles of construction adopted in this branch of the law, because, in the first place, the words " who shall be lawfully begotten " were rendered ineffectual ; and, in the second place, as there was to be no payment till the majority of the first child, there appears to have been no reason compelling the ascertainment of the class prior to that time. The opinions appear to rest the decision on the ground that the bequest must be taken as vesting at the testator's death, whereas in most of the cases the rule has been adopted that the ascertainment of the class is to be governed by the directions as to the payment or distribution of the fund. In English Law all children born before the majority of the eldest would have been admitted.[1]

Where payment is postponed.

(b) *Where the Period of Distribution is postponed.*—Where a gift is made to a liferenter and to a class in fee, the gift vests in the children alive at the testator's death, subject to defeasance *pro tanto* in favour of other children who come into existence before the period of distribution.[2] The principle on which this rule is based is expounded in *Douglas* v. *Douglas*.[3] The estate in that case was given to trustees in trust for the testator's widow in liferent and for his nephews and nieces in fee. In delivering the judgement of the Court, namely, that children predeceasing the liferentrix had acquired vested interests, Lord Curriehill said : " It is true that the provision is in favour of a class, but this means, not that it was in favour of a corporate or aggregate body as a separate person in law, but that an equal *pro indiviso* share of the residue was provided to each individual included in that class ; and the vesting of the right to such a share in each of these individuals at the death of the testator was quite consistent with their number being either diminished by deaths or increased by births before the arrival of the term of payment. In the former of these alternatives, the effect of the death of any one or more of the twenty-one

[1] Jarman on Wills (7th Ed.), p. 1650. *Post*, p. 197.

[2] Cf. Lord Davey in *Hickling's Trs.* v. *Garland's Trs.* (1898), 1 F. (H. L.) 7 ; *Miller* v. *Finlay's Trs.* (1875), 2 R. (H. L.) 1 ; *Corbet's Trs.* v. *Elliott's Trs.* (1906), 8 F. 610 ; and the rule was recognised in the cases of *Scheniman* v. *Wilson* (1828), 6 S. 1019 ; *Shaw* v. *Shaw*, 6 S. 1149 ; and *M'Pherson's Trs.* v. *Hill* (1902), 4 F. 921.

[3] (1864), 2 M. 1008. Stated *post*, 215.

nephews or nieces would only have been that the legal testamentary or conventional succession of each of such defuncts would take his or her $\frac{1}{21}$st share. And in the latter alternative, it might be a question whether any nephew or niece born during the survivance of the widow would have been entitled to share in the residue. But even assuming that he or she would have been entitled to share in the residue at the testator's death, the only effect would be that the shares of the others, although vested in the meantime, would be diminished in amount. The fallacy in the opposite view lies in not distinguishing between suspensive and resolutive conditions."

This principle of construction was sanctioned and applied in the very important case of *Carleton* v. *Thomson*.[1] In this case the testator directed that his estate should be " vested in my said trustees for behoof of my daughter A. . . . in liferent and her children in fee, to be kept in trust for them till they in their discretion shall see proper to settle it in the most safe and secure manner on her and her children ; and in the event of her decease without issue," [2] for others. At the testator's death A. had two children ; subsequently other children were born, who all predeceased her. The question raised in the case was whether these children had acquired a vested interest. The Court decided the question in the affirmative. " The circumstance," said Lord Colonsay, " that some of the members of the favoured class were unborn at the testator's death is no obstacle to the right vesting in each of them as soon as they respectively come into existence, although the amount of the benefit to accrue to each may not then be ascertainable. That is quite settled."

The effect of this decision is, it will be observed, that members of the class in existence at any time between the time of vesting and the time of distribution are entitled, although they may not be alive at either of these times.

The above rule appears to be applicable in all cases where the time of distribution is postponed beyond the time of vesting indicated by the terms of the will.[3] If there is

---

[1] (1867), 5 M. (H. L.) 151 ; L. R. 1 Sc. App. 232.

[2] As to the effect of these words, see *post*, p. 207.

[3] *Hardman* v. *Guthrie* (1828), 6 S. 920 (where a gift to A. and his children to be paid twenty years after the testator's death, was held to vest *a morte*

no child alive at the testator's death, the gift will vest in the child first coming into existence for behoof of himself and of the later born children if there are any such.[1]

The vesting in the class may, however, be suspended if the gift is qualified by a destination-over,[2] or by a clause of survivorship ; [3] or if the objects are described as those alive or surviving at the end of the liferent.[4] The absence of these elements (which are the usual indications of an intention to suspend vesting) leads to the inference that vesting was meant to take place at the testator's death.[5] And the circumstance that the gift appears in the form of a direction to pay to the class at the end of the liferent is *in itself* not sufficient to suspend vesting.[6]

Children born after the time of distribution excluded.

The rule as to the ascertainment of the class has the effect not only of admitting all members of the class coming into existence before the time appointed for the distribution of the fund,[7] but also of excluding *postnati*. Thus, in *Wood* v. *Wood*,[8] the liferent of a fund was given to the testator's wife, and the capital was at her death " to be given to my nephews and nieces—that is, the children of A. and B." It was held that a nephew born after the widow's death was not an object of the bequest, there being no provision for the prolongation of the trust after the widow's death.

The same principle was applied in *Ross* v. *Dunlop*,[9] where the distribution of the fund was postponed till the deaths of certain annuitants. The testator, in this case, instructed his trustees to set apart a large capital to secure two

---

testatoris, subject to defeasance in favour of other children born in that time. The decision was given in accordance with an opinion obtained from English counsel).

[1] *Per* Lord Curriehill in *Carleton* v. *Thomson, supra* ; Ld. Pres. Inglis in *Christie* v. *Wisely* (1874), 1 R. 436 ; Lord M'Laren in *Cunningham* v. *Cunningham* (1889), 17 R. 218 ; *Scott's Trs.* v. *Dunbar* (1900), 2 F. 516 ; Lord Adam in *Steel's Trs.* v. *Steedman* (1902), 5 F. 239.

[2] See Chapter IV., p. 49.

[3] See Chapter IV., p. 45.

[4] See Chapter IV., p. 49.

[5] *Douglas* v. *Douglas, Carleton* v. *Thomson, supra*.

[6] Chapter II., p. 24. *Halbert* v. *Dickson* (1853), 15 D. 609 ; *Home's Trs.* (1891), 18 R. 1138.

[7] As in *Hay Cunningham's Trs.* v. *Blackwell*, 1909 S. C. 219.

[8] (1861), 23 D. 338. See to the same effect *Murray's Tr.* v. *Murray*, 1919 S. C. 552. Cf. *Stewart's Trs.* v. *Stewart* (1868), 7 M. 4 (but the judgement of the Court proceeded on the special terms of the deed, and not on any general principle of construction).

[9] (1878), 5 R. 833.

annuities, and instructed them to divide the residue of his estate, " including the sum set apart to meet the said annuities, at the termination thereof equally " among his nephews and nieces and their descendants, one share being given to the children of A. It was also provided that the provisions in favour of minors were not to vest or be payable till their majorities ; but that the interest should be paid to their guardians. At the death of the truster, A. had eleven children, of whom three were in majority. The residue remaining after the setting-apart of the capital necessary for the annuities was distributed on the testator's death ; thereafter an annuitant died, and the capital of her annuity was then paid over. Subsequently, but before the remaining annuitant died, a child was born to A. It was held that the testator had intended three times of distribution, and that the objects were to be ascertained at these times respectively. Hence A.'s twelfth child was not entitled to participate in the two payments made before his birth ; but he was admitted to share in the capital of the annuity which became payable after his birth. The circumstance that certain shares in the first two sums remained in the hands of the trustees (for behoof of the minor children) at the birth of the twelfth child was considered immaterial. In this case the truster had treated his estate as consisting of three separate portions, and it was in no way improbable that he had intended the objects of the gift to be ascertained at the respective times at which these funds fell in.

This decision was followed in *Potter's Trs.* v. *Allan*.[1] That case was one in which the testator directed his trustees to hold and apply or pay a share of the residue of his estate to, or for behoof of, his daughter and her children, or any of them, in such portions and at such times as the trustees might consider to be for their advantage. There were two children of the daughter at the testator's death, but two others were born before any portion of the residue was distributed. It was held that the objects of the power were not limited to the children alive when the testator died, and that the power might be exercised, in whole or in part, in favour of any of the children of the daughter who might be alive at the date of its exercise.

[1] 1918 S. C. 173.

Where the gift to the children is burdened, not with a liferent, but merely with an annuity, *Buchanan's Trs.* v. *Buchanan* [1] is an authority to the effect that the subsistence of the annuity does not keep open the class.

Thus, in *Davidson's Exrs.* v. *Davidson*,[2] the class was held to be fixed at the death of the testator although the gift was subject to an annuity. The trustees were directed to divide the residue, on the annuitant's death, among the testator's grandchildren " then surviving " ; and this direction was followed by a declaration that the residue was to vest on the testator's death, but that the shares were not to be payable till the respective majorities of the grandchildren, the interest in the meantime being employed for their maintenance. On a consideration of these obscure and inconsistent terms, the Court held that the vesting declaration fixed the recipients as at the testator's death, and that a child born thereafter was excluded. Further, the circumstances that an annuity only was given, and that the surplus income was to be expended on the grandchildren during the annuitant's lifetime, were considered strongly to support the view that the testator intended to benefit only those grandchildren who were alive at his death.

Effect of a fiduciary fee.

It must be observed, however, that, if the subject of the gift is heritage, a direction to trustees to convey it to a person in liferent allenarly, and his or her issue in fee, does not necessarily close the class at the time when the conveyance is to be made. In such cases the parent takes a fiduciary fee, and the Court holds that the creation of this fiduciary right is equivalent to trust management as regards the ascertainment of the class. Thus, in *Simpson* v. *Marshall*,[3] where trustees were directed on the testator's death " to dispone and convey " a heritable subject to his daughter in liferent only and to her issue in fee, it was held that a child born after the death of the testator was comprehended in the class, the Court observing that the rules of

---

[1] Stated *post*, p. 198. This is so in England ; Jarman on Wills (7th Ed.), vol. iii., p. 1645.

[2] (1871), 9 M. 995.

[3] (1900), 2 F. 447. See the opinion

of the Lord Ordinary (Stormonth Darling) in this case. Cf. *Beattie's Trs.* v. *Cooper's Trs.* (1862), 24 D. 519 ; *Robertson* (1869), 7 M. 1114 ; *Douglas* v. *Thomson* (1870), 8 M. 374.

Wood v. *Wood* were not applicable to directions to convey heritage. Similarly, where trustees were instructed " as soon as convenient " after the testator's death to convey residue (of a mixed character) to a person in liferent and to her issue in fee, it was found that all the children born before the end of the liferent were entitled.[1] And this would seem to be the case wherever there exists a fiduciary fee.

(c) *Gifts to Children at a Given Age.*—If in a gift to children the condition is annexed that the members shall attain majority, the subject will vest in the first member attaining majority, subject to defeasance *pro tanto* as the other members reach majority or marriage. Thus, in *Burnett* v. *Burnett*,[2] a party by his marriage contract provided a sum of money to the younger children of the marriage,—namely, £2000 if there was one child, £4000 if there were two, and £6000 if there were three or more,— and he declared that these provisions should be payable at the " first term . . . after the majority or marriage of such children." Seven children survived their father, and all save one attained majority. On a construction of the terms of the deed, it was held that vesting was dependent on the children attaining majority ; that some of the children having reached majority, the class-gift had vested ; and that the share of the child dying in minority accresced to the others. Lord Ivory explained the principle of the decision in these words : " The arrival of each child at majority or marriage fixes directly the time of payment to him, and indirectly the amount which each shall receive if any of the others predecease that term. But, having reached the term at which the provision is to be distributed, it is enough to satisfy the vesting of the provision that any one of the children shall become major ; for, although all the others of the class shall have been taken away, if there had been three at the time of the dissolution of the marriage, the maximum provision of £6000 goes to the class of three ;

Where gift depends on attainment of an age.

---

[1] *Christie* v. *Wisely* (1874), 1 R.436 .
[2] (1854), 16 D. 780. This case is noticed (on the question of accretion) by Lord Colonsay in *Carleton* v. *Thomson* (1867), 5 M. (H. L.) 151 ; L. R. 1 Sc. App. 232, *ante,* p. 193. On the question of the vesting of the gift, see *Alves' Trs.* v. *Grant*, Chapter III., *ante.* Cf. also Lord Rutherfurd's opinion in *Baillie* v. *Seton* (1853), 16 D. 216.

and if two of these shall predecease the term of payment and one reach majority, the sound construction of this deed is that the whole goes to the survivor."

Ascertainment of the class.

Where the testator in making a gift to a class directs that the shares of the members shall be payable as they respectively attain majority or marriage, the selection of the members of the class may be affected by this direction. According to English Law, if each child is entitled to payment of his or her share on his or her majority or marriage, the time for fixing the class is the time when the first child becomes entitled to payment, and children subsequently coming into existence are excluded.[1] This rule was referred to (with approval) in *Buchanan's Trs.* v. *Buchanan.*[2] The circumstances of that case were these : the testator instructed his trustees to pay the interest of a sum of £20,000 to his sister A., and on her death to pay an annuity of £300 to her husband B. " Upon the decease " of A. the trustees were to " hold and apply the said principal sum of £20,000 and the income thereof to and for behoof of all the lawful children of my brother " C., " procreated or to be procreated . . . equally among them, . . . payable the several children's shares to the sons on their attaining twenty-five years, and to the daughters on their attaining that age or being married." There was also a gift-over " in the event of the decease of any one or more of the said children, whether before or after their aunt " A. It was held that vesting took place as the children attained twenty-five after the death of A. A. died survived by her husband B. ; on her death C. had nine children, of whom two had reached the age of twenty-five. In a multiplepoinding raised to determine the rights of the beneficiaries, it was held that vesting was postponed during the lifetime of A. (because the trustees were to hold for the children only after her decease) and until the children reached twenty-five (because of the gift-over) ; that the subsistence of the annuity did not prevent the distribution of the capital, beyond what was required to secure it ; and that each child was entitled to payment of his or her share at twenty-five. " It is unnecessary,"

---

[1] *Gimblet* v. *Purton* (1871), L. R. 12 Eq. 427 ; *Whitbread* v. *Lord St John* (1804), 10 Ves. 152. Jarman on Wills (7th Ed.), p. 1650.

[2] (1877), 4 R. 754.

the Lord Justice-Clerk [1] observed, " for us to decide whether there must be any divestiture and repayment in the event of other children coming into existence. It will be time enough to determine that question when other children are born. But I must say that I am strongly of opinion that no children except those actually in existence at the death of the liferentrix are entitled to participate in this fund." In confirmation of his opinion his Lordship founded on *Wood* v. *Wood* [2] and the rule of English Law. Lord Gifford, with some hesitation, concurred in holding that no part of their shares could be withheld from the children on their respectively attaining twenty-five, but was disposed to avoid deciding absolutely against unborn children. Lord Ormidale, on the other hand, was of opinion that payment should be made to the children only on caution to repeat so much as might be necessary to satisfy the claims of future children if there were any such, a proposition which the majority (the Lord Justice-Clerk and Lord Gifford) rejected as inconsistent with the terms of the testator's directions.

In England, this principle of construction has been the subject of much adverse criticism ; [3] and in *Hope-Johnstone* v. *Sinclair's Trs.*,[4] Lord M'Laren declared that it had not been adopted in our law. But since the date of that case decisions in accordance with the rule have been pronounced in two cases. In *Scott's Trs.* v. *Scott* [5] the Second Division decided that under a bequest in terms similar to those in *Buchanan's Trs.* only those children alive when the eldest child attained majority were entitled to participate, the Lord Justice-Clerk remarking " the only way in which the matter can be worked out is by holding that the class of beneficiaries is to be determined at the time when the first payment comes to be made " ; and in *Howden's Trs.* v. *Macpherson*,[6] Lord Ormidale applied the same " hard rule."

[1] Lord Moncreiff.

[2] *Ante*, p. 194.

[3] See Lord Thurlow's opinion in *Andrews* v. *Partington* (1791), 3 B. C. C. 401. *Watson* v. *Young* (1885), 28 Ch. D. 436. Cf. also *Hoste* v. *Pratt* (1798), 3 Ves. 729. In *In re Emmet's Estate* (1880), 13 Ch. D. 484, Sir George Jessel, M.R., speaks of the rule as one " of convenience, not founded on any view of the testator's intention."

[4] (1904), 7 F. 25. The judgement in *Hayward's Exrs.* v. *Young* (1898), 22 R. 757, *ante*, p. 191, is certainly not favourable to the extension of the principle. Cf. also *Mackinnon's Trs.* v. *M'Neill* (1897), 24 R. 981, stated *ante*, p. 41.

[5] 1909 S. C. 773.

[6] 1911 2 S. L. T. 308.

As the rule is based on the necessity for ascertaining the respective shares of the beneficiaries at the time when the trustees are required to make the first payment, there is, in any case, no ground for its application if the trustees are not directed to pay the shares on the respective majorities of the members of the class. Thus, in *Hope Johnstone* v. *Sinclair's Trs.*,[1] a testatrix directed her trustees to hold part of her estate for her nephew's wife, who was to receive one-third of the income thereof, and, subject to the trust in her favour, for all the children of the nephew, who, being sons, should attain majority, or, being daughters, should attain that age or be married. There were at the date of the case six children of the nephew, of whom three were major. The nephew and his wife were alive, and the latter agreed to restrict her *nexus* on the fund to one-third thereof. The three major children sought to have it declared that one-sixth of the fund had vested in each of them. But the Court dismissed the action, the main ground of the decision being that, as the trustees were merely instructed to hold the subject for the children, no direction as to payment being given, it could not be held that children born thereafter would be excluded.

Further, there is no occasion for limiting the class at the majority of the eldest if payment is otherwise deferred till a subsequent time. Hence it is held in England, that if a bequest be made to A. for life, and after her death to the children of B., payable at twenty-one, the period for fixing the class is the later of these two events : that is to say, if the eldest child attains twenty-one during A.'s life, all the children born in A.'s lifetime are included ; and if A. die and no child is major, all children born before the first child reaches twenty-one are admitted.[2]

Bequest on majority of youngest of class.

(*d*) *Gifts to Children on the Majority of the Youngest.*— The term " youngest " refers to the period of distribution, and not to the testator's death. In such gifts all children whenever born are admitted. Thus in *Scheniman* v. *Wilson* [3]

---

[1] (1904), 7 F. 25.

[2] *In re Emmet's Estate* (1880), 13 Ch. D. 484.

[3] (1828), 6 S. 1019. Observe that there was here a direction to pay subject to the liferent, an element which might be considered as favourable to the argument which was rejected. The rule is the same in England, *vide Mainwaring* v. *Beevor* (1849), 8 Hare, 44.

a testator bequeathed his estate to his children in liferent and to their issue in fee, payable " on the majority of the youngest child of any of my said children . . . subject always to the liferent of their parents." The children of a daughter sought payment of the portion due to that family. All these children were in majority, and it was argued on their behalf that the provision as to the majority of the youngest was satisfied when all the children in existence at any time were major ; but the Court rejected this argument, and permitted payment only on condition that caution should be found by these children for repetition in the event of other children being born.

The rules of construction to be applied to gifts in this form, where the condition as to the majority of the youngest cannot be fulfilled, owing either to the circumstance that only one child survives the testator, or to the accident of the youngest child dying in minority, have been noticed in a previous chapter.[1]

(e) *Where Members of the Class are dead at the date of the Will.*—A question which has been raised in several cases is, whether, under a gift to a class, members who are dead at the date when the will is made are included as objects of the gift. This question may arise where a fund or subject is given to the members called by a class description in liferent and to their issue in fee, or where the gift is made with a provision calling issue in the event of any of the members predeceasing, in which cases the right of issue of a member dead at the date of the making of the will will depend on the construction to be put on the gift to the class.

In *Sturrock* v. *Binny*,[2] the testator declared that the residue of his estate should belong equally to all his nephews and nieces in liferent and to their children in fee ; and provided that " in case any of my said nephews or nieces shall have predeceased me leaving children," the children were to have right to a share in the same way as if their parent had survived him ; and if any nephew or niece died after him without issue, his or her share was to pass to the survivors. When the testator made his will, there were alive issue of a niece, who had died more than twenty years before

Where members of class dead at date of will.

---

[1] See Chapter IV., *ante*, p. 89.   [2] (1843), 6 D. 117. See also *Wishart* v. *Grant* (1763), M. 2310.

its date ; and a special legacy was given to those children. They sought to participate also in the residue, but the Court repelled their claim. The decision was based on various grounds. At the outset of his opinion the Lord Justice-Clerk (Hope) distinguished the case from one in which the objects of the bequest were children of the testator, for in that case the bequest was considered to be made by the parent in discharge of his natural duty and hence it received the most extended construction.[1] Further, under the terms of the deed, the fee was destined to the children of life-renters, and there could be no liferent contemplated in the case of a niece who was dead at the date of the deed ; and, finally, the fact that a special legacy was given to the children of the deceased niece and the terms of the destination-over to the children of predeceasing nephews and nieces were held to be against the inclusion of the niece's children. The destination-over, prefaced as it was by the words " in case " was considered to refer to a contingency which might or might not occur after the date of the deed. The decision was a narrow one for the interlocutor of the Lord Ordinary (Cunninghame) was reversed, and Lord Moncreiff dissented from the opinions of the other members of the Court (the Lord Justice-Clerk and Lord Cockburn).

It was, however, followed in *Stewart's Trs.* v. *Walker*,[2] where the gift was to the truster's own children. By his will the testator directed his trustees to hold his estate for behoof of all his lawful children equally in liferent and for their respective issue *per stirpes* in fee, and in case any of his children should die leaving issue, his or her share should belong to the issue, and if any died without issue the share was given over to the survivors. At the date of the will there were three children alive and the daughter of a deceased child. This daughter, to whom a specific legacy was given, was held, on grounds very similar to those founded on in *Sturrock* v. *Binny*, not to be entitled to participate in the residuary bequest.

---

[1] See to the same effect Lord Cowan's opinion in *Rhind's Trs.* v. *Leith* (1866), 5 M. 104.

[2] (1905), 12 S. L. T. 801 (Second Division). For the rule in England see Jarman on Wills (7th Ed.), Vol. II., p. 1308 *et seq.* ; *In re Walker* [1930], 1 Ch. 469.

In *Rhind's Trs.* v. *Leith* [1]—where the question was as to the application of the *conditio si institutus sine liberis decesserit*—Lord Cowan observed : " The established rule of law is, that a legacy lapses by the predecease of the legatee when children are not called to the succession ; but where a legacy is bequeathed to a class, and not *nominatim*, only those falling within the description can be held included who are in existence when the legacy is bestowed. When a legacy is given to the children of A. B., the natural meaning of the term is children then in existence. They alone can take as legatees under the general description. A legacy to a person who is dead at the date it was bestowed can have no legal effect given to it. And, on the same principle, one of a class who has previously died cannot take any legal interest under a legacy to the class. There can be no distinction in this respect between a *nominatim* and a class legatee. And as little can the issue of such a party claim the share their parent if alive would have received, unless there be words in the settlement conferring such an interest, or room *ex presumpta voluntate testatoris* for holding such right and interest to have been conferred. . . . There must be a legatee instituted in the first instance, otherwise there can be no conditional institute either under the express terms of the deed or under the implied condition." [2]

The foregoing cases were reviewed and distinguished in *Baird's Trs.* v. *Crombie.* [3] The bequest in this case was made by the testatrix to " all my brothers and sisters, and in the event of any of my brothers or sisters predeceasing me leaving lawful issue, such issue shall be entitled equally among them to the share to which their parent would have been entitled, if in life, and, in the event of any of my brothers and sisters predeceasing me without leaving lawful issue, the share of such deceaser " was to fall to the sur-vivors and the issue of predeceasers. When the settlement was executed three brothers and sisters were, to the know-ledge of the testatrix, dead and had left issue ; others survived her. The issue of the three brothers and sisters were held to be entitled to shares of the bequest. It was pointed out that from the terms of the deed it appeared

---

[1] (1866), 5 M. 104.
[2] See Chapter XVII.
[3] 1926 S. C. 518.   The Lord Justice-Clerk dissented.

that the intention of the testatrix was to make a stirpital division of her estate as at the date of her death among her brothers and sisters and their issue, each *stirps* receiving an equal share. The bequest to the children was a direct and independent one irrespective altogether of whether the death of the parent occurred before or after the date of the settlement ; and the only difficulty felt as to the construction of the deed was due to the earlier decisions.

It is made clear by this case that there is no hard and fast rule excluding the issue of beneficiaries who are dead at the date of the will, but that in each case the question is to be determined in the light of the language used by the testator.

On the other hand, it is a settled rule that the *conditio si institutus sine liberis decesserit* cannot be invoked in favour of the issue of children dead at the date of the will.

(f) Where the Class is enumerated in the Will.—If a testator makes a gift to a class stating the number of the members, and that number corresponds with the actual number in existence at the date of the will, those members form the whole class of beneficiaries. The testator has afforded the means of selecting the objects of the gift, and there is no need to resort to the rules of law as to the ascertainment of the class.

This was assumed in *Millar's Trs.* v. *Rattray*,[1] where, however, the mode of expression led to the statement of the number of the class being disregarded. There the testatrix made a bequest to " the children of my said brother A., of whom there are ten," with a provision that if any died before payment his or her share should go to his or her issue, whom failing to the survivors. A. had at the date of the will ten children. Three were afterwards born in the lifetime of the testatrix. It was held that the thirteen were entitled to participate, because, although the number was correctly stated, yet the form of expression showed that it was intended to be demonstrative and not limitative. The Court in this case observed that there was such

Bequest to enumerated class.

---

[1] (1891), 18 R. 989. See also *In re Emery's Estate* (1876), 3 Ch. D. 300. In this case the gift was to three children, and, there being three alive at the date of the will, another child then *in utero* was held not to be entitled to participate.

improbability that a testator, in making a gift in general terms to a class, should intend to confine the benefit to those members alive at the date of the will, that in order so to limit the objects of the gift the Court must find clear evidence or a clear implication to that effect.

But where the number stated does not correspond with the actual number at the time when the will was made, a difficult question arises. In these cases the general principle on which the Court proceeds is that all the members are to be admitted rather than that the gift should fail on the ground of uncertainty. The rule was thus expressed by Lord Lindley in *In re Stephenson* :[1] " If the Court comes to the conclusion from a study of the will that the testator's real intention was to benefit the whole of a class, the Court should not and will not defeat that intention because the testator has made a mistake in the number he has attributed to that class. The Court rejects an inaccurate enumeration."

The cases on this point in Scotland are not numerous. In *Maclehose* v. *Bogles*,[2] the rubric bears that " a bequest of a sum certain (£400) to each of the daughters of a marriage, being stated as amounting in all to a sum (£1200), which implied that there were only three, and there being in reality four, it was found that each of them was entitled to the full amount legated." This case does not raise the question altogether purely, for the total sum appeared in the margin, and the Court in its decision invoked the principle that clear words of gift occurring in the will were not to be defeated by a marginal marking. Under the decision the residuary legatee was deprived of a larger sum than would have been the case had the summation governed the amount. This necessarily results from the general rule where specific legacies are given and where the actual number exceeds that specified, but this is not a reason for excluding its application.[3]

In *Bryce's Trs.*[4] a sum of £2000 was given to " each of the other three children of A." A. had four children besides

---

[1] [1897], 1 Ch. 75.
[2] 28 Feb. 1815, F. C. ; Hume's Decs. 274.
[3] See *Daniell* v. *Daniell* (1849), 3 De G. & Sm. 337.
[4] (1878), 5 R. 722. This is in accordance with the English authori-ties. In *Garvey* v. *Hibbert* (1812), 19 Ves. 125, a legacy of £600 was be-queathed to each of the three children of D. At the date of the will D. had four children and all four were held entitled to legacies ; and see also *In re Bassett's Estate* (1872) L. R. 14 Eq. 54.

the excepted child, and all four were held entitled to a legacy of that amount.

According to the English authorities where the Court finds a dominant intention by the testator to benefit persons who answer a particular description or class, coupled with a mistake in the enumeration of the persons answering the description or composing the class, the inaccurate enumeration is rejected, whether the actual number in existence at the date of the deed is less or more than that specified in the will. Thus, where the testator directed that the residue of his estate should be divided among five legatees and the six children now living of the late O., and at the date of the will five of these children were dead, it was held that the surviving child took the whole sum bequeathed to O.'s children.[1] On the other hand, in *In re Groom* [2] the number specified was less than the true number, a sum of £4000 being bequeathed to the two children of W., whereas there were four children alive at the date of the deed, and it was held that the sum was divisible among the four children.

The rule rejecting the enumeration of the beneficiaries is applied as the best means of carrying out the testator's apparent intention, and in order to save the gift. When the testator affords a means of determining which of the members he intended to benefit by adding some description or in any other way, and the Court finds that the number falling within that description corresponds with that given in the will, it will carry out the testator's intention and give the subject of the gift to those members. In an English case, the objects of the bequest were described as the two children of A. living at X.; A. had three children, but only two resided at X.; and the Court held that these two alone were entitled under the bequest.[3] So also, where, in addition to the enumeration, the beneficiaries were named, the bequest being in favour of the testator's three children by his first wife, namely, A., B., and C., and C. was dead (but the testator believed him to be alive) it was held that the bequest to C. lapsed.[4]

[1] *In re Sharp* [1908], 2 Ch. 190.
[2] [1897], 2 Ch. 407.
[3] *Wrightson* v. *Calvert* (1860), 1 J. & H. 250.

[4] *In re Whiston* [1924], 1 Ch. 122; *Campbell's Trs.* v. *Berry*, 1921 2 S. L. T. 199 (Lord Blackburn).

It is a question which has apparently not been decided Whether only the members alive at the date of the will take. either in England or in Scotland, whether, when the class is wrongly enumerated, the Court departs from the enumeration to the extent of admitting all the children who would take were no number given, or only to the extent of admitting the members alive at the time when the will was made.[1] In *Millar's Trs.* v. *Rattray*,[2] Lord M'Laren expressed the opinion that only those alive at the date of the will would be included. The reason to be advanced for this construction would seem to be that where a testator gives a number, whether correct or erroneous, he must at least have had in view a class then capable of enumeration.

III. Gifts-over in Case of Death without Issue or Death without leaving Issue.

The words " die without issue " " Die without issue." may mean " die without *having had* issue, or die without *leaving children surviving*," but it is settled that *primâ facie* they bear the first of these meanings.[3] On this construction the effect of the words on vesting is clearly distinguishable from that of destinations-over which, as in *Young* v. *Robertson*,[4] are designed to regulate the rights of the objects *inter se*, or of destinations-over which, as in *Bryson's Trs.* v. *Clark*,[5] are annexed to gifts to named legatees, and can therefore refer to no other event than the legatee's predecease of a given period. Accordingly, where trustees are directed to hold a subject for A. in liferent and for his issue, and in case of his death without issue for other parties in fee, the subject will vest, and the gift-over will be defeated, whenever a child comes into existence.[6]

And the same meaning attaches to the words " failing " Failing issue." issue." Thus, in *Cunningham* v. *Cunningham*,[7] where the testator, after distributing his estate among his children, directed his trustees to hold the shares of daughters for

---

[1] Theobald on Wills (8th Ed.), 331.

[2] (1891), 18 R. 989, *supra*. See Hawkins on the Interpretation of Wills (3rd Ed.), p. 79 (cited with approval by Jessel, M.R., in *Newman* v. *Piercey* (1876), 4 Ch. D. 41), to the same effect.

[3] *Carleton* v. *Thomson* (1867), 5 M. (H. L.) 151 ; L. R. 1 Sc. App. 232, stated *ante*, p. 193 ; *Steel's Trs.* v.

Steedman (1902), 5 F. 239 ; *Johnston* v. *Johnston* (1868), 7 M. 109. Cf. *Robertson* v. *Richardson* (1843), 5 D. 1117.

[4] *Ante*, p. 46.

[5] *Ante*, p. 50.

[6] *Carleton* v. *Thomson*, *supra*.

[7] (1889), 17 R. 218 ; see also *Scott's Trs.* v. *Brown & Co.* (1882), 9 R. 798, *per* Ld. Pres. Inglis, at 801.

them in liferent, " the principal sum or share itself after
their death to be divided . . . among the deceaser's lawful
issue, and failing issue " to the testator's surviving children,
it was held that the case fell within the principle of *Carleton*
v. *Thomson*, and that the children of daughters took vested
interests as they were born. The construction, it will be
observed, was not altered by the circumstance that the only
gift was contained in a direction to the trustees to pay to
the children on their mother's death. In this case Lord
Adam (speaking of the words " failing issue ") said : " No
one disputes that the words are capable of two meanings.
They may mean ' without having issue surviving ' or
' without having had issue.' In the first case it rather
appears that vesting might be postponed. In the second
case there is vesting *a morte testatoris* in the children as a
class ; and I think the case of *Carleton* v. *Thomson*, etc.,
settled that unless something is to be found in the deed
leading to a contrary inference, the latter is the proper
interpretation to be put upon the words."

Influence of
the context. But while " failing issue " and " without issue " are, in
their primary sense, equivalent, the former phrase, it is
thought, points less distinctly than the latter to the non-
existence of issue as the condition of the destination-over
taking effect, and it may more easily be construed, under
the influence of its context, as providing also for the case of
issue coming into existence, but predeceasing their parent.
In a case [1] which arose before the date of *Carleton* v. *Thomson*,
the latter sense was attributed to the phrase. In that case
trustees were instructed to settle a portion of the truster's
estate on his daughter A. and her husband in liferent only,
and to hold it " in fee as trustees for the children of the
said A. of her present or any subsequent marriage equally
among them, and failing of children, to and for behoof of
the said A.'s other heirs or assignees," and the House of
Lords agreed with the Court of Session in holding that the
vesting of the children's right was postponed until the
termination of the liferent. Of A.'s four children two predeceased leaving issue, and two without issue. The decision
was that the issue of the children took the whole subject
under the *conditio*, to the exclusion of assignees of the

[1] *Thomson* v. *Scougalls* (1835), 2 S. & M'L. 305 ; 8 S. J. 102.

children. The reports do not disclose at all clearly the grounds on which this decision went, but it seems to have been based on the special features of the will.[1] One element of the case was that A. had children at the date when the will was made, and therefore it could not be supposed that the testator had any other intention than to provide for the case of the children dying before some period, and that period was, in accordance with the authorities, the time of payment. On this construction the vesting would necessarily be suspended. This peculiarity of the case probably distinguishes the decision from the decisions in *Carleton* v. *Thomson* and *Cunningham* v. *Cunningham* ; but if it is not so distinguished it is inconsistent with, and therefore overruled by, these cases.

As a further example of the primary sense being displaced by the context, the case of *Normand's Trs.* v. *Normand* [2] may be cited. In that case trustees were directed to pay at the termination of a liferent to the liferenter's issue, whom failing to his assignees. The gift-over to the liferenter's assignees was held to indicate that by failure of issue was meant failure not at the testator's death (at which time the liferenter could not know that he had anything to assign), but at the liferenter's death, and the objects of the gift were accordingly held to be the issue who survived the parent.

Again, in *Scott's Trs.* v. *Dunbar*,[3] the testator instructed his trustees to settle a sum on A. in liferent and his children in fee, " and failing the said A. and his children " the capital was to revert to the testator's next-of-kin. As the leading direction to settle the fund was to be carried out at the testator's death, the Court held without difficulty that the destination-over referred to that event. Hence children then alive acquired a vested right although they predeceased their parent. It was pointed out in Lord Adam's opinion, that the result might have been otherwise had the gift to the children depended on a direction to trustees to pay to them at the expiry of the liferent. Had the direction taken the form of a direction to the trustees to settle on A. in liferent and his children equally in fee, whom failing, etc., Lord Adam thought that vesting would still have been

Form of the gift.

---

[1] See the Jurist Report.
[2] (1900), 2 F. 726.
[3] (1900), 2 F. 516.

immediate ; but on this point Lord M'Laren reserved his opinion.

Where the subject of the gift is heritage (or where trustees are directed to invest the funds in heritage), the words " failing issue " (following a gift to issue) are presumed to import a substitution, and not merely a conditional institution.[1]

Failing Heirs of my Body.—This term, it has been said, is to be understood as primarily meaning failure at the death of the testator, for it is only at that time that the heirs can be ascertained. It may possibly refer to another time, as, for example, if it appears that the testator has used the term as meaning simply issue or children ; " but in the ordinary case, when, after a direction to hold for behoof of children, and still more, if to hold for children in fee, there is introduced another purpose by the term ' and failing heirs of my body,' that expression is construed to be failure at the death of the truster." [2]

Die without leaving Issue.—If a gift be made to the issue of A. with a gift-over in the event of his dying without leaving issue, it is clear that the point of time referred to is the death of A.[3] The destination-over will be defeated only in the event of the existence of issue at A.'s death ; and as it remains operative in the meantime, the class-gift (in favour of issue) is affected by the contingency. Thus, in *Halliday* v. *M'Callum*,[4] heritage was disponed by a *mortis causâ* deed under burden of a sum of £500 in favour of the children of the testator's daughter. There was a destination-over " if my said daughter shall die without leaving any living child." The daughter had two children ; but, as these predeceased her, it was decided that the bequest had not vested in them.

But the circumstance that it cannot be ascertained till A.'s death whether the gift will take effect in favour of the issue, does not necessarily confine the gift to the issue then in existence, to the exclusion of children who have

[1] *Brown's Trs.* v. *Smith* (1900), 2 F. 817.

[2] L. J.-C. Hope in *Robson* v. *Shirreff* (1853), 15 D. 297.

[3] *Hickling's Trs.* v. *Garland's Trs.* (1898), 1 F. (H. L.) 7.

[4] (1867), 8 M. 112 ; and cf. *Paul* v. *Warrand* (1896), 3 S. L. T. 251 (Lord Moncreiff).

predeceased.[1]   The case of *Hickling's Trs.* v. *Garland's Trs.*[2] is the authority on this point.   In this case the testator directed his trustees to hold a sum of money for his daughters in liferent, and " on the death of my said daughters respectively, *leaving lawful issue*, I hereby direct my trustees to divide equally amongst the issue of each of my said daughters " the sum liferented by their parent.   One of the daughters had (at the testator's death) four children.   Two of these children predeceased their mother, and two survived her.   It was not disputed that as the mother was survived by the children the class-gift had vested.   The only point in controversy was whether the two predeceasing children had acquired vested rights.   On the authority of certain English cases, the House of Lords (reversing the Court of Session's decision) decided that these children were included in the class.   Lord Shand said : " Another principle which it is of importance to bear in mind in the determination of this case is, that although the bequest may be dependent on a contingency, this will not necessarily prevent the vesting.   The time at which the contingency happens in a bequest to a class does not determine the vesting in the individuals composing the class.   If the contingency should apply to the individual and relate to his capacity to take, as, for example, a bequest left subject to the condition that the legatee should attain the age of twenty-one years, there can be no vesting till he or she shall reach that age ; but where the contingency applies to a class, and not as a condition of the capacity of the legatee to take, the contingency

---

[1] Prior to *Hickling's Trs.* v. *Garland's Trs.*, *infra*, the law appears to have been that a gift-over of this nature limited the gift to children alive at the death of the party spoken of.   Thus, in *Robertson* v. *Houston* (1858), 20 D. 989, a testatrix directed her trustees to hold certain shares of her estate for her daughters in liferent and for their children in fee ; and declared that it should be " in the power of such of my daughters *as may not leave children* . . . to bequeath or settle and dispone *mortis causa* the provisions . . . to any persons they may think fit."   One daughter had four children, of whom one predeceased her.   It was held that no share had vested in this predeceasing child.   The implication of the clause was considered to be that, as a full power of disposal was conferred if issue did not survive the daughter, the primary gift was confined to children who should survive ; and the gift to the class was to " derive its whole operative qualities from the event of survivorship."   But this reasoning appears to be inconsistent with *Hickling's Trs.* v. *Garland's Trs.*

[2] (1898), 1 F. (H. L.) 7.

is not to be imported into the constitution of the trust so as to suspend vesting till the death of the liferenter." And Lord Davey remarked : " I think it is equally clear that when the gift is made to depend on the happening of a contingency, that contingency is not imported by implication into the description of the class so as to confine the gift to those members of the class who survive the contingency." Lord Watson and Lord Herschell dissented from the decision.

If, however, in the case of a gift dependent on a party leaving issue, the objects are described as *such* issue (*e.g.* on the death of A. leaving issue I direct my trustees to divide . . . . among *such* issue),[1] or as the issue alive at the death of the parent,[2] the gift will be confined to the members of the class surviving the parent. In these cases the testator has by his language introduced the contingency into the composition of the class.

The decision in *Hickling's Trs.* has not been received with much favour in the Scottish Courts, and there is no disposition to extend it to cases which do not come directly within its authority. Thus, it has been decided more than once [3] that it does not apply to cases in which there is a destination-over in the event of the liferenter dying without leaving issue. In *Graham's Trs.* v. *Lang's Trs.*[4] trustees were directed to retain a share of residue for the purpose of paying the income to a daughter and of conveying the capital on her death to her issue in such shares as she might appoint ; and, if she died without leaving issue, the capital was to be conveyed to the testator's other surviving children. On the daughter's death survived by children, it was held that the surviving children were alone entitled to the capital to the exclusion of a predeceasing child.[5] It was pointed out that there was no destination-over in *Hickling's Trs.*, and the presence of a destination-over in this case was held to

[1] See *Crichton's Trs.* v. *Bell* (1900), O. H., 8 S. L. T. 177 (Lord Kincairney).

[2] See opinions in *Hickling's Trs.* v. *Garland's Trs.*, *supra*.

[3] *Binnie's Trs.* v. *Prendergast*, 1910 S. C. 735 ; *Graham's Trs.* v. *Lang's Trs.*, 1916 S. C. 723 ; *Craik's Trs.* v. *Anderson*, 1932 S. C. 61.

[4] *Supra*.

[5] The predeceasing children left issue and it was held that the issue took under the *Conditio*. It may be noted that the admission of the *Conditio* tempers to some extent what might be regarded as the hardship of excluding predeceasing children from participation in the bequest.

postpone vesting in the individuals composing the class until the termination of the parent's liferent. In a later case,[1] in which this decision was followed, Lord Hunter, delivering the opinion of the Court, observed : " The case "—*Hickling's Trs.*—" is an illustration of the view—of which more examples are to be found in English cases than in Scottish cases—that there is no rule that, where there is a gift to a class upon a contingent event, the time of the happening of the contingency determines the individuals composing the class. In other words, vesting may take place in a class subject to a resolutive clause in the event of no member of the class surviving a specified date. This, however, does not constitute a contingency personal to each member of the class, so that if the condition is satisfied by the survivance of one member of the class, predeceasing members are entitled to participate. In *Hickling's* case, however, there was no destination-over such as is to be found in the present case. I think the presence of the words giving the interest of a daughter dying without leaving lawful issue to the surviving members of the family effectively prevents the application of the doctrine applied in *Hickling's* case. In such circumstances it appears impossible to hold that vesting took place at a date prior to the expiry of the liferent, at which date alone the ascertainment of the class can be made." [2]

There would indeed be a certain theoretical difficulty in holding a destination-over to be not inconsistent with the application of the doctrine. Assume that the bequest is made in the simple form of a direction to trustees to hold a sum for A. in liferent and for her children in fee, and, if she does not leave children, for X. If there is applied to this bequest the doctrine of *Taylor* v. *Gilbert's Trs.*,[3] the result is that there is vesting in X. *a morte testatoris* subject to defeasance if A. is survived by children. On the other hand, the result under *Hickling's Trs.* is that there is vesting in the children at birth subject to defeasance in the same

---

[1] *Craik's Trs.* v. *Anderson, supra.*

[2] In Theobald on Wills (8th Ed., p. 665) the author, after citing *Hickling's* and other similar cases, adds : " There may, however, be indications of intention, such as a gift-over if A. dies without children living at his death, which may lead to the conclusion that only members of the class living when the event happens are to take."

[3] 5 R. (H. L.) 217, *ante,* p. 130.

event. The doctrines of the two cases thus come into conflict, for there cannot be vesting at one and the same time in two persons. But, while this theoretical difficulty exists, it causes no embarrassment in the practical working out of the bequest, for the final determination of the rights of the parties must await the termination of the liferent and at that date the facts on which the construction of the bequest depends have been ascertained.

Another instance in which the gift has been held to be limited to the children who survive the liferenter is where the provision as to his leaving issue appears in conjunction with a personal condition. Thus, in *Wilson's Trs.* v. *Wilson*,[1] the trustees were directed to hold a residue for the testator's children in liferent and " for behoof of the issue . . . in fee ; . . . and failing any of my said children by decease without leaving issue who may attain to the age of majority or be married," then for the surviving children and their issue. One of the testator's children died survived by three children who attained majority, and predeceased by two who had also attained majority. It was decided that the representatives of the predeceasing children had no claim to participate in the bequest, and that the surviving three children took the whole. But it is somewhat difficult to reconcile this decision with the principle established in *Taylor* v. *Gilbert's Trs.*,[2] where a gift to a class of children on their majorities and subject to a contingency was held to vest in the children when they reached majority, although it remained uncertain whether the contingency would or would not occur.[3]

Implication in favour of issue.

In *Douglas* v. *Douglas* [4] the Court was called on to consider the implication of the words " decease without lawful issue " where there was no prior gift to the issue. In that

[1] (1901), 3 F. 967. Cf. *Neill's Trs.* v. *Neill* (1902), 4 F. 636.

[2] (1881), 5 R. (H. L.) 217 ; 3 App. Cas. 1287, *ante*, p. 130.

[3] In England the doctrine of *Hickling's* case is applied in circumstances in which it has not as yet been admitted in Scotland—see *In re Walker* [1917], 1 Ch. 38 and *In re Stephens* [1927], 1 Ch. 1. In the former case Younger, J. (Lord Blanesburgh) said : " There

are many cases in which the Courts have struggled against what may be called the orthodox construction," *i.e.* the construction in *Hickling's* case " in order to give effect to what may be presumed to have been the real intention of the testator, namely, that only children living at the death of the tenant for life are to take."

[4] (1843), 6 D. 318, *ante*, p. 14.

case the testatrix directed her trustees to pay the interest of a sum of £300 to her son, and " in the event of his decease without lawful issue " the trustees were to pay the capital to his reputed daughter and to the testatrix's next-of-kin. The son died (after the testatrix) survived by a lawful child. It was held that by implication the lawful child was entitled to the whole gift.

IV. Provision that the Child succeeding to other Property shall not participate in the Class-Gift.—A clause of this nature came under the consideration of the Court in the leading case of *Douglas* v. *Douglas*, which has been referred to above.[1] In this case the testator gave to his widow one-third of the residue of his estate in fee and the liferent of the other two-thirds and of his property of X. On her death he directed his trustees to deliver the two-thirds of the residue to his nephews and nieces, the children of his brother and three sisters and their heirs, executors, and successors with the exception of the person who should succeed to the estate of X. He also directed his trustees to convey that estate on the death of his widow to the eldest son, whom failing to another son, of his brother, whom failing to others, whom failing to the eldest daughter of his brother. The widow survived the testator, and during her life some of the nephews and nieces died. The Lord Ordinary held that this clause providing for the exclusion of the person taking X. operated to suspend vesting until the end of the liferent, but the First Division reversed his judgement. It was held that, even assuming that the vesting of the estate of X. was delayed till the widow's death, this did not suspend the vesting of the two-thirds of the residue in the nephews and nieces, but operated merely as a resolutive condition, affecting the rights of the parties *inter se* and the amount of the fund to be taken by each child.

Does not suspend vesting.

This decision was followed in *Johnston* v. *Johnston*,[2] and

---

[1] (1864), 2 M. 1008, *ante*, p. 192. See also as to such clauses, *Ewing* v. *Ewing's Trs.* (1860), 22 D. (H. L.) 5 ; 32 S. J. 344 (better report) ; *Dickson* v. *Dickson* (1854), 1 Macq. 729 ; *Erskine* (1850), 12 D. 649 ; and *Bell's Trs.* v. *Bell*, 1916 2 S. L. T. 250 (Lord Hunter).

[2] (1868), 7 M. 109. And cf. Lord Rutherfurd's opinion in *Baillie* v. *Seton* (1853), 16 D. 216, where he held (1) that a power of apportionment, (2) a clause of forfeiture, and (3) a provision for children of another marriage, did not prevent vesting.

in *Robertson*.[1] In the latter case, Mrs Robertson by her marriage contract conveyed her estate to her husband in liferent and to her children in fee, excepting the eldest or other child " in the event only of his or her happening to succeed, exclusively of the other children, to any estate in right of his or her father." Mrs Robertson died, survived by her husband and four children. The eldest son A. predeceased the father, and the next son B. succeeded to an estate on his father's death. It was decided that A. took an interest on his mother's death, subject to defeasance in an event which had not happened, and that therefore his share went to his representatives ; and that B. was excluded.

But the general rule suggested in these cases was adversely criticised by Lord President Inglis in *Morin's Trs*.[2] Here the trustees were instructed to divide the residue on the death of the survivor of the truster's widow and his son, and on the majority of the youngest of the son's children. A heritable property (Allanton) was to be settled on the eldest of these children at the same time, and the residue was to be paid to these children, or their issue ; and it was declared that at the final division the party acquiring right to the heritage should not be entitled to a share with the other children in the residue. The youngest child attained majority and survived the widow, but died before her father., She therefore, it was held, had no vested interest, because vesting was postponed till the occurrence of all three events. There were various elements which led to this result, but that to which most importance was attached was the clause of forfeiture. Lord President Inglis said : " As it remained uncertain whether a share should go to one child or another, that indicates very strongly that no right could vest in any of them, for it might be that at the period of division any one might be found to have succeeded to the estate of Allanton. This is a circumstance of great importance, and its importance is not diminished by the case of *Welwood's Trs*.,[3] or even the earlier case of *Douglas* v. *Douglas*.

---

[1] (1869), 7 M. 1114, referred to by Ld. Pres. Inglis in *Haldane's Trs*. v. *Murphy* (1881), 9 R. 269, at 279, as an instance of vesting subject to defeasance.

[2] (1872), 10 S. L. R. 65.

[3] Cited above *sub nom Johnston* v. *Johnston*.

Although in these cases there were indications of opinion that the fact of a person succeeding to a heritable estate, and whose succession could only be definitely ascertained at the period of division of the moveable estate, would not prevent the vesting of the moveable estate, still that opinion was not necessary for the decision in either of these cases, and I cannot hold it as a doctrine applicable to all cases."

Despite the great weight to be attached to the remarks in this last case, it may be submitted that clauses excluding members of the class can have no greater influence on vesting than powers of appointment ; and it is thought that the decisions in regard to such powers (since the Act of 1874), establishing the rule that these are consistent with vesting, tend to support the principle laid down in the cases of *Douglas* v. *Douglas* and *Johnston* v. *Johnston*.

In the more recent case of *Yeats* v. *Paton*,[1] it was ruled that a clause of exclusion operates *intra familiam*, and ceases to have effect when the class consists of, or is reduced to, one member. In that case the truster directed his trustees to divide his estate on the death of his widow among the " children then alive of my brothers and sisters equally *per capita* ; but always secluding the eldest son of each family who may have succeeded to any heritable property of his father's." On the widow's death a deceased brother was represented by one child, who had succeeded to an estate on his father's death ; and it was held that this child was entitled to participate along with the other families.

Again, the member of a class " succeeding or entitled to succeed " to a property is to be ascertained at the term of distribution of the subject of the gift. In *Cunningham* v. *Moncreiff*,[2] the testator instructed his trustees to convey his estate of X. to his eldest son A., whom failing to his son B., and to divide the residue of his estate among B., C., D., E., F., his younger children, on the majority of the youngest ; but in the event of any of his younger children succeeding to property of a certain amount, the bequest conceived in favour of such younger children should cease and determine, and their shares should be divisible equally among the other children. X. was conveyed to A. ; he died, and B. took as substitute. Thereafter (and before the majority of the

Construction of clauses of exclusion.

---

[1] (1880), 8 R. 171. [2] (1858), 20 D. 1214.

youngest of the children) B. brought an action to have it declared that he was entitled to participate in the residue when it became divisible. It was argued for him that the provision as to the succession referred to a succession opening before the testator's death, and that as the shares of the residue vested *a morte testatoris*, they could not thereafter be affected by that provision. But the Court rejected this argument, and held that B., having succeeded to the estate before the period of distribution, was excluded.

So also, in *Clarke* v. *Clarke*,[1] where a fund was to be distributed at the close of a liferent among the children of A. other than the " heir entitled to succeed " to a property held by A. in fee-simple, it was held that the eldest of the children alive at the liferenter's death was excluded by this clause, although, A. being alive, he had no more than a *spes successionis*.

V. Distribution *Per Capita* and *Per Stirpes*. — When a legacy is given to a plurality of persons, the natural and simple mode of distribution is that which gives each legatee an equal share in the subject of the gift. Accordingly, the

Presumption in favour of *per capita* distribution.

general rule of law is that legatees take *per capita* unless the will supplies evidence that the testator intended that the division should be *per stirpes*.[2] Beyond this, there are few rules on this matter, nor, it has been observed,[3] would it be desirable that there should be any system of rules, for the decision of this question must depend in an eminent degree on the particular terms used by the testator in making his bequest. It is impossible, therefore, to do more than

---

[1] (1832), 11 S. 220. See *Lord and Lady Strathmore's Trs.* v. *Lord Glamis*, 1932 S. C. 458. Cf. also *Fenton Livingstone* v. *Waddell's Trs.* (1899), 1 F. 831 (a marriage contract case). As to the meaning of the words " eldest " and " younger " in clauses of this kind, see M'Laren's Wills and Succession (3rd. Ed.), vol. ii., p. 1072. The general rule is that where provisions for younger children are made in a deed either destining an estate, or framed with reference to the destination of an estate, to the " eldest " son, this expression is to be construed as meaning the child succeeding to the estate, and the expression " younger children " as meaning those who do not succeed to the estate.

[2] *M'Courtie* v. *Blackie* (1812), Hume's Decs. 270 ; Lord Cowan in *MacDougall* v. *MacDougall* (1866), 4 M. 372 ; 38 S. J. 187 ; rev. 6 M. (H. L.) 18 ; 40 S. J. 466 ; Lord M'Laren in *Allen* v. *Flint* (1886), 13 R. 975 ; Lord Stormonth-Darling in *Inglis* v. *MacNeils* (1892), 19 R. 924.

[3] Lord Young in *Inglis* v. *MacNeils*, *supra*.

adduce examples of the manner in which different forms of bequest have been interpreted, noticing the main considerations which have guided the Court in their decisions on the question.

In the first place, it is clear that the mere fact that the legatees are called under class descriptions does not warrant a departure from the general rule. " If you have an original bequest, it will not signify that the parties favoured are called or nominated as members of a class. In that case, although others come in, it may be, and is a just rule, that the division should be *per capita*," [1] Thus, in *M'Kenzie* v. *The Legatees of Holte*,[2] where a testatrix conveyed her estate to A. in trust for his children, and directed that in case of the death of one of them (which happened) the sum of £700 should be paid to the children of A., and the children of B., and the children of C., it was held that this sum was divisible among these children *per capita* ; and this decision was followed in *Hay Cunningham's Trs.* v. *Blackwell*,[3] where the testator directed that the residue of his estate should be divided " among my cousins the Blackwells (leaving out Mrs B.) and among the children of my uncle, J. H."

Similarly, in *Bogie's Trs.* v. *Christie*,[4] where the will provided that the testatrix's estate should be divided equally between the children of the testatrix's late sister and the children of her late brother, the members of these families were held to take *per capita*. In strict accuracy, the word " between," it was pointed out, applied only to a division between two participants, but the Court took cognisance of the fact that the word was popularly used as synonymous with " among," and construed the word in that sense.[5]

---

[1] L. J.-C. Moncreiff in *Laing's Trs.* v. *Sanson* (1879), 7 R. 244.

[2] 1781, M. 6602. See also *Grant* v. *Fyffe*, 22nd May 1810, F.C., and *Young's Trs.* v. *Young* (1869), 6 S. L. R. 454.

[3] 1909 S. C. 219.

[4] (1882), 9 R. 453.

[5] The New English Dictionary states that the word " between " imports " division between two (or more) "; see also *Cobban's Exrs.* v. *Cobban*, 1915 S. C. 82 ; *In re Walbran* [1906], 1 Ch. 64 ; *In re Harper* [1914], 1 Ch.

70 ; and *In re Cossentine* [1933] Ch. 119. As to "among," see *Hay Cunningham's Trs.* v. *Blackwell*, *ante*, and *Searcy's Trs.* v. *Allbuary*, 1907 S. C. 823. In the last of these cases the direction to the trustees was to divide the residue " in equal proportions amongst the families of A. and B. in equal proportions share and share alike." A. and B. were the brothers respectively of the testator's first and second wives. It was held that the division fell to be made *per stirpes*.

And the general rule apparently holds also where the bequest is to a relative of the testator and to the children of a deceased person who stood in the same relationship to the testator,[1] as, for example, to my son A. and the children of my deceased son B.

Gift to named legatees and to a class.

Nor is the general presumption displaced by the fact that some of the legatees are called *nominatim* while others are called under a class description. Thus, in *M'Courtie* v. *Blackie's Children*,[2] the testator gave pecuniary legacies of various amounts to legatees *nominatim*, and a sum to the children procreated or to be procreated of A. and B. equally among them on their respectively attaining majority, and to the survivors of these children, and then directed that the residue of the estate should be divided among these legatees and the children of A. and B. The question arose as to the distribution of the residue, and it was held that the children took *per capita* along with the other legatees, because the gift was made to them not as representing their parents, but " of their own proper and original right."

In *Renny* v. *Crosbie*,[3] the testator gave a part of his estate to the children procreated or to be procreated of his daughter, and A. and B. (who were the children of a deceased daughter), and the survivors of them, share and share alike. It was decided that these took the estate *per capita*, the Court laying stress on the provision as to survivorship as apparently indicating that the testator had been influenced by favour for the beneficiaries as individuals.

Where issue are called in room of their parent.

But the presumption is displaced by any evidence that the testator called the children as representing and in room of their parents. Thus, in *Thomson* v. *Cumberland*,[4] where money was bequeathed to the testator's sisters' children, whom failing to their descendants, it was held on this ground that the descendants took only the shares their parents would have taken had they survived.

Similarly, in *Laing's Trs.* v. *Sanson*,[5] the will directed

---

[1] See Lord Stormonth - Darling's opinion in *Inglis* v. *MacNeils* (1892), 19 R. 924. His Lordship founded on this circumstance as strengthening the other evidence in favour of a division *per stirpes*, although not in itself a sufficient ground for that construction.

And see *Galloway's Trs.* v. *Galloway* (1897), 25 R. 28.

[2] (1812), Hume's Decs. 270.

[3] (1822), 2 S. 60.

[4] 16 Nov. 1814, F. C.

[5] (1879), 7 R. 244. So also *Murray* (1873), 45 S. J. 574 (" to my brothers

that the testator's estate should be divided among his "surviving brothers and sisters and the lawful issue of those who may be deceased, share and share alike." Here the division was *per stirpes*, the provision in favour of issue being construed as meaning that the issue should be substituted for their parent in the event of his predeceasing, and should take the share which would have been his had he survived.

So also, although the words *per stirpes* do not appear in the bequest, it may be inferred from the whole conception of the will that division in this mode was intended. In *Robertson's Trs.* v. *Horne*,[1] a testator, who had one brother and six sisters, of whom two were dead, divided his estate into seven parts, of which one was given to each of the surviving brother and four sisters and one to the children of one of the deceased sisters, and then directed that the remaining share should be "divided equally between A., B., and C. (the children of my deceased sister M. H.) and the children of F. the deceased daughter of the said M. H." It was held that this share was divisible *per stirpes*, the Lord President observing : "He (the testator) did not in terms make the division stirpital ; but he did what appears to me to be—so far as evidence of intention goes—the same thing ; that is to say, he indicated in a parenthesis the reason for including the three survivors (viz., because they were the surviving children of his sister), and went on to include the children of the predeceasing child—again indicating his reason (viz., because their mother was also a child of his sister). I think in these circumstances if the testator had had any intention of giving the family of grandchildren more than he gave to each surviving child he would have said so."

Further, in cases where an estate or fund is given to

Gifts to parties in liferent, and their issue in fee.

and sisters and their children, and the children of my said deceased sister " —*per stirpes*), and *Still's Trs.* v. *Hall* (1899), 36 S. L. R. 390. In *M'Meekan's Trs.* v. *M'Clelland*, 1918, 1 S. L. T. 193 (Lord Hunter), where there was a destination-over to the issue equally among them of any predeceasing beneficiary, and a beneficiary pre-

deceased leaving a daughter and the children of a deceased daughter, it was held that the share of the beneficiary was divisible *per stirpes* among her daughter and her grandchildren.

[1] 1921 S. C. 817. The case was thought to be similar to *Galloway's Trs.* v. *Galloway*, 25 R. 28.

parties in liferent and to their issue in fee, the connexion between the liferent and the fee indicates that the measure of the one right is to be the measure of the other also. In such cases the division is therefore *per stirpes*. Thus, in *Home's Trs.* v. *Ramsays*,[1] a father left his estate to his three daughters in liferent, and provided that their issue should be entitled to the one-third share liferented by their mother ; and that, if any daughter died without issue, her one-third share was to be held for the liferent use of the surviving daughters, " and failing them or either of them, then the said one-third share shall be divided equally amongst their lawful children, share and share alike, on their respectively attaining majority." A daughter having died childless, it was held that her share fell to be divided among the children of her surviving sisters *per stirpes*. In delivering judgement, Lord President Inglis said : " Upon the authorities in a bequest of this kind, where a share of residue, whether original or lapsed, is given in liferent and fee to a person named, and his or her children respectively, the rule of construction is that the division is *per stirpes* and not *per capita*. I think this is settled by the case of *Richardson* v. *MacDougall*.[2] If there had been no liferent, a different question would have arisen. If we were to omit the words constituting the liferent here the case would have been different. The fund would then have been held by the trustees for the purpose of equal division among the children of the surviving sisters. But it is because of the introduction of a liferent that I think the division should be *per stirpes* and not *per capita*."

It should be observed that in this case the liferents were several and not joint. This element is favourable to a stirpital distribution, because if the fee is to be divided at the termination of the liferent, it is to be presumed that the testator intended that the class should then be fixed, and it would be an awkward arrangement if, notwithstanding that the interest was disengaged, the fee should be retained in order to be divided at the termination of all the liferents among a class that could only then be ascertained.

---

[1] (1884), 12 R. 314. See also *Allen* v. *Flint* (1886), 13 R. 975 ; *Tristram* v. *M'Haffies* (1894), 22 R. 121.

[2] (1868), 6 M. (H. L.) 18. Stated *ante*, p. 100.

The rule thus established in *Home's Trs.* v. *Ramsays* was applied in *Low's Trs.* v. *Whitworth*,[1] where the special feature of the deed was that the liferent was given to three parties and the fee to the issue of two only of these. The circumstances of the case were that the testator gave annuities to his two sisters and his sister-in-law, and provided that the families of the annuitants were to get the interest that fell to their parents until the death of the last annuitant, when the estate was to be divided into two parts, one part being given to the family of each sister. Although the absence of correspondence between the liferents and the fees certainly would appear to weaken the argument for stirpital division, the case was held to fall within the principle of *Home's Trs.* v. *Ramsays*. And the same construction prevailed in *Ramsay's Trs.* v. *Ramsay*,[2] where the residue of the estate was given to the truster's brothers and sisters in liferent respectively, the share of the estate liferented by each to be paid to his or her issue, and failing issue to the issue of the survivors in fee. A liferenter having died childless, it was held that the disengaged share of the estate was to be distributed among the issue of the other legatees *per stirpes*, although there was no liferent of the devolving share given to the parent.

Again, where a testator provides for a division of the estate among all the beneficiaries, and then adds words importing that there is to be a second division among the members of any class, the division is held to be *per stirpes*, for otherwise there would be no necessity for more than one division. The difficulty, however, is to determine what words amount to an instruction to subdivide the subject. In *Inglis* v. *MacNeils*,[3] trustees were directed to divide the residue of an estate equally between A. and the children of B. equally between them. The repetition of the words " equally between " was held to point to two divisions, and on this ground the Court held that the estate was to be divided into two shares, one going to A. and the other to B.'s children ; but it may be, as in *Binnie's Trs.* v.

Where there are words importing that two divisions are to be made.

---

[1] (1892), 19 R. 431. See *Swan* v. *Holmes* (1854), 19 Beav. 471.

[2] (1876), 4 R. 243. Lord Gifford dissented.

[3] (1892), 19 R. 924. See also *Campbell's Trs.* v. *Dick*, 1915 S. C. 100 and *Searcy's Trs.* v. *Allbuary*, 1907 S. C. 823.

Prendergast,[1] that the language is merely a redundant mode of describing how the division of the estate is to be carried out, once and for all, and with no further significance.

Effect of the
word "re-
spectively."

So, in English law, the word " respective " or " respectively " has been held to indicate that the parties were to be collected into classes and a portion allotted to each class—that is to say, a stirpital division of the subject.[2]

Gift to next-
of-kin.

In *Hogg* v. *Bruce,*[3] two spouses by mutual will gave their estate to the survivor, and after the death of the survivor to their nearest-of-kin equally. The estate was held to be divisible *per capita,* on the ground apparently that the terms of the deed did not displace that rule of division, and that the deed was a joint deed taking effect at the death of the survivor in favour of all the next-of-kin as one class.

But, on the other hand, in *Cunningham's Trs.* v. *Cunningham,*[4] a direction to trustees to divide the residue of an estate amongst all the testator's relatives, but so that one of these (his sister) should get a half more than the others, was held to import a gift to the heirs *in mobilibus* " in the same manner as if he had died intestate," that is to say, *per stirpes.*

Gift to
relatives.

And in *Cobban's Exrs.* v. *Cobban,*[5] a bequest in these rather special terms, " I bequeath the remainder of my estate . . . to be divided equally between P. and his children and my brother G. and his children," was held to import a division *per capita* among all the beneficiaries. The bequest to each brother and his children was construed as giving the parent an equal share with each of his children, and, as the word " and " when first used did not create a stirpital division as between the parent and his children, there was no ground for attributing a different effect to the word when used in the second instance.

---

[1] 1911 S. C. (H. L.) 6. See also *Hay Cunningham's Trs.* v. *Blackwell,* 1909 S. C. 219, where the repetition of the word " among " was held not to import division *per stirpes.*

[2] *Davis* v. *Bennett* (1862), 4 De. G. F. & J. 327 ; *Kekewich* v. *Barker* (1903), 88 L. T. 130 ; *Re Moore's Settlement Trust* (1862), 31 L. J. (Ch.) 368. Cf. Lord M'Laren's opinion in *Tristram* v. *M'Haffies* (1894), 22 R. 121, at 126.

[3] (1887), 14 R. 887. See *Rook* v. *The Att.-Gen.* (1862), 31 Beav. 313.

[4] (1891), 18 R. 380. In *Stewart's Trs.* v. *Stewart,* 1917 2 S. L. T. (Lord Cullen) a bequest to " my relatives mentioned already in my will " was held to be divisible *per capita.*

[5] 1915 S. C. 82, *ante,* p. 50.

VI. Gifts to Heirs, Executors, or Next-of-Kin. Ascertainment of these Classes.—When a testator makes a gift to his own heirs, or next-of-kin, the rule as to the ascertainment of the parties described by these terms was thus expressed by Lord Watson in *Gregory's Trs.* v. *Alison* : [1] " The rule, as I understand it, is simply this, that in cases where a testator or settlor, in order to define the persons to whom he is making a gift, employs language commonly descriptive of a class ascertainable at the time of his own death, he must *primâ facie*, and in the absence of expressions indicating a different intention, be understood to refer to that period for the selection of the persons whom he means to favour. In my opinion the rule has no other effect than to attribute to the words used their natural and primary meaning, unless that meaning is displaced by the context." Under the rules of intestate succession, the heirs of a person are ascertained at his death ; [2] and accordingly the presumption is that the testator, in employing the law of intestate succession as a means of selecting the objects of his bounty, intended that these should be ascertained at that time.

This is the earliest time, indeed, at which they can be ascertained. In *Nimmo* v. *Murray's Trs.*,[3] the Intestate Moveable Succession of 1855 having been passed between the date of the will and that of the testator's death, it was contended that the testator's " nearest heirs and successors " to whom his estate was bequeathed should be ascertained in accordance with the rule of succession in force at the date of the will ; but it was pointed out that the testator must be held to have known of the change in the law, and, if he did not make any alteration on his will to show that he intended the old rule to apply, the new law must govern the construction of the bequest.

Marginal notes: Gifts to the testator's heirs. Heirs ascertainable at the testator's death.

---

[1] (1889), 16 R. (H. L.) 10 ; 14 App. Cas. 124.

[2] *Lord* v. *Colvin* (1865), 3 M. 1083 ; *Hutton's Trs.* v. *Coates* (1868), 6 S. L. R. 146 ; *Wilson's Trs.* v. *Wilson's Trs.* (1894), 22 R. 62 ; *Logan's Trs.* v. *Logan* (1896), 23 R. 848 ; *Hamilton's Trs.* v. *Boyes* (1898), 25 R. 899 (affd. (1899) 1 F. (H. L.) 79) ; *Young's Trs.* v. *Janes* (1901), 3 F. 616. A testator does not, by making a bequest to his heirs, throw the subject of the bequest into intestacy ; the law of intestate succession is invoked for the purpose of ascertaining the beneficiaries, but they take *provisione hominis*.

[3] (1864), 2 M. 1144 ; see also *Maxwell* v. *Maxwell, ante*, p. 92.

Though payment be postponed.

The rule referred to by Lord Watson holds, although the period of distribution is deferred until the expiry of a liferent. If the liferenter is himself one of the heirs or next-of-kin, the gift of the liferent does not exclude him from participating also in the gift of the fee. Thus, where a testator gave the residue of his estate to his three sisters in liferent, and on their death to " the heirs who by law would have been entitled to succeed to my heritable property " in fee, it was held that the fee vested on the death of the testator, and that the sisters (who were, with others, his heirs) had taken, in addition to the liferent, a share of the fee.[1]

So also where the gift to the testator's heirs is affected by a contingency of the kind which does not suspend vesting, the heirs, in the event of the gift in their favour taking effect, will be ascertained at the testator's death, and their right under the bequest will vest subject to defeasance if the contingency occurs. Thus in *Anderson's Trs.* v. *Forrest*,[2] the trustees under a marriage contract were directed to pay the income of the wife's settled funds to her, and after her death to her husband, if he survived, and upon the death of the survivor of the spouses and upon the youngest of the children of the marriage attaining the age of twenty-one, to make over the funds to the children. It was declared that the provision to the children should not vest until the occurrence of both events and, in the event of the children dying before the period of vesting, the funds were to be made over to the wife's " heirs or assignees." The wife died intestate survived by her husband, and the only child of the marriage predeceased the husband and, therefore, acquired no right under the provision in favour of the children of the marriage. The question as to the construction of the final destination in the marriage contract was

---

[1] *Maxwell* v. *Wyllie* (1837), 15 S. 1005 ; 12 Fac. 928 ; *Balderston* v. *Fulton* (1857), 19 D. 293. See the opinions of the minority of the judges in *Haldane's Trs.* v. *Murphy* (1881), 9 R. 269 (stated *ante*, p. 133), which were approved in *Gregory's Trs.* v. *Alison* (1889), 16 R. (H. L.) 10. And cf. *Blackwood* v. *Dykes* (1833), 11 S. 443, in which case a testator, after giving an annuity to his eldest son and excluding him from all claim on his estate, gave the estate on a contingency to his (the testator's) heirs and assignees, and the son being heir, it was held that the clause of exclusion would not prevent him taking on the occurrence of the contingency ; and see also *Aitken's Trs.* v. *Aitken*, 1927 S. C. 374 on this point.

[2] 1917 S. C. 321 ; for a similar decision, see *G.'s Trs.* v. *G.*, 1937 S.C.141.

submitted to the Court in a special case, and as there were
two recent decisions which were in conflict,[1] was remitted to
the Whole Court. It was held, after an exhaustive consideration of the earlier authorities, that the wife's heirs
were to be ascertained at her death.[2]

It will be observed that the result of this decision was
that the child of the marriage acquired the funds as the
heir of the wife. It might be thought to be improbable
that the spouses should have intended to make a provision
for their children and at the same time to include them
among the heirs who were to take only on failure of the
children ; but, as Lord Watson observed in *Gregory's Trs.* v.
Alison [3] (where the circumstances were similar), " that is a
kind of probability which has frequently been put forward
without success in cases of this description, and whenever it
is, as here, unsupported by the context, it can only afford
material for conjecture."

In the case of *M'Donald's Trs.* v. *M'Donald*,[4] trustees
were directed on the death of the liferentrix to dispone
heritable subjects " to my (the testator's) son, whom failing
without lawful issue, to my heir-at-law." The son (who was
the testator's only lawful child) survived the testator, but
predeceased the liferentrix. It was held that the son, as
the testator's heir-at-law at the date of his death, had
right to the subjects. " The presumption—the strong presumption— " Lord Kyllachy observed, " is that by heir-at-
law is meant the person who possesses that character at the
truster's death." As the son might have left issue at his
predecease, the right could vest in him only subject to
defeasance, but there was nothing to suspend vesting for the
further destination to the heir-at-law was in the circumstances ineffective. Had the destination to the heir been
read as a substitution, as in *Smith's Trs.* v. *Smith's Trs.*,[5]

---

[1] *Muirhead's Trs.* v. *Torrie*, 1913
S. C. 85, and *Hannay's Trs.* v. *Graham*,.
1913 S. C. 476. The former decision
was over-ruled in *Anderson's Trs.* v.
Forrest.

[2] This decision is in accordance with
Gregory's Trs. v. *Alison* ; *Howe's Trs.*
v. *Howe's Jud. Factor* (1903), 5 F.
1099 (stated *post*, p. 243). In *Gregory's*

Trs. the English cases of *Bulloch* v.
Downes (1860), 9 H. L. C. 1, and
Mortimore v. *Mortimore* (1879), 4
App. Cas. 88, were referred to.

[3] *Supra.*

[4] 1907 S. C. 65.

[5] (1905), 7 F. 815. See also
Baillie's Trs. v. *Whiting*, 1910 S. C.
891 (stated *ante*, p. 98).

the heir could not have been ascertained till the death of the child.

It is, however, " a question of construction in each case whether the class is to be ascertained at the death of the testator or at a later date. It is for those who assert that the class is to be ascertained at a date other than that of the death of the testator to show that this is the fair result of the language of the will. If by the use of an adverb of time or otherwise the will shews that the class is to be ascertained on the death of the holder of some antecedent interest, this settles the point." [1] Thus, if a testator directs his trustees to distribute his estate at the expiry of a life-rent, or at some other period subsequent to his death, among his heirs " then living," [2] or among his " then next-of-kin " [3] or among his " heirs alive at the period of distribution," [4] the parties answering the description cannot be discovered until the time appointed for distribution.

Moreover, although the bequest to the testator's heirs is made without qualification, if it appears that under the structure of the bequest vesting is suspended, the weight of authority is to the effect that the heirs are to be ascertained at the date of vesting. This was the construction put on such bequests in the opinion of Lord Kyllachy in *Thomson's Trs.* v. *Jamieson*,[5] an opinion which was referred to with approval by Lord Dundas in *Anderson's Trs.* v. *Forrest*,[6] and by the First Division in *G.'s Trs.* v. *G.*,[7] the Lord President (Normand) observing in the last case : " If the settlement prescribes a postponed vesting in the testator's heirs, then these heirs fall to be ascertained at the period of vesting. . . . Accordingly I think that before we can determine in this case the date at which the testator's own heirs are to be ascertained, we must find the date of vesting in them."

---

[1] *Hutchinson* v. *National Refuges for Homeless and Destitute Children* [1920], A. C. 794 *per* Viscount Finlay, at p. 802.

[2] *Black* v. *Valentine* (1844), 6 D. 689.

[3] See the Lord President's opinion in *Hendry's Trs.* v. *Hendry* (1872), 10 M. 432.

[4] As in *Cockburn's Trs.* v. *Dundas* (1864), 2 M. 1185.

[5] 2 F., at 484. The passage in the opinion bearing on this point is quoted *ante*, p. 94.

[6] 1917 S. C., at 326.

[7] 1937 S. C. 141.

The effect of these authoritative statements of the law is that the heirs of the testator are to be ascertained in the same way as if he had died at the date of the vesting ; that is to say, the legatees are not those who actually were his heirs, but an artificial class existing at a later date. There is, however, another possible view. Let it be assumed that a bequest is made to the testator's heirs *simpliciter*, but that for some reason the vesting is postponed till a later date than his death, *e.g.* the termination of a liferent ; in a bequest of this kind, as the rules in regard to the ascertainment of the class are designed to fix the class of favoured legatees and the rules of vesting refer to the acquisition by the legatees of their right under the will, it might be considered that the effect of combining these rules was that the heirs should be fixed as at the testator's death and that the bequest should take effect in favour of such of these heirs as survived the date of vesting. The possibility that this construction might in a suitable case be adopted seems to have been present to the mind of Lord Cowan in *Cockburn's Trs.* v. *Dundas*,[1] and it is apparently adopted in English Law ;[2] but it was rejected in that case and also, it would seem, by Lord Kyllachy in *Thompson's Trs.* v. *Jamieson*.[3] It is open to the objection that it exposes the bequest to the risk of lapse.

The rule which refers the ascertainment of the heirs to the death of the testator or grantor does not hold in the case of a destination which is to be inserted in the disposition of the heritage to be granted by the trustees ; the heirs called in the destination are ascertained at the date when the succession opens.[4]

Under the Common Law the expression " next-of-kin " denoted those persons who were entitled to succeed to the

Bequests to next-of-kin.

---

[1] (1864), 2 M. 1185, at 1191.

[2] " In a gift to a class of next-of-kin of the testator, or his nearest relatives, or similar class living at a future period of distribution, the entire class is ascertained at the testator's death, but those only of the class take who survive the period of distribution "—Halsbury's Laws of England, vol. xxviii., p. 756. See also

In re Nash (1894), 71 L. T. 5, and *In re Winn* [1910], 1 Ch. 278.

[3] 2 F., at 483. In *Anderson* v. *Cunningham's Trs.* (1907), 14 S. L. T. 588, Lord Ardwall rejected this construction in the case of a bequest to the heirs of a legatee.

[4] *Baillie's Trs.* v. *Whiting*, 1910 S. C. 891 ; *Cripps's Trs.* v. *Cripps*, 1926 S. C. 188, at 203.

testator's moveable estate, but, since the Intestate Moveable, Succession Act of 1855, this is no longer so ;[1] and, therefore the expression has not now the same direct reference to intestate succession. In *Johnston's Trs.* v. *Dewar*,[2] Lord Kinnear observed that in his opinion there could be no presumption founded on what was supposed to be the primary meaning of these words for they conveyed " no significance whatever except that of propinquity of blood at whatever time it is necessary to look for the persons who answer the description." This opinion was uttered with reference to a destination which clearly had the effect of postponing vesting beyond the date of the testator's death. But, where there is nothing to postpone the vesting, the next-of-kin would naturally fall to be ascertained at the testator's death.[3]

The decisions as to the ascertainment of the heirs, not of the testator, but of a legatee, as in the case of a bequest to A. whom failing his heirs, have been noticed in an earlier chapter.[4]

---

[1] See *ante*, p. 183.

[2] 1911 S. C. 722.

[3] *Andrew's Trs.* v. *Andrew*, 1918 2 S. L. T. 12 (Lord Hunter). It may be noted that the marriage contract under consideration in *Gregory's Trs.* v. *Alison* was entered into before the date of the Intestate Moveable Succession Act ; and this was also the case in *Ferrier* v. *Angus* (1876) 3 R. 396.

[4] See *ante*, p. 92.

CHAPTER IX.

GIFTS SUBJECT TO POWERS OF APPOINTMENT.

I. Gifts to a Class subject to a Power of Apportionment, with a Gift-over to the Members in default of the exercise of the Power.

II. Gifts to a Class, subject to a Power of Appointment with no Provision in default of the exercise of the Power.

III. Gifts subject to a General Power of Disposal.

IV. Gifts subject to a Power of Encroachment on Capital bestowed on a Liferenter.

WHEN a gift is made subject to a power of appointment, and that power is exercised in a manner not strictly in accordance with the terms of the instrument by which it is given, there is a considerable body of authority as to the effect of the variance upon the validity of the deed exercising the power. As these cases do not actually involve the question of vesting, it is not proposed to consider them here. The case of *M'Cormack* v. *Barber* [1] may, however, be noticed. In that case the testator instructed his trustees (of whom A. was one), on the death of A. and B., and in case A. had no issue, to divide part of his residue " among my relations in such proportions as they shall think proper." A. survived the other trustees, and died without issue, having by a deed executed eleven years before her death appointed the fund among certain parties related to the testator. These parties were not the testator's next-of-kin either at his death or at the death of A. It was argued that the objects of the power were the testator's next-of-kin at the time of distribution (A.'s death), and that, the power having been exercised before the contingency on which it

Exercise of the power.

---

[1] (1861), 23 D. 398. In this case all the judges founded on the circumstance that it was the testator's intention that the power might be exercised prior to the contingency.

See Farwell on Powers (3rd Ed.), pp. 166 *et seq.*; Lord St Leonards in *Eden* v. *Wilson* (1852), 4 H. L. C. 257, at 283.

was to operate the appointment was invalid. It was held
that A. had validly exercised the power. This decision
proceeded on the view that by " relations " the testator
intended to call all who might at any time prior to the
distribution be able to trace a relationship with him ; and
that as the power had been exercised in favour of such
parties, the appointment was not rendered nugatory by the
fact that it had been executed prior to the contingency on
which it was to take effect. But if a deed make a gift to
parties who are to be ascertained, and who are to take
vested interests, at a time mentioned (or indicated), subject
to a power of apportionment, the exercise of the power prior
to that time will not have the effect of accelerating the
time of vesting, and entitling the objects in whose favour
it is exercised to obtain immediate payment.[1]

I. Gifts to a Class subject to a Power of Apportionment, with a Gift-over to the Members of the Class in default of the exercise of the Power.

—It is well settled that in gifts
of this description the existence of the power does not suspend
vesting in the class, but merely renders the vesting defeasible
if, and in so far as, the power is exercised.[2] In several
cases it has been said that the existence of the power is
favourable to vesting.[3]

Vesting takes place subject to defeasance.

Thus, in *Sivright* v. *Dallas*,[4] subsequently to a marriage,
the husband's mother and the wife's father entered into an
agreement whereby they obliged themselves to convey
funds to trustees for behoof of the children to be born of
the marriage. A power was given to the spouses, or either
of them, to divide at any time the provision among the

---

[1] *Cuming's Tr.* v. *Cuming* (1896), 24 R. 153. Cf. *Stevenson's Trs.* v. *Taylor* (1895), 3 S. L. T. 102.

[2] Cf. Lord Blackburn's opinion in *Chamber's Trs.* v. *Smith* (1878), 5 R. (H. L.) 151 ; and Lords Fullerton and Cunninghame's opinions in *Crawcour* v. *Graham* (1844), 6 D. 589. In *Smith's Trs.* v. *Graham* (1873), 11 M. 630, the opinion was expressed that such a power told against vesting, but in that case there were other and conclusive features in the deed.

[3] " A power of apportionment rather implies vesting " (L. J.-C. Moncreiff in *Sandbach & Others* (1874), 12 S. L. R. 96). Cf. also *Angus' Trs.* v. *Angus* (1880), 17 S. L. R. 536 (*ante,* p. 58) ; *Johnston* v. *Johnston* (1868), 7 M. 109.

[4] (1824), 2 S. 643 (N.E.) 543 ; 27th Jan. 1824, F. C. As to a father's right to apportion provisions at common law, see Ersk. *Inst.* iii. 8. 49.

children, and failing division it was to be divided equally among them. There were two children (a son and daughter) both of whom survived their mother, but predeceased their father ; the son left a child and the daughter had assigned her interest. The power was held not to have been exercised. The Court had no doubt that the fee had vested in the two children, and that the funds were divisible in equal shares between the son's child and the daughter's assignee.

In *Watson* v. *Marjoribanks*,[1] Mrs Ramsay bequeathed a legacy to her daughter in liferent and to the daughter's children in fee, " in such proportions as she may appoint, and failing thereof equally among such of them as survive me." Nine children were alive at the testatrix's death, of whom three predeceased their mother. The mother executed a deed of appointment, which was held to be inept in respect that it allotted no shares to two of the predeceasing children.[2] The judgement bears that " a fee *pro indiviso* vested in the several children . . . who should survive Mrs Ramsay, with a power to Dame A. Marjoribanks of distribution " ; and, accordingly, the surviving children and the representatives of those who had predeceased were found entitled to equal shares.

The cases of *Brodie's Trs.* v. *Mowbray's Trs.*,[3] *Romanes* v. *Riddell*,[4] and *Beattie's Trs.* v. *Cooper's Trs.*,[5] all involved the construction of marriage contracts, and support the rule of law stated above. In the first of these the provision was to the children who should be in existence at the dissolution of the marriage, subject to a power of apportionment in the father, and failing apportionment to the children equally. The wife predeceased, and the provision was held to have vested in the children on her death. Lord Moncreiff observed : " I think it very clear that the power of division in the father could not prevent the vesting of the provision in the two children existing at the dissolution. The right of each no doubt was subject to modification in

---

[1] (1837), 15 S. 586 ; 12 Fac. 553.
[2] The Act 37 & 38 Vic. c. 37, has changed the law upon this point.
[3] (1840), 3 D. 31 ; 16 Fac. 8.
[4] (1865), 3 M. 348.

[5] (1862), 24 D. 519. Cf. also Lord Rutherfurd's opinion in *Baillie* v. *Seton* (1853), 16 D. 216 ; and *Young's Trs.* v. *Young* (1869), 6 S. L. R. 454.

the amount, but only by giving more to the other. But the right itself was vested in each according to its nature under the contract." In *Romanes* v. *Riddell* the point was again very sharply raised. A fund was to be held for the wife and the husband, if he survived her, in liferent and the children in fee.[1] It was to be paid to the fiars on the death of the survivor of the spouses, and " in such proportions . . . as the father and mother or the survivor of them may direct by any deed, . . . and in case of no such deed being executed, equally between or among them." There was one child, who survived the mother but predeceased the father. The Lord Ordinary (Ormidale), founding chiefly on the existence of the power, decided that there was no vesting of the fund in this child ; but this decision was reversed in the Inner House. " The fourth and main consideration which the Lord Ordinary assigns for his judgement against vesting is," said Lord Deas, " the power of apportionment or division among the children which was reserved to the spouses and the survivor of them. But I agree with your Lordships, that if we were to countenance this as a reason for holding that there was no vesting, we should be throwing loose one of the most important and best settled principles in the law of provisions for children as a class, namely, that the provisions vest in them as a class notwithstanding of there being a power of apportionment or division." The question of vesting was not, he added, " affected in the slightest degree by the existence of the power of apportionment, whether reserved by the parents in their marriage contract or conferred by a third party." It was, however, unnecessary in the circumstances of the case to decide whether the right vested on the child's birth or at the dissolution of the marriage. But in *Beattie's Trs.* v. *Cooper's Trs.* this point was raised, and it was ruled that the fee vested in the children on their birth, although the parent was alive to whom the power was given.

Again, in *Johnston* v. *Johnston*,[2] the testator directed his trustees to hold half of the residue of his estate for A. in

---

[1] There was a destination-over in this case, which was held, however, to refer to the dissolution of the marriage.

[2] (1868), 7 M. 109.

liferent, " and upon her decease, in case she survives me, they shall pay over the foresaid half of the said residue to and among her children . . . in such proportions as she shall appoint by a writing under her hand, and failing such appointment to them, share and share alike." A. survived the testator ; it was held that vesting took place in the children *a morte testatoris* as a class. The Lord Ordinary [1] (whose opinion was adopted by the Second Division) remarked that " the power of appointment may be said to be conclusive against the idea of the fee not vesting till after the death of the mother ; for it implies a class of fiars existing, with a right in the class, anterior to the mother's death. The mother could not apportion the fortune amongst fiars becoming such after her death ; for she could not know who these would be."

These cases all occurred before the Powers of Appointment Act, 1874,[2] which enacts that no appointment made in exercise of any power to appoint shall be invalid on the ground that any object has been excluded. The circumstance that the interest is liable not merely to be reduced, but to be totally withdrawn, does not, it is thought, render inapplicable the law laid down in the cases already quoted.[3] In principle, the case of a gift subject to a power of appointment does not appear to differ from one in which the party's interest is liable to be displaced by the birth of issue,[4] the only distinction being that the event on which defeasance is to take place is in the one case the possible existence of appointees, and in the other the possible existence of issue.

In all of the cases hitherto considered, the power had not been exercised, and the effect of the decisions is to establish that the existence of the power is not inconsistent with vesting in the class. It is hardly necessary to remark that the gift in default of appointment may be so expressed

Effect of the Powers Act.

---

[1] Lord Kinloch.

[2] 37 & 38 Vic. c. 37. Prior to the Act, the exclusion of an object rendered the exercise invalid—*Watson* v. *Marjoribanks, supra* ; *Campbell* v. *Campbell* (1878), 5 R. 961. There was no case of a deed exercising the power being held invalid because an illusory share had been given—*Smith's Trs.* v. *Graham* (1873), 11 M. 630.

[3] Cf. *Whyte* v. *Robertson* (1890), 17 R. 708 ; *Weir* v. *Young* (1898), 5 S. L. T. 233 (Lord Kyllachy).

[4] See cases under Vesting subject to Defeasance.

as (under the general rules of vesting) to suspend vesting ; as, for example, by the introduction of a survivorship clause [1] or destination-over [2] referring to the death of the donee of the power or some other period. But in such cases the suspension of vesting is due, not to the subsistence of the power, but to other conditions of the bequest.

It may be, however, that the power is exercised, and that the question is as to the effect of the appointment in conferring a vested right on the member or members of the class in whose favour the appointment is made. The power may be so expressed as to put it within the power of the donee to fix the date of vesting ; but, in the ordinary case where there is no such power given, the effect of the appointment must depend on the terms in which the bequest to the class to which the power relates is expressed.

In *Hamilton's Trs.* v. *Hamilton,*[3] a father executed an irrevocable *inter vivos* deed conveying his estate to trustees in trust for himself in liferent and his children born and to be born in fee, and for the issue of such as might die. Under the deed the father retained a power of apportioning the fee among the children, and failing apportionment the children were to take equally among them. The father renounced his liferent over a portion of the funds, and apportioned it among the children then in existence. It was held that this was a valid apportionment, and that the children were entitled to immediate payment ; the grounds of the decision being that the fee had vested in the children, and that, although other children might be born, their possible interest did not invalidate the appointment, because the parent under the statute had power to appoint the subject to the children then alive, to the exclusion of other members of the class that might come into existence.

Again, in *Chancellor's Trs.* v. *Sharples' Trs.*[4] Mr Chancellor, the heir in possession of an entailed estate, in terms of a power in the deed of entail, by his marriage contract bound

---

[1] *Smith's Trs.* v. *Graham, supra*; *Cuming's Tr.* v. *Cuming* (1896), 24 R. 153 ; *Blackburn's Trs.* v. *Blackburn* (1896), 23 R. 698 ; *Stirling's Trs.* v. *Stirling* (1898), 1 F. 215.

[2] *Robertson* v. *Houston* (1858), 20 D. 989.

[3] (1879), 6 R. 1216. Lord Ormidale dissented. See for a similar trust *Miller* v. *Finlay's Trs.* (1875), 2 R. (H. L.) 1.

[4] (1896), 23 R. 435.

the succeeding heirs to pay a sum to trustees for behoof of
the children of the marriage not succeeding to the entailed
estate " in such shares or proportions, and subject to such
conditions, if more than one " as he should appoint, and,
failing appointment, for behoof of the younger children alive
at his death and the issue of predeceasers.   By an irrevocable
and delivered deed the father appointed a portion of the
funds to a younger son who subsequently predeceased him.
The Lord Ordinary (Kyllachy) held that no right in this
portion had vested in that son on the ground that it was
not " possible to construe the deed as giving a power to
appoint to a class of objects larger than the class of objects
taking in default of appointment."   But this decision was
reversed in the Inner House. Lord Trayner pointed out
that at the date of the appointment Robert was, and, had
he survived, would have been at his father's death, a younger
child, adding : " There was nothing in the Shieldhill entail
or in Mr Chancellor's marriage contract to prevent him
dividing or apportioning the fund so as to make it vest
during his lifetime. The only reference in the marriage
contract to any right to be conferred after Mr Chancellor's
death is the equal division of the fund among the objects
of the power, failing apportionment by Mr Chancellor himself.
This provision cannot affect the question before us, seeing
that *quoad* Robert there had been no failure to appoint."

So also in *M'Dougal's Tr.* v. *Heinemann*,[1] where the
testator directed that farm leases should be made over to
his sister and her husband in liferent, and, on the death of
the survivor, to such of their sons as she might appoint,
and, failing appointment, to her eldest son or, if he would
not accept them, to the next eldest son alive at the death
of the survivor of the liferenters, it was held that a renunciation of her liferent and an appointment by her in favour of
a son who predeceased her was effectual to transfer to him
the right to the leases.

In the two last mentioned cases it will be observed that
the objects of the power were not limited to the class in
whose favour the subject was destined in default of appointment.   It by no means follows from the circumstance that
the testator has thought fit to prescribe how the funds

*Effect of
Bequest failing
appointment.*

[1] 1918 S. C. (H. L.) 6.

shall be disposed of, if no appointment is made, that his intention is that the donee of the power shall be restricted in the exercise of it to those who are to take if he does not avail himself of the power.[1] Whether the power is to be so restricted is a question depending on the construction of the terms of the deed conferring the power.[2] In the following cases there are expressions of opinion in favour of the construction which was rejected in *Chancellor's Trs.* v. *Sharples' Trs.* and *M'Dougal's Tr.* v. *Heinemann*, viz., that the gift in default of appointment defined the objects of the power.

In the first of these [3] a father was bound by his marriage contract to make payment on the death of the survivor of the spouses " to the child or children that may happen to be procreate of this marriage " of a sum the amount of which was to depend on the number of the children. This sum was to be divisible among the children in such proportions as the father should at any time of his life appoint ; and, failing such appointment, it was to be divided amongst the survivors of them and the issue of predeceasers. The father exercised the power by dividing the fund among all the children, but in terms which suspended vesting till the death of the survivor of the spouses ; and this exercise was challenged on the ground that the fund vested under the terms of the marriage contract not later than the dissolution of the marriage and that there was no power to postpone the vesting. As the appointment favoured the same class as was called in default of appointment, the decision in favour of its validity does not bear on the question now under consideration. But in the course of

---

[1] " The intention of a settlor is not to be ascertained merely from the manner in which the fund is given over in default of appointment. The settlement says, that in favour of certain objects, the donee of the power shall have an absolute control over the fund ; but if he does not exercise his power, then the funds shall go in a particular specified manner. To say that because the settlement specifies the manner in which the fund is to go if unappointed,

the power must necessarily be partially cut down, so as to prevent the donee from disappointing those to whom the property is to go in default of appointment, does not appear to me to be a fair conclusion." *Fearon* v. *Desbrisay* (1851), 14 Beav. 635, *per* Romilly, M. R., at 642 ; Sugden on Powers (8th Ed), 639, 640.

[2] *M'Dougal's Tr.* v. *Heinemann*, *supra, per* Lord Skerrington.

[3] *Blackburn's Trs.* v. *Blackburn* (1896), 23 R. 698.

his Opinion Lord M'Laren said : " I see no reason to doubt that the persons amongst whom the fund is to be apportioned are the same as those who would take under the provision for equal division in case of the power not being exercised. The meaning of any power of apportionment is that the fund is to be divided, but may be divided unequally, amongst the members of the class who would take failing apportionment. Any other construction, if not exactly a contradiction in terms, would at least involve a departure from the principle of apportionment."

Cuming's Tr. v. *Cuming* [1] also involved the construction of a marriage contract. By that contract the wife assigned funds to trustees in trust to pay the funds on the death of the survivor of the spouses to " the child or children of this intended marriage in such shares or proportions, if more than one child, as may be appointed by " the spouses or the survivor ; and, if no appointment was executed, the trustees were to pay the funds to the children equally and the issue of such " as may have predeceased," and if there were no children or " in case of their predeceasing their parents " to the wife and her heirs and assignees. The wife survived her husband and executed a deed of appointment in favour of the children then alive. The wife and the daughters then called on the trustees to denude of the funds. But this claim was rejected on the ground that the objects of the power were the children alive at the death of the wife, and that until that event it was impossible to say who were entitled to take or among whom the appointment would have to be made.

II. Gifts to a Class subject to a Power of Appointment, but with no Provision in default of the exercise of the Power.—If the deed contain a bequest to a definite class, burdened with a power in a liferenter or trustee of appointing the subject among the members, the gift vests in the members, subject to defeasance as and when the power is exercised ; and if the power is not exercised, or is exercised invalidly, the testator's general intent in favour of the class takes effect, although the special intent as to the mode of

Effect of non-exercise of the power.

[1] (1896), 24 R. 153.

distribution has failed.[1] Thus, in *Hill's Trs.* v. *Thomson*,[2] the testatrix directed her trustee to retain and apply a share of residue for behoof of a family of grandchildren, " and that at such time or times and in such way and manner as my said trustee . . . may think most conducive to the welfare of said children, with full power to her [3] to divide and apportion the said provision among the said children " ; and it was declared that the children should meantime have no vested interest in the subject. After making certain payments, the trustee became insane. It was held that the amount undistributed was to be divided among the children so that there should be (taking into account the shares paid by the trustee) ultimate equality between them. In the opinion of the Court, there was a gift to the family, and the power was merely a burden thereon, which, as it could not be exercised, flew off, leaving the initial gift unburdened. The declaration as to vesting was held to refer to the individual shares, and not to the class-gift.

But if the terms of the gift to the class are such as cannot receive effect, then, in the case of the power not being exercised, the gift will lapse. Thus, in *Robbie's Judicial Factor* v. *M'Crae*,[4] trustees were directed to pay the residue " to such charitable or religious purposes . . . as they . . . may think proper, according to their or his discretion." After the death of all the trustees, a portion of the funds remained undistributed. It was held that this portion fell to the heir *ab intestato* of the testatrix, the

---

[1] For English Law cf. *Lambert* v. *Thwaites* (L. R. 2 Eq. 151), *Bradley* v. *Cartwright* (L. R. 2 C. P. 511), *Wilson* v. *Duguid* (24 Ch. D. 244); *In re Llewellyn's Settlement* [1921], 2 Ch. 281. In *Lambert* v. *Thwaites* Kindersley, V.C., states the law thus : " The general principle seems to be this : If the instrument itself gives the property to a class, but gives a power to A. to appoint in what shares and in what manner the members of that class shall take, the property vests, until the power is exercised, in all the members of the class, and they will all take in default of appointment ; but if the instru-ment does not contain a gift of property to any class, but only a power to A. to give it as he may think fit among the members of that class, those only can take, in default of appointment, who might have taken under an exercise of the power. In that case the Court implies an inten-tion to give the property, in default of appointment, to those only to whom the donee of the power might give it." In the last case, that is to say, if the power were testamentary, only those alive at the donee's death take.

[2] (1874), 2 R. 68.

[3] *i.e.*, the trustee.

[4] (1893), 20 R. 358.

gift to the charitable or religious purposes being too vague to receive effect.

And, similarly, in the early case of *Dick* v. *Ferguson*,[1] a direction to trustees to apply a sum for the "support of such of the granter's descendants as should happen to be in want," was held to be ineffectual on the refusal of the trustees to accept the trust.

Lastly, it may be noticed that in an Outer House case,[2] where a gift was made to A. "to be divided among those of his children whom he may think most needful," it was held by the Lord Ordinary [3] that (A. having predeceased the testator) the gift fell to be divided among the children equally. There was no gift to the children here except through the exercise of the power, but the decision apparently proceeded on the view that the testator had intended to benefit the class, and that, the power having failed, the testator's general intention must receive effect.

III. Gifts subject to a General Power of Disposal.— Power does not suspend vesting.

In *Balderston* v. *Fulton*,[4] the testator conveyed his estate to trustees for behoof of his widow in liferent, and on her death for behoof of his only child (a daughter) in liferent also. On the death of the widow and daughter, the trustees were instructed to make over the property to the testator's nearest heirs. Further, a power was conferred on the widow, "by any deed to be executed by her, and to take effect after her death, to destine and convey the whole estate . . . in such way and manner as she shall think fit." The widow predeceased the daughter without having exercised the power. Thereafter the daughter brought an action to have it declared that the fee was vested in her as her father's heir. The question raised in the case was, whether the heirs were to be ascertained on the death of the longest liver of the daughter and widow (in which case the daughter would, of course, be

---

[1] (1758), M. 7446.

[2] *Weir* v. *Young* (1898), 5 S. L. T. 233.

[3] Lord Kyllachy. Contrast the English cases of *In re Weekes' Settlement* [1897], 1 Ch. 289, and *In re Combe* [1925], Ch. 210.

[4] (1857), 19 D. 293. See the English cases: *Cunningham* v. *Moody*, 1 Ves. Sen. 174, *Doe* v. *Martin*, 4 T R. 39, 65, and *Heron* v. *Stokes*, 2 Dr. & War, 89.

excluded), or whether they might be ascertained during the lives of the daughter and widow. The Lord Ordinary (Neaves) decided in favour of the first of these views, largely because of the existence of the power of disposal in the widow. This judgement was reversed by the First Division. The widow's power of disposal is not discussed save in the Opinion of Lord Deas, who remarks : " The power reserved to the wife could only render the fee defeasible, or, at the utmost, suspend the vesting till her death. But even this latter view would create no practical difficulty, as the daughter has survived the mother." But, although it was immaterial for the decision of the case whether vesting was at the truster's or his widow's death,[1] the inclination of the opinions is towards vesting *a morte testatoris*.[2]

But whatever doubt there might be as to the effect of *Balderston* v. *Fulton*, standing alone, as a decision on the effect of a power of disposal on vesting is removed by the observations on it in subsequent decisions. In *Haldane's Trs.* v. *Murphy*,[3] Lord President Inglis said : " The case of *Balderston* v. *Fulton* furnishes another example of the vesting of a fee of moveables subject to defeasance. The widow in that case had an absolute power of disposal of the whole estate during her viduity. She survived her husband for four years, and enjoyed the liferent of the estate, and might have disposed of the fee as she thought fit at any time during these four years ; and if she had done so to the prejudice of her daughter, the result would have been that the right of fee, which the Court held to vest in the daughter *a morte testatoris*, would have suffered defeasance. I am not able to make any distinction in principle between the possible exercise of a power of alienating the fee belonging to a survivor of the testator, and the possible existence of issue of a liferenter, as a reason for preventing the vesting of the fee in the heir-at-law, or to hold that

[1] Cf. Lord Young's Note in *Boyd* v. *Denny's Trs.* (1877), 9 R. 299 at 307.

[2] Thus Lord Curriehill asks : "And is it credible . . . that in the event of Mrs Balderston (the daughter) predeceasing her mother leaving children, these children, although his legal representatives, should have no right to even the fee of his estate unless they should survive their grandmother ? " And Lord Ivory agrees that " she (the daughter) is vested with a fee *a morte testatoris*."

[3] (1881), 9 R. 269. Lord President Inglis (with Lords Mure and Shand) dissented.

the one is a suspensive while the other is a resolutive condition." [1]

A decision in accordance with these opinions was pronounced in *Howe's Trs.* v. *Howe's Judicial Factor*.[2] In that case the husband, in his marriage contract, assigned his estate to his wife in liferent, and to the issue of the marriage, and failing issue to his " heirs whomsoever," in fee. A power was given to the widow in the event (which occurred), of failure of issue " to test upon or execute conveyances *inter vivos* or settlements *mortis causa* . . . so as to sopite the above destination to the heirs whomsoever." The wife survived, but died without exercising the powers. It was held that the fee vested on the death of the husband in his heirs.

IV. Gifts subject to a Power of Encroachment on the Fee or Capital thereof.—A power of this nature affects the amount of the gift of the capital. As, however, a right may be assigned or otherwise disposed of whatever be its present or ultimate value, there is no reason (it is submitted) why such a power should in any way prevent vesting. The case of a power of absolute disposal, considered in the previous section, would seem to be *a fortiori* of a power of encroachment ; and if vesting in the former case is possible, the same reasoning would lead to vesting in the latter. The decisions on this point, which are not numerous, support this view, although a decision in the Outer House suggests that the rule that powers of encroachment are not inconsistent with vesting cannot be stated in unqualified terms.[3]

In *Reddie's Trs.* v. *Lindsay*,[4] the testator gave his widow a liferent, with " full power to use or encroach on the funds, means, and estate . . . and also to test or dispose, by any deed or writings *mortis causa*, of any part not otherwise

---

[1] The Lord President's view in this case was subsequently approved in *Gregory's Trs.* v. *Alison* (1889), 16 R. (H. L.) 10 ; L. R. 14 App. Cas. 124, in which Lord Watson referred to *Balderston* v. *Fulton* in these terms : " The power reserved to Dr. Gregory to make another disposition of his estate in the events which have since occurred need not be taken into account. In *Balderston* v. *Fulton* it was held that the existence of such a power does not impede vesting."

[2] (1903), 5 F. 1099.

[3] *Roberton's Trs.* v. *White* (1904), 11 S. L. T. 566 (Lord Kincairney).

[4] (1890), 17 R. 558.

conveyed away or tested on by " the testator. This curiously vague clause was construed to mean that the widow might use the capital freely for herself ; but could only use it for herself, and could not dilapidate the estate or give any part away without consideration.[1] The fee was held to have vested in the parties to whom it was given at the testator's death, although the widow survived. Lord M'Laren in his opinion guarded the import of the decision in these terms : " I should assent to the proposition that where a gift of residue is made, subject to the exercise of an unqualified power of disposal given to some other person, it is impossible that the right to the residue should vest so long as that power subsists, because the amount to be taken by the legatee is wholly uncertain—indeed, it is in doubt whether he will receive anything. But when the power of disposal is confined to certain specified purposes, and is only to be used in certain circumstances, then I think it is consistent with previous decisions that vesting may exist concurrently with the existence of the power." [2]

These words were founded on by Lord Kincairney in a case in which the power was held to postpone vesting.[3] The power was thus expressed in the will : " Declaring that in the event of the revenue of my said estates being inadequate for the sufficient maintenance and support of my said spouse, on which point she shall be sole and uncontrolled judge," the trustees might pay to her the whole or such part of the estate as she should deem necessary. Lord Kincairney considered that this clause fell within the exception noticed by Lord M'Laren, and decided that vesting was therefore postponed till the end of the liferent. There was another element in the case—namely, that the gift was expressed in a direction to pay at the death of the liferentrix —which also pointed towards postponement of vesting.

Ross's Trs. v. *Ross* [4] differs from these cases in that the power was very carefully and precisely limited. The truster gave his estate to trustees, to hold for his widow in liferent

---

[1] Cf. Ld. Pres. Inglis' opinion.

[2] In *Barr's Trs.* v. *Barr's Trs.* (1891), 18 R. 541, there was a power similar to that in *Reddie's* case, but the question of vesting was not under consideration. The effect of such powers as regards the donee's interest in the estate is considered in Chapter XVIII., *post.*

[3] *Roberton's Trs.* v. *White, supra.*

[4] (1897), 25 R. 65.

and his children in fee ; the will then proceeded : " I direct my trustees . . . to pay over to my said wife, during all the days of her lifetime and while she remains unmarried, the free annual proceeds of my whole remaining property, heritable and moveable ; and in the event of the said free annual proceeds falling short of the sum of £150, then my trustees are hereby required to apply as much of the principal of the trust funds and estate as will make up the sum of £150 to my said wife, year by year." It was held that this power did not prevent vesting *a morte testatoris* in the children.[1]

---

[1] See also *Ferrier* v. *Angus* (1876), 3 R. 396, where a power to the liferentrix " to sell, use, or dispose thereof (*i.e.*, the capital), for onerous causes," but with no power gratuitously to dispose of it, was held not to be inconsistent with vesting of the capital at the death of the testator.

CHAPTER X.

VESTING AS DEPENDENT ON THE ACTION
OF TRUSTEES.

I. Gifts made through the Medium of a Discretionary Trust.

II. Destinations-over referring to " Payment."

I. Gifts made through the Medium of a Discretionary Trust.—A testator, in making a bequest to a party through the hands of trustees, may give to the trustees a power of determining whether the bequest shall or shall not take effect in favour of the legatee. Where this intention is expressed, the trustees are not, as in other cases, merely the agents for carrying out the dispositions made by the testator ; they are arbiters as to whether the party shall or shall not receive the legacy. They cannot be controlled in the exercise of the power entrusted to them by the testator, and consequently the party has no claim to, and no vested interest in, the subject of the gift, unless and until the trustees determine that he shall receive it.

Thus, in *Paterson's Trs.* v. *Paterson*,[1] trustees were directed, upon the testator's natural son A. attaining twenty-one years of age, and being of the character and capacity which, in their estimation, would render the same prudent, to dispone, assign, and convey to him the whole or such part as they might consider proper of the testator's estate ; they were also authorised to withhold the conveyance either for a time or absolutely ; and, in the event of their not making payment to A., they were instructed to convey the subject to his issue or to other parties. Further, it was declared that they should have a full and uncontrolled discretion as to the disposal of the subject. A. attained majority and received a portion of the estate, and thereafter died leaving

[1] (1870), 8 M. 449.

issue. On a consideration of the special terms of the deed, it was held that the unpaid portion had not vested in him. The legatee's conduct had not been discreditable, but this was quite immaterial, because payment was made by the will a condition of vesting; and the partial payments that had been made did not deprive the trustees of their discretionary power as to the remainder of the legacy, for the testator authorised them to give a part only if they deemed this expedient.

Similarly, where trustees were instructed to pay a sum to a legatee "in the event of their considering it proper," and at such times and in such portions as they deemed fit, it was decided that the legacy lapsed owing to the legatee's death before payment was made.[1] The same construction prevailed where the direction was that the subject should "be given in such sums and ways and times as the trustees may think best."[2]

Again, a testator may direct his trustees to hold a subject or portion of his estate for a legatee, giving them at the same time a power to withdraw the legatee's right; and in such cases the legatee's interest is defeasible at the discretion of the trustees. Examples of such gifts will be found in a subsequent chapter.[3]

II. Destinations - over referring to "Payment." — In the cases already cited the substance of the gift was affected by the powers given to the trustees; the legacy was or was not to be given according to the judgement of the trustees as to the merits or circumstances of the legatee. In the cases now to be considered, no discretionary power over the rights of the beneficiaries is entrusted to the trustees, and the only reference to their action is to be found in a destination-over, survivorship clause or declaration as to vesting relating to the payment of the legacy.

---

[1] *Burnside* v. *Smith* (1829), 7 S. 735; 4 Fac. 1003. See Lord Cowan's observations on this case in *Sanderson's Exr.* v. *Kerr* (1860), 23 D. 227. Cf. *Sorley* v. *Martin* (1890), 27 S. L. R. 880; *Arkley* v. *Paterson* (1893), 1 S. L. T. 336 (Lord Kyllachy); *Dun* v. *Angus* (1894), 1 S. L. T. 158 (Lord Wellwood).

[2] *Smith's Trs.* v. *Smith* (1883), 10 R. 1144. See also *Haldane's Trs.* v. *Sharp's Trs.* (1890), 17 R. 385.

[3] XV., *Chambers' Trs.* v. *Smiths* (1878), 5 R. (H. L.) 151, and other cases cited in that Chapter.

In its literal sense the word " payment " would denote actual transfer to, and receipt by, the beneficiary of the subject bequeathed. But it is so improbable that a testator should desire to make the right of the beneficiary dependent on the date at which payment is made, however dilatory or culpable the conduct of the trustees in the administration of the trust may have been, that the Court will not adopt this construction unless compelled to do so by conclusive evidence that this was really intended. " A power to trustees to hasten or postpone the period of vesting at their pleasure is not readily to be reared up by implication." [1]   There is no instance of this construction in our reports ; [2] for, while it is true that in some cases a legatee has been held to have had no vested right because he died before receiving payment, it will be found that in all of these the Court was careful to point out that there had been no undue delay on the part of the trustees.

The disinclination to adopt a construction of a deed which would result in leaving the rights of beneficiaries to depend on the course of the trust administration greatly influenced the opinions of Lord Watson and Lord Davey in *Bowman* v. *Bowman*.[3] In that case there occurred a destination-over *primâ facie* referable, in their opinion, to the time of distribution. But the time of distribution was the termination of a partnership, and under the will the trustees had power to prolong the partnership. Lord Watson pointed out that if the period of distribution " were taken as the date of ascertaining survivorship, then the testator

[1] *Per* Lord Deas in *Spens* v. *Monypenny's Trs.* (1875), 3 R. 50. Cf. Ld. Pres. Inglis's opinion in *M'Elmail* v. *Lundie's Trs.* (1888), 16 R. 47.

[2] But in *Johnson* v. *Crook* (1879), 12 Ch. Div. 639, where the gift-over was " in case A. shall die before he shall have actually received the whole of his share, . . . whether the same shall have become due and payable or not, such part or parts as he shall not have actually received " to be paid to another, Sir George Jessel, M.R., held that it referred to actual payment, even although payment should be delayed by the fraud or negligence of the trustees. The words " whether the same shall have become due and payable or not " showed that actual receipt was meant ; and as A. died without receiving payment, he had no vested interest in the legacy. See also *In re Goulder* [1905], 2 Ch. 100. But cf. *Minors* v. *Battison* (1876), 1 App. Cas. 428, where Lord Selborne said that a gift-over referring to actual receipt was too indefinite to receive effect.

[3] (1889), 1 F (H. L.) 69 ; stated *ante*, p. 74. Cf. *Henderson's Trs.* v. *Henderson* (1876), 3 R. 320.

must be held to have delegated to his trustees the duty and right of determining by their action at what date the shares of his trust-estate are to vest, and it may be of settling whether these shares are to be taken by his children as institutes, or by their heirs as conditionally instituted to them. To make the operative part of his settlement, the selection of the persons who were to succeed to the corpus of his estate, dependent in a great measure upon the option of his trustees was certainly an unusual if not a capricious provision ; and that is one of the considerations which may fairly be taken into account in judging of the time at which the testator intended that survivorship should be ascertained." On this ground Lord Watson and Lord Davey were enabled to concur with the majority of the House in holding that there was vesting *a morte testatoris*, despite the destination-over which otherwise, in their opinion, would have operated to prevent this.

Influenced by these considerations, the Court seeks to find from the terms of the settlement some definite time or event which the testator may be supposed to have had in view when referring to " payment " of the legacy ; and the usual construction is to treat the word as meaning the time at which the subject of the bequest was set free for payment and might have been paid. Thus, if the testator has burdened the subject with a liferent [1] or has appointed the time at which it is to be divided among the legatees,[2] a destination-over or survivorship clause dependent on payment will generally be referred to the termination of the liferent or the time so appointed ; and even where the direction is that the trustees shall make payment " as soon as convenient " after the termination of the liferent or the appointed time, this will not postpone vesting beyond these times.[3] This construction of the word " payment " is that adopted in so large a majority of the decisions that it may be regarded as the normal one.

---

[1] As in *Steel's Trs.* v. *Steel* (1888), 16 R. 204 ; and *Muirhead* v. *Muirhead* (1890), 17 R. (H. L.) 45.

[2] As in *Brown* v. *Campbell* (1855), 17 D. 759 ; *Chalmers' Trs.* (1882), 9 R. 743 ; and *Neville* v. *Shepherd* (1895), 23 R. 351 ; *Howat's Trs.* v. *Howat*, 1922 S. C. 506, *per* Ld. Pres. Clyde.

[3] See, *e.g.* *Henderson's Trs.* v. *Henderson* (1876), 3 R. 320.

The following cases are cited as examples of this construction :—

In *M'Call's Trs.* v. *Murray*,[1] the trustees were directed, on the death of the truster's widow (to whom a liferent of the estate was given), or " so soon thereafter as deemed proper," to divide the residue, and there was a provision that the share of any residuary legatee predeceasing " the said term of payment and division among them " should lapse. It was held here that a portion of the residue had vested in a legatee, who survived the liferentrix, but died without having received payment. " It appears to me," Lord Trayner observed, " that the period of division and payment among the residuary legatees contemplated by the truster was the death of the liferentrix, and although it is added ' or so soon thereafter ' as the trustees should deem proper, these words appear to me only to provide for a reasonable time being allowed the trustees to realise and distribute the estate."

In *Scott* v. *Scott's Exr.*,[2] the testator gave his estate, which was wholly heritable, to his trustees, directing them to pay a small annuity to his widow. Certain debts affected the property, and the truster enjoined the trustees to hold it until the time appointed for its division. The will continued : " My said trustees . . . upon the decease of my said spouse in the event of her surviving me, so soon thereafter as the whole heritable debts . . . shall be paid off and discharged, in the event of the same not having been discharged during my lifetime," shall sell and convert, and divide the estate among my five children. There was a destination-over " in the event of any of my said children above mentioned deceasing before or after me and before the division shall take place of my said means and estate." The postponement of division, however, was made " without prejudice to my said trustees selling my said heritable subjects, under the burden of the heritable debts affecting the same, at any time after the death of my said spouse, without waiting until they shall be in possession of funds

---

[1] (1901), 3 F. 380.
[2] (1877), 4 R. 384. This case was distinguished in *Bleakley's Trs.* v. *Johnston, post,* p. 256 ; see also *Seton's* *Trs.* v. *Seton* (1886), 13 R. 1047. As to directions to trustees to make over an estate when debts are realised or paid off, see p. 306, *post.*

from my said general estate to enable them to clear off said debts as aforesaid, provided they shall think such a course expedient and for the interest of my estate." The wife survived the truster, and at her death there were five children alive. The debts were not discharged at her death, and were still in part unpaid when the trustees eight years later sold the property. One child died in this period. The Court held that there had been vesting at the widow's death, and that therefore this child's share passed to his representatives. But for the clause authorising, in the discretion of the trustees, a sale under burden of the debts, vesting might have been held as postponed till the discharge of the debts ; but, as under that provision the trustees might have divided the whole estate at the widow's death, the Court declined to make vesting depend on the trustees' course of action. It was not said that the trustees had unreasonably delayed the sale or the payment of the debt.

Again, in *M'Elmail* v. *Lundie's Trs.*,[1] the trustees were enjoined to set aside a capital sum to secure an annuity to the testator's widow, which sum he directed should, " upon the death of " his spouse, " be divided into six shares " among his children. In regard to the residue, the trustees were instructed to divide it among the children " as soon as my estate shall be realised." The daughter's shares were to be held for them in liferent ; and as to the sons' shares, it was declared that they should not " become vested interests in them until the respective terms of payment thereof." The trustees were also empowered to hold the share of one son, or a part thereof, for such time as they should think fit, the interest in the meantime being paid to him. The case was raised to ascertain whether the share of this son had vested in him although he had not received payment. The Court decided that it had. Under the will there were three terms of payment, namely, the widow's death in regard to the sum set apart for her annuity, the daughters' deaths in regard to their shares, and the truster's death in regard to the sons' shares of residue. It was to one or other of these, as the case might be, that the testator referred when he spoke of " terms of payment." The Court rejected the argument that vesting depended on actual payment.

[1] (1888), 16 R. 47

In *Maclean's Trs.* v. *Maclean*,[1] the payment was post-poned in order to provide for the possible existence of grandchildren of the testator. The trustees were instructed, if the truster's son died without issue, to divide the residue among the children of his brother " within twelve months after that event, or so soon thereafter as circumstances will permit." A declaration was added that " the share of succession effeiring to the said residuary legatees shall become vested interest in their persons at and only upon the period of payment above mentioned." The son died without issue, and six months after his death a child of the brother died without having received payment. The provision as to the time of payment was construed as meaning that the trustees were to make the division as soon after the son's death as they could, and in any event not later than a year thereafter.[2] The period was allowed merely for the purposes of realisation, and as the trustees might have paid at the death of the son, vesting was referred to that time. Had the estate not allowed of division owing to its nature or to other circumstances, it was said in the opinions delivered that the decision might have been otherwise.

Payment on the legatee's majority.

In *Chalmers' Trs.*,[3] Mr Chalmers left a legacy to his son " payable on his attaining the age of twenty-one years." He further provided that if the son or any of his other children " should die previous to payment," his or her share should go over to the other children. The son was major at the testator's death, but died before receiving payment. It was found that he had acquired a vested interest, the destination-over being construed as referring to death under age.

Gifts dependent on actual payment.

But the language of the destination-over or survivorship clause or the frame of the settlement may exclude the construction adopted in these cases. It is doubtful whether a reference to the legatee's death before " receiving payment " would have this effect.[4] A reference to death before " actual

[1] (1889), 16 R. 1095.
[2] Contrast the interpretation given to similar words in *Howat's Trs.* v. *Howat, post*, p. 255.
[3] (1882), 9 R. 743. Followed in *Howat's Trs.* v. *Howat*, 1922 S. C.

506. See also *Graham* v. *Russell* (1791), 3 Pat. 210; and *Walker's Trs.* (1870), 8 M. 870.
[4] In *Steel's Trs.* v. *Steel* (1888), 16 R. 204, Ld. Pres. Inglis observed with reference to a destination-over in these

payment " is more explicit and has been held sufficient to exclude the construction. In *M'Dougall* v. *M'Farlane's Trs.*[1] the testator directed his trustees, upon the death of the survivor of himself and his wife, and upon the youngest of his children attaining the age of forty, to divide his estate among his children then alive ; adding, that if any of these should " die before receiving implement of their claims under these presents," and leaving issue, their issue should have their parent's share. There followed a declaration that the provisions were not to vest till " *actual payment and conveyance* " ; and if any of the children died " *before receiving payment or conveyance* of their share, and without leaving issue, such share " should " be divided among my surviving children and the issue of deceasers," etc. The youngest child survived the parents, and died after attaining the age of forty, but without having received his share. It was decided that no right had vested in him. It was noticed in the Lord Ordinary's [2] opinion that the delay in payment was not due to fault on the part of the trustees. Again, in *Stephen's Trs.* v. *Stephen's Trs.*[3] the testator directed that the capital set apart to secure certain annuities should be divided as soon as it was set free among his children and the issue of predeceasing children. He declared that the shares " shall not vest in them until actual payment or conveyance shall have been made by my trustees to them respectively, and, in the event of a partial payment being made to any of them to account of their said shares and interests, then the vesting shall take place to the extent only of such partial payment." One of the children died a month after the date at which the capital sums were set free by the death of the last annuitant. As payment had not been made to this child, it was held that no right had vested in him.

---

terms : " I do not, of course, construe the words ' before receiving payment ' as referring to the fact of payment being made, but only to the time when payment ought to be made, or, in other words, to the term or terms of payment specified in the deed." See also *Howat's Trs.* v. *Howat* (*post*, p. 255) ; *White's Trs.* v. *White* (1896), 23 R. 836 ; *Howat's Trs.* v. *Howat*, 1922 S. C. 506 ; and *Yuill's Trs.* v. *Yuill* (1901), 8 S. L. T. 324 (Lord Low). See also *M'Elmail* v. *Lundie's Trs.* (1888), 16 R. 47, at 55.

[1] (1890), 17 R. 761. See also *White's Trs.* v. *White, supra.* Contrast *Yuill's Trs.* v. *Yuill, supra.*

[2] Moncreiff.

[3] 1928 S. C. 16.

It will be observed that not only was the word " actual " used, but that partial vesting was contemplated, and the extent of the vesting was to be determined by the extent of the payment.

So also the settlement may be so framed as to exclude vesting *a morte testatoris* and yet afford no means of referring the word " payment " to any other fixed time or event. Of the cases of this kind *Howat's Trs.* v. *Howat* [1] has been most frequently discussed. But the decision in that case followed on two earlier cases, *Thorburn* v. *Thorburn* and *Wilkie* v. *Wilkie.*

In the first of these [2] the trustees were directed, *as soon after the truster's death as should be thought most prudent* and expedient, to separate and *divide* the remainder of his means and estate into nine equal shares, and to allocate these among his brothers and sisters. It was declared that the shares should be delivered and paid over to them *as soon as the estate should be converted into cash*, or otherwise brought into such a situation as to enable the trustees to make a general division ; and, further, that if any legatee should *die before the truster " or before the foresaid period of division,"* leaving issue, his or her share should pass to the issue, and, failing issue, should accresce to the general fund to be divided among the survivors. The estate consisted almost wholly of heritable property. The lands were sold five years after the truster's death, and in that interval a brother had died. It was decided that no share had vested in him, because no division had been made. It will be observed that, as the truster had referred to his own death and to the period of division as alternative events on which, in the case of the legatee's predecease, the gift-over was to come into operation, it followed that effect could be given to the latter term only by referring it to a time subsequent to the testator's death. The ground of the decision is succinctly summed up in the following sentence from Lord Corehouse's opinion : " As predeceasing the period of division is therefore put on exactly the same footing as predeceasing the truster, it seems to follow that the right was not to vest in the one case more than in the other." Seeing that the trustees were empowered to let the lands for any period

[1] *Post*, p. 255. [2] (1836), 14 S. 485 ; 11 Fac. 419.

they might think fit, instead of bringing them to sale, it was possible (on the principle of the decision) that vesting might have been postponed till a remote date.

The second case is *Wilkie* v. *Wilkie*.[1] The trustees were to hold a certain heritable estate for fourteen years, the rents being paid in the meantime to the testator's children. At the end of that period, but not before, they were to sell it ; and " as soon after the sale of said lands as possible, to divide " the proceeds among " the children then in life, or their issue . . . the share of predeceasers without issue always accrescing to the survivors equally." It was provided—in a clause which was almost tantamount to a declaration as to vesting—that the " shares shall not be liable to be affected or attached by their debts or deeds while in the hands of my said trustees." The fourteen years expired in January 1834. Three sons and three daughters were then alive. In the following August a Minute of Sale was executed, under which the daughters were to purchase the sons' rights in the estate, the price to be paid and entry given at the Martinmas following. One son died before Martinmas, and before the disposition was drawn up or signed. It was decided that no share had vested in him. The very clear language of the will excluded the idea that the testator meant to refer to the expiry of the period of fourteen years during which the trustees were to hold the fund. This construction, then, being inadmissible, it followed that the gift had not vested, for, if vesting depended on actual transfer, the legacy had not been paid, and, if the time of vesting was the time at which the trustees were, or ought to have been, able to make payment, that period had not arrived, for the legatee died within a year of the date at which the trustees became entitled to sell the lands, and therefore they could not be charged with negligence.

The third case is *Howat's Trs.* v. *Howat*.[2] The will provided that the trustees should " at the expiry of twelve months after my decease, or so soon thereafter as my trustees may be able to realise said estates, and upon my youngest child attaining twenty-one years of age, . . . divide the free residue " among four younger children. There followed a devolution

[1] (1837), 15 S. 430 ; 12 Fac. 377   [2] (1869), 8 M. 337.
(the better report).

clause in favour of issue or survivors " in the event of any of my said children predeceasing me or dying before receiving payment of their shares." All the children were major at the testator's death, and therefore the clause as to the majority of the youngest did not come into operation. A son died two years after his father ; he had received several payments, but certain properties were not realised until two years after his death. This son's portion was held not to have vested in him. The majority of the Court construed the direction to the trustees as meaning that they were to make payment as soon as they realised the estate, but in any case not before one year from the testator's death. There had been no undue delay on the part of the trustees, for they had found it impossible to sell the subjects before the son's death, and it followed, under the construction put on the will, that he had acquired no right in these. Lord Deas dissented, holding that the true construction of the direction to the trustees was that the realisation was to be effected as soon as possible after the truster's death, and at least not later than one year thereafter.

These decisions were followed in *Bleakley's Trs.* v. *Johnston*.[1] There the testator directed his trustees to dispone a house to his niece in liferent and to her children in fee. The house was to be sold or let after the niece's death, and the proceeds, when the house was sold, were to be divided among the children ; but, if any child died " before division is made," his or her share was to pass to the survivors. The Court read the will—which was holograph—as enjoining the trustees in certain circumstances not to realise and divide the proceeds on the niece's death ; and accordingly the construction which would have referred the division to that event was not permissible.

It is plain from the comments passed on these decisions in later cases that they are regarded as exceptional and to be followed only where the explicit language or the frame of the deed precludes any other construction.[2] In *Ferrier*

[1] 1907 S. C. 593.

[2] " The case of *Howat's Trs.* must be considered so special as not to rule the present or any other case not the same as regards the terms of the settlement on which it depends."— Lord Ormidale in *Scott* v. *Scott's Exr.* (1877), 4 R 384 ; " The two cases of *Howat's Trs.* and *Thorburn* were special."—Lord Shand in *Chalmers' Trs.* (1882), 9 R. 743 ; " I should not like to say anything which could be

v. *Ferriers*,[1] the trustees were instructed to retain a sum of £500 and pay the interest thereof to the testator's sister. And after the death of his sister, or after his own death (in the event of her predeceasing him), the trustees were directed, " as soon thereafter " as they should " find it convenient," to pay the capital of that sum to his nephew, whom failing to his issue. If the nephew died " before the period of payment " without issue, the legacy was given over to others. The sister predeceased the testator, and the nephew died five months after him. It was held that the estate had vested in the nephew on the testator's death. *Thorburn* v. *Thorburn*, *Wilkie* v. *Wilkie*, and *Howat's Trs.* v. *Howat* were distinguished. " The case differs from the cases quoted," said Lord Justice-Clerk Moncreiff, " in this, that the provision . . . does not relate to any general period of division, nor was any sale or other thing directed to be done by the trustees before the funds were to be applied to that purpose." " Payment " is not the word which a testator naturally uses in referring to his own death ; but in this case the legacy was to be paid on the testator's death if his sister predeceased him, and on her death if she survived him, and the obvious convenience of denoting these alternative events by one term supplied a reason for the use of the word " payment " ; and therefore the Court was enabled to construe it as relating to the testator's death in the events which had happened. It appeared in this case that the trustees could not have paid the legacy before the legatee's death, but this was immaterial, because the word was treated as pointing to the time at which the fund was liberated for payment.[2]

supposed to add to the authority of that decision . . . the principle of it is well worthy of reconsideration "— Lord Young in *M'Dougall* v. *M'Farlane's Trs.*, 17 R. 761 ; " A somewhat special case."—Ld. Pres. Clyde in *Howat's Trs.* v. *Howat*, 1922 S. C. 506 ; and see *Stephen's Trs.* v. *Stephen's Trs.*, 1928 S. C. 16.

[1] (1872), 10 M. 711. Cf. *Rutherford* v. *Easton's Trs.* (1904), O. H., 12 S. L. T. 184 (Lord Kyllachy) and *Jamieson* v. *Allardice* (1872), 10 M. 755. See also *Henderson's Trs.* v. *Henderson* (1876), 3 R. 320 ; stated *ante*, p. 65 ; *Wood* v. *Neill's Trs.* (1896), 24 R. 105 ; *ante*, p. 65 ; and *Hunter's Trs.* v. *Hunter* (1888), 15 R. 399.

[2] In the English case of *In re Arrowsmith's Trusts* (1860), 2 De G. F. & J. 474 ; 29 L. J. (Ch.) 774, where the facts were similar to those of *Ferrier* v. *Ferriers,* a different conclusion was reached. In that case the testator made a gift to those of his nephews and nieces who should be living at his death, with a gift-over to the survivors in the event of any

In his dissenting opinion in *Howat's Trs.* v. *Howat*, Lord Deas considered that vesting was not postponed beyond the period of twelve months after the testator's death, and in support of this construction invoked the principle of *Stair* v. *Stair's Trs.*[1] In that case trustees were instructed, after the payment of all the truster's debts and legacies, to lay out the residue of the estate, and the interest and proceeds thereof, in the purchase of lands to be entailed ; but for some years after the testator's death the trustees were not able to invest the whole of the funds. The person on whom the lands were to be settled as the first heir of entail brought an action claiming the interest which had accrued since the testator's death on the portion not invested. This claim was rejected both in the Court of Session and in the House of Lords. Thereafter the heir, founding on certain expressions in the opinions delivered in the House of Lords, raised another action claiming the interest arising from and after the expiry of one year from the testator's death. The Court of Session rejected this claim also, on the ground that it had not been shown that the trustees had been guilty of any negligence, or that any serious delay had occurred in implementing the instructions of the will.[2] On this view the rights of the parties under a bequest of this kind would be determined on an inquiry into the actual facts of the case. But the House of Lords overturned this decision, and admitted the heir's claim. The principle of the judgement was that, as the truster had fixed no period within which the investment was to be made, but had intended that the

dying before " receiving their respective shares." This gift-over was treated as relating not to the testator's death, nor to the time of actual payment, but to the period of twelve months from the testator's death. It could not mean the testator's death, because the only objects of the gift were those of the nephews and nieces who were then alive, and in order to give a meaning to it, some other period had to be taken. Again, there was no subsequent time mentioned in the will, and therefore the period of twelve months, being the time which is granted to trustees for

the ingathering of the estate and the payment of legacies, was selected as being that to which the gift-over must be held to refer. No decision was given on the question whether, had it appeared on inquiry that the trustees were at an earlier date in a situation to pay, the legacy would have vested at that time, but Turner, L.J., expressed an opinion to that effect. See also *In re Wilkins* (1881), 18 Ch. D. 634.

[1] (1826), 2 W. & S. 414 and 614 ; reversing 5 S. 475 ; 2 Fac 281. See also 1 W. & S. 68.

[2] Lords Alloway, Eldin, Cringletie, and Gillies dissenting.

beneficiary should enjoy the subject as soon as the directions in the will could be carried out, he must have meant that the investment should be made within a reasonable period ; that, in order to avoid the difficulty of fixing in the particular circumstances of each case what that reasonable period was, it was desirable that a certain period should be fixed for that purpose in all cases in which a different intention was not expressed ; and that that period was to be taken as twelve months from the testator's death.[1] This principle is not without its bearing on the construction of destinations-over in case of the legatee's death before payment ; but it has not been applied in any of the cases on the point.

The time at which the trustees are to be considered as having been in a position to pay will in all cases depend on the character of the truster's directions and the nature of his estate. If the trustees make payment to one beneficiary of his whole share, then, as they have been able to set aside and hand over that part of the estate, it will, as a general rule, be inferred that they were able, or ought to have been able, to denude of the shares of the other beneficiaries called along with the beneficiary who has been paid, and the rights of these others will be fixed as at the date of payment to that one. That is to say, trustees cannot arbitrarily vary the

Payment to one of a class vests the rights of all.

---

[1] See Lord Curriehill's opinion in *Dickson's Tutors* v. *Scott* (1853), 16 D. 1 ; and Lord Gifford's in 1 W. & S. 68. See also *Moncreiff* v. *Menzies* (1857), 20 D. 94 ; Lord Deas in *Love's Trs.* v. *Love* (1879), 7 R. 410 ; and *Howat's Trs.* v. *Howat, ante* ; Lord M'Laren in *Hay's Trs.* v. *Hay* (1890), 17 R. 961 ; *Wood* v. *Neill's Trs.* (1896), 24 R. 105, *ante,* p. 65. The rule of *Stair* v. *Stair's Trs.* does not hold where no accumulation of interest is directed—*Macpherson* v. *Macpherson* (1852), 1 Macq. 243 ; *Howat's Trs.* v. *Howat* (1838), 16 S. 622 ; 13 Fac. 501. As to the period within which legacies (where payment is not postponed by the testator) are payable by trustees, Lords Eldin and Alloway in *Stair* v. *Stair's Trs., supra,* and Lord Jeffrey in *Howat's Trs.* v. *Howat, supra,* observe that legacies are not payable till six months after the testator's death ; and in *Stewart's Trs.* v. *Evans* (1871), 9 M. 810, L.J.-C. Moncreiff says that trustees may safely pay legacies after the lapse of that period. Unless the period of payment is postponed by the testator, the modern rule is that in the general case interest is due from the testator's death. (*Kirkpatrick* v. *Bedford* (1878), 6 R. (H.L.) 14 ; *May's Trs.* v. *Paul* (1900), 2 F. 657 ; and *Waddell's Trs.* v. *Crawford,* 1926 S.C. 654, at 658, 663, and 668), although in *M'Innes* v. *M'Allister* (1827), 5 S. 862 (aff. on another point, 4 W. & S. 142), it was given only from the lapse of one year from the testator's death.

interests of parties equally favoured by the truster. Thus, in *Sutherland's Trs.* v. *Clarkson*,[1] trustees were instructed to divide the residue among the testator's children and his widow " when the same can be conveniently done . . . declaring that in the event of any one of my children predeceasing me or dying without issue before receiving his share under trust," his share was to pass to the widow and the other children. The truster died in 1856. In 1857 the trustees paid the shares of one daughter and of the widow. There were two other children, and one of these, a son, died in 1872 without having received his share. The fact that the trustees had before his death made payments to others was considered to prove that the whole division might then have been " conveniently done "; and the son was held to have had a vested interest.

On the other hand, in *Stephen's Trs.* v. *Stephen's Trs.*,[2] it was held that the language of the deed was so explicit in requiring actual payment as to displace this rule.

The time at which trustees resolve to pay is the time of payment.

Again, in *Leighton* v. *Leighton*.[3] " payment " was construed as meaning the date at which the trustees resolved to make payment. The facts of this case were these : the testator instructed his trustees on his death (as it happened) to divide the estate, and set aside a one-third share for each of his sons. But he empowered them to retain any share, and pay the proceeds to the son whose portion was so retained ; and other powers were also given them, including that of making advances in the event of any share being retained. There followed a clause " declaring that the above provisions for my said sons shall not become vested interests in them until actually paid," and a destination-over to issue and survivors referring to death " before payment or application " of the shares. A son died, having received by way of advance (and as a loan) more than the amount of his share. Prior to his death the trustees had decided to wind up the estate if they could lawfully do so, and to convert the son's loan into a payment of his share. When the son died this resolution had not been carried out ; and after his death, a question as to his right in these circum-

---

[1] (1874), 2 R. 46.

[2] Stated *ante*, p. 253. See especially Lord Blackburn's opinion.

[3] (1867), 5 M. 561.

stances was submitted to the Court. It was held that the son's portion had vested in him at the date of the resolution " I consider it to be a principle in the law of trusts," said Lord Cowan, " that however large the discretion of trustees may be with regard to the application of trust funds, still, if they once have come to a positive resolution, the rights of the beneficiaries cannot be affected by any delay that may accidentally arise in carrying out such resolution." And Lord Neaves said : " A resolution once taken is to be held in law as carried out ; and the party's rights shall be judged of as at the date of the resolution, without reference to a supervening accident." [1] The effect of the resolution was to convert what was a loan to the son into a payment of his share.

Two subsequent decisions, however, shew that this case is not to be regarded as establishing a hard-and-fast rule that in all cases a resolution by trustees has the effect of fixing the rights of the beneficiaries. In *Stephen's Trs.* v. *Stephens' Trs.*[2] and *Stewart's Trs.* v. *Hay*,[3] *Leighton* v. *Leighton* was distinguished, partly on the ground that the decision turned on the fact of advances to the beneficiary having been made, and partly also because the language of the will did not so clearly require actual payment as a condition of vesting.

[1] And cf. *Weller* v. *Ker* (1866), 4 M. (H. L.) 8 ; and *Macfarlane's Trs.* v. *Macfarlane* (1903), 41 S. L. R. 164.

[2] *Ante*, p. 253.
[3] 1930 S. C. 772.

CHAPTER XI.

THE VESTING OF LEGACIES PAYABLE ON THE OCCURRENCE OF A DOUBLE CONTINGENCY.

Gift to a
legatee on
majority on
the expiry of
a liferent.

THE usual case in which the effect of a reference to a double contingency requires to be considered is that of a legacy to a person payable on his majority and on the expiry of a liferent. Where the gift in this form is made simply and without the adjection of any conditions, the construction will depend on the manner in which reference is made to the legatee's majority. If it appear that that direction is merely administrative and is inserted with the purpose of protecting the legatee during his minority, and not with the view of depriving him of the power of using the subject in the meantime as a fund of credit, then, in accordance with the law stated in a previous chapter,[1] it will be presumed that the intention was that the legacy should vest *a morte testatoris*.[2] But if, on the other hand, the will shows that the testator intended that the legatee's attainment of majority should be a condition of his acquiring a right to the legacy, there can be no vesting till that event ; but it does not follow that vesting will also be suspended till the expiry of the liferent. Payment being deferred till the arrival of a *dies certus* (the expiry of the liferent) and a *dies incertus* (the legatee's attainment of twenty-one), then, as the latter term alone has power to suspend vesting, it results that on the legatee's attainment of majority his right is purified and vesting takes place, although the liferent has not then come to an end.[3]

But where the gift is made subject to a survivorship clause, or destination-over, or to any other condition which, according to the general rule of law, is treated as relating to

---

[1] Chapter III.
[2] *Matthew* v. *Scott* (1844), 6 D. 718.
[3] *Per* Lord Fullerton in *Matthew* v.

Scott, supra. Boyd's Trs. v. *Boyd* (1905), 7 F. 576.

the time of payment, or if there is a specific reference in the will to " payment," the construction of the gift causes difficulty. There is apparently a strong disposition on the part of the English Courts to hold, on grounds of expediency, that a gift of this kind, forming part of a family settlement, was intended to vest on the legatee's attainment of majority, although the subject should not then be relieved of the life interest.[1] But no such principle is recognised by the Scots Courts,[2] and the general rule—in so far as any general rule can be deduced from the decisions—would appear to be that the time of payment to which conditions appearing in the gift are *primâ facie* referable, is the time at which the legacy becomes payable by the death of the liferenter and the attainment of majority by the legatee, whichever of these events shall last happen.[3] This is the case, at least, where the gift takes the form of a direction to trustees to pay to the legatee on, or to hold for him after, the liferenter's death, the provision as to the legatee's majority and the survivorship clause or destination-over being engrafted on this leading direction.[4]

Thus, in *Richardson's Trs.* v. *Cope*,[5] the testator directed his trustees to pay the interest of the residue of his estate to his sister, and after her death to make over the principal to her children A. and B., and in the case of the death of either of them without issue, his or her share was to pass to the survivor ; but in case they or the survivor had not then attained majority, the interest was to be paid to him or them in the meantime, and the capital on majority. The testator further made a gift-over in the event of both children dying without issue before attaining majority, and declared that the children's shares should not vest before their

[marginal note: Vesting suspended till the close of the liferent and the legatee's majority.]

---

[1] Jarman on Wills (7th Ed.), pp. 1377-78 ; Theobald on Wills (8th Ed.), 656 ; *Partridge* v. *Baylis* (1881), 17 Ch. D. 835. In *Young* v. *Stewart* (1875), 13 S. L. R. 5, Lord Shand refers to this principle of construction.

[2] *Vide* Lord Shand's opinion in *Chalmer's Trs.* (1882), 9 R. 743.

[3] Cf. *M'Alpine* v. *Studholme* (1884), 10 R. 837.

[4] *Vide Melrose* v. *Melrose's Trs.*

(1869), 7 M. 1050, 593 (where a gift-over in case of death " before the said respective terms " was held to refer to death under age, or before the expiry of the liferent (whichever last happened), because the direction to the trustees was to hold " after the death of " the liferenter) ; *Lockhart* v. *Scott* (1858), 20 D. 690 ; and *Brown* v. *Warden* (1905), 12 S. L. T. 670 (Lord Stormonth-Darling).

[5] (1850), 12 D. 855.

majorities. One of the children attained majority but died before the liferentrix ; the other also attained majority and survived her. The Lord Ordinary,[1] considering that the conditions of the gift referred solely to their attainment of majority, held that both children had acquired vested interests. But the Second Division reversed this decision. It was observed in the opinions delivered that, although the testator mentioned only the period of majority in the declaration as to vesting, yet throughout the will he always referred to majority as occurring after the death of the liferentrix, and therefore it was clear that he had intended that both events should occur before the legatee became entitled to the subject. There was a survivorship clause which was referable in law to the termination of the liferent ; and there was a destination-over relating to the legatee's death before attaining majority ; hence, in order to give effect to the combination of these elements, it was necessary to hold vesting to be postponed until the occurrence of both events.

Again, in *Forbes* v. *M'Condach's Trs.*,[2] trustees were instructed to hold one-third of the residue for behoof of the truster's daughter in liferent ; and upon her death this third part was " to be uplifted and equally divided at the time after specified " among the daughter's children. It was declared that the shares of these children should be payable as they respectively attained majority : if all had reached majority on the daughter's death, the shares were to be paid as soon as convenient thereafter ; but if they should die " before receiving payment of his or her share respectively," it was to pass to his or her issue, and failing issue to the survivors. At the time at which the case was brought, all the children were major, but the daughter was alive. The case was held to fall within the rule of *Bryson's Trs.* v. *Clark*,[3] and the time of vesting was referred to the death of the liferentrix.

The same construction was adopted in *Bogle's Trs.* v. *Cochrane*,[4] where trustees were instructed to hold a fund for

---

[1] Wood.

[2] (1890), 18 R. 230. See to the same effect *Hunt's Trs.* v. *Hunt* (1906) 8 F. 764, where vesting was held to be suspended till the death of the life-renter, although all the children were major, and, owing to the liferenter's re-marriage, the liferent had been reduced to one-third of the income of the residue.

[3] (1880), 8 R. 142 ; *ante*, p. 50.

[4] (1892), 20 R. 108. As to the construction of the word " entitled," see *In re Maunder* [1902], 2 Ch. 875. In

the truster's sister in liferent and for her children in fee. Payment was to be made to the children on their mother's death if they had then attained majority ; but, if not, as soon thereafter as they should attain majority. Then followed a declaration that if any child should predecease the time at which he would have been " entitled to the benefit " of his share, it should go to his issue, and failing issue to the survivors. The words " entitled to the benefit of " were construed as meaning " entitled to the possession of " the subject, and vesting was accordingly held to be suspended until the termination of the liferent. A child, therefore, who attained majority but predeceased his mother took no share of the estate.

In *Swan's Trs.* v. *Swan*,[1] trustees were directed to hold the shares of residue for the testator's children in liferent and for their respective children in fee with a declaration that the share of any child who died without leaving issue should accresce to the other children then surviving in liferent and their issue in fee, that the shares should not be paid to any of the fiars until the age of twenty-five and that the fee should not vest in any of them " until the period of payment has arrived." The Court, rejecting the contention of certain grandchildren that by " period of payment " was meant the attainment of the specified age, decided that vesting was suspended till the occurrence of that event and the expiry of the liferent of the share. In *Gray's Trs.* v. *Gray*[2] a similar declaration as to vesting was held to have the effect of suspending vesting till the majority of the youngest child and the expiry of a liferent.

To this consistent train of authorities in favour of referring declarations or destinations-over depending on payment to the time at which payment became possible, *M'Kay's Trs.* v. *Gray*[3] forms an exception. On the death or re-marriage of the testator's wife, in the event of her surviving him (which occurred), the trustees were instructed to make over the residue to the children who survived him as they

---

Banks' Trs. v. *Banks' Trs.*, 1907 S. C. 125, where the same result was reached the survivorship clause referred to death " without having acquired a vested interest."

[1] 1912 S. C. 273.
[2] 1907 S. C. 54. See also *M'Ewan's Trs.* v. *Macdonald's Trs.* (1909), 46 S. L. R. 31.
[3] (1903), 5 F. 1086.

respectively attained majority or (if daughters) were married.
It was declared that the shares of residue should not vest
" until the respective terms of payment " ; and that, if any
child died before or after the testator without having
acquired a vested interest, his or her share should pass to
his or her issue, and, if there were none, to the surviving
children and the issue of predeceasers. It was held that one
of the children who had attained majority but died before
his mother had taken a vested interest in his share. The
ground of decision was that " respective terms " must be
such as might be different in the case of the several legatees,
and could not, therefore, be referred to the death of the
widow. In delivering the opinion of the Court in *Swan's
Trs.* v. *Swan*,[1] Lord Skerrington commented adversely on
this decision. " I cannot," he said, " regard that decision
as an authority, seeing that no argument was (so far as
appears from the report) offered in favour of what seems to
me to have been the natural meaning of the will. The
Judges were asked to elect between the views that vesting
took place at the beneficiary's majority, or alternatively at
the death of the widow. It does not appear to have been
argued that the period of payment could not arrive without
the concurrence of both events."

Destination-
over referring
only to the
legatee's
majority.

In all of the above cases the destination-over or other
qualification of the bequest was capable of being read as
applicable throughout the whole period before payment
became possible. But, if the destination-over is expressly
limited to the legatee's death before majority, there would
seem to be no justification for introducing the further condition of survivance of the liferenter ; indeed, the limitation
of the destination-over to the legatee's death in minority
would point strongly to vesting on his majority. Thus, in
M'Alpine v. *Studholme*,[2] the gift was made in the form of a
direction to trustees to pay the residue on the death of the
liferenter, with a destination-over expressly referring to the

---

[1] *Supra*. As to the meaning of
" respective terms of payment," cf.
Ld. Pres. Inglis's observation in
M'Elmail v. *Lundie's Trs.* (1888) 16 R.
47, at 54 : " It is quite clear that the
testator had in his mind more than
one period of payment, and also that

these terms of payment were applicable either to different persons or to
different portions of the estate.
That is the idea suggested by the
word " respectively."

[2] (1883), 10 R. 837. See also *Boyd's
Trs.* v. *Boyd* (1905), 7 F. 576 ; and

deaths of the residuary legatees in minority. A share of the residue, it was held, vested in a legatee who attained majority but died before the expiry of the liferent. In this case, apart from the destination-over, there was nothing to suspend vesting ; but then the destination-over referred solely to the period of the legatees' minorities, and therefore, when that period elapsed, it became inoperative, and there remained nothing to exclude immediate vesting.

Again, where the legacy is burdened with an annuity merely, vesting will, in the general case, take place on the legatee's majority. In *Fairgrieve* v. *Stirling*,[1] the truster directed that his children should have the residue of his estate equally among them, " their respective shares thereof being payable on their attaining majority, but subject always to the annuity in favour of my said wife," and declared that the shares of any of the children who died before " their shares respectively become payable," should pass to the survivors. It was decided that the share of a child (including his portion of the capital retained for the annuity) vested in him on his becoming major, although he died before the annuitant.

Where the legacy is given subject to an annuity.

To the same effect is the decision in *Howat's Trs.* v. *Howat*.[2] An annuity was provided to the testator's wife, and, subject to this annuity, the residue of the estate was to be held for the testator's son and any other children that might be born or the survivors of them or their issue. The portion of the estate retained for the annuity was made payable to the children as they respectively attained majority ; and there was a bequest to a charity if the children died " before receiving payment " of their shares without leaving issue. The only child, the son, attained majority, but died before his mother. It had been found necessary to retain the whole of the residue in order to meet the annuity, and no payment had, or could have, been made to the son. Nevertheless, the destination-over before receiving payment was held to relate to the time appointed for payment, viz., the son's majority ; and accordingly vesting was held to have taken place at that time.

Carruthers v. *Eeles* (1894), 21 R. 492. Stated *post* p. 291. *Sinclair* v. *Sinclair's Trs.* (1867), 5 S. L. R. 133.
[1] (1896), 34 S. L. R. 80 ; *Young* v.

Stewart's Trs. (1875), 13 S. L. R. 5, see p. 62, *ante*.
[2] 1922 S. C. 506.

CHAPTER XII.

THE VESTING OF PROVISIONS IN MARRIAGE CONTRACTS AND BONDS OF PROVISION.

Purpose of a marriage contract.

I. Marriage Contracts.—The proper and primary purpose of a marriage contract is to regulate the rights of the spouses and of the issue of the marriage.[1] . The stipulations directed to this purpose are onerous, because they form conditions of the marriage, and because the party undertaking obligations in favour of the other party or of the issue of the intended marriage receives as consideration " the paramount boon of a spouse." [2] The deed may, and frequently does, contain provisions which are outwith this purpose, as, for example, provisions in favour of parties other than the spouses and the issue ; but such purposes do not partake of the onerous character which attaches to the proper purposes of the deed, and, although contractual in form, are generally understood not to be so in substance.[3]

Provisions to children by destinations.

The reports in the Dictionary show that formerly matrimonial provisions were usually made by way of a simple destination. The father obliged himself to provide a subject or a sum of money to the children. Under such deeds the rights of the parent and of the children were of a peculiar nature. On the one hand, the father retained the fee of the subjects, and the essence of a fee is the power of disposal. On the other hand, the marriage had taken place on the faith of the marriage contract, and it would have been inequitable had the rights of the children remained at the

---

[1] *Per* Lord Young in *Wardlaw* v. *Wardlaw's Trs.* (1880), 7 R. 1070. See also *Advocate-General* v. *Trotter* (1847), 10 D. 56.

[2] *Per* Lord Curriehill in *Romanes* v. *Riddell* (1865), 3 M. 348.

[3] *Ramsay* v. *Ramsay's Trs.* (1871),

10 M. 120 ; *Murray's Trs.* v. *Murray* (1901) 3 F. 820, at 827 ; *Lord Advocate* v. *Stewart* (1906), 8 F. 579. But it is not beyond the power of the spouses to confer a contractual right on parties other than the issue of the marriage. See the cases cited on p. 283, *post*.

mercy of the parent and resting on no higher security than his disposition to fulfil his undertaking. To reconcile the rights of the parties, a somewhat anomalous view of these was adopted by the law, namely, that the issue were *quodam-modo* creditors—heirs among creditors and creditors among heirs—and that the parent could not defeat their right by a gratuitous deed, although no restraint was laid on his power of disposal for onerous causes. In other words, the obligation of the father was onerous in respect of the contract by which it was created, but it was ineffectual to restrain him in the free administration of the property during his lifetime.[1]

The nature of the respective rights of parent and child under such contracts was considered in the very important case of *Arthur and Seymour* v. *Lamb*.[2] In that case the father, by antenuptial marriage contract, bound himself to settle and secure, and for that purpose to take the rights and securities of, one-half of the estate then belonging to him, or which he should conquest or acquire during the marriage, in favour of himself in liferent and of the children of the marriage in fee. Under this provision the father was fiar, and the nature and effect of his obligation was thus described in the interlocutor pronounced : " He had the same absolute power of use, administration, disposal, dilapidation, and spending that any owner of property has, subject only to the condition that he could not defeat or prejudice the children's right of succession by any merely gratuitous alienation, whether by deed *inter vivos*, by disposition *mortis causâ*, or by testament. The right of the children under the provision is not a proper *jus crediti* on the one hand, nor a bare hope of succession on the other. It does not make the children creditors of the father during his lifetime, or creditors at all at any time, in competition with his creditors in onerous debts and obligations, but makes them creditors against the estate of their father after his decease for performance of the obligation contained in the marriage contract."

Protected rights of succession.

---

[1] *Per* Lord Benholme in *Wilson's Trs.* v. *Pagan* (1856), 18 D. 1096. Ersk. iii. 8. 38.

[2] (1870), 8 M. 928. See *Earl of Wemyss* v. *Earl of Wemyss' Trs.*

28th Feb. 1815, F. C. ; affd. 6 Pat. 390 ; *Macdonald* v. *Hall* (1893), 20 R. (H. L.) 88 ; *Gillon's Trs.* v. *Gillon* (1890), 17 R. 435.

In this case the only child of the marriage predeceased the father. As his right under the contract was no more than that of a protected succession, it followed that he had acquired no vested interest in the provision.[1] There was, however, a grandchild alive at the death of the granter of the provision, and this grandchild was admitted under the *conditio*.[2]

The theory of protected succession was applied to testamentary bequests in *Massy* v. *Scott's Trs.*[3] and *Gibson's Trs.* v. *Ross.*[4]

Children may have a *jus crediti* in their provisions. But the contract may give the issue a higher right than a right of succession. They may have a *jus crediti* enabling them to compete with creditors, and giving them a preference if their right is secured by diligence or perfected by seisin. If a party on his marriage could, while giving the issue of the marriage no claim against himself, introduce them in preference to, or in competition with, his creditors, this form of disposition of his estate would obviously be liable to grave abuse. Hence, in a question with creditors, the law scrutinises the nature of the provision in favour of the issue. A party cannot, it is settled, confer upon his children a right which shall be good against all the world except himself ; if the provision to issue is to stand in competition with creditors, there must be a claim also, not merely against the parent's estate on his death, but against himself during his lifetime. The conditions under which children will have a *jus crediti* are summarised in the following passage from Lord Moncreiff's opinion in *Goddard* v. *Stewart's Children*[5] :—

" (1) I understand the rule of law to be, that under such marriage contracts the children have a *jus crediti* giving them such a right against the creditors of their father, if the provision is so conceived as that there was or might be a direct interest accruing to them in the lifetime of the father. As, for example, if the provision is made payable on the marriage or majority of the child, though such event should

---

[1] *Maconochie* v. *Greenlee* (1870), M. 13040 ; *Rattray* v. *Blair* (1790), Hume's Dec. 526.

[2] See *Hughes* v. *Edwardes* (1892), 19 R. (H. L.) 33.

[3] (1872), 11 M. 173.

[4] (1877), 4 R. 1038. But see *post*, p. 328.

[5] (1844), 6 D. 1018. See *Herries* v. *Brown* (1838), 16 S. 948 ; 13 Fac. 567.

happen in the lifetime of the father ; or if the provision is declared to bear interest from any such term which might be in his lifetime ; or if it is declared to be payable at the dissolution of the marriage, or to bear interest from and after that event, which may happen by the wife's predecease. (2) But, on the other hand, that if the provision is so conceived that the principal is not payable till after the father's death, and does not bear interest from any earlier term, and where no actual benefit or interest can be claimed or taken in his lifetime, there is no *jus crediti* vested in the children as against onerous creditors. In respect of the father and his heirs, they are, no doubt, creditors ; but in respect of his creditors, they are merely heirs, having no more than a *spes successionis*. (3) I understand it also to be a fixed rule, that it has no effect in conferring a *jus crediti* on the children, that, instead of the husband being simply bound to pay a sum to the children, he engages to provide and secure a sum so payable. (4) But if he actually lends out the money, or constitutes a trust, or grants heritable security to the wife, or any other person in name of the children, with absolute warrandice, it constitutes a fee in the children, which will prevail against onerous creditors."

Although the provision in favour of the issue does not fall within any of the above categories, the issue may yet have a *jus crediti*, if the obligation in their favour has been purchased by some consideration over and above that implied in all marriage contracts. Thus, where a father in his son's marriage contract bound himself to provide a sum after his death to the issue of the intended marriage, and the son renounced in favour of the father a lease which he had from him, it was held that, in consideration of the renunciation of the lease, the issue had a right enabling them to compete with the creditors of the father.[1]

But where the subject of the contract is conquest, the issue have no *jus crediti*.[2] The conquest is to be ascertained at the father's death, and not at the dissolution of the

Rights of children in provisions of conquest.

---

[1] *Thomson* v. *Gourlay* (1824), 2 Sh. Apps. 183 ; *Cannan* v. *Greig* (1794), M. 12005 ; *Gordon* v. *Murray* (1833), 11 S. 368.

[2] *Anderson* v. *Anderson* (1684), M.

12960 ; *Cruickshanks* v. *Cruickshanks* (1685), M. 12964 ; Lord Fullerton in *Advocate-General* v. *Trotter* (1847), 10 D. 56.

marriage,[1] and the father is not so strictly bound as he is where a special provision is made. A provision of conquest is "little better than a simple destination, so that the subject may be affected not only by the father's onerous or rational deeds, but even gratuitous, provided they be granted for small sums, perhaps to a child of another marriage." [2] In *Champion* v. *Duncan*,[3] spouses by antenuptial contract disponed each to the other, in case of the other's survivance, their whole property "pertaining or belonging, or that shall pertain and belong to them, or either of them, at the dissolution of the marriage," in liferent, and in regard to the fee it was provided that, failing issue, the whole should be divided on the survivor's death, and one-half should go to the husband's heirs and one-half to the wife's. After the marriage the husband took out a policy of insurance on his life, the premiums of which he paid from the income of his estate. He afterwards assigned this policy. In a competition between the assignees and the wife's representatives, who claimed a half of the benefit under the policy, the former were preferred. Taking the terms of the disposition literally, the property carried was that belonging to the husband either at the date of the contract or at his death, and the policy was not part of his estate at either of these dates. Moreover, as Lord Curriehill pointed out, a technical meaning attached to a marriage contract which conveyed an *universitas*. "When," he said, "an *universitas* is provided by an antenuptial marriage contract to the wife and children, even *per verba de præsenti*, the rule is that, on the one hand, the husband remains the absolute owner, with right of administration and power of disposal for onerous causes, and even gratuitously, unless his alienation be of such a character as to be a fraud on the marriage contract."

The vesting of children's provisions. But, although the issue may have a *jus crediti*, it does not appear to follow as a necessary consequence that they have also a vested interest, that is to say, a transmissible interest, in the provision in their favour, during the parent's

[1] *Anderson* v. *Anderson* and *Cruikshanks* v. *Cruikshanks*, *supra*.

[2] Ersk. iii. 8. 43.

[3] (1867), 6 M. 17 ; *Cowan* v. *Young* (1669), M. 12942 ; *Oliphant* v. *Finnie* (1629), M. 3066 ; *Ormiston* v. *Ormiston* (1809), Hume's Decs. 531. See also Ld. Pres. Inglis's opinion in *Haldane* v. *Hutchison* (1885), 13 R. 179.

lifetime. The obligation may be binding and at the same time contingent—indeed, it must in any case be contingent, until it is seen whether children will come into existence. The features which go to show that the children have a *jus crediti* may be favourable to early vesting,[1] but the question must ultimately depend upon the terms in which the provision is conceived. *Grindlay* v. *The Merchant Company of Edinburgh*,[2] for example, is an instance where the terms of the contract were such as to confer a *jus crediti*, but where vesting was suspended until the children's majorities. In that case a father bound himself to pay a sum to his children on their respective majorities whether they became major before or after his death. This undertaking, as it was prestable during his lifetime, created a *jus crediti*. But the provision was dependent on the arrival of a *dies incertus*, the majority of each child, and accordingly the vesting was held to be suspended until the children became major.

Where the father has merely a liferent with a fiduciary fee for behoof of the children, the children will take a vested interest on birth, unless the provision in their favour is so expressed as under the general rules of vesting to exclude this result. Thus, in *Beattie's Tr.* v. *Cooper's Trs.*,[3] the father bound himself at the first term after the marriage to lend out a sum and take the securities for himself and his wife and the longest liver of them in liferent allenarly, and for the children of the marriage, and, failing children of the marriage, for the wife and her heirs and assignees, in fee. A bond was granted in these terms. It was held that the provision vested in the first child born, for behoof of himself and any other children that might be born, and that the shares were transmissible although the children died before the dissolution of the marriage.

It was laid down, however, in the subsequent case of *Grant's Tr.* v. *Anderson's Tr.*,[4] that the general presumption in regard to marriage contract provisions in favour of children was that vesting took place at the dissolution of

Vesting in cases where the parent is liferenter and fiduciary fiar.

---

[1] See *Walkinshaw's Trs.* v. *Walkinshaw* (1872), 10 M. 763 ; and *Allardice* v. *Lautour* (1845), 7 D. 362.

[2] 1st July 1814, F. C.

[3] (1862), 24 D. 519 ; *Falconer* v. *Wright,* 20th Jan. 1825, F. C. ; 3 S. 455. See *Robertson* (1869), 7 M. 1114.

[4] (1866), 4 M. 336. See *Brodie's Trs.* v. *Mowbray's Trs.* (1840), 3 D. 31, stated *ante*, p. 233.

the marriage, and that in accordance with this presumption vesting was excluded where the children died before that event. There a father, in the marriage contract of his daughter, bound himself to lay out a sum of money, which sum was to be payable after his death to the daughter and her husband for their liferent use allenarly and for the children of the marriage in fee, whom failing, for his own heirs and assignees. There was one child of the marriage, who predeceased the granter and both of the parents. The Lord Ordinary [1] held that there was no vesting in the child, because the sum was payable only on the granter's death, and the child predeceased him. This judgement was sustained by the First Division ; but, although the feature of the case on which the Lord Ordinary founded was noticed, the decision was rested, not on that ground, but on the circumstance that the child had not survived the dissolution of the marriage. The Lord President [2] observed : " The general doctrine in reference to cases of this kind is, that the dissolution of the marriage is to be taken as the period of vesting. Under that general doctrine, I think it may be held here that the provision did not vest in the child." The destination-over in case of failure of the children of the marriage was treated as referring to the contingency of no children being alive at the dissolution of the marriage.[3]

On the other hand, in *Walkinshaw's Trs.* v. *Walkinshaw*,[4] it was held that a sum, which the father undertook to pay to his children on the death of the longest liver of himself and his wife, vested in the children although they all predeceased both their parents, the Court relying upon the circumstance that the father had bound himself to provide and secure the sum, and to insure his life at the sight, and in the name, of trustees in security of the provision.

Marriage contract provisions secured by a trust.

In modern practice, provisions in marriage contracts are usually secured by the constitution of a trust. The vesting of the beneficiary interests will depend in such cases upon the terms in which the trust conveyance is made, and the canons of vesting discussed in the previous chapters with reference to testamentary gifts are applicable in determining the time at which the vesting of the provisions takes place.

[1] Lord Mure.
[2] Lord Colonsay.
[3] See Lord Deas' opinion.
[4] (1872), 10 M. 763.

There is, however, a presumption that the children's interests under an antenuptial contract vest at the dissolution of the marriage, and, although this presumption may be displaced, distinct evidence in favour of vesting at a subsequent period is required for this purpose.[1] This presumption corresponds with the presumption in favour of vesting *a morte testatoris* in the case of legacies, and has the effect of casting the onus on the party maintaining that the vesting of matrimonial provisions in favour of children is deferred to a period subsequent to the dissolution of the marriage by the death of the first deceaser of the spouses. But the presumption has also in some cases [2] been treated as meaning that *primâ facie* vesting is suspended during the subsistence of the marriage. It may be doubted, however, whether the presumption in this sense can be considered as a principle of general application in the construction of marriage settlements. If a party in his marriage contract assigns to trustees the property belonging to him at the time of the marriage, or a sum of money, or specific subjects, there would seem to be no sufficient ground for holding that vesting in the children as they come into existence is excluded merely because the trust conveyance is contained in a marriage contract. The vesting in a case of this kind would appear to depend upon the same considerations as apply in regard to the vesting of beneficiary interests under other trusts.[3] On the other hand, if the trust is to come into operation only on the death of the parent, and he is not divested, the vesting would seem to be suspended during the parent's lifetime ; [4] and vesting would also apparently be suspended if the parent conveyed to the trustees merely the property belonging to him at his death,[5] or possibly if he

---

[1] *Romanes* v. *Riddell* (1865), 3 M. 348, *per* Lord Deas ; *Wardlaw's Trs.* v. *Wardlaw* (1880), 7 R. 1070 ; *per* Lord M'Laren in *Blackburn's Trs.* v. *Blackburn* (1896), 23 R. 698.

[2] *Grant's Tr.* v. *Anderson* (1866), 4 M. 336, *supra*, p. 273 ; *Lord and Lady Strathmore's Trs.* v. *Lord Glamis*, 1932 S. C. 458, *per* Ld. Pres. Clyde, at 464.

[3] Cf. *Miller* v. *Finlay's Trs.* (1875), 2 R. (H. L.) 1 ; *Beattie's Tr.* v.

Cooper's Trs. (1862), 24 D. 519 ; *ante*, p. 273 ; *Turnbull* v. *Tawse* (1825), 2 W. & S. 80 ; *Smitton* v. *Tod* (1839), 2 D. 225 ; and *Spalding* v. *Spalding's Trs.* (1874), 2 R. 237.

[4] See Lord M'Laren's opinion in *Dowie* v. *Hagart* (1894), 21 R. 1052.

[5] *Hagart's Trs.* v. *Hagart* (1895), 22 R. 625 ; *Somerville* v. *Somerville*, 18th May 1819, F. C. See also Lord Fullerton's opinion in *Advocate-General* v. *Trotter* (1847), 10 D. 56.

conveyed by the same words of conveyance the property belonging to him at the date of the marriage or which should belong to him at his death,[1] because the conveyance is in form testamentary.

Vesting at birth.

In *Sivright* v. *Dallas*,[2] which has already been stated,[3] the parents of the spouses conveyed to trustees sums of money to be held for behoof of the spouses in liferent and for the children of the marriage in fee, and it was held that the children acquired vested rights as they were born.

Vesting not deferred beyond the dissolution of the marriage.

In *Romanes* v. *Riddell*,[4] vesting was held not to be postponed beyond the dissolution of the marriage. In the antenuptial contract the wife conveyed the half of the property then belonging to her, and the property she should acquire, to trustees for behoof of herself in liferent and of her husband also in liferent if he survived her, and for behoof of the children of the marriage, whom failing herself and her heirs and assignees in fee. The only child of the marriage survived his mother but predeceased his father. In these circumstances it became necessary to determine the rights of the child in the estate conveyed to the trustees by his mother. The Court, without deciding whether vesting took place on his birth or on the dissolution of the marriage, held that at all events it was not deferred beyond the latter event. Lord Deas observed : " As regards provisions to children under an antenuptial marriage contract, it is generally to be presumed that these provisions vest at the dissolution of the marriage. In some cases the provisions vest at the birth of a child, and it is necessary to look narrowly into the terms of the contract to see which

---

[1] In *Hall's Trs.* v. *Macdonald* (1892), 19 R. 567, where this form of expression was used, Lord Kinnear observed : " He (*i.e.* the father) remains the undivested owner of his whole estate during his life, with full and unrestricted power of control and disposal, because the condition that the estate which is to be carried by his conveyance shall belong to him at his death is applicable to *acquisita* as well as to *acquirenda*, when, as in the present case, the former are included in the same general words of conveyance as the latter." This statement does not appear to be affected by the reversal of the decision in the case (20 R. (H. L.) 88). See also *Fernie* v. *Colquhoun's Trs.* (1854), 17 D 232 ; *Grant* v. *Robertson* (1872), 10 M. 804 ; *Wyllie's Trs.* v. *Boyd* (1891), 18 R. 1121 ; *Buchanan's Trs.* v. *Whyte* (1890), 17 R. (H. L.) 53 ; and contrast *The Lord Advocate* v. *Hagart's Exrs.* (1870), 9 M. 358 ; affirmed 10 M. (H. L.) 62, with *Moir's Trs.* v. *The Lord Advocate* (1874), 1 R. 345.

[2] 27th Jan. 1824, F. C. ; 2 S. 643.

[3] *Ante*, p. 232.

[4] (1865), 3 M. 348.

of the two periods was intended, or to find good grounds for holding that the parties had reference neither to the one period nor the other. . . . But whatever may be said of vesting at birth, there is no presumption in favour of postponement of vesting beyond the dissolution of the marriage. On the contrary, the reasons and presumptions in favour of vesting upon that event (if not previously) are so strong and palpable, that they require to be overcome by something leading pointedly to an opposite conclusion." The provision for failure of issue was treated as meaning failure by non-existence, or at all events non-existence at the termination of the marriage.[1]

The question which was noticed but not decided in *Romanes* v. *Riddell*, namely, whether the issue acquired a vested right at birth or only on the dissolution of the marriage, was raised in the subsequent case of *Wardlaw's Trs.* v. *Wardlaw*.[2] There the husband bound himself to provide one-half of the whole estate belonging to him at his death for behoof of his wife in liferent, if she outlived him, and of the children of the marriage in fee, and that by vesting the same in trustees ; and the wife conveyed to the trustees all lands and funds then belonging to her or which she might succeed to, for behoof of herself and her husband in conjunct fee and liferent, and for behoof of the children in such proportions as the husband should appoint. Of the children of the marriage some died before both spouses, and others survived their father, but died before their mother. It was held that the provisions vested in all the children alive at the dissolution of the marriage, to the exclusion of those who died before that event. The only difficulty experienced by the Court arose from the terms in which the wife's estate was settled. Had the wife taken a fee, it was said in several of the opinions that the decision must have been otherwise, for vesting would necessarily have been suspended until the death of the fiar ; but the tenor of the deed, and especially the power of apportionment conferred on the husband, convinced the Court that no more than a liferent was reserved to her, and therefore it was possible to hold that vesting took place during her life. The vesting

Vesting at the dissolution of the marriage.

---

[1] As to the meaning of "failing issue," see *ante*, p. 207.   [2] (1880), 7 R. 1070.

of the husband's estate was postponed till his death, because he conveyed what he should conquest, and accordingly the contributions of both vested at the same time, namely, on the death of the husband.

Vesting on the respective deaths of the spouses.

But the estates of the spouses may vest at different times. In *Murray's Trs.* v. *Bloxsom's Trs.*[1] it was conceded that the estate conveyed by the wife in the marriage contract did not vest until her death. The husband, on the other hand, had assigned a specific sum to the trustees to be held for the issue, under the declaration that, if the children died before the survivor of the spouses without issue, the provision should pass to the husband's heirs and assignees. It was decided that the sum contributed by the husband vested at his death although his wife survived him, the destination-over to the husband's heirs and assignees being apparently deemed insufficient to suspend the vesting.

The fact that the provision to the children is contained in a direction to the trustees to make payment to them on the death of the longest liver of the spouses, is obviously, in itself, not sufficient to suspend vesting.[2] But the other terms of the deed may show that the parties intended to postpone vesting till that event.

Whether marriage contracts are to be more favourably construed than wills.

The remark has been made in some cases,[3] that marriage contracts are to be construed more favourably, as regards early vesting, than testamentary deeds ; that is to say, that stronger language is required to postpone vesting in the case of matrimonial provisions to children than where the gift is made in a will. This principle of construction was carried very far in *Pretty* v. *Newbigging.*[4] In that case a marriage contract provided that in the contingency which occurred, namely, the husband's death survived by his wife and children, the trustees should hold a fund in security of an annuity given to the widow, and should pay the principal on her death to the children then alive ; and it was declared that if any child should die before the provision became payable, his or her issue should have right to his or her

[1] (1887), 15 R. 233.

[2] *Boyd's Trs.* v. *Boyd* (1905), 7 F. 576.

[3] By Lord Cowan, Lord Rutherfurd, Lord Curriehill, Lord Benholme, and Lord Deas, in *Pretty* v. *Newbigging* (1854), 16 D. 667 ; and by Lord Cowan and Lord Benholme in *Rogerson's Trs.* v. *Rogerson* (1865), 3 M. 684.

[4] (1854), 16 D. 667—a case before the whole Court.

share. If the husband had in his lifetime made provision for the widow's annuity (which he did not do), then the principal was to be paid to the children on his death. It was decided by a very narrow majority of the Court, that the only surviving child of the marriage had a vested interest during the widow's life, and that he was entitled, with her concurrence, to receive payment of the trust funds. In this case the destination-over to the issue of the children pointed to the death of the widow as the date of vesting, and it was admitted in the opinions of the majority that a provision of this kind occurring in a testamentary deed would probably be sufficient to suspend vesting ; but then the deed under construction was a marriage contract, and the destination was deemed insufficient to overcome the presumption in favour of vesting arising from the nature of the deed.

In view of the powerful dissenting opinions in this case,[1] it may be doubted whether the same influence would now be allowed to this consideration. Later cases show that, if in a marriage contract trustees are directed on the death of the longest liver of the spouses, or on the termination of his or her liferent, to pay the principal to the children of the marriage then alive,[2] or to the children and the survivors,[3] vesting is suspended until the death of the survivor of the spouses or the termination of the liferent. The presumption in favour of vesting at the dissolution of the marriage gives way in these cases to the plainly expressed conditions of the obligation.

Thus, in *Scott's Trs.* v. *Brown & Co.*,[4] the interest of the wife's estate was given to her and to her husband if he survived her, and after the death of the survivor of them the capital was to be paid by the trustees to the children of the marriage. If there were no children of the marriage, or

Vesting suspended till the death of both spouses.

---

[1] By the Lord President (Colonsay), the Lord Justice-Clerk (Hope), Lords Handyside, Wood, and Cowan. See also L. J.-C. Hope's opinion in *Allardice* v. *Lautour* (1845), 7 D. 362 ; and L. J.-C. Inglis's opinion in *Rogerson's Trs.* v. *Rogerson* (1865), 3 M. 684.

[2] *Vines* v. *Hillou* (1860), 22 D. 1436 ; *Boyle* v. *The Earl of Glasgow's Trs.* (1858), 20 D. 925 ; *ante,* p. 88 ;

Robertson v. *Houston* (1858), 20 D. 989 ; *Hughes* v. *Edwardes* (1892), 19 R. (H. L.) 33.

[3] *Blackburn's Trs.* v. *Blackburn* (1896), 23 R. 698 ; *Cuming's Trs.* v. *Cuming* (1896), 24 R. 153. But cf. *Angus' Trs.* v. *Angus* (1880), 17 S. L. R. 536, stated *ante,* p. 58.

[4] (1882), 9 R. 798.

if there were children but all of them should die before the term of payment, then the wife's assignees, and failing these her heirs, were to receive the capital. The First Division, following the case of *Lockhart* v. *Scott*,[1] held that there was no vesting till the death of both spouses. The clear reference in the destination-over to the term of payment as the time at which it was to become operative in the case of there being then no issue, put the matter almost beyond question. In distinguishing the decision in *Romanes* v. *Riddell*, Lord President Inglis remarked : " There the only event in which the money was to revert was if there was a failure of issue of the marriage in the sense of no issue having ever existed. That was the construction put on the deed by all the judges who heard the case, and it is, I think, a legitimate construction. It would be a strained construction to say that the words ' failing a child or children ' could include the death of a child or children before the term of payment ; if that is meant it is always expressed. The case of *Romanes* then only settled that the words ' failing a child or children ' in that deed meant that no child or children should ever have existed."

In *Lockhart* v. *Scott*,[2] the construction was more difficult than in the last case, because the direction to pay the funds to the children on the death of the longest liver of the spouses was followed by a declaration that the shares should be payable on majority, or, in the case of daughters, marriage. A subsequent destination-over in the event of children dying before the term of payment of their respective provisions was treated as suspensive of vesting until the death of both spouses, although the children attained majority before that event.

Vesting on majority. The postponement of vesting in this case was due to the clear reference in the destination-over to the time of payment, coupled with the direction to the trustees to make over the subject on the death of the survivor of the spouses. If, however, the destination-over refers merely to the death of the children in minority, then, in the general case, the provision will vest not later than the dissolution of the marriage if there be then any major child, or, if all the children are then in minority, when the first child attains majority. It was

[1] (1858), 20 D. 690.   [2] *Supra.*

so decided in *Boyd's Trs.* v. *Boyd*,[1] where the trustees under the marriage contract were directed to pay the principal of the sum put in settlement by the husband to the children of the marriage on the death or re-marriage of the survivor of the spouses, and it was declared that the share of any child dying before attaining majority should pass to his or her issue, and failing issue to the surviving children.

So far the construction of marriage contracts and the vesting of the rights given under this class of deeds have been considered with reference to provisions in favour of the issue of the marriage. But the parties not infrequently provide for the destination of the property in the event of there being no children. The stipulations in favour of such parties may be as onerous and irrevocable as provisions to children if this is part of the contract between the parties, as, for example, if a stipulation in favour of the relatives or next-of-kin of one of the spouses is the counterpart of an obligation in favour of the other.[2] But in the general case the substitutes called after the issue of the marriage are understood to have no indefeasible right : the substitution is a simple destination, and is alterable by the parties.[3]

Provisions to parties other than the children.

So strictly was this rule enforced in the Court of Session in a leading case,[4] that it was held that children alone—sons and daughters—were within the consideration of the marriage. In the case referred to, a husband by antenuptial contract

Grandchildren are within the consideration of the marriage.

---

[1] (1905), 7 F. 576 ; *Burnett* v. *Burnett* (1854), 16 D. 780 ; stated *ante*, p. 197 ; Lord Rutherfurd's Note in *Baillie* v. *Seton* (1853), 16 D. 216. The whole provision will vest in the first child for behoof of himself and the other children who may attain majority, but the individual shares will vest in the children only as they reach majority, *ante*, p. 197.

[2] In *Hall's Trs.* v. *Macdonald* (1892), 19 R. 567, Lord Kinnear observed : " It is, no doubt, perfectly competent for the spouses, contracting with each other before marriage, to stipulate for benefits to other persons or classes of persons besides themselves and their children, and if a destination to the heirs or to other relatives of one of the spouses is the counterpart of an obliga-

tion in favour of the other, it will be just as onerous and irrevocable as the mutual provisions in favour of the spouses themselves." Provisions to the respective heirs of the spouses may be contractual as between them but testamentary *quoad* the heirs— *Ferguson's Curator Bonis* v. *Ferguson's Trs.* (1893), 20 R. 835. There are, of course, numerous cases in which provisions in marriage contracts in favour of the relations of one of the spouses have been held irrevocable after his or her death by the other spouse— *Kinsman* v. *Scot* (1687), M. 12980 ; *Yorkston* v. *Simpson* (1693), M. 12981.

[3] See the cases cited in note 3, p. 268, *ante*.

[4] *Macdonald* v. *Hall* (1893), 20 R. (H. L.) 88.

conveyed his estate to his wife in liferent allenarly, and to the issue of the marriage and the issue of their bodies in fee, whom failing to his own heirs and assignees. The only child of the marriage predeceased both his parents, leaving a child. The father by his testamentary trust settlement gave his estate to other parties, and the question in the case was whether the grandchild had an indefeasible right. It was decided in the House of Lords, contrary to the judgement of the First Division, that in a question as to a marriage contract grandchildren were within the consideration of the marriage, and were, like children, heirs *in obligatione*.

Provisions to substitutes are testamentary. When the usual form of matrimonial provision was a simple destination, there were obvious grounds of expediency for holding that the rather anomalous restraint imposed on the father should not be extended beyond the provisions in favour of the children of the marriage. But it is not so clear why the distinction between provisions in favour of issue and provisions in favour of other parties should obtain where the parties constitute a trust and insert in the trust purposes the provisions conceived in favour of those other parties. But it is settled that the rule that strangers to the marriage are merely substitutes obtains also in the case of trust conveyances. The parties are understood to contract merely with reference to the rights of themselves or of the issue, and provisions outwith these purposes are considered to be merely testamentary.[1]

Provision to the heirs of one of the spouses. Thus, in *Macleod* v. *Cunninghame*,[2] a lady in her antenuptial contract conveyed her estate to trustees in trust for herself in liferent, and for the issue of the marriage in fee, whom failing, for such persons as she should appoint or otherwise for her nearest heir-at-law. On the dissolution of the marriage without issue, the lady made another disposition of the subjects, and it was held that this disposition was effectual to sopite the destination to her heir contained in the contract. In this case it was thought the contract really contained no proper destination beyond the issue,

---

[1] See Lord Watson's opinion in *Mackie* v. *Gloag's Trs.* (1884), 11 R. (H. L.) 10; and Lord Young's in *Wardlaw's Trs.* v. *Wardlaw* (1880), 7 R. 1070.

[2] (1841), 3 D. 1288; affirmed 5 Bell's Apps. 210; *Martin* v. *Bannatyne* (1861), 23 D. 705; *M'Lean's Trs.* v. *M'Lean* (1878), 5 R. 679.

for the provision in favour of the heir was, as Lord Jeffrey pointed out, not a destination, but the negation of all destination.

Similarly, in *Montgomery's Trs.* v. *Montgomery*,[1] where the wife's estate was held by trustees for herself and her husband and the survivor of them in liferent, and for the children of the marriage in fee, and in the event of there being no children alive at the wife's death, then for her assignees, executors, or nearest of kin, it was held that, as all the children died before her, the wife retained the fee of the estate and might dispose of it by her will. It is a settled rule in the construction of trust-deeds that the truster is divested of the property which is the subject of the conveyance to the trustees only in so far as is required by the purposes of the deed.[2] Hence, as the wife had directed the trustees to make over the estate to the beneficiaries only in the event of their surviving her, and as this contingent disposition failed because of the children's death before her, her radical right of fee was not displaced.

On the other hand, an example of the rights of strangers to the marriage being indefeasibly secured by the provisions of the contract is afforded by *Mackie* v. *Gloag's Trs.*[3] In that case a widow on entering into a second marriage became a party to an antenuptial contract. By the contract she conveyed certain heritable and other property to trustees in trust for her own liferent use allenarly, and for her children procreated and to be procreated in fee. There were no children of the second marriage, but there were three of the first. The question in the case was whether the lady could defeat by testamentary disposition the provisions in the contract in favour of these three children. The Second Division held that these provisions were testamentary as regards these children, although onerous as regards any children that might have been born of the second marriage. But on appeal this decision was reversed. The general rule

Rights of strangers indefeasibly secured.

---

[1] (1895), 22 R. 824. See p. 177, *ante*, for a fuller statement of the effect of this decision. See also *Ramsay* v. *Ramsay's Trs.* (1871), 10 M. 120, *per* Ld. Pres. Inglis, at 124.

[2] *Higginbotham's Trs.* v. *Higginbotham* (1886), 13 R. 1016 ; Lord

M'Laren's and Lord Low's opinions in *Smith* v. *Stuart* (1894), 22 R. 130.

[3] (1884), 11 R. (H. L.) 10. See Lord Watson's observation on this case in *Macdonald* v. *Hall* (1893), 20 R. (H. L.) 88 ; and *de Mestre* v. *West* [1891], A. C. 264.

that provisions in favour of substitutes other than the children of the marriage are testamentary, was held to be inapplicable, because the children of the first marriage were not substitutes, but were favoured in the first instance, and were called along with the children of the marriage in contemplation of which the contract was made. Lord Selborne observed : " The considerations of the contract, though founded on marriage, must, I apprehend, extend to all the terms of the contract on which depend the interest of those who are within the consideration of the marriage, and when they take only on terms which admit to a participation with them others who would not otherwise be within the consideration, then, not the matrimonial consideration properly so called, but the consideration of the mutual contract, extend to and comprehend them."

In this case it will be observed that the subject of the conveyance was specific property, and it was to be held by the trustees from the date of the conveyance for behoof of existing beneficiaries.[1] But the same result was reached in *Leslie's Trs.* v. *Leslie*,[2] where the marriage contract dealt with the property which should belong to the spouses at the date of their deaths. On his second marriage the husband entered into this marriage contract by which the parties directed the trustees to hold their estates for themselves and the survivor of them in liferent, and on the survivor's death to divide the estates equally *per capita* among the issue of the marriage and the son of the husband by his former marriage. Subsequently the spouses executed a postnuptial contract by which they provided that the wife's estate should be divided among the issue of the marriage alone. It was held that the interest of the son of the first marriage was contractual and irrevocable in like manner as was the interest of the children of the parties, and that consequently the alteration made by the postnuptial contract was ineffectual.

It will be noted that in both of these cases the third

---

[1] See Lord Kinnear's opinion in *Barclay's Trs.* v. *Watson* (1903), 5 F. 926. See also *Turnbull* v. *Tawse* (1825), 1 W. & S. 80 ; *Smitton* v. *Tod* (1839) 2 D. 225 (reviewed in

Spalding v. *Spalding's Trs.* (1874), 2 R. 237).

[2] 1921 S. C. 940. See also *Allan's Testamentary Trs.* v. *Allan's Marriage Contract Trs.* (1907), 15 S. L. T. 73 (Lord Dundas).

party was called as an institute along with the issue of the marriage, and the decisions in no way touch the construction of provisions in favour of persons who are called as conditional institutes on the failure of issue. In the latter case, indeed, the presumption is that the general rule as to the construction of such provisions is applicable. In *Barclay's Trs.* v. *Watson* [1] the facts were these : By her marriage contract a wife conveyed her estate to trustees in trust for behoof of the spouses in liferent, and, on the death of the survivor of them, to pay the capital to the children of the marriage and their issue, and failing these to the wife's brothers and sisters *nominatim*. There were no children of the marriage, and after her husband's death the wife executed a deed altering the destination to her brothers and sisters. It was held that this deed was effectual. *Mackie's* case was distinguished on the ground that the brothers and sisters were no more than conditional institutes. Lord M'Laren observed : " Looking to the authorities—which in this branch of the law are perfectly consistent—I think it is established that no one who is without the consideration of the marriage can claim to have received an indefeasible right under the marriage contract, unless (1) he takes as an institute, and (2) there is in the deed an expressed intention to create in his favour an indefeasible right."

A postnuptial contract is intended to serve the same purpose as an antenuptial contract, and although in a question with creditors it may not have the same effect, it should be construed, it would seem, in any question as to the vesting of the rights of the parties or the children, according to the principles of construction discussed in this chapter. In *Peddie* v. *Peddie's Trs.*,[2] Lord Rutherfurd Clark, delivering the opinion of the Court, observed : " In a question with creditors, a postnuptial marriage contract may not have the same power as an antenuptial marriage contract. But, *intra familiam*, I think that it has." *Postnuptial marriage contracts.*

II. Bonds of Provisions.—In bonds of provision, the natural presumption is in favour of the provisions vesting *Presumption for vesting at the father's death.*

---

[1] (1903), 5 F. 926. For a similar case, see *Montgomerie's Trs.* v. *Alexander*, 1911, S. C. 856.

[2] (1891), 18 R. 491.

at the death of the parent, because the parent maintains the children during his lifetime, and the object of the bond is, generally speaking, to provide for the children after his or her death.[1] The rules of vesting applicable to provisions of this nature are not different from those already stated in regard to legacies. According to *Ainslie* v. *Elliots*,[2] provisions if *statim debeantur* do not fall by the child's predeceasing the father, but if the provision is payable only on the father's death, the mere fact that the bond is irrevocable and is out of the hands of the granter is not alone sufficient to confer a vested right on the children during the father's lifetime. The fact of delivery has, however, been referred to in subsequent cases as an element in favour of immediate vesting.[3]

In *Allardice* v. *Lautour*,[4] a divorced husband, in pursuance of an agreement between himself and his wife, bound himself to make payment of a sum of money to the younger children of the marriage (who were named) and the heirs of their bodies and the survivors on the death of the longest liver of himself and the mother. Interest was to run on this provision from the mother's death. The granter having died before the mother, it was held that vesting took place on his death. The features of the deed which conduced to this result were that the father bound himself by a direct obligation in favour of the children ; that interest was given from an event which might have occurred during his lifetime ; and that the deed bore to have been delivered, and was delivered, to a party for behoof of the children.[5]

In the less common case, where the granter is divested of the property during his lifetime, the children may acquire vested interests before the granter's death. In *Napier* v. *Orr*,[6] for example, a lady by a disposition and settlement disponed lands to her son, burdening the subjects with sums of money to be paid to her daughters. One half of the sum was to be paid to each daughter after the mother's death, the other half ten years after her death, and it was provided

---

[1] *Marjoribanks* v. *Marjoribanks* (1752), M. 13046.

[2] (1749), M. 13044. See also *Downie's Trs.* v. *Cullen* (1882), 9 R. 749.

[3] *Allardice* v. *Lautour, infra.*

[4] (1845), 7 D. 362.

[5] Lord Cockburn dissented.

[6] (1864), 3 M. 57 ; *Greig* v. *Moodie* (1839), 2 D. 169. See *Erskine* v. *Wright* (1846), 8 D. 863.

that if any daughter died before the said terms of payment, the sum was to go to the heirs of her body, and failing heirs to the surviving daughters. The son was infeft on this deed. The question raised in the case was, whether vesting took place in the daughters at the time when the deed was delivered, or whether it was suspended till the granter's death. The Court held that vesting took place on delivery, founding on the circumstances that the deed was irrevocable and that the granter was divested.

A bond of provision is understood to be granted for the personal benefit of the child, and, although it bears to be in favour of the child or his heirs, the heirs have no claim to the subject in the event of the child predeceasing the father. In this respect a bond of provision differs from a legacy.[1] Thus, in *Russel* v. *Russel*,[2] where a father granted a bond of provision for a sum payable after his decease to his son, his heirs, executors, and assignees, it was held that, as the son predeceased the father, the provision was not exigible by the son's heir. In a later case,[3] a husband by his trust-disposition and settlement, on the narrative that he wished to make a provision for his wife in the event of her surviving him, over and above the provisions conceived in her favour in their marriage contract, disponed and assigned to her and her heirs and assignees whomsoever, the whole effects which should belong to him at his death. The provisions of the marriage contract were to take effect only if the wife survived the husband. It was held that the same condition was by implication attached to the supplemental provisions of the will, and that accordingly the gift lapsed on the wife's predecease. Lord Deas, after referring to *Russel* v. *Russel*, observed : "The law thus applicable to provisions to children has been long quite settled. Heirs and assignees are held to mean heirs and assignees of the child, if the implied condition of survivance is implemented, but not otherwise. The provision is held to have been made from affection for the particular child, and to provide for the maintenance of that child after the death of the father. Much of

Under a provision to a party or his heirs the heirs are not conditional institutes.

---

[1] See p. 69, *ante*.
[2] (1769), M. 6372 ; *Bell* v: *Davidson*, (1730), M. 6342 ; *Gordon* v. *Ross*, (1757), M. 6343 ; *Wood* v. *Aitchison* (1789), M. 13043.
[3] *Findlay* v. *Mackenzie* (1875), 2 R. 909 ; *Russell's Trs.* (1887), 14 R. 849.

the same reasoning is applicable to the provisions for a widow."

The decision in this case was followed in *Baillie's Exr.* v. *Baillie*,[1] where in a mutual settlement a husband and wife granted and disponed their whole property then belonging to them, or which might belong to them at their deaths, each to the other in the event of the other surviving him or her.

Substitutions in bonds.

In the case of *Macreadie* v. *The Executors of Macfadzean*,[2] a substitution contained in a bond was held to imply that gratuitous alienations were barred. The father in that case assigned a bond to his two daughters " equally between them, and failing either of them by decease without heirs of their bodies, or conveyance in a contract of marriage, to the survivor of them." Both daughters survived their father. The one who first died assigned her interest in the bond to her husband. It was held, in a competition between him and the assignee of the surviving daughter, that the cross substitution could not be defeated by gratuitous alienation, and the assignee of the surviving daughter was preferred. The reference to assignation in a marriage contract was considered to be equivalent to a prohibition of gratuitous alienations. But in the cases of *Wauchope* v. *Gibson*[3] and *Wallace* v. *Smith*,[4] provisions in favour of the surviving children, in the event of any of the children dying without issue, were held to be merely substitutions and defeasible by the children who survived the parent.

[1] (1899), 1 F 974.
[2] (1752), M. 4402.
[3] (1752), M. 4404.
[4] (1710), M. 4332.

CHAPTER XIII.

DECLARATIONS AS TO VESTING.

A DECLARATION as to vesting may take the form of a state- Forms of
declarations.
ment that the legacy is to vest on the arrival of a time
mentioned ; or it may appear as a provision that the gift
is not to vest before a specified time, which will generally
be construed as a direction that vesting is to take place then.[1]
So also a statement that the subject shall not be affected
by the legatee's debts or deeds before the time of payment,
appears to have much the same effect as an express declaration as to vesting, because it excludes the powers characteristic of, and implied in, a vested right.[2]

In questions arising on wills containing such clauses, the
Court will, so far as possible, give effect to the testator's
intention as thus expressed. If the other features of the
deed are consistent with the testator's declaration, no
difficulty will arise. But if the context points to a time of
vesting other than that indicated in the testator's declaration, it becomes a difficult task to determine whether the
testator's intention will be realised by adhering to his express
declaration, or by adopting that construction which is called
for by the other clauses of the deed. When the context does
not markedly point to a period other than that mentioned
in the will, the declaration as to vesting will probably be
the decisive element in the decision of the case.[3] But, on
the other hand, if the terms in which the legacy is conferred
or the conditions attached to it distinctly require that
another time shall be selected, it is obvious that the

---

[1] *Miller's Trs.* v. *Miller* (1890), 18
R. 301 ; *M'Elmail* v. *Lundie's Trs.*
(1888), 16 R. 47 ; *Hunter's Trs.* v.
Hunter (1888), 15 R. 399. Cf. *Swan's
Trs.* v. *Swan*, 1912 S. C. 273, at 279.

[2] As in *Wilkie* v. *Wilkie* (1837), 15
S. 430 ; 12 Fac. 377, *ante*, p 255.

[3] See *e.g.* *M'Laren* v. *M'Alpine*,.
1907 S. C. 1192.

declaration merely defeats the purpose which it was intended
to serve. The embarrassment caused in such cases by the
declaration led Lord President Inglis in *Croom's Trs.* v.
Adams [1] to observe that it was a " very doubtful remedy "
for the difficulties which beset the construction of wills in
regard to vesting.

Construction
of " vesting."

The primary meaning of the word " vesting " is vesting
in point of interest.[2] But the word is employed in popular
language in more than one sense. This being so, the Court
holds itself free to depart from the primary meaning if by
doing so it is enabled to reconcile the declaration with the
other clauses of the will. Thus, the word may be interpreted
in the sense which the judges in *Young* v. *Robertson* [3] declared
to be the natural one, at least when the word is employed by
a testator in his will, namely, as referring to the time at
which the legatee is to become entitled to the possession of
the subject of the gift ; [4] or it may signify vesting subject to
defeasance ; [5] or it may even be treated, in the case of a
class-gift, as meaning the time at which the gift is to vest
in the class generally, although the respective shares of the
members are not then vested.[6] But, unless it appears that
the testator has used the term in another sense, the Court
will attribute to it its primary meaning in law, namely,
vesting in point of interest.

Where the declaration as to the time of vesting and the
other provisions of the will cannot be reconciled, it is obvious
that one part of the will must be sacrificed. Whether the
declaration or the inconsistent clauses are to be rejected
can be determined only with reference to the whole terms
of the will in regard to which the question arises. The
following cases are, therefore, cited merely as illustrating
the manner in which the Courts have treated questions of
this kind.

[1] 22 D. 45. Stated *post*, p. 293.
See Lord M'Laren's opinion in *Macfarlane's Trs.* v. *Macfarlane* (1903),
6 F. 201.
[2] See Chapter I.
[3] (1862), 4 Macq. 314.
[4] *Popham's Trs.* v. *Parker's Exrs.*
(1882), 10 R. 888 ; *King* v. *Cullen*
(1848), 2 De G. & Sm. 252 ; *Williams*
v. *Haythorne* (1871), L. R. 6 Ch. 782 ;

Simpson v. *Peach* (1873), L. R. 16
Eq. 208.
[5] Cf. *Chamber's Trs.* v. *Smiths*
(1878), 5 R. (H. L.) 151 ; *M'Laren* v.
M'Alpine, 1907 S. C. 1191 ; *Taylor*
v. *Frobisher* (1852), 5 De G. & Sm.
194 ; *In re Edmonson's Estate* (1868),
L. R. 5 Eq. 389 ; *Armytage* v. *Wilkin-
son* (1878), 3 App. Cas. 355.
[6] *Croom's Trs.* v. *Adams, supra.*

In *Bowes' Trs.*[1] the trustees were charged to realise the
estate on the majority of the youngest of the truster's
children, and to divide the proceeds among the children.
It was declared that the shares of the sons should become
vested interests on their attaining the age of twenty-one,
and that the daughters' shares should also vest at that age
or on marriage, but that the shares were not to be payable
until the majority of his youngest child. So far the provisions of the will were quite consistent, but there occurred
later in the will a destination-over to issue and survivors in
the event of any child dying before his or her share should
" have vested or become payable." On a construction of
these clauses, the First Division held that vesting took place
at the respective majorities or marriages of the children,
and that the term of payment was the majority of the
youngest. The destination-over, seeing that it expressly
referred to vesting and payment as alternative events, was
inconsistent with this construction of the gift, but it was
not permitted to overcome the effect of the leading provisions in favour of the legatees. *Croom's Trs.* v. *Adams* [2]
was distinguished.

Marginal note: Vesting declaration construed in its primary sense.

Again, in *Smith's Trs.*[3] the testator bequeathed one-half
of the residue of his estate to his sons, and directed his
trustees, as soon as practicable after his death, to make
payment of two-thirds of their respective shares on their
respectively attaining the age of twenty-five, and the remaining third at the winding up of the estate on his widow's
death. He declared that this half of the residue should
vest and bear interest from and after his death, and he
added a survivorship clause referring to the event of any
son dying *either before or after him*. Taken by itself, this
survivorship clause might have operated to suspend vesting
till the winding up of the estate in regard to one-third of
each share. But some part of the will had to be sacrificed,
and the Court preferred rather to reject this clause than to
set aside all the other provisions of the will. Accordingly
the whole share of each child was held to vest at the testator's
death.

In *Carruther's Trs.* v. *Eeles*,[4] the testator gave a liferent

[1] (1870), 42 S. J. 382.
[2] (1859), 22 D. 45.
[3] (1894), 31 S. L. R. 538.
[4] (1894), 21 R. 492.

of his whole estate to his widow. On the death of the
longest liver of the spouses. the trustees were instructed to
set apart a sum for the maintenance of his children until they
attained majority or were married ; and on the death of
the surviving spouse or on the majority of the youngest child
(whichever of these events happened last). the estate was
to be paid to the children " *and the survivors and survivor*
equally on the following conditions : *the share of each
child shall be a vested right at majority*. though not payable
till the youngest reach majority." There was. further. a
destination-over to issue *if any child predeceased the* " *said
period of division.*" When the wife (who survived her
husband) died. all the children were major. A son predeceased her. having attained majority. A special case was
brought to ascertain whether this son had taken a vested
interest. Lord Rutherfurd Clark considered that the words
of survivorship and the vesting clause should be reconciled
by reading the latter as designed to provide that, if on the
widow's death a child was major. the vesting of his share
should not be postponed till the majority of the youngest
of his brothers and sisters—a construction which he thought
was suggested by the qualification " though not payable till
the youngest reach majority " attached to the declaration
as to vesting ; and that the death of the widow was in any
case a condition precedent of vesting. But the majority
of the judges refused to depart from the express declaration,
and held that on majority. whenever occurring. the rights
of the children vested, and that therefore the predeceasing
son had had a vested right.[1]

In all of these cases it will be observed that the testator
had in the will distinguished between the time of payment
and the time of vesting. and consequently it was not possible
to remove the difficulty by construing the declaration as
referring to vesting in possession.

Vesting
construed as
referring to
payment.

On the other hand. in *Popham's Trs.* v. *Parker's Exrs.*,[2]
the Court. by departing from the strict interpretation of the
word " vest," was enabled to reconcile all the terms of the
settlement under construction. In this case the testator left
legacies in simple terms,—terms, that is to say, that indicated

[1] Cf. also *M'Kay's Trs.* v. *Gray*   [2] (1882), 10 R. 888.
(1903), 5 F. 1086.

vesting *a morte testatoris*. He added, however, a declaration that " unless I otherwise expressly desire, no legacies left by me *shall vest or be payable* to the legatees till after the death of my wife, who during her life shall derive the benefit of all interest or income therefrom." In two subsequent holograph writings he referred to the legacies " to be paid after my dear wife's decease." On construing these deeds, the Court adopted the view that by *vesting* the testator meant payment, and decided that a legacy had vested in a legatee who had died in the lifetime of his widow.[1]

Again, in *Croom's Trs.* v. *Adams* [2] and *Davidson's Trs.* v. *Davidson*,[3] the Court referred the declaration to the class-gift, and not to the interests of the individuals forming the class. In the former of these cases, the testator enjoined his trustees at the end of twelve months after his death, or on the eldest survivor of the residuary legatees attaining twenty-one years of age, to divide the residue among A., three children of B. *nominatim*, and the children of C. and the survivors and survivor of them. He declared that the shares of C.'s family should be paid " on their respectively attaining the age of twenty-one years, or on the death of their father, whichever of these events shall last happen " ; and declared, further, that the whole of the legacies *should vest on the majority of the eldest of the residuary legatees* ; but that, if any of the children of C. should " die after the said period of division and before *the respective terms of payment* without issue," his or her share should go to the survivors. One of C.'s children survived him and also the period of division (the majority of the eldest legatee), but died under age. It was decided that no interest had vested in her. The Court considered that the reference to vesting at the majority of the eldest anuitant meant that the shares should be set aside for the children, and should vest in them as a class ; and that the shares of the individual members were not at that time fixed or vested, but remained subject to the contingency of any of them dying under age. " I can understand," said Lord President Inglis in a subsequent case,[4]

Marginal note: Vesting declaration referred to the gift to the class.

---

[1] Lord Rutherfurd Clark dissented.
[2] (1859), 22 D. 45.
[3] (1871), 9 M. 995 ; *Macfarlane's Trs.* v. *Macfarlane* (1903), 6 F. 201.
[4] *Bowe's Trs.* (1870), 42 S. J. 382, *supra.*

" the interest of a family becoming vested so that the share of each shall not be transmissible or assignable by him, and yet the whole fund vest in the family as a class. The case of *Croom's Trs.* is a good example of that kind of vesting in a class, without any particular share vesting." [1]

The same interpretation was adopted in *Davidson's Trs.* v. *Davidson.* In that case the trustees were directed to divide the residue on the death of the truster's widow among his " whole grandchildren *then surviving.*" He declared that *the residue should vest at his death.* A child was born after the truster's death. It was decided that as vesting was declared to be at the truster's death, this child was necessarily excluded from sharing in the bequest.[2] Lord Cowan remarked that the declaration as to vesting was to be interpreted in the same sense as in *Croom's Trs.*, and that therefore only those children who were alive as well at the widow's death as at the testator's were entitled to participate in the family gift.

It will be observed that in the two last cases it would not have been possible to read the vesting declaration as a direction in regard to payment only.

Vesting construed as vesting subject to defeasance. Lastly, in *Chambers' Trs.* v. *Smiths,*[3] a declaration that the share of a beneficiary was to vest at the testator's death was (owing to subsequent clauses) construed as meaning that the share was to vest then, subject to defeasance.[4]

Destinations-over in case of death before "vesting." In *Young* v. *Robertson,*[5] a destination-over to survivors if any of the legatees should " die before his or her share vest," was construed as referring to the time of payment. It was

---

[1] *Croom's Trs.* v. *Adams* was referred to by Lord Gordon in *Chambers' Trs.* v. *Smiths* (1878), 5 R. (H. L.) 151.

[2] Contrast with this case *Williams* v. *Haythorne,* L. R. 6 Ch. 782, where the gift was to the children of a niece " who should be living at the time of her decease," declaring that the same should be " a vested interest in him or them respectively on their respectively attaining the age of twenty-one years." Lord Hatherly decided that a child who died before the niece, aged twenty-one, took no vested interest.

[3] *Supra.* Stated *post,* p. 337; *M'Dougall's Trs.* v. *M'Dougall's Trs.* (1902), 39 S. L. R. 375, *supra.*

[4] Cf. *Love's Trs.* v. *Love* (1879), 7 R. 410, for a very special declaration as to vesting.

[5] (1862), 4 Macq. 314. Stated *ante,* p. 46. The case was discussed and distinguished in *Richardson* v. *Power* (1865), 19 C. B. N. S. 780.

observed in the opinion of Lord Justice-Clerk Inglis,[1] that the testator, in employing these words, did not mean to indicate a time to be determined by a course of judicial reasoning, but intended to describe a time known to himself and fixed under the terms of the will. That time might be the date of his own death ; but " the circumstance that the testator refers to a particular time as the time of vesting creates a presumption that that time was not to be his own death, because, when a testator refers to the time of his death, he generally speaks of it as ' the time of my own death,' or refers to it in some similar manner." In this case the only time mentioned was in the direction to the trustees to pay the legacies at the expiry of a liferent ; and this was held to be the period of vesting. As the presumption in any event is that a survivorship clause relates to the time of payment, the decision would have been the same had the words " before his or her share vest in the party or parties so deceasing " been omitted.

It is obvious, indeed, that a reference to the legatee's death before vesting as the contingency on which the gift-over is to take effect, cannot exercise any great influence on the construction of the will. It shows that the testator intended the gift-over to operate as a conditional institution and not as a substitution, and so far it serves a useful purpose ; but in itself it affords no means of determining the time of vesting. That time must be ascertained from the other provisions of the will ; and although in *Young* v. *Robertson* the destination-over led to a suspension of vesting, the result would probably be different where the frame of the will was not inconsistent with vesting *a morte testatoris*.

Thus, in *Alston's Trs.* v. *Alston*,[2] a gift-over in terms similar to those in *Young* v. *Robertson* was, on the special terms of the will, referred to the testatrix's death. The trustees were directed to hold and apply two sums of money for four persons (who were named) after the death of a liferenter, and there was a destination-over to issue and survivors in the event of any of the beneficiaries " dying

---

[1] (1860), 22 D. 1527, at 1542. This was a dissenting opinion. See to the same effect Lord Kinloch, at p. 1539 and Lord Cowan, at p. 1546. The remarks of the Lord Justice-Clerk were referred to with approval in the opinion of the Lord Chancellor.

[2] (1902), 4 F 654.

before the vesting of the provisions herein conceived in their favour.'' Thereafter the will provided that in the event of one of the legatees not having more than three children at the date of the testatrix's death, his share should pass to another of the legatees and his issue. This last clause was held to differentiate the case from that of *Young* v. *Robertson* ; and, as it was difficult to perceive why the testatrix should have referred to her death in this branch of the settlement, unless she intended vesting at her death, the Court, on the strength of the clause, decided that the share of one of the beneficiaries who died before the liferenter was carried by his will.

CHAPTER XIV.

ACCELERATION OF VESTING OR PAYMENT.

I. Acceleration of Payment.—In the foregoing chapters the question of vesting has been considered as arising upon the terms of the will or deed. It may happen, however, that something unforeseen by the testator occurs to disturb the provisions of the will and the arrangements made for the disposal of the estate ; and the question may be raised as to the manner in which the testator's directions are to be carried out in the unforeseen circumstances, and whether, in particular, the time of the vesting or payment of the gifts in the will is altered by the alteration of circumstances.

A case which frequently arises is that in which the testator gives a liferent and the liferenter renounces his liferent. In a series of cases, the Courts have been called on to determine whether the liferenter's renunciation of his interest has the effect of accelerating the vesting or payment of the legacies given in the will. It is not doubtful that if all the persons who are, or may be, interested in a bequest concur in seeking payment from the trustees under the will, and there are no trust purposes which require the maintenance of the trust administration, payment may be made and the trust may be terminated, although the testator contemplated that the trust should be continued until a subsequent date. For example, if the residue of an estate is burdened with a legacy to A. in the event of her attaining majority or being married, A., on acquiring the interest of the residuary legatee, will be entitled to payment although she may be in minority and unmarried ; because, supposing that A. should not live to become major or marry, yet as the legacy would in that event fall into residue, it is obvious that all the possible interests in the subject are united in her person when she acquires the contingent right of the residuary legatee.[1]

When the fee is vested absolutely, payment may be accelerated. It is no more than a corollary of this general proposition that, if a testator directs his trustees to hold a subject for a liferenter and to make over the capital to another, the person to whom the fee is given will be entitled, provided he has a vested right, to immediate payment if the liferenter renounce the liferent.[2] In a case of this kind, payment is accelerated for the benefit of one who has at the time the power of disposing of the subject ; and, no other party being interested, the Court merely relieves his right of a cumbrous and unnecessary trust administration. This is the general rule. But even although the right of fee is vested, payment will not be accelerated if the continued retention of the subject by the trustees is required by other purposes of the will.[3]

Where the fee is not vested, no acceleration allowed. If the vesting of the fee is postponed until the termination of the liferent, or if the right of the fiar is subject to a possible defeasance until the arrival of that time, it does not signify in what position the interest of the liferenter stands, and the death of the liferenter must be regarded as a time appointed by the testator at which the rights of the parties favoured in the will are to be ascertained.[4] In this case there are contingent interests—whether of conditional institutes, or of the residuary legatees, or of the heirs *ab*

---

[1] *Grant* v. *Dyer* (1813), 2 Dow 73, at 85.

[2] *Roberton* v. *Davidson* (1846), 9 D. 152 ; stated *ante*, p. 53 ; *Rainsford* v. *Maxwell* (1852), 14 D. 450 ; *Pretty* v. *Newbigging* (1854), 16 D. 667 ; stated *ante*, p. 278 ; *Foulis* v. *Foulis* (1857), 19 D. 362 ; *Grant* v. *Grant's Trs.* (1876), 3 R. 280 ; *Archibald's Trs.* v. *Archibald* (1882), 9 R. 942 ; *Finlay's Trs.* v. *Finlay* (1886), 13 R. 1052 ; *M'Murdo's Trs.* v. *M'Murdo* (1897), 24 R. 458 ; *Crawford* v. *Crawford's Trs.* (1873), 11 S. L. R. 2 ; *Mackay's Trs.* (1878), 16 S. L. R. 197 ; *Knox* v. *Knox's Trs.* (1887), 24 S. L. R. 282. In several of these cases it must be

observed that the Court proceeded on the doctrine that a destination-over to issue did not affect vesting ; but as to this doctrine, see *ante*, Chapter IV. *Annandale* v. *Macniven* (1847), 9 D. 1201 ; (for an explanation of which see *Scott* v. *Scott* (1847), 9 D. 1264), was questioned in *Muirhead* v. *Muirhead* (1890), 17 R. (H. L.) 45. *Alexander's Trs.* v. *Waters* (1870), 8 M. 414, followed *Annandale*, and its authority appears also to be affected by the observations in *Muirhead*.

[3] See *post*, p. 302.

[4] Per L. J.-C. Moncreiff in *Alexander's Trs.* v. *Waters* (1870), 8 M. 414.

intestato of the testator—which must be considered. The renunciation of the liferent does not accelerate the vesting of the gift ; and if the Court were to sanction payment, the effect might be to defeat prematurely these contingent interests. In other words, there is the risk that the subject may be given to parties other than those who would have been entitled had the trust been allowed to subsist during the period contemplated by the testator.

" Where there is an absolute and indefeasible right vested in a legatee, the disappearance of the liferenter will entitle him to claim payment, even although payment is, in words, directed to be made at the liferenter's death, because there is no testamentary interest to interfere with his immediate payment ; but, on the other hand, where vesting and not mere payment is dependent upon the death of the liferenter, nothing that the liferenter does in the way of abandoning his or her right can accelerate the period of vesting, because the testator has fixed it finally, and it is not for anybody else to make a new will for him." [1]

The law on this point is settled by the decisions of the House of Lords in *Muirhead* v. *Muirhead* [2] and *Hughes* v. *Edwardes*.[3]

In the first of these, the truster directed his trustees to pay an annuity to his widow, and to accumulate the balance of the income during her life. On the widow's death the trustees were directed to distribute the residue among the testator's children, and it was provided that the share of any child predeceasing the term of payment should go to his or her issue, and, failing issue, should fall into residue. The wife survived the testator, repudiated the annuity, and claimed her legal rights. Founding on the disappearance of the annuity the children claimed immediate payment of the residue. The Lord Ordinary [4] held that vesting took place at the time at which the Thellusson Act prevented further accumulation, and that the children became at that date entitled to payment. This interlocutor was varied by the Second Division, their Lordships finding that vesting took

---

[1] *Jacks's Trs.* v. *Jacks*, 1913 S. C. 815, *per* Lord Kinnear at 826.

[2] (1890), 17 R. (H. L.) 45. See also *Ferrie* v. *Ferries* (1849), 11 D. 704 ; and *Cattanach* v. *Thom's Exrs.* (1858), 20 D. 1206.

[3] (1892), 19 R. (H. L.) 33.

[4] Lord Fraser.

place on the truster's death. On appeal, the House of
Lords agreed with the Second Division in holding that the
operation of the Thellusson Act had no effect on vesting,
but reversed their interlocutor on the ground that vesting
was suspended until the widow's death. Lord Watson said :
" I see no reason to doubt that, in cases where the final
distribution of a trust estate is directed to be made on the
death of an annuitant, and it clearly appears that in postponing the time of division the testator had no other object in
view than to secure payment of the annuity, it may be within
the power of the Court, upon the discharge or renunciation
of the annuitant's right, to ordain an immediate division.
But in order to the due exercise of that power, it is, in my
opinion, essential that the beneficiaries to whom the trustees
are directed to pay or convey shall have a vested and
indefeasible interest in the provisions. That principle
appears to me to be just in itself, and to be firmly established
by *Roberton* v. *Davidson*, *Rainsford* v. *Maxwell*, and *Pretty* v.
Newbigging.[1] I cannot conceive that it should be in the
power of any Court to give the testator's estate to persons
other than those whom he has appointed to take. It may
also be that in the circumstances supposed, the Court would
be justified in directing distribution, although no beneficial
interest had vested, if application were made to that effect
by the entire class of persons to whom, or to one or more
of whom, the beneficial interest must eventually belong,
but no such case is presented in this appeal."

The rule laid down by Lord Watson was treated as
absolute, and was followed in *Ross's Trs.* v. *Ross*,[2] where the
circumstances of the case were so far favourable to acceleration, in that it was provided in the will that vesting and
payment should take place as well on the liferenter's second
marriage as on her death.

In Hughes v. *Edwardes*, the circumstances of the case
were these : By a marriage contract it was provided, that in
the event of the wife predeceasing the husband, the trustees
should hold a fund for his liferent alimentary use : if there
were children alive at the wife's death, the trustees were to

---

[1] Cited in note 2, p. 298.
[2] (1894), 21 R. 927. See also
Whitehead's Trs v. *Whitehead* (1897),

24 R. 1032 ; *Hunt's Trs.* v. *Hunt*
(1906), 8 F. 764 ; and *Jacks's Trs.* v.
Jacks, 1913 S. C. 8 15.

convey the capital to them at the first term after their
father's death, and on their attaining (in the case of sons)
majority or (in the case of daughters) on majority or marriage ; and it was declared that the provisions in favour of
the children were not to vest or be payable till the father's
death and the majority or marriage (as the case might be)
of the children.   If there were no children at the wife's
death, or, if there were, " in case of the death of all of them
before the terms of payment of their provisions as aforesaid,"
the capital was to be subject to any dispositions made by
the wife.   The wife died survived by her husband and a
son, and leaving a will in favour of the husband.   Twenty-
seven years after the wife's death, the son and husband
claimed payment, maintaining that in any event the sum
would fall to one or other of them—to the son if he survived
his 'father, and to the father under the wife's will if the son
predeceased.   The House of Lords (reversing the interlocutor
of the First Division) repelled the claim.   Had the father
and son alone been interested, their claim would have been
sustained, but there was one possible contingency in which
other interests might emerge, namely, in the event of the
son's predecease of the father leaving issue, in which case
the issue would be entitled under the *conditio si institutus
sine liberis decesserit*.   As this contingent interest could be
secured only by the continuance of the trust until the time
contemplated by the truster, it was held to be impossible to
order payment before that time.

In this case the liferent was declared to be alimentary, An alimentary
and this provision in itself was sufficient to prevent accelera- be renounced
tion of payment.[1]   A liferenter whose interest is alimentary
cannot assign his interest ; and a renunciation of his liferent
in favour of the party in right of the subject over which
the liferent is constituted is equivalent to an assignation to
the fiar.   This rule obtains even where the liferenter is at the
same time vested in the fee.[2]   The alimentary liferent, unlike
a simple liferent, does not coalesce in these circumstances

---

[1] Cf. *White's Trs.* v. *Whyte* (1877),
4 R. 786 ; *Duthie's Trs.* v. *Kinloch*
(1878), 5 R. 858 ; *Smith & Campbell*
(1873), 11 M. 639 ; *Cosens* v. *Stevenson* (1873), 11 M. 761 ; *Curror* (1874),
11 S. L. R. 507 ; *Barron* v. *Dewar*
(1887), 24 S. L. R. 735.

[2] *Eliott's Trs.* v. *Eliott* (1894), 21 R.
975 ; *Barron* v. *Dewar, supra* ; *Main's
Trs.* v. *Main*, 1917 S. C. 660 ; *Howat's
Trs.* v. *Howat*, 1922 S. C. 506.

with the fee ; they continue as two distinct estates ; and,
although the party may assign the fee, he cannot discharge
his liferent, which remains protected for his behoof during
his lifetime. In *Balderston* v. *Fulton*,[1] where trustees were
directed to hold an estate for behoof of a married woman in
liferent, exclusive of the *jus mariti* and right of administration of her husband, it was decided that the trust could not
be terminated by the woman during her coverture, as its
continuance was required for her protection.

Further trust
purposes
prevent
acceleration.
As previously noticed, although the person claiming
payment has a vested and indefeasible right, his claim will
fail if there are trust purposes which require the continuance
of the trust administration.

In *Lucas' Trs.* v. *The Lucas Trust*,[2] for example, where
the trustees were instructed to accumulate the income of
the residue of the estate during the lifetime of the testator's
widow and on her death to make over the funds to trustees
for the establishment of a charity, the Second Division
authorised payment to these trustees although the widow
was alive. The right of the beneficiaries here had vested,
but in *Muirhead* v. *Muirhead*[3] doubt was expressed by
Lord Watson and Lord Herschell whether this departure
from the testator's directions was justified.

A different conclusion was reached in *Haldane's Trs.* v.
Haldane.[4] In that case the provisions of the trust settlement were that the trustees should pay certain annuities to
the truster's five children during his widow's life, and the
surplus of the income to her. On her death the son was to
receive £18,000, and the four daughters £8000 each, and the
residue was given to the son. The son, with the consent of
the widow, claimed payment of a share to account of his
provision (leaving a sum more than sufficient as it stood to
meet the daughters' provisions). The Court declined to

---

[1] (1857), 19 D. 293 ; stated *ante*,
p. 207. See *Williamson* v. *Williamson's Trs.* (1881), 19 S. L. R. 276
(O. H., Lord M'Laren). But an
exclusion of the marital rights was
held to be effectual although the gift
was made directly and not through
the medium of a trust—*Young* v.
Loudoun (1855), 17 D 998.

[2] (1881), 8 R. 502.
[3] (1890), 17 R. (H. L.) 45. Lord
Bramwell thought the decision was
sound.
[4] (1895), 23 R. 276 ; *Grieve's Trs.*
v. *Bethune* (1830), 8 S. 96 ; *Souter
Robertson* v. *Robertson's Trs.* (1900),
8 S. L. T., 50 (Lord Kyllachy). Cf.
Macculloch v. *M'Culloch's Trs., infra.*

order payment. It was pointed out that in all the cases in which advances had been authorised, the beneficiaries claiming payment were alone interested in the fund, whereas here the son was entitled only to share *pari passu* with the daughters ; and therefore the trustees were bound to retain the whole fund as security for the shares of the daughters during the lifetime of the widow.

In *Macculloch* v. *M'Culloch's Trs.*[1] the trustees were directed to hold the estate for the testator's children in liferent and their issue in fee ; the income was to be divided among the children equally, and, if any died the deceaser's share of the income was to be paid to his issue, and, if there were no issue, to the survivors and the issue of predeceasers ; and on the death of all the children the estate was to be wound up and the proceeds divided among the children of the testator's sons and daughters *per stirpes*. Of the testator's four children one died unmarried and another died leaving one child, who claimed payment of one-third of the estate notwithstanding the survivance of two of the testator's children. The trustees were of opinion that a better return was obtained from certain heritage than would be obtained by a sale and they had not, therefore, exercised a discretionary power of sale which was entrusted to them in the will. All the beneficiaries, except the grandson, were against a sale. In these circumstances the grandson's claim failed. The Lord Chancellor (Halsbury) stated the ground of the decision in these words : " The testator has intended that the estate should be kept together, and that until the period of distribution, which he has himself ordained to be that which the will discloses, there should be the payment of the income to each of the persons entitled. It is enough to decide my view upon this matter that, in the events which might have occurred, the trustees would have paid so much that by so doing they would have withdrawn from the whole of the estate the power of giving their aliquot part to each of the persons entitled to it for the time being, so that when the period of distribution which the testator part contemplated has ultimately arrived, the distribution of the whole of the estate would not have been that which he determined and expressly directed by his

[1] (1903), 6 F. (H. L.) 3.

will.   To my mind that is enough, without reference to any
authority, to establish the proposition that you must adhere
to the words of the testator because there are ulterior
purposes to be served upon the arrival of the period of
ultimate distribution." [1]

Again, in *White's Trs.* v. *White*,[2] an annuity was given to
the testator's widow and the surplus income was to be
accumulated and added to the residue.   On the widow's
death legacies of £4000 were to be paid ; and after payment of these the residue was to be divided into four shares
and paid to the residuary legatees.   The widow claimed her
legal rights in place of the annuity.   During her lifetime one
of the residuary legatees sought payment of his share of the
residue, subject to provision being made for the legacies of
£4000 ; but this was opposed by the other residuary legatees.
It was held that, although the residue had vested at the
testator's death, payment of the share could not be accelerated.   If the directions of the will remained undisturbed,
the income of the £4000 during the widow's life would go
to augment the residue, and, while it might have been
possible to ordain payment if all the residuary legatees had
united in applying for this, one of them alone was not
entitled to withdraw his share.   It was also argued that it
was impossible to authorise payment, as the widow, after
the amount paid to her in respect of her legal rights had been
replaced from the income might (under the doctrine of
equitable compensation [3]) be entitled to receive her annuity
thereafter, but the Court found it unnecessary to deal with
this argument.

A somewhat similar point occurred in *Rose's Trs.* v.
Rose [4] in regard to the acceleration of a liferent interest.
There a liferent was given to the testatrix's son, and, after
his death, to his daughter.   The son having elected to claim
his legal rights and having thereby forfeited the liferent, the
daughter maintained that the liferent had opened to her,
but it was held that this was not so, seeing that the income

---

[1] See the observations of the Lord
President (Dunedin) on this case in
Baxter v. *Baxter*, 1909 S. C. 1027.

[2] 1916 S. C. 435.   Lord Salvesen
dissented.

[3] As in *Macfarlane's Trs.* v. *Oliver*
(1882), 9 R. 1138.

[4] 1916 S. C. 827.

during her father's lifetime fell to be applied in compensating those who had suffered through his action in claiming his legal rights.

In the above-mentioned cases the truster had fixed the time of payment by a reference to a determinate event. In the two following cases payment was to be made when the trust purposes were fulfilled, and the question was as to the construction of this direction. In *Scott* v. *Scott*,[1] the testator gave a legacy to the family of A., on his (A.'s) death. All the other legacies were prestable on the death of the testator. The residuary clause was expressed thus : " In case of any residue being left in the hands of my said trustees after the purposes of the trust shall be fulfilled, I hereby appoint the same to be made over and paid to my nearest relations then alive." When all the trust purposes had been satisfied save the legacy to A.'s family, A. came to an agreement with his children whereby they agreed to discharge their claim to the legacy, and thereafter he sought payment of the residue as being at that time the testator's nearest relative. Lord Fullerton thought that the meaning of the words " after the purposes of the trust shall be fulfilled " was that the residue was to be distributed whenever the purposes of the will were satisfied, whether by the death of A. or by arrangement between the parties interested in the trust funds, and that A. was, therefore, in the circumstances entitled to payment ; but the majority of the Court held that the period indicated by these words was the time when the purposes would in due course be fulfilled on the death of A. Accordingly A.'s claim was rejected, and this decision was sustained in the House of Lords. Lord Brougham observed : " If a gift be to a class or to an individual by a description which cannot be ascertained till some future time, those who may answer the description at an earlier period cannot by any arrange-ment among themselves exclude those who may become entitled at such future date or upon such future event happening."

On the other hand, in *L'Amy* v. *Nicholson*,[2] similar words were construed as merely amplifying the word " residue " and not as defining a time at which payment was to be

[1] (1850), 7 Bell's Apps. ; affg. 9 D. 1264.   [2] (1850), 13 D. 240.

made. In that case the residue of an estate was to be paid by the trustees " after all the other purposes of the present trust are attained " to A. and B. and to the heirs of their bodies, whom failing to the survivor. All the purposes having been fulfilled save the payment of one annuity, A. and B. sought payment. The annuitant agreed to discharge the annuity, but the children of A. opposed the claim. The Court authorised payment to A. and B. This case appears to be distinguishable from the previous case by reason of the different construction put on the words of gift, and by the fact that the legatees were named individuals and not a class. A similar construction of such words was adopted in *Scott's Trs.* v. *Scott*,[1] and *Maclean's Trs.* v. *Maclean*.[2]

Payment on discharge of debts.

A similar problem is presented in cases where the testator directs that his estate is to be made over to an institute, whom failing, to others, when the debts affecting the estate have been discharged, and the institute comes forward with an offer to discharge these. In such cases the question is whether the testator intended the disponee to be selected when the estate was disencumbered, however that might be accomplished ; or, on the other hand, was it his intention that the selection of the disponee should be postponed till the debts were discharged by the method appointed in his will—usually by the accumulation of rents—and in no other way ? [3] If the latter is the sound construction of the testator's directions, an offer to discharge the debts by other means will not have the effect of accelerating the conveyance of the estates, for the result of acceleration might be to put one person in the place of another as the disponee favoured in the will.[4]

In *Scarlett* v. *Lord Abinger's Trs.*,[5] trustees were enjoined to continue to hold the testator's landed estates and to apply the free income towards payment of the debts charged on them until the whole of these were absolutely discharged and extinguished. After these debts had been paid and discharged, " as aforesaid," the estates were to be disponed

---

[1] (1891), 18 R. 1194, *ante*, p. 67.
[2] (1897), 24 R. 988.
[3] See Lord Hunter's opinion in *White's Trs.* v. *Nicol*, 1923 S.C. 859.
[4] See Ld. Pres. Clyde's opinion in *Home's Trs.* v. *Fergusson's Exr.*, 1921 S. C. 474.
[5] 1907 S. C. 811.

by a deed of entail to the person who should, at the time
when the debts were discharged, be in right of a certain
peerage. Two years after the testator's death the person
who would be entitled to the disposition if it were then to
be executed offered to provide funds to meet the debts.
It was held here that it was part of the testator's scheme
that the debts should be discharged by the application of
the surplus income and in no other way, and that there
could be no disposition of the estates till that scheme had
been carried out. The pursuer's right, it was observed,[1]
was " contingent on his survival of a period defined by
reference to the time required for payment of the debts out
of the trust funds, because it is perfectly clear that the
payment referred to is the payment under the course of
administration which the testator has himself prescribed.
The proposition which we are invited to affirm in effect
involves an anticipation of the period of vesting of the fee
by an arbitrary interference with the prescribed administration, and such an anticipation is, I think, contrary to
settled principles of vesting, as these are expounded in the
decision of the House of Lords in the case of *Muirhead*." [2]

The cases of *Home's Trs.* v. *Fergusson's Exr.* and *White's
Trs.* v. *Nicol* stand in contrast with this decision.

In the former the testator directed his trustees to collect
and accumulate the income of his landed property " and
from time to time as they shall consider expedient to pay
and apply the same in and towards payment *pro tanto* of
the debts secured upon the said lands," and as soon as the
property was " entirely freed and disencumbered thereof "
to dispone it to a nephew and his heirs. Thirty-nine years
after the testator's death, only one third of the debt had
been paid off, and the heir of the nephew at that time

[1] By Lord M'Laren.

[2] There were also other purposes
than payment of debt for which the
trust had to be kept up. It was
noted that the pursuer did not say
that he had money to meet the debt ;
he might have obtained a loan, and,
after receipt of the disposition might
have reimposed the debt on the estate.
See also *Colt* v. *Colt's Trs.* (1868), 5
S. L. R. 660.

In *Stainton's Trs.* v. *Stainton*
(1850), 12 D. 571, trustees were
directed to entail and convey an
estate after payment of the testator's
debts and obligations to his son and a
series of heirs. When all the debts
were paid, except a sum due to the
son under his father's marriage contract, it was held, by a majority of
the Court, that he was entitled to a
conveyance of the estate.

offered to provide a sum sufficient to enable the trustees to pay off the remaining debt. It was held that the trustees were bound to accept this offer and execute a disposition of the property. The testator here had doubtless contemplated that the debts would be met out of the accumulated rents, but there did not appear to have been any intention on his part to exclude other sources of payment should such become available.

In *White's Trs.* v. *Nicol* this decision was followed. The direction in this case was that the rents of the property should be accumulated until all debts incurred by the testator or the trustees were discharged, and that, as soon as these were discharged, the trustees should execute a deed of entail in favour of a nephew and the heirs of his body.[1]

In certain of these cases the trustees stated that they saw little or no prospect of paying off, or even materially reducing, the debt out of the accumulation of income. No case has arisen in which the testator's direction as to the payment of the debts has become definitely impossible of fulfilment ; but some light on the problem created by such circumstances is afforded by the decision in *Colquhoun* v. *Colquhoun's Trs.*[2] The direction in this case was that the mineral rents from an estate should be accumulated till they reached the sum of £25,000, when they were to be paid over to the heir in possession of certain lands. When the accumulated rents amounted to a little more than £12,000, the period allowed for accumulation by the Thellusson Act terminated, and further accumulation became impossible. This being so, as the sole purpose of the postponement of payment was that the accumulated rents should reach the specified amount and the statute had frustrated this purpose, the heir was held entitled to payment of the £12,000.[3]

---

[1] In *Sinclair's Trs.* v. *Sinclair*, 1913 S. C. 178, trustees were directed to hold the estate for ten years or such further period as, having in view the freeing of the estate from debt, " in so far as this may be reasonably attained " they might consider necessary ; and then to make over the estate to the testator's son, whom failing, to others. After thirty-six years there was no prospect of the estate being disencumbered within any period that could be specified. The Court held that the estate must be made over burdened with the existing debt.

[2] (1892), 19 R. 946.

[3] No case has occurred in Scotland as to the effect on a direction of this kind of the debts being paid out of

A question which has been raised in a number of cases regarding acceleration of payment is, whether there is any presumption recognised in the law of Scotland as to the age at which a woman may be considered to be past child-bearing. If a gift be made to a woman in liferent and to her children in fee, it is obvious that, in the general case, payment cannot be made to the fiars until it is certain that the class will not be increased. Unless, therefore, the Courts are able to hold that the possibility of issue has become extinct when the liferentrix attains a certain age, the fund cannot be distributed during her lifetime. In two Scots cases [1] which came before the Second Division, the Court assumed that women above the age of sixty were beyond the age of child-bearing, and sanctioned payment to their children then alive ; in other cases payment to children during their mother's lifetime was allowed on condition of their taking out an insurance policy or finding caution to repeat to the extent necessary to provide shares to *nascituri*.[2] But in later decisions [3] the weight of authority was in favour of " the hard rule of the law " [4] that there is no presumption that a woman becomes at any age incapable of bearing children, and that the Court must act on the assumption that a woman, whatever be her age, may give birth to children. Finally, this question came before a Court of Seven Judges

---

the capital either under diligence by heritable creditors or otherwise. The result of the English cases is stated in Theobald on Wills (8th Ed., 635) in these terms : " If a testator creates a trust for payment of mortgage or other debts out of the annual income of his estate, and the debts are, in fact, paid out of the *corpus*, there is no equity to compel the tenant for life out of annual income to make good what has been so paid, and if a fund has been accumulated out of income to pay mortgage debts as directed by the will and the mortgagees are paid by sales of the mortgaged estates under order of the Court or out of Court, the tenant for life is entitled to the accumulated fund." See *In re Green* (1888), 40 Ch.

D. 610 ; *In re Brandon*, 49 T. L. R. 48.

[1] *Louson's Trs.* v. *Dickson* (1886), 13 R. 1003 ; *Urquhart's Trs.* v. *Urquhart* (1886), 14 R. 112 ; and see *De la Chaumette's Trs.* v. *De la Chaumette* (1902), 4 F. 745.

[2] *Turnbull* v. *Turnbull's Trs.* (1907), 44 S. L. R. 843 ; *M'Pherson's Trs.* v. *Hill* (1902), 4 F. 921 ; *Gordon* v. *Young* (1873), 45 S. J. 272 ; *Scheniman* v. *Wilson* (1828), 6 S. 1019 ; and *Shaw* v. *Shaw*, 6 S. 1149.

[3] *Anderson* v. *Ainslie* (1890), 17 R 337 ; *Beattie's Trs.* v. *Meffan* (1898), 25 R. 765 ; *Gollan's Trs.* v. *Booth* (1901), 3 F. 1035 ; *Rackstraw* v. *Douglas*, 1917 S. C. 284 ; *Inland Revenue* v. *Bone*, 1927 S. C. 698.

[4] *Per* Lord Sands in *Inland Revenue* v. *Bone, supra.*

in *G.'s Trs.* v. *G.*[1] and it was laid down by the majority of the Court, on a review of all the previous cases, that the Court would, unless the rights of parties other than the issue might be adversely affected, proceed on the presumption that a woman of fifty-three years of age and upwards was past the age of child-bearing and could have no issue.

Divorce equivalent to death of the guilty spouse. **II. Effect of Divorce.**—" Marriage dissolved by divorce, either upon wilful non-adherence (or wilful desertion) or adultery, the party injurer loseth all benefit accruing through the marriage (as is expressly provided by the foresaid Act of Parliament, 1573, c. 55, concerning non-adherence), but the party injured hath the same benefit as by the other's natural death." [2] Thus the legal rights of terce and *jus relictæ*, or courtesy, as the case may be, become due. The sole exception occurs in regard to *jus relicti*. The Act [3] which creates that right gives it to the husband only on his wife's death, and the rule which obtains with respect to the other legal rights has not been extended by analogy to this more recently created right.[4]

Where both spouses are divorced, neither can claim the benefit of the statute.[5]

The operation of the statute is not confined to the legal rights. It affects also the provisions made by the spouses in their marriage contract. The offending spouse is bound to make good to the other all the obligations undertaken by him or her in favour of the other, and loses (for the benefit of the other) all provisions in his or her favour.[6] Thus, where a provision was made in a marriage contract in favour of the spouses " in conjunct fee and liferent and to the longest liver of them two in liferent," the husband, on divorcing the wife, became entitled to the liferent of the whole ; [7] and, where a father in his son's marriage contract

---

[1] 1936 S. C. 837. The decision in *Beattie's Trs.* v. *Meffan, supra,* was disapproved.

[2] Stair, i. 4. 20. The Act provides : " the said partie offender to tyne and lose their tocher and *donationes propter nuptias.*"

[3] The Married Women's Property Act, 1881, 44 & 45 Vict. c. 21.

[4] *Eddington* v. *Robertson* (1895), 22 R. 430.

[5] *Fraser* v. *Walker* (1872), 10 M. 837.

[6] See Lord Kinnear's opinion in *Somervell's Tr.* v. *Dawes* (1903), 5 F. 1065.

[7] *Thom* v. *Thom* (1852), 14 D. 861.

undertook to pay an annuity to him, whom failing to his wife, it was held that after the husband was divorced on the ground of adultery the wife had right to the annuity, and that an assignation by the husband prior to the divorce did not exclude the wife's claim.[1] The rights provided to the innocent spouse under a marriage contract to which he or she becomes entitled on divorce are those, and those only, which he or she takes in succession to, and following upon a forfeiture incurred by, the guilty spouse ;[2] and the statute takes nothing from the guilty spouse except that which it gives to the innocent spouse. The interest of the children of the marriage in the matrimonial provisions is not enlarged or accelerated by divorce ; it is only *quoad* the injured spouse that the offending party is treated as dead.[3] This qualification of Lord Stair's statement of the law is illustrated in *Harvey* v. *Farquhar*,[4] a case which contains almost all the law on this topic. By antenuptial marriage contract the husband assigned to trustees a sum of money, and the wife conveyed the property she should receive from her father. The purpose of the trust was that the income of the estate should be paid to the husband during the marriage, and on the dissolution of the marriage to the surviving spouse, and that on the death of the survivor the capital should be made over to the children of the marriage, and, if there were no children, or if they should all predecease the survivor, to others. The husband having been divorced, it was treated as settled law, both in the Court of Session and in the House of Lords, that the wife was entitled to the income of the whole estate. On the death of the wife, a second case[5] was raised in order to ascertain the respective rights of the husband, who survived, and the child of the marriage. The child contended that in respect of the divorce the wife was to be considered as the surviving party

The interests of children not affected.

---

[1] *Johnstone - Beattie* v. *Johnstone* (1867), 5 M. 340 ; *Johnstone-Beattie* v. *Dalzell* (1868), 6 M. 633.

[2] *Drummond* v. *Bell-Irving*, 1930 S. C. 704. A power of apportioning a fund among the children of the marriage exercisable under the terms of the marriage contract by the guilty spouse is not lost on divorce, whatever be the source of the fund—*M'Grady's Trs.* v. *M'Grady*, 1932 S. C. 191.

[3] *Montgomery* v. *Zarifi*, 1918 S. C. (H. L.) 128, *per* Viscount Haldane, at 133, Lord Dunedin, at 138.

[4] (1872), 10 M. (H. L.) 26.

[5] *Harvey's Jud. Factor* v. *Spittal's Curator* (1893), 20 R. 1016. See *Macalister* v. *Macalister* (1854), 26 S. J. 597.

and that on her death the right of the children was purified, and the provision became exigible. But this claim was rejected. It was held—(1) that the father was entitled to the income of the estate which he had put in settlement, seeing that it was relieved of the wife's liferent ; (2) that the vesting of the children's right was suspended until the father's death, and that it was not accelerated by the divorce ; and (3) that the income of the wife's part of the trust estate, as it was not disposed of by the contract in the circumstances which had occurred, formed part of her estate.

In this case the children had no vested interest until the death of both parents. But had their right been vested the decision would not have been different. In *Dawson* v. *Smart*,[1] the trustees were directed by the marriage contract to pay the income of the estate conveyed by the wife to her during her life, and on her death to her husband, and to make over the capital to the children. There was a destination-over which probably had the effect of suspending the vesting until the time of payment, but no decision was pronounced as to its effect, and the case was treated on the assumption that the children had a vested right. The circumstances of the case were that the wife was dead, and that the husband who had been divorced survived. The child of the marriage claimed payment of the trust funds on the death of her mother, but without success. Under the contract, the children had the right to receive their provision on the death of both of their parents and nothing more, and the divorce, whatever might be its effect as between the parties to the contract, did not entitle the children to the possession of the subjects at an earlier period. The income accruing on the wife's estate during the husband's lifetime fell back into her estate.

The statute mentions "tocher and *donationes propter nuptias*." Provisions made in a marriage contract, and even by one of the spouses in favour of the other after marriage,[2] fall within these words. But in no case has the rule of the statute been applied to testamentary bequests.[3]

The statute does not affect testamentary gifts.

---

[1] (1903), 5 F. (H. L.) 24.
[2] *Ritchie* v. *Ritchie's Trs* (1874), 1 R. 987; *Hedderwick* v. *Morison* (1901), 4 F. 163.

[3] *Lacy* v. *Morrison* (1869), 7 S. L. R. 45 ; *Countess of Argyle* v. *The Tenants of Dollar* (1573), M. 327 and 6184 ; Lord Kinloch's opinion in *Johnstone-*

When a legacy is given to a wife in the event of her husband predeceasing her, the words receive their natural interpretation, and the condition is not satisfied by divorce of the husband.[1] Similarly, if the gift is given over to others in case the wife does not survive her husband, the rule cannot be applied so as to defeat the contingent right of the conditional institutes.[2]

III. Effect of Accumulations Acts. — The Thellusson Act [3] provides that no person shall by will, deed, or otherwise settle or dispose of real or personal property in such manner that the rents, issues, profits, or produce thereof shall be wholly or partially accumulated for any longer term than—(1) the life of the granter or settlor ; [4] or (2) the term of twenty-one years from the death of the grantor, settlor, or testator ; or (3) during the minority or respective minorities of any person or persons, who shall be living, or *en ventre sa mère* at the time of the death of the grantor or settlor ; or (4) during the minority or respective minorities only of any person or persons who, under the uses or trusts of the deed or will, would for the time being, if of full age, be entitled unto the rents, profits, dividends, or annual produce directed to be accumulated. This period differs from the third in that it is not required that the minor should have been alive at the grantor's death.[5]

By section 2 of the Act accumulation for payment of debt or for raising portions was excepted from its operation, but the Entail (Scotland) Act, 1914,[6] enacts that this section shall not apply to Scotland.

This statute, it is settled,[7] applies both to the case where

Beattie v. *Johnstone* (1867), 5 M. 340. See *Drummond* v. *Bell-Irving*, 1930 S. C. 704, at 716.

[1] *Mason* v. *Beattie's Trs.* (1878), 6 R. 37 ; *Taylor's Trs.* v. *Barnett* (1893), 20 R. 1032.

[2] *Mason* v. *Beattie's Trs.* and *Taylor's Trs.* v. *Barnett, supra.*

[3] 39 & 40 Geo. III. c. 98. The exception as to heritable property was abolished by 11 & 12 Vic. c. 36, sec. 41. The repeal of the Act by the Law of Property Act, 1925, does not affect the operation of the Act in Scotland—*Smith's Trs.* v. *Gaydon*, 1931 S. C. 533.

[4] As in *Stewart's Trs.* v. *Stewart*, 1927 S. C. 350 ; *Union Bank* v. *Campbell*, 1929 S. C. 143.

[5] *In re Cattell* [1914], 1 Ch. 177.

[6] 4 & 5 George V. c. 43, sec. 9

[7] *Lord* v. *Colvin* (1860), 23 D. 111 ; *Logan's Trs.* v. *Logan* (1896), 23 R. 848. Cf. *Mitchell's Trs.* v. *Fraser*, 1915 S. C. 350, a case which is explained in Lord Dundas's opinion in *Innes's Trs.* v. *Bowen*, 1920 S. C. 133, and Lord Skerrington's opinion

accumulation is directed by the will, and to the case where, although not so directed, accumulation necessarily results from the provisions of the will ; as, for instance, where a testator makes a disposition of his estate which is dependent on the occurrence of a future contingency, but gives no directions as to the income in the meantime, for in that case the income must perforce be accumulated until the time at which it can be ascertained whether the contingency on which the disposition depends will or will not occur. Nor is the operation of the statute at the termination of the period of twenty-one years from the testator's death, excluded by the circumstance that there has been no accumulation during that period, for what is prohibited is not merely the accumulation of income for twenty-one years, but any accumulation after the expiry of that period from the testator's death.[1]

The Act, beyond preventing accumulation, does not affect the construction of wills. Beyond prohibiting accumulation after the prescribed periods, the Act does not affect the construction of the will or alter the dispositions of the testator's property ; and, in particular, it has not the effect of accelerating the period of the vesting of the subject, the income of which is to be accumulated, if under the will it is postponed beyond the time at which the accumulation must cease.[2] " Although the trust for accumulation is cut down and reduced to a limited period, the whole of the rest of the will remains, in point of disposition, in point of the meaning, effect, and true interpretation of its language, precisely as if there had been no such operation performed by the statute." [3] In other words, the will is to be read as if it had contained a direction that the income should be accumulated for twenty-one years and no longer.[4]

Disposal of interest liberated by the statute. The question which has been mainly agitated in the

in *Watson's Trs.* v. *Brown*, 1923 S. C. 228. The Act does not apply to savings made by trustees out of a fund in their hands—*Lindsay's Trs.*, 1911 S. C. 584, or to accumulation of income under a scheme prepared on remit from the Court for the purpose of effecting equitable compensation for loss occasioned by a claim for legal rights—*Moss's Trs.* v. *Bramwell*, 1936 S. C. (H. L.) 1.

[1] *Campbell's Trs.* v. *Campbell* (1891), 18 R. 992.

[2] *Muirhead* v. *Muirhead* (1890), 17 R. (H. L.) 45.

[3] *Per* Lord Westbury in *Green* v. *Gascoyne* (1865), 34 L. J. (Ch.) 268.

[4] See Lord Kyllachy's opinion in *Elder's Trs.* v. *The Treasurer of the Free Church of Scotland* (1892), 20 R. 2 ; *Smith* v. *Glasgow Royal Infirmary*, 1909 S. C. 1231.

Scots cases concerning the application of the statute is as to the disposal of the income directed to be accumulated beyond the permitted periods. The Act declares that " where any accumulation shall be directed otherwise than as aforesaid, such direction shall be null and void, and the rents, issues, profits, and produce of such property so directed to be accumulated shall, so long as the same shall be directed to be accumulated contrary to the provisions of this Act, go to and be received by such person or persons as would have been entitled thereto, if such accumulation had not been directed." The determination of the parties entitled under this provision depends on the character of the gift and the nature of the instructions given by the testator as to the disposal of the subject on which the income arises.   In *Maxwell's Trs.* v. *Maxwell*,[1] Lord Justice-Clerk Moncreiff stated the general rule on this point in terms which have been approved in later cases.[2] " If the fund directed to be accumulated," he said, " is not the subject of any present gift, then the right of the eventual beneficiary will not be accelerated or arise at the term of twenty-one years, but the heirs-at-law *in mobilibus* will take it as intestate succession. But if there be a present gift of the fund itself, and the direction to accumulate be only a burden on the gift, then the burden will terminate at the expiration of twenty-one years, and the gift will become absolute in the person of the donee."

The rules as to the disposal of the income directed to be accumulated beyond the period allowed may be summarised as follows :—

1. Where there is a present gift of the principal, conferring on the beneficiary an interest vested at the testator's death or prior to the termination of the permitted period, and burdened with a direction to trustees to withhold the subject and accumulate the income, the income released by the statute will fall to the beneficiary.[3] The initial gift bestows on the legatee all right in the subject, save in so far

---

[1] (1877), 5 R. 248.

[2] *Logan's Trs.* v. *Logan* (1896), 23 R. 848 ; *Mackay's Trs.* v. *Mackay*, 1909 S. C. 139.

[3] *Ogilvie's Trs.* v. *Kirk Session of Dundee* (1846), 8 D. 1229 ; *Mackenzie* v. *Mackenzie's Trs.* (1877), 4 R. 962 ; *Maxwell's Trs.* v. *Maxwell*, *supra* ; *Combe* v. *Hughes* (1865), 34 L. J. (Ch.) 344 ; *Trickey* v. *Trickey* (1832), 3 M. & K. 560.

as the other provisions of the will effectually limit that right ; and the income liberated by the statute goes to the legatee as an accessory of the prior gift. It will not escape notice that a legatee, having an absolute right to a subject, can put an end to an accumulation in which no one has any interest save himself, and which is not required by the other provisions of the will, and can at once, under the doctrine of repugnancy,[1] claim payment of the subject without requiring the aid of the statute.

In *Stewart's Trs.* v. *Whitelaw*,[2] a liferent was conferred on a child with a provision that until he was twenty-five the trustees should pay him such part of the income as they should think proper and accumulate the balance. The child here was fully vested in the liferent and the discretionary power was merely a rider on that interest, the consequence being, therefore, that, when the statute prevented further accumulation, it became the duty of the trustees to pay over the whole income to the child.

2. Where the right to the bequest, whether it be of residue or of a particular fund or subject, is not vested or is subject to a possible defeasance,[3] at the time when the accumulation is terminated by the statute, the legatee is not entitled to the income thereafter accruing. If the gift is not residuary, the income will fall into residue, if there is in the will a bequest of residue, and if the residuary legatees are ascertained and are in a position to receive the income as it arises.[4] If there is no bequest of residue, or if the vesting of the residuary gift is suspended, the income falls to the testator's heirs *ab intestato* ; and if the subject of the bequest is residue, and is not vested, the heirs will in this case also be entitled to the income.[5] The general rule is that a bequest of residue, whether vested or contingent,

---

[1] *Post,* Chapter XV.

[2] 1926 S. C. 701.

[3] *Eyre* v. *Marsden* (1838), 2 Keen 564 ; *M'Donald* v. *Bryce* (1838), 2 Keen 276.

[4] *Ellis* v. *Maxwell* (1841), 3 Beav. 587 ; *Jones* v. *Maggs* (1852), 9 Hare 605 ; *In re Pope* [1900], 1 Ch. 64.

[5] *Pursell* v. *Elder* (1865), 3 M. (H. L.) 59 ; *Keith's Trs.* v. *Keith*

(1857), 19 D. 1040 ; *Lord* v. *Colvin* (1860), 23 D. 111 ; *Smyth's Trs.* v. *Kinloch* (1880), 7 R. 1176 ; *Cathcart's Trs.* v. *Heneage's Trs.* (1883), 10 R. 1205 ; *Campbell's Trs.* v. *Campbell* (1891), 18 R. 992 ; *Logan's Trs.* v. *Logan* (1896), 23 R. 848 ; *Moon's Trs.* v. *Moon* (1899), 2 F. 201 ; *Muir's Trs.* v. *Jamieson* (1903), 10 S. L. T. 701 (Lord Kincairney).

carries all income undisposed of by the will.[1]   But that rule cannot govern the destination of income set free by the statute, because the statute makes it imperative that the trustees shall not retain the income, but shall pay it away as it accrues, and therefore it cannot be kept to await the final distribution of the residue.

3. But, although the beneficiary's right has vested, it cannot be said that he is entitled to the income arising after the period permitted for accumulation, if the gift in his favour is contained in a direction to hold for, or pay to, him from and after a time which is subsequent to the expiry of that period.   The expression used in the passage from Lord Justice-Clerk Moncreiff's opinion quoted above is " present gift " ; and in all the cases in which the legatee has been preferred to the income there has been a bequest operating in his favour at the testator's death or before the time at which the statute put an end to the accumulation.[2] In *Smith* v. *Glasgow Royal Infirmary*[3] the testator instructed his trustees to pay certain annuities, and out of the accumulation of the income to discharge a bond.   When the bond was paid off the accumulations of income were to be invested, and after the death of the last survivor of the annuitants the trustees were to realise the estate and pay over the proceeds to the Directors of the Infirmary " to whom I leave, bequest and destine the same."   On the expiry of twenty-one years from the testator's death some of the annuitants were alive.   It was held that the income accruing thereafter was not due to the Infirmary, but fell into intestacy.   It is clear that the right to the residue had vested *a morte testatoris* ; but, although the Infirmary was the residuary legatee because it eventually took the residue, " it is not residuary legatee by way of present gift, because the only gift given to it is a gift which is to take effect at the death of the last annuitant."[4]

---

[1] *Pursell* v. *Elder, supra* ; *Sturgis* v. *Meiklam's Trs.* (1865), 3 M. (H. L.) 70 ; Lord Cottenham's opinion in *Turnbull* v. *Cowan* (1848), 6 Bell's Apps. 222.

[2] See the cases in note 3, p. 315.

[3] 1909 S. C. 1231.   The Lord President (Dunedin) referred to the English case of *Weatherall* v. *Thornburgh* (1877), 8 Ch. D. 261, which was followed in *In re Travis* [1900], 2 Ch. 541 ; *Re Parry* (1889), 60 L. T. 489. See *Wharton* v. *Masterman* [1895], A. C. 186 ; *Burgh of Ayr* v. *Shaw* (1904), 12 S. L. T., 126 (Lord Low).

[4] *Per* the Lord President.

This decision was followed in *Wilson's Trs.* v. *Glasgow Royal Infirmary*.[1] The will in this case was in the simple form of a direction to trustees to pay an annuity to the testator's widow and to hold the residue and all accumulations thereof until her death, and on that event to pay over the same and all accumulations to the Infirmary. Here, also, it was held that the fact that the residue had vested did not entitle the Infirmary to the income accruing after the lapse of twenty-one years from the testator's death.

The election by a beneficiary to claim his legal rights in place of a legacy may have the effect, according to *Innes's Trs.* v. *Bowen*,[2] of bringing the statute into operation with regard to accumulation of income following upon the election. In that case the testatrix bequeathed the income of the residue to her only child, a daughter, and the residue after the daughter's death to her children with a further destination. The daughter claimed legitim, and the trustees for twenty-one years accumulated the income of the residue for the purpose of compensating the beneficiaries injured by the withdrawal of the legitim. It was held that the statute prohibited further accumulation, and that the daughter as heir *ab intestata* was entitled to the future income. The ground of judgement was shortly stated by the Lord Justice-Clerk (Scott-Dickson) in these words : " When the claim to legitim had been enforced, there came into operation, in respect of the terms of the trust-deed, the doctrine of equitable compensation, whereby, in respect of these terms, accumulation of income had to take place. That accumulation was the direct result of the trust-deed ; and it was the result which I think the truster must be held to have known would inevitably follow if the second party's claim to legitim were made and pressed to payment. I think, therefore, that the accumulation was directed by the trust-deed, so as to be struck at by the Act."

Accumulations Act, 1892. The policy of the law which found expression in the Thellusson Act has been further extended by the Accumulations Act, 1892,[3] which provides that " no person shall, after the passing of this Act, settle or dispose of any property

---

[1] 1917 S. C. 527.

[2] 1920 S. C. 133. In this case Lord Hunter's decision to the same effect in the Outer House case of

Hutchison v. *Grant's Trs.*, 1913 S. C. 1211 was approved. See *Moss's Trs.* v. *Bramwell*, 1936 S. C. (H. L.) 1.

[3] 55 & 56 Vic. c. 58.

in such manner that the rents, issues, profits, or income thereof shall be wholly or partially accumulated for the purchase of land only, for any longer period than during the minority or respective minorities of any person or persons who under the uses or trusts of the instrument directing such accumulation would for the time being, if of full age, be entitled to receive the rents, issues, profits, or income so directed to be accumulated." In the only case [1] which has arisen in Scotland in regard to the Act it was ruled that its effect is not to nullify the whole provisions of the settlement relating to the accumulation and the purchase of lands, but merely to annul the direction for accumulation. Hence, where the testator had directed his trustees to hold the residue of his estate, to accumulate the income for fifteen years, and then to apply the whole in the purchase of lands to be settled on a series of heirs, it was held that the effect of the Act was to prevent the accumulation of the income and that in all other respects the testator's directions stood unimpaired. The conveyance of the lands was not accelerated, and the income during the fifteen years fell to be disposed of as intestate estate. In England it has been decided that the Act applies to a will made before it was enacted by a testator who dies after that date.[2]

IV. Statutory Restrictions on the Creation of Liferents.— During the last century the whole tendency of the legislation in regard to entails was towards affording in increasing measure means whereby entailed lands might be set free from the fetters of the entail. But this legislation would have been largely defeated had it remained possible to tie up lands in perpetuity by the creation of a series of liferents. " A series of liferents," Lord Mackenzie observed in *Erskine* v. *Wright*,[3] " is the most proper entail, and, if competent, would soon supersede all others." Accordingly the authors of the Entail Amendment Act of 1848 [4] found it necessary to supplement the sections dealing with entails by making provisions controlling the creation of liferents.

---

[1] *Robertson's Trs.* v. *Robertson's Trs.*, 1933 S. C. 639.

[2] *In re Baroness Llanover* [1903], 2 Ch. 330.

[3] (1846) 8 D. 863. But the majority

of the Court held that a series of annuities was validly constituted a real burden on an estate.

[4] 11 & 12 Vic. c. 36.

Section 48 of the Act provides that it shall be competent to grant an estate limited to a liferent interest in favour only of a party in life at the date of such grant, and, where any land or estate shall by virtue of any deed dated on or after 1st August 1848 be held in liferent by a party of full age, born after the date of such deed, he shall not be affected by any prohibitions, etc., contained in the deed and shall be deemed the proprietor in fee simple of such estate. This section, as was pointed out in *Crichton-Stuart's Tutrix*,[1] "makes neither settlements in liferent nor settlements in entail illegal or void ; nor does it make either of them necessarily inoperative. It only provides means by which the liferenter and the heir of entail alike can get relief from the limitations of their titles." If, therefore, the liferenter is content with his liferent, he may leave the settlement to take its course in accordance with the provisions of the deed.

Section 17 of the Entail Amendment Act of 1868,[2] made a provision on similar lines with regard to moveable estate. This section is now repealed and re-enacted by the Trusts (Scotland) Act, 1921,[3] (sec. 9), which provides :— "It shall be competent to constitute or reserve, by means of a trust or otherwise, a liferent interest in moveable and personal estate in Scotland in favour only of a person in life at the date of the deed constituting or reserving such liferent, and, where any moveable or personal estate in Scotland shall, by virtue of any deed dated after the 31st day of July 1868 (the date of any testamentary or *mortis causa* deed being taken to be the date of the death of the grantor, and the date of any contract of marriage being taken to be the date of the dissolution of the marriage), be held in liferent by or for behoof of a person of full age born after the date of such deed, such moveable or personal estate shall belong absolutely to such person, and where such estate stands invested in the name of any trustees, such trustees shall be bound to deliver, make over, or convey such estate to such person."

The difficulties in the way of reconciling the two portions of this section are pointed out in the Lord President's

[1] 1921 S. C. 840.
[2] 31 & 32 Vic. c. 84.
[3] 11 & 12 George V. cap. 58.

opinion in *Reid's Trs.* v. *Dashwood.*[1] In so far as they are inconsistent, " the second," it was observed, " as the operative part of the section must prevail over the first part, and must receive effect." The effect of the second part is to convert the liferent into a fee : and the section is not, therefore, susceptible of the construction adopted in *Crichton-Stuart's Tutrix*,[2] viz., that the liferenter is given, not the fee, but the power to acquire the fee.

The section does not apply where the interest is not a liferent but an annuity [3] or a right to receive the income of a fund, not for the lifetime of the recipient, but until the occurrence of a certain event.[4] In *Shiell's Trs.* v. *Shiell's Trs.*[5] the income of the testator's estate was bequeathed to his four children, and, if any one of them predeceased the last survivor, his issue were to be entitled to his share of the income. On the death of the last survivor of the four children the estate was to be divided among the surviving grandchildren and the issue of predeceasers. A grandson (J. A. Shiell), who was born after the death of the testator, became entitled on the death of his father to a share of the income, and this was paid to him until his death, which occurred before the death of all the testator's children. This grandson's representatives having claimed the fee under this section, it was held that the claim failed in respect that the grandson's interest was not a liferent in the sense of the section.

The right of the grandchild was, said Lord Kyllachy, " really a right of a somewhat complex and quite innominate character,- embracing as it did (1) a contingent fee in a certain share of the trust-estate, and (2) a right (subject to certain burdens) to enjoy the income of the share in question until the right to the fee became absolute upon the death of the last survivor of the truster's immediate children— J. A. Shiell's uncles and aunts. That was really the substance of the right, and being so, it appears to me that, however it may be described, it cannot be described as a right of liferent."

(margin note: Acts apply only to liferents.)

[1] 1929 S. C. 748.
[2] *Supra.*
[3] *Drybrough's Trs.* v. *Drybrough's Trs.*, 1912 S. C. 939.
[4] *Shiell's Trs.* v. *Shiell's Trs.* 1906, 8 F. 848.
[5] *Supra.*

It is clear that effect cannot be given to the section without defeating the rights of those to whom the fee is destined under the testator's settlement, and, therefore, if these are the only persons prejudiced, there would appear to be no reason why the liferenter should not be entitled to demand that the subject liferented be made over to him.[1] But there may be other interests involved which exclude any demand by the liferenter for transference of the subject to him before the time appointed for payment by the testator. In *Macculloch's Trs.* v. *McCulloch*,[2] where the testator had provided that his estate should be held as a *unum quid* until the death of all his children, a grandchild who had a vested right in a *pro indiviso* share of the fee and a right also to a proportionate share of the income, claimed in the lifetime of certain of the children that he was entitled under the statute [3] to have his share of the trust estate paid over to him at once. In regard to this claim, Lord Davey observed : " The statute apparently (I express no opinion upon what may be the construction of it) converts a person with a limited interest into one holding a larger interest, and says that the trustees, notwithstanding any directions to the contrary in the will, are to transfer his share to him ; but it says nothing at all as to the time when it is to be transferred, nor is there anything in the statute which in the least degree overrides any apt and competent provisions in a will for the purpose of fixing the period." What the pursuer was seeking in this case was accelerated payment ; and, in the absence of any provision in the statute as to the time at which payment could be demanded, he could succeed only by shewing that the conditions under which the Court permits acceleration of payment were satisfied.[4] These conditions were not satisfied, seeing that acceleration would cause injury to other parties, and accordingly the claim failed.

Of this decision it was said by Lord Stormonth-Darling [5]

---

[1] See Lord Stormonth - Darling's opinion in *Shiell's Trs.* v. *Shiell's Trs.* (1906), 8 F. 848, at 853 ; Ld. Pres. Dunedin's opinion in *Baxter* v. *Baxter*, 1909 S. C. 1027, at 1031 ; and cf. the opinions in *Mackenzie's Trs.* v. *Mackenzie*, 1922 S. C. 404.

[2] (1903), 6 F. (H. L.) 3. This case is stated *ante*, p. 303.

[3] The 1868 Act.

[4] See *ante*, p. 297.

[5] In *Shiell's Trs.* v. *Shiell's Trs.*, *supra*.

that " the view taken by the House of Lords seems to imply that the kind of ' liferent interest ' contemplated by the section is not to be extended beyond the simple case where, coming to be held by trustees for behoof of a person of full age, it is capable of being converted into a fee without interfering with the legitimate interest of others." [1]

In the cases [2] in which the liferenter has been held entitled, as fiar by reason of the statute, to payment of the share of the trust estate held for him in liferent, his interest extended to the whole of the estate or his share was severed from the rest of the estate or appropriated so that no one except the ultimate fiars was prejudiced by his claim for payment. In the most recent of these cases [3] the claimant was *in utero* at the death of the testator. In *Stewart's Trs.* v. *Whitelaw* [4] the Court reserved its opinion on the question whether a liferent conferred by a deed executed by the donee of a special power of appointment on one who was not in life at the time of the death of the donor of the power would fall within the operation of the section.

---

[1] This must mean apparently others who are not the prospective fiars.

[2] *Baxter* v. *Baxter; Mackenzie's Trs.* v. *Mackenzie; Reid's Trs.* v. *Dashwood, supra;* and *Davie* v. *Davie's Trs.* (1900), 8 S. L. T. 28 (Lord Low). See also *Downie's Trs.* (1901), 38 S. L. R. 755.

[3] *Reid's Trs.* v. *Dashwood, supra.*

[4] 1926, S. C. 701.

CHAPTER XV.

REPUGNANT AND INEFFECTUAL CONDITIONS.

A TESTATOR may annex to his bequests such conditions as he chooses, and these will, as a general rule, receive effect. *Uti quisque rei suae legassit, ita jus esto.* The legatee is not entitled to enjoy the testator's bounty save under the conditions he has imposed. But it may happen that the condition, because of some inherent vice, or for some other reason, is ineffectual to restrict the legatee's interest. The condition or limitation may be inoperative, for example, either because the truster has failed to provide the necessary machinery for carrying it into effect ; or because it is repugnant to, or inconsistent with, the policy of the law ; or because it is, or becomes, incapable of fulfilment.

Fee cannot be rendered alimentary.

I. Declarations that the Legacy is given for the Legatee's Alimentary Use.—Where an absolute and un-limited right of property in the subject of the bequest is conferred on the legatee, a declaration that it is given for his alimentary use only is of no effect.[1] If the legatee has the *dominium plenum,* he cannot be fettered in his

---

[1] *Wilkie's Trs.* v. *Wight's Trs.* (1893), 21 R. 199 ; Ld. Pres. Inglis and Lord Shand in *Young's Trs.* v. *M'Nab* (1883), 10 R. 1165 ; *Johnston* v. *Johnston's Trs.* (1903), 40 S. L. R. 757 ; *Watson's Trs.* v. *Watson,* 1913 S. C. 1133. In *Gray* v. *Gray's Trs.* (1877), 4 R. 378, a doubt was expressed as to whether periodical payments out of capital could be made alimentary. See also *Elliot* v. *Bowhill* (1873), 11 M. 735.

enjoyment or use of that which is his own property, or protected from the diligence of creditors.

It is otherwise in the case of a liferent. A liferenter is Continuing
trust necessary
to secure
alimentary
liferents. entitled only to the income of the subject over which the liferent is constituted, and he can assign to a purchaser nothing more than the right to receive that income in his room and place. A testator may, for example, provide that the liferent shall terminate if the liferenter attempts to sell it ; [1] or he may declare that it is given for alimentary purposes, the effect of this declaration being that the proceeds, in so far as they are not in excess of a reasonable aliment, cannot be attached save for alimentary debts. These conditions are valid and effectual. The only question which arises is whether the testator has provided the means for carrying out his purpose. According to the older authorities,[2] a liferent might be rendered alimentary although no trust was set up by the testator ; but the modern view is that the legatee's interest can be protected only by means of a continuing trust.[3] When a trust of this kind is provided, the legatee has merely a claim to receive from the hands of the trustees, and under the conditions imposed by the truster, the income as it accrues.

But the Court has no power to create a trust ; [4] and if No power in
Court to
create a trust
for this
purpose. a testator direct his trustees to make payment of a subject to a legatee, and then declares that his or her right shall be alimentary, the direction to pay must be obeyed, although the result may be that the provision for the legatee's right being alimentary is thereby frustrated. Thus, in *Allan's Trs.* v. *Allan*,[5] the testator directed his trustees to divide and pay over the capital of the residue to and among the

---

[1] *Chaplin's Trs.* v. *Hoile* (1890), 18 R. 27.

[2] *Lewis* v. *Anstruther* (1852), 14 D. 857 ; *Muirhead* v. *Miller* (1877), 4 R. 1139 ; *Urquhart* v. *Douglas* (1738) M. 10,403. In *Dunsmure's Trs.* v. *Dunsmure*, 1920 S. C. 147, Lord Skerrington expressed the opinion that it ought not to be held that a trust was essential for the creation of an alimentary liferent. (See also his Lordship's opinion in *Dempster's Trs.* v. *Dempster*, 1921 S. C. 332.)

[3] See the *dicta* in *White's Trs.* v.

Whyte (1877), 4 R. 786 ; *Eliott's Trs.* v. *Eliott* (1894), 21 R. 975 ; *Murray* v. *Macfarlane's Trs.* (1895), 22 R. 927 ; *Kennedy's Trs.* v. *Warren* (1901), 3 F. 1087 ; *Brown's Trs.* v. *Thom*, 1916 S. C. 32 ; *M'Dougal's Trs.* v. *Heinemann*, 1918 S. C. (H. L.) 6, *per* Lord Dunedin, at 12 ; *Forbes's Trs.* v. *Tennant*, 1926 S. C. 294. See further as to alimentary liferents, p. 301 *ante*.

[4] *Per* Lord M'Laren in *Murray* v. *Macfarlane's Trs.* ; and Lord Dundas in *Brown's Trs.* v. *Thom*, *supra*.

[5] (1872), 11 M. 216.

children who might survive him, payable, as to the daughters' shares, on their attaining majority or being married ; and he declared that the provisions to daughters should be alimentary and exclusive of the *jus mariti* or *jus administrationis* of their husbands, and not affectable by the debts of them or their husbands.   On a question being raised as to the manner in which these provisions were to be secured, it was held that the daughters were entitled to receive their shares in accordance with the clear direction to the trustees to pay, and that the only effect of the declaration was that there should be inserted in the receipts granted by the daughters a clause excluding the *jus mariti*.[1]   The Lord Justice-Clerk [2] observed : " Now, the fund is declared alimentary and inalienable, and if that had been consistent with the other direction to pay over, I do not say but that the Court might have taken steps to enforce the truster's intention. If this condition had related to a sum payable annually, it would perhaps have been proper that the Court should exercise its equitable jurisdiction for the purpose of carrying into effect such an intention. But in the present case I do not think this is practicable. The testator has attempted to do two inconsistent things. He has ordered his trustees to pay over, while he has endeavoured to limit the full right of property in the payees, and that without a trust, and without creating a separate or resulting right in anyone else."

This decision has been followed in a series of cases.[3]   An absolute direction to trustees to pay will not be withdrawn by mere inference : there must be a clear statement that the trustees are to hold the shares if an intention to that effect is to be operative.[4]   Thus, in the case of *Clouston's Trs.* v. *Bulloch*,[5] the truster directed his trustees to pay over certain shares of his estate to his daughters, " to be at (their) absolute disposal."   By a codicil he directed that the daughters, in respect of one half of their shares,

Direction to pay not controlled save by clear words.

---

[1] But the restrictions have no effect. Lord M'Laren in *Murray* v. *Macfarlane's Trs.* (1895), 22 R. 927.

[2] Lord Moncreiff.

[3] *M'Nish* v. *Donald's Trs.* (1879), 7 R. 96 ; *Clouston's Trs.* v. *Bulloch* (1889), 16 R. 937 ; *Jamieson* v. *Lesslie's Trs.* (1889), 16 R. 807 ; *Murray* v. *Macfarlane's Trs., supra* ; *Mitchell's Trs.* v. *Smith* (1880), 7 R. 1086.

[4] Lord Shand in *Clouston's Trs.* v *Bulloch, supra.*

[5] *Supra.*

should not " have power to deal with it during their respective lifetimes beyond the interest or revenue derived from it," but should have power to dispose of it after their deaths ; " my object in making this restriction being, that they shall not by any act on their part deprive themselves of a fair livelihood during their lifetime." It was held that this clause was insufficient to reduce their interests to a liferent,[1] and the principle of *Allan's Trs.* was applied.

Similarly, a direction to trustees " to see to the investment in such manner as shall to them appear best to secure " the provisions,[2] and a direction in a codicil that shares were " to be invested for the legatees " and not paid in cash, were held insufficient to reduce the legatees' rights or qualify a previous instruction to pay.[3]

But the direction to pay will be superseded if the subsequent declarations have the effect of reducing the legatee's interest to a liferent. Thus, in *Duthie's Trs.* v. *Kinloch*,[4] the testator, after directing his trustees to pay certain legacies at his death, proceeded to declare that these were to be " invested by the said trustees " for behoof of his married daughters, " exclusive of the *jus mariti* . . . and the annual proceeds thereof paid to such legatees during their lives, *and thereafter divided amongst their children* " ; here it was held that the rights of the married daughters were by these words restricted to a liferent, and that the trust was to be continued in order to secure these. As a mere declaration that the rights shall be alimentary or exclusive of the *jus mariti* does not reduce a right of fee previously given, the distinctive feature of this case appears to be the gift of fee to the children.[5]

Again, in two cases [6] where the truster directed his trustees to make over a share of his estate to a daughter and her children, the Court, in order to give effect to the testator's intention, directed that there should be inserted in

Protected rights of succession.

[1] Lord Adam dissented, on the ground that these words reduced the daughter's interest to a liferent.

[2] *Jamieson* v *Lesslie's Trs.*, *supra.*,

[3] *Murray* v. *Macfarlane's Trs.*, *supra.*

[4] (1878), 5 R. 858.

[5] Cf. *Gibson's Trs.* v. *Ross* (1877), 4 R. 1038.

[6] *Massy* v. *Scott's Trs.* (1872), 11 M. 173 ; *Gibson's Trs.* v. *Ross, supra.*

the titles of the legatees words constituting a protected right
of succession in the children.

In *Massy* v. *Scott's Trs.*,[1] the trustees were directed to
pay a legacy to the truster's grandniece and her heirs,
" to be settled on herself and her issue, with power to her
of disposal in case of no issue, and failing issue and disposal
by her " to her own heirs.   It will be observed that there
was no course of trust management instituted here by the
testator, and therefore the grandniece was entitled to
immediate payment ; but, in order to reconcile the interests
of all the parties, the Court directed that the sum bequeathed
should be invested in securities for the grandniece, " subject
to the condition that the right of succession of the said
children . . . shall not be defeated by any gratuitous act
or deed " of the grandniece, and with power to her, failing
issue, to dispose of the subjects.

Whether the application of the doctrine of protected
succession should have been thus extended may be open to
question, and it is " hard to reconcile " this decision [2] with
Houston v. *Mitchell* [3] and *Newall's Trs.* v. *Inglis's Trs.*[4]
In *Allan's Trs.* v. *Allan* [5] the Lord Justice-Clerk distinguished
Massy v. *Scott's Trs.* on the ground that in *Massy* third
parties were introduced in the declarations that followed
the primary gift ; and in *Houston* v. *Mitchell* the Court
declared that the doctrine was not to be further extended.

Provision that
a gift shall
not pass into
a marriage
contract trust.

Again, in this connexion may be noticed the decisions
regarding the effect of a declaration by a testator that the
subject of a bequest made by him shall not fall under the
operation of a conveyance to trustees made by the legatee
in his marriage contract.   If a person in his marriage contract conveys to the trustees under it all the property which
he shall acquire, any subject falling to him during the
subsistence of the marriage is carried to the trustees by
virtue of the contract.   It is, as already observed, a general
rule of law, deeply founded in equity and expediency, that
property cannot be held and enjoyed in fee and at the same
time remain exempt from the claims of the owner's creditors,
and as the trustees are creditors in the obligation contained

---

[1] *Supra.*

[2] *Robertson* v. *Hay-Boyd*, 1928
S. C. (H. L.) 8, *per* Viscount Dunedin.

[3] (1877) 5 R. 154.

[4] (1898) 25 R. 1176.

[5] *Supra.*

in the contract, the debtor is bound to make forthcoming to them what is given to him in absolute property, whatever may have been the intention of the donor. If the subject of the gift would otherwise pass to the trustees, a mere declaration or expression of intention by the testator will not bring about a different result.

In *Douglas's Trs.* v. *Kay's Trs.*,[1] the testator conveyed his estate to his daughter, with a direction that it should not fall under his daughter's marriage-contract trust, and that his trustees should take the necessary steps to carry out this provision. But the daughter had, in her marriage contract, assigned to trustees all that should accrue or belong to her during the subsistence of the marriage. Hence, as the testator had failed to guard his daughter's right by creating a trust and limiting her interest, it was held that the gift fell into the marriage contract trust, despite the anxious provision to the contrary.

It appears from this and the subsequent case of *Simson's Trs.* v. *Brown*,[2] that the only manner in which a fund can be prevented from falling under a marriage contract is by the creation of a separate and continuing trust, and by the restriction of the legatee's interest to some right short of an absolute fee, as, for example, a liferent, with or without a power of disposal.[3]

II. Directions to purchase Property or an Annuity for the Beneficiary.—If a testator directs his trustees to purchase an estate or annuity for A., the Court will not insist on that direction being carried out, if A., on receiving the annuity or the estate, would have an unlimited power of disposal thereof. The principle of the cases on this point is " that wherever a beneficiary, totally unfettered by the truster, can at once undo what the trustees have done, or what the trustees are directed to do, and wherever there is no limitation of the beneficiary's right, and no restraint imposed upon the beneficiary, but only a direction to trustees, the Court will never insist upon the trustees carrying out the direction, for the only result of this would be to put the beneficiary to the expense, trouble, and inconvenience of undoing, in a

---

[1] (1879), 7 R. 295.
[2] (1890), 17 R. 581.

[3] Cf. opinion of consulted judges in *Simson's Trs.* v. *Brown, supra.*

circuitous way and entirely at his own pleasure, what the trustees had fruitlessly done." [1]

Thus, in *Spens* v. *Monypenny's Trs.*,[2] the testator directed his trustees, as soon after his death as they might think proper, to invest the whole residue and remainder of his estate in the purchase of lands ; and, on the funds being so invested, " to execute a valid disposition thereof in favour of . . . A., and the heirs whomsoever of his body in fee," whom failing to others. Two years after the testator's death, A. claimed payment of the funds remaining in the hands of the trustees. The Lord Ordinary [3] repelled this claim, holding that the right of A. was qualified by a conditional institution in the event of his death before receiving a conveyance, and that no part of the residue had vested in him.   But the First Division reversed this decision, holding that A.'s right vested *a morte testatoris* ; and that, as the directions merely provided for the manner in which the residue was to be made over, and in no way controlled A.'s right, his claim to the funds must be sustained.

On the same principle, a direction to trustees to lay out a certain portion of the estate in purchasing an annuity for behoof of a beneficiary, or to purchase an annuity of a specified amount and to make over the same to the beneficiary, has been set aside as ineffectual in a series of cases.[4] In the case of *Kennedy's Trs.* v. *Warren*,[5] the application of the principle was discussed as follows in the opinion of the Court : " It is not disputed that where a trust is constituted with a direction to the trustees to hold the estate and pay over the income to a beneficiary for life, subject to the usual conditions of an alimentary trust, the beneficiary must be content to take the income under the conditions on which it is given.   In the case supposed, the capital is protected by means of the trust, and the income, being declared alimentary, is subject to the rule that alimentary creditors have a qualified preference.   But Mrs Kennedy's will does not contemplate a continuing trust for the protection of her legatees.   The capital is to be employed in the purchase

---

[1] *Per* Lord Gifford in *Dow* v. *Kilgour's Trs.* (1877), 4 R. 403.

[2] (1875), 3 R. 50.   Cf. also *Gordon* v. *Gordon's Trs.* (1866), 4 M. 501.

[3] Lord Shand.

[4] *Dow* v. *Kilgour's Trs.*, *supra* ; *Kippen* v. *Kippen's Trs.* (1871), 10 M. 134 ; *Tod* v. *Tod's Trs.* (1871), 9 M. 728 ; *Turner's Trs.* v. *Fernie*, 1908 S. C. 883.   [5] (1901), 3 F. 1087.

of annuities in their favour, and the only protection which she proposes to give them is that in each case the bond of annuity is to contain a condition in the terms already referred to.[1] Now, if we suppose the direction to be carried out, it is clear that no one but the annuitant himself has any interest in the bond, and in the event of his being unable to meet his engagements, the bond is part of his estate, which may be attached by his creditors, who are in no way affected by the condition under which he receives it, that he is to treat it as an income-producing subject. It is, I think, also clear in principle that a purchaser of the annuity would not be bound by the condition, because he is not a party to the supposed contract between the testator and the legatee. That being so, the question is, whether the legatee ought to be put to the disadvantage of receiving the bequest in the form of an annuity, which he can sell for something less than the sum expended in purchasing it, when he prefers to receive the bequest in money. It has been held by the other Division of the Court, in a series of cases which were cited to us, that he ought not to be put to this disadvantage, and in the principle of these decisions I entirely concur. I know of no authority in support of the proposition that an alimentary interest can be secured in any way except by a continuing trust ; and in principle it is clear that when an individual is put into possession of the full enjoyment of a fund of any kind, that fund is subject to his acts and deeds, and to the diligence of his creditors."

It was thought to be doubtful, in some of the earlier cases,[2] whether the beneficiary could demand the purchase-money if the testator declared that the annuity was to be alimentary, but it is now settled that, if no continuing trust is set up, a declaration of this kind is not an obstacle to the claim. Thus, in *Brown's Trs.* v. *Thom*,[3] trustees were directed to purchase an alimentary annuity for the testator's sister, exclusive of the rights of her husband and

---

[1] In the will it was provided that the annuities should be purchased "subject to the condition that the same are for the personal support and subsistence only of the annuitants."

[2] See *Dow* v. *Kilgour's Trs.* and *Kippen* v. *Kippen's Trs., supra,* and

Lord Cowan's opinion in *Dunbar* v. *Scott's Trs.* (1872), 10 M. 982.

[3] 1916 S. C. 32. See also *Murray* v. *Macfarlane's Trs.* (1895), 22 R. 927 and *Dempster's Trs.* v. *Dempster*, 1921 S. C. 332.

creditors. The sister having died two days after the testator, it was found that the right to the purchase price of the annuity had vested in her and passed under her will.

On the other hand, if the direction is that trustees shall purchase an annuity in their own names which is to be paid to the beneficiary for his alimentary use, this is effectual and the beneficiary cannot claim the price of the annuity.[1] In *Hutchinson's Trs.* v. *Young*,[2] a direction to apply sums in the purchase of Government or Savings Bank annuities was sustained against a claim for payment of the price on the ground that by statute such annuities are not (save in insolvency or bankruptcy) assignable by the annuitant.[3]

The doctrine of repugnancy.

III. Directions to Trustees to retain the Subject for behoof of the Legatee after the Period of Vesting.— Where a beneficiary is vested in the full right of property in a legacy, a provision by the testator that the subject shall be retained and administered for his behoof by the trustees is not enforceable as against the legatee or those claiming in right of him. Such attempts to fetter the legatee are inconsistent with the idea of a proprietary right, and are therefore legally impossible. Further, as (in the case supposed) the legatee has everything but the possession of the subject, he can assign or burden his interest ; and to maintain the trust administration would have no other effect than to place him under the disadvantage of having recourse to indirect and circuitous modes of taking the benefit of the subject actually held for him by the trustees. There are only two exceptions **Exceptions.** to this principle—(1) The case of a legatee who is in minority or is mentally incapable ;[4] and (2) the case of a married woman. When a woman in her marriage contract conveys her estate to trustees to be held by them for proper matrimonial purposes, the trust must be maintained till, and even after,[5] the death of her husband ; for it is the only means of

---

[1] *Branford's Trs.* v. *Powell*, 1924 S. C. 439 ; *Arnold's Trs.* v. *Graham*, 1927 S. C. 353.

[2] (1903), 6 F. 26.

[3] See the comments on this case in *Turner's Trs.* v. *Fernie*, and *Brown's Trs.* v. *Thom*, *supra*. It was distinguished in *Dempster's Trs.* v. *Dempster*, *supra*, where the direction was to purchase an annuity from Government or a Scottish Insurance Co.

[4] See cases in Chapter III. ; and Lord M'Laren's opinion in *Miller's Trs.* v. *Miller*, *infra*.

[5] *Burn Murdoch's Trs.* v. *Tinney*, 1937 S. C. 743.

protecting her against not only her husband but also herself and her own acts.[1]   In both of these cases the exception is founded on the beneficiary's need for protection.

The doctrine of repugnancy under consideration was discussed and authoritatively expounded in the two leading cases of *Miller's Trs.* v. *Miller* [2] and *Yuill's Trs.* v. *Thomson.*[3]

In the first of these the testator directed his trustees to hold an heritable estate for his son A.   He declared that the same should not vest in A. till he attained twenty-five, or married after attaining the age of twenty-one with the approval of the trustees ; and, as this clause clearly implied that the gift was to vest on the occurrence of either of these events, there was no difficulty as to the time of vesting. The will proceeded to declare that the trustees should manage the property " as absolute proprietors " until the son was twenty-five, when they were to denude in his favour. There was also a gift of a share of the residue of the moveable estate, under similar conditions.   The son, having come of age and married with the approval of the trustees, demanded a conveyance of the estate and the residue from the trustees.   The question was thus raised whether the trustees could withhold the property, in accordance with the testator's directions, until the son was twenty-five, or whether this direction was liable to be set aside by the son after the right had vested in him.   It was decided that the direction was ineffectual, and that the trustees were bound to make over the properties.   Lord President Inglis based the decision on the ground " that where by the operation of a testamentary instrument the fee of an estate or parts of an estate, whether heritable or moveable, has vested in a beneficiary, the Court will always, if possible, relieve him of any trust management that is cumbrous, unnecessary, or expensive."   " Where," he added, " there are trust purposes to be served which cannot be secured without the retention of the vested estate or interest of the beneficiary in the hands of the trustees, the rule cannot be

---

[1] *Anderson* v. *Buchanan* (1837), 15 S. 1073 ; 9 S. J. 509 ; *Pringle* v. *Anderson* (1868), 6 M. 982 ; *Ramsay* v. *Ramsay's Trs.* (1871), 10 M. 120 ; *Menzies* v. *Murray* (1875), 2 R. 507 ; *Barron* v. *Dewar* (1887), 24 S. L. R. 735 ; *Reid* v. *Reid's Trs.* (1899), 1 F. 969. Cf. also *Balderston* v. *Fulton* (1857), 19 D. 293.

[2] (1890), 18 R. 301.

[3] (1902), 4 F. 815.

applied, and the right of the beneficiary must be subordinated to the will of the testator.   But I am not aware of any case in which the mere maintenance of a trust management without any ulterior object or purpose has been held to be a trust purpose in the sense in which I have used that term." [1]

Lord Rutherfurd Clark remarked :   " I do not think that the law allows of any restriction on the owner of an absolute fee, and in my opinion the direction that the trustees shall manage the estate till A. reaches twenty-five is just as repugnant to the right of fee which is vested in him as a direction to manage the estate till he reaches any other age, or it might be till his death." [2]

The decision in this case has been regarded, in a series of subsequent cases, as establishing a principle of construction of general application.[3]   In consequence, however, of the dissenting opinions delivered in several cases, the Second Division, in *Yuill's Trs.* v. *Thomson*,[4] submitted the question for reconsideration by the whole Court.   In this

---

[1] See also Ld. Pres. Dunedin's opinion in *Millar's Trs.* v. *Millar* (1907), 45 S. L. R. 6.

[2] Lords Young and Trayner dissented.   In *Macculloch* v. *M'Culloch's Trs.* (1903), 6 F. (H. L.) 3. Lord Davey expressed approval of the principle of *Miller's* case.   The English Law agrees with *Miller's Trs.* ; *Wharton* v. *Masterman* [1895], A. C. 186 ; *Saunders* v. *Vautier* (1841), 4 Beav. 115 ; *Rocke* v. *Rocke*, (1845), 9 Beav. 66 ; *Curtis* v. *Lukin* (1842), 5 Beav. 147.   " The principle of this Court has always been, to recognise the right of all persons who attain the age of twenty-one to enter upon the absolute use and enjoyment of the property given to them by a will, notwithstanding any directions by the testator to the effect that they are not to enjoy it until a later age— unless, during the interval, the property is given for the benefit of another. If the property is once theirs, it is useless for the testator to attempt to impose any fetter upon their enjoyment of it in full so soon as they attain twenty-one "—Wood, V.C., in *Gosling* v. *Gosling* (1859) John. 265 ; *In re Couturier* [1907], 1 Ch. 470.

[3] The cases of repugnancy are : *Mackinnon's Trs.* v. *The Official Receiver in Bankruptcy* (1892), 19 R. 1051 ; *Wilkie's Trs.* v. *Wight's Trs* (1893), 21 R. 199 ; *Ritchie's Trs.* v. *Ritchie* (1894), 21 R. 679 ; *Ballantyne's Trs.* v. *Kidd* (1898), 25 R. 621 ; *Greenlees' Trs.* v. *Greenlees* (1894), 22 R. 136 ;   *Brown* v. *Brown's Trs.* (1890), 17 R. 517 ; *Stewart's Trs.* v. *Stewart* (1897), 25 R. 302 ; *Hargrave's Trs.* v. *Schofield* (1900), 3 F. 14 ; *Watson's Trs.* v. *Watson*, 1913 S. C. 1133 ;   *Veitch's Trs.* v. *Rutherford*, 1914 S. C. 182.   Cf. also *Lawson's Trs.* v. *Lawson* (1890), 17 R. 1167 ; and the cases of *Christie's Trs.* v. *Murray's Trs.* (1889), 16 R. 913 ; and *Campbell's Trs.* v. *Campbell* (1889), 16 R. 1007 (all prior to *Miller*).

[4] *Supra.* *Diss.* Lords Young and Moncreiff ; Lord Trayner acquiescing in view of prior authorities. See *Veitch's Trs.* v *Rutherfurd*, 1914 S. C. 182.

case the testator conveyed his estate to trustees in trust, to provide a liferent of the residue of his estate to his widow, and " to hold and apply the whole . . . for behoof of, and to make over the same to and among my brothers and sisters." There was a clause of survivorship, under which the issue of predeceasing legatees were called to their parent's shares ; and the shares were made payable on the majorities of the parties (with a power to the trustees to retain them till a later time). By a codicil the truster directed that in case the children of two sisters should become entitled, their shares should be retained during the lives of their respective fathers. On the death of the testator's widow, these children had become entitled to their parents' shares ; they sought payment from the trustees, their fathers being still in life, and the Court by a majority sustained the claim, on the authority of *Miller's Trs.*

" The principle of that decision," it was said, " is that when a vested, unqualified, and indefeasible right of fee is given to a beneficiary of full age, he is entitled to payment of the provision, notwithstanding any direction to the trustees to retain the capital of the provision, and to pay over the income periodically, or to apply the capital or income in some way for his benefit. The proposition is qualified, in the opinion of Lord President Inglis, by the addition that, where there are trust purposes to be served which cannot be secured without the retention of the vested estate or interest of the beneficiary in the hands of the trustees, the rule cannot be applied, and the right of the beneficiary must be subordinated to the will of the testator. This is a necessary qualification, because there may be contingent liabilities, the amount of which cannot be precisely ascertained, and for which it may be necessary to retain such a sum as the trustees judge to be sufficient. The rule only applies to a gift of an absolute or unqualified right of fee, because, if the fee is burdened with annuities or other charges, a sufficient sum must be retained to provide for these charges out of the income of the portion retained. Further, the rule supposes an indefeasible right of fee, because it may be that where, as in the case of *Chambers' Trs.* v. *Smith*, the trustees are empowered, in certain circumstances, or in their discretion, to reduce the right of fee to a liferent, it may be their duty to retain the fund until they shall be satisfied that the necessity will not arise for exercising the power.''

The conditions recognised in these statements of the principle may be summarised as follows :—

Conditions of application of principle.

1. There must be an initial gift sufficient to take the subject out of the estate of the truster and vest the right of property therein in the legatee.[1] It is an essential condition of the application of the doctrine of repugnancy, that there should be found in the settlement words of gift such as would, apart from the subsequent directions given to the trustees, confer on the beneficiary a vested right at, or prior to, the time at which he seeks to set aside those directions.[2]

2. The legatee's right must be unqualified. Thus it is plain that, if the estate is burdened with a liferent, the legatee cannot obtain payment while the liferent subsists ; in a case of this kind he has not the full right of property.

3. If the subsequent directions so qualify the original gift as to show that no right of fee was intended to be conferred,[3] or if they withdraw the right of fee previously given or render it defeasible, they are not within the rule of *Miller's Trs.* v. *Miller.* In the cases in which that rule has been applied, the directions did not affect the fee ; they were directions to retain the subject of the bequest, or to retain it and pay the legatee the interest [4] or to hold it for the alimentary use of the beneficiary.[5]

The following cases are examples of directions which have been found to be effectual :—

Principle inapplicable where subsequent directions withdraw the fee.

(a) Where the directions to the trustees limit the

---

[1] Cf., as to the necessity for an initial gift, the cases on vesting subject to defeasance, *ante,* p. 144 ; also such cases as *M'Donald* v. *M'Donald* (as to exercise of a power) (1875), 2 R. (H. L.) 125, and see Chapter XVIII., *post.*

[2] *Peden's Trs.* v. *Peden* (1903), 5 F. 1014 ; *Millar* v. *Millar's Trs.* (1907), 45 S. L. R. 6.

[3] Cf. *Muir's Trs.* v. *Muir* (1895), 22 R. 553.

[4] Lord M'Laren in *Mackay's Trs.* v. *Mackay* (1897), 24 R. 904, observes :

" An original gift on partition of a residue amongst the members of a family will not be cut down to a liferent by the effect of a subsequent direction to pay the income to one or more of the objects of the gift for life " ; and cf. also his Lordship's remarks in *Greenlees' Trs.* v. *Greenlees* (1894), 22 R. 136.

[5] As in *Wilkie's Trs.* v. *Wight's Trs.* (1893), 21 R. 199 ; *Watson's Trs.* v. *Watson,* 1913 S. C. 1133. A direction making a right of fee alimentary is ineffectual—see *ante,* p. 324.

beneficiary's interest in the subject to a liferent. Thus, in *Miller Richard's Trs.* v. *Miller Richard*,[1] the testator by his will bequeathed the residue of his estate to his children declaring that it should be payable to them as soon as conveniently might be after his death, with a survivorship clause referring to payment. By a codicil he instructed his trustees to pay to one son a part only of the share apportioned to him, and " to hold the remainder of the share so apportioned to my said son and invest the same in suitable investments, paying him, for his liferent alimentary use, the income thereof at such intervals as they may find convenient " ; and he declared that the sum retained should not be affectable by the son's debts, but that he should have a power of disposal of the capital " by will or deed of provision." There was no further disposal of the capital. It was held that the effect of this provision was to reduce the son's interest to a liferent.[2]

The construction here was aided by the circumstance that the directions appeared in a codicil, for a revocation may more readily be presumed in such cases than when the original gift and the instructions to the trustees appear in the same deed.

(*b*) Where the trustees have the power to suspend vesting, or to withdraw the fee and settle it on other parties. In such cases the legatee has not a vested and indefeasible right. *Where subsequent directions affect the vesting of the right.*

Thus, in *Chambers' Trs.* v. *Smiths*,[3] the testator directed his trustees to hold and apply the residue of his estate for behoof of his children, " with and under the exceptions and modifications to be afterwards stated." He then declared that the shares should vest on his death, but he authorised the trustees to postpone payment of the shares for so long as they should think fit, and to pay the income of the shares during the postponement to the children ; and he also

---

[1] (1903), 5 F. 909.
[2] See also *Russell* v. *Bell's Trs.*, *post*, p. 339.
[3] (1878), 5 R. (H. L.) 151, followed in *White's Trs.* v. *White's Trs.* 1917, 1 S. L. T. 272 (Lord Hunter). In this case an alimentary liferent was given by the truster to his son and the fee to his issue. The trustees were empowered to withhold payment of the income to the son and to accumulate it and add it to the capital. It was held that this power might be exercised by the trustees as against creditors of the son.

empowered the trustees by a deed under their hands to secure the share of any child so that he should receive only the interest thereof, and that the capital should be settled on him and his issue. A creditor of a son arrested the portion of his share remaining in the hands of the trustees. After the arrestment the trustees restricted the son's interest, and settled his share on him in liferent only and on his issue in fee. It was held that the effect of the directions in the will was to render the vesting in the son defeasible at the discretion of the trustees, and that the arrestment was not effectual against the fee. The feature which distinguishes this case from *Miller's Trs.* is the contingent right of the issue.[1]

As Lord Kinnear points out in *Watson's Trs.* v. *Watson*,[2] " the ground of judgement was that the trustees were entitled to divest the children to a certain extent by giving them an alimentary liferent instead of the fee. But a condition of that being done is that the trustees should be entitled to do something which would take away the fee previously, according to the form of the language of the deed, vested in the beneficiaries."

Direction to settle on marriage.

Similarly, a direction to trustees to hold the subject of the gift for behoof of a woman, and, in the event of her marrying, to settle the same on her as her separate estate, and on the issue of the marriage, is effectual ; and the beneficiary, although unmarried, cannot demand payment of the subject, because her right is liable to be affected by the exercise of this power by the trustees.[3]

Again, in *White's Trs.* v. *White*,[4] the subsequent directions were held to be effective, because they operated to suspend the vesting of the gift previously made.

Postponed vesting.

The testator here directed his trustees to divide the residue of his estate in certain shares among, *inter alios*, his sons on their attaining majority, and in the event of any son dying in minority, his share was to devolve on his issue, whom failing on the other children or their issue. By a later clause he declared that one half of each son's share was not

---

[1] Cf. the opinion of the Court in *Kenmond's Trs.* v. *Mess* (1898), 25 R. 819.

[2] 1913 S. C. 1133, at 1139.

[3] *Mackay's Trs* v. *Mackay's Trs.* (1897), 24 R. 904 (stated p. 148).

[4] (1896), 23 R. 836.

to be paid before the age of twenty-five, with a power, however, to the trustees to pay over the share on or at any time after the son's majority, or to retain it for so long as they thought expedient ; but so that " in case any of my sons shall die after me and after attaining majority but without having received payment," then the capital, " or so much as shall remain in the hands of the trustees," should go to their issue, whom failing, to appointees of the sons, etc. In the initial gift the element of survivance implied in the destination-over suspended vesting till the legatee's majority ; and so, when the same destination-over was, by the subsequent clause, referred to a later event, namely, payment, the result was further to suspend vesting till that event. The words last quoted showed that the truster, in speaking of payment, alluded to actual payment, and not (as the Court inclines to construe such destinations-over) to the time when the trustees became entitled to pay. Hence, vesting being postponed, the power was held to be effectual.

A similar decision was pronounced in *Walker* v. *Buchanan*,[1] where to a bequest to a legatee was added a provision empowering the trustees to withhold payment of the legacy " in whole or part " and apply the income, or such part of the capital as they might think proper, for behoof of the legatee, but with a further gift-over if he died with or without issue, which the Court construed as referring to death before payment by the trustees in the exercise of the power entrusted to them.

In these cases the terms of the clause authorising retention of the legacy, referring as it did to the portion remaining in the hands of the trustees, made it clear that postponement of payment was to entail postponement of vesting. But where, under the scheme of the original bequest, vesting is dependent on the arrival of the time appointed for payment, and the later clause merely empowers the trustees to retain the subject of the bequest, it may often be a question of difficulty whether the action of the trustees in withholding payment was meant to have the effect of altering the date of vesting.

In *Russell* v. *Bell's Trs.*,[2] the residue was bequeathed to the testatrix's children. The shares were to be paid twelve

[1] (1905), 8 F. 201.   [2] (1897), 24 R. 666.

months after her death, and there was a destination-over should any child die "before the said residue becomes payable." A codicil expressed the testatrix's desire that a son's share should not be handed over to him, but that he should draw the interest, provided that at any time the trustees, if they considered it for his benefit, might hand over his share to him. It was held that only the portion of the capital paid to this son had vested in him. The judgement is a singularly hesitant one. The effect of the codicil was considered to be that the son's interest was thereby restricted to a liferent, and that the destination-over was operative so long as any part of the share had not been made over to the son.

But the authority of this decision is gravely impaired by *Graham* v. *Graham's Trs.*[1] In this case 'the direction to the trustees to retain the subject was held to be repugnant, although the terms of the deed were very nearly the same as those in *Russell* v. *Bell's Trs.* ; indeed, Lord Sands thought that it was impossible satisfactorily to distinguish the two cases. The trustees were instructed to pay the fee of the residue to three of the testator's children (as it happened) on their respectively attaining majority, with a destination-over in the event of any of the children predeceasing "the said period of payment." The purport of a codicil dealing with the share of one child was the same as in *Russell's* case. Lord Sands indicated that there might be a difference, although "a very thin one," between the expressions "becomes payable" (used in *Russell's* case) and "said period of payment," as used in this case ; and Lord Blackburn relied on the word "said" in this expression as definitely attaching the destination-over to the period of vesting fixed by the will. The tenuity of these distinctions suggests that the Court came as near as possible to over-ruling *Russell's Trs.* v. *Bell* without in terms doing so.

4. Lastly, if there are trust purposes that cannot be served without the retention of the subject, the legatee is not in a position to enforce immediate payment.

Where there are further trust purposes.

Thus, in *Macculloch* v. *M'Culloch's Trs.*,[2] Lord Davey

---

[1] 1927 S. C. 388.

[2] (1903), 6 F. (H. L.) 3. The facts of this case are stated, *ante*, p. 303.

In *Miller Richard's Trs.* v. *Miller Richard* (1903), 5 F. 909 Lord Moncreiff stated that he was disposed to

pointed out that the principle of *Miller's Trs.* was inapplicable to the case in hand because, although the claimant had a vested interest, he had no present right to receive his share of the estate and that that share could not, according to the terms of the will, be ascertained until the death of other beneficiaries.

Again, *Graham's Trs.* v. *Graham* [1] presents a further example of the exception stated in the Lord President's observation, that the subject cannot be paid if trust purposes require its retention. In this case the residue was to be divided among the testator's sons when his youngest daughter attained twenty-five years of age. A legacy of £4000 was left to a son A., payable when he attained thirty years of age, with interest at 4 per cent. from the age of twenty-five. A legacy in similar terms was given to each of two daughters. It was held that A. was not entitled to immediate payment at the age of twenty-five, because the daughters, being still under thirty, were entitled to receive interest at four per cent. ; and the state of the funds was such, that to continue the payment of this interest involved an encroachment on the capital. Accordingly, as it could not be foretold how far the application of capital for payment of the interest might reduce the amount of the legacy to each beneficiary, it was impossible to permit immediate payment of any share.

IV. Impossible and Illegal Conditions.—In accordance with the doctrine of the civil law,[2] a condition which from its nature is impossible is treated *pro non scripto*, and the legacy is held to be pure. In this respect there is a marked distinction between legacies and obligations.

Impossible conditions held pro non scripto.

think that " we must now hold that in order to warrant retention where a fee is given the trust purposes must be connected with other objects and persons than the beneficiary whose share is in question ; and that if the purposes are concerned solely with the management of the estate or bequest and the protection of the beneficiary against his own improvidence, they must be entirely disregarded, and immediate payment must be made to the fiar free of all restrictions." The decision in *Ballantyne's Trs.* v *Kidd* (1898), 25 R. 621, is affected by the alteration in the view as to the effect of a clause calling the issue of a predeceasing legatee (see *ante*, p. 149) and in any case is difficult to reconcile with *Macculloch's* case.

[1] (1899), 2 F. 232.

[2] Dig. xxxv. 1. 3 ; xxviii. 7. 14. Stair, iii. 8. 24 ; Ersk., iii. 3. 85 ; Bell's Prins. § 1785.

If, however, the condition is not in itself impossible, but becomes in the course of events incapable of fulfilment, it is a more difficult question whether the legacy is to be considered as having failed or lapsed, or whether the condition is to be disregarded so as to allow of the legacy receiving effect.

Apparently this question is to be determined in accordance with what may appear from the provisions of the will and the character of the condition to have been the testator's intention.[1] There are decisions which indicate that if a legacy be given to A. in the event of B.'s marrying [2] or attaining a certain age,[3] the death of B. without having married or under that age will not defeat A.'s right : A. will acquire a vested interest on B.'s death. The testator's primary purpose in favour of A. is not to be frustrated by the circumstance that the condition of his acquiring a right in the subject has been rendered impossible of fulfilment by the act of God.

But, according to the civil law, if the legacy were given to A. in the event of his marrying B., the legacy would not take effect if by B.'s death A. were prevented from marrying her.[4] Here the nature of the condition shows that the testator's purpose was to benefit A. only in the circumstances prescribed, and the condition therefore is of the essence of the gift.

This distinction seems to be recognised in the remarks made in *Dunbar* v. *Scott's Trs.*[5] In that case a testatrix bequeathed a sum of money to her nephew " to purchase a captain's commission in his regiment." The system of purchase in the army was abolished after the date of the will, but before the testatrix's death, and the fact that the testatrix had not availed herself of the opportunity of revoking or altering her will weighed with the Court in deciding the case. It was held in the circumstances that the general rule that impossible conditions are to be disregarded was applicable, and the legacy was given to the nephew. Lord

---

[1] Domat, iii. 1. 8. § 19.

[2] *Parlane's Trs.* v. *Parlane* (1902), 4 F. 805.

[3] *Graham's Trs.* v. *Graham* (1899), 2 F. 232 ; *Maitland's Trs.* v.

MacDiarmid (1861), 23 D. 732, *ante* pp. 89 *et seq.*

[4] Cod. 6. 46. 4.

[5] (1872), 10 M. 982.

Cowan observed : " Viewed either as a condition or a purpose, I do not think that the argument of the trustees should prevail. Viewed as a condition, if the condition becomes impossible, the legacy is good and the condition flies off. Viewed as a purpose, it raises a more delicate question. The purpose may be so wrought into the substance of the bequest that, unless it can be carried out, the bequest fails. If the purpose be such that the legatee only is concerned in it, then the purpose ceases to have any effect."

Similarly, where a legacy was given to discharge the debts on an estate, and the legatee prior to the time at which the legacy became payable to him had sold the estate, part of the bargain of sale being that he should discharge the debts, it was held that the legacy was due.[1]

Conditions which offend against public policy, or are *contra bonos mores*, are void and the legacy is pure. In *Reid* v. *Coates*,[2] the effect of a condition annexed to a legacy that the legatee should not reside with his mother, was considered, but no decision was given on the point. In subsequent cases, it has been decided that conditions that a wife shall not live with her husband, or that a child shall not live with its parents, are ineffectual as being *contra bonos mores*, unless there be something in the circumstances or character of the spouse or parent which affords a justification of the condition.[3] *{Conditions contra bonos mores.}*

Again, conditions in restraint of marriage are invalid and are disregarded. A provision that the legatee shall never marry, is void.[4] But a condition that the legatee is to receive the legacy only if he or she marries,[5] or does not marry, a certain person,[6] is valid ; and so also is the *{Conditions in restraint of marriage.}*

[1] *Sutherland's Trs.* v. *Sutherland* (1870), 8 M. 716.

[2] 5th March 1813, F. C. ; 10th March 1809, F. C.

[3] *Fraser* v. *Rose* (1849), 11 D. 1466 ; *Grant's Trs.* v. *Grant* (1898), 25 R. 929 ; Bell's Prins. §§ 49, 1785. See also *Barker* v. *Watson's Trs.*, 1919 S. C. 109 ; *Wemyss* v. *Wemyss' Trs.*, 1921 S. C. 30 ; and *Balfour's Trs.* v. *Johnston*, 1936 S. C. 137. See also the discussion of the law in *Aitken's Trs.* v. *Aitken*, 1927 S. C. 374. " The force of any objection on the ground of policy depends upon the tendency of the testamentary dispositions to affect conduct "—*per* Lord Kinnear in *Earl of Caithness* v. *Sinclair*, 1912 S. C. 79.

[4] Fraser on Husband and Wife (2nd ed.), vol. i., pp. 464 *et seq.* ; *Ommaney* v. *Bingham* (1796), 3 Pat. 448

[5] Stair, iii. 8. 24 ; Fraser on Husband and Wife, 474.

[6] *Forbes* v. *Forbes' Trs.* (1882), 9 R. 675 ; *Ommaney* v. *Bingham* (1796), 3 Pat. 448 ; *Hepburn* v. *Cockburn* (1687), M. 3253.

condition that a person's liferent shall terminate on his or her second marriage,[1] or that a right of fee shall suffer defeasance in that event.[2] It is competent for a testator to give the interest of an estate to ladies for so long as they remain unmarried.[3]

Legacies *ob turpem causam*.

If a legacy be given *ob turpem causam*, it is invalid.[4]

Potestative conditions.

As regards potestative conditions, Erskine says these " are held as fulfilled if he (the creditor) has done all he could to fulfil them. If, for instance, an obligation be granted under the condition that the grantee shall inter-marry with a particular lady, law considers the condition as purified if he has made addresses to her, though she should have rejected them. But if he shall put off performing his part till performance becomes impossible, the obligation in the grantee's favour is extinguished." [5] Beyond this it is difficult to extract from such decisions as there are any rule of general application as to the construction of such conditions. In *Pirie* v. *Pirie*,[6] Lord Justice-Clerk Moncreiff observed that " it is essential to look to the relation of the condition to the subject of the gift, and the effect which it was intended by the testator to operate. Such conditions need not always be performed in terms, or specifically. In some cases equivalents may be sufficient implement. In others, fulfilment of part may suffice instead of complete fulfilment, and in others, again, the condition need not be performed at all. These results all depend on the substance of the condition more than on the mere words in which it may be expressed."

In this case the testator bequeathed the residue of his estate to his eldest son. A sum had been advanced by the father to a younger son, and in his will he directed that this son should have the right to refrain from repaying the sum for a period of eight years in the event of the eldest son being throughout a director of a company carrying

---

[1] *Kidd* v. *Kidd's Trs.* (1863), 2 M. 227.

[2] *Smith's Trs.* v. *Smith* (1883), 10 R. 1144, *ante*, p. 43.

[3] *Sturrock* v. *Ranken's Trs.* (1875), 2 R. 850.

[4] *Johnston* v. *M'Kenzie's Exrs.* (1835) 14 S. 106 ; 11 Fac. 79 ; *Young*

v. *Johnston & Wright* (1880), 7 R. 760 ; *Troussier* v. *Matthew*, 1922, S. L. T. 670 (Lord Murray).

[5] iii. 3. 85. See also Stair, i. 3. 8.

[6] (1873), 11 M. 941. See for another instance of a potestative condition, *Reids* v. *M'Phedran* (1881), 9 R. 80.

on a business in which the father and sons were interested. A few months after the father's death the eldest son resigned his directorship for the avowed purpose of calling up the loan to his brother, and brought an action concluding for payment.   In this action he was unsuccessful on the ground that in the circumstances the condition must be held as accomplished.   This decision is an example of the application of the principle that, if the person whose interest it is that the condition shall not be fulfilled intentionally and by his voluntary act makes fulfilment impossible, the condition is treated as implemented.[1]

This feature was absent in *Simpson* v. *Roberts*.[2]   The bequest in that case was made by a testatrix to her housekeeper " provided she is in my employment at the time of my death, or in that of my husband at his death should he survive me."   The housekeeper continued in the service of the testatrix till her death and thereafter in that of the husband till his re-marriage when he terminated her engagement.   The housekeeper had been willing to remain in his service ; and, this being so, the Court, having regard to the nature of the condition and the motive which was thought to have inspired it, held that the legacy was due.

If a bequest is made on condition of the legatee doing some act or following some course of conduct, he will not be held to have lost his right by reason of non-compliance if he was not made aware of the condition.[3]

---

[1] Dig. xxxv. 1. 57, 78, 81 ; xl. 4. 55.
[2] 1931 S. C. 259.   See also *Robertson's Trs.* v. *White* (1904), 11 S. L. T. 566 (Lord Kincairney).

[3] *Rodger's Trs.* v. *Allfrey*, 1910 S. C. 1015 ; *Balfour's Trs.* v. *Johnston*, 1936 S. C. 137.   Cf. also *Stirling* v. *Miller*, 29th June 1813, F. C.

CHAPTER XVI.

VESTING IN THE RESIDUARY LEGATEE OR HEIR
AB INTESTATO.

The vesting
of residue.

I. Residuary Bequests.—As a gift of residue comprises the entirety of the estate not required for the antecedent purposes of the will,[1] it follows that, save in the exceptional case where these purposes are to be satisfied immediately on the death of the testator, the amount of the fund is liable to variation, according as, for example, the prior gifts fail or take effect. But this liability to variation does not suffice to prevent vesting. The residue—save in very special cases—is regarded as a mass, and the residuary legatee takes it irrespective of what its amount may turn out to be. The time of vesting is determined in accordance with the rules applicable to other bequests.

The leading authority on the point is *Storie's Trs.* v. *Gray.*[2] In this case trustees were directed to hold a sum of money for two persons successively in liferent, and on the death of the survivor of them to pay the capital to their children " then alive." All the children predeceased their parents, and accordingly the gift to them failed. The residuary bequest was in the form of a direction to the

---

[1] Lord Westbury in *Sturgis* v. *Campbell* (1865), 3 M. (H. L.) 70 ; Lord Kinloch in *Donald's Trs.* v. *Donald* (1864), 2 M. 922 ; and Lord Watson in *Duchess of Montrose* v. *Stuart* (1887), 15 R. (H. L.) 19. In *Aitken's Trs.* v. *Aitken*, 1927 S. L. T. 308, Lord Sands says: " Law attributes to a residue clause an intention to sweep in everything not effectually disposed of, and that altogether irrespective of what items the testator may have contemplated as possibly falling within this category. The rule has, I think, been expressed somewhat as follows :—When there is a general residue clause operative as from the date of death, partial intestacy is impossible except on failure of a residuary legatee." This passage does not appear in the Session Cases report. See also *White's Trs.* v. *White*, 1936 S. L. T. 562 (Lord Robertson).

[2] (1874), 1 R. 953. See also *Watson's Trs.* v. *Brown*, 1923 S. C. 228, at 241.

trustees to divide the residue among three persons (one of them being one of the liferenters) " and their respective heirs." The survivor of the liferenters died ten years after the testator, predeceased by two of the residuary legatees. The question in the case was whether the subject of the bequest which had lapsed vested in the residuary legatees *a morte testatoris*, or whether vesting was suspended until the death of the survivor of the liferenters, when it was ascertained that the legatees called in the first instance had failed. It was held that the subject passed with the general residuary fund, and that, as the gift of residue was made in simple terms, the whole vested *a morte testatoris*. The ground of the decision was thus explained by Lord President Inglis : " The argument of the reclaimer is based on a fallacy, which consists in supposing that every contingent bequest is a bequest to the special legatee, with a conditional institution of the residuary legatee. That is not so : the true theory is, that the estate is given to the residuary legatee, but he is burdened with the contingent bequest in certain events. If that point be once settled, there is an end to the question, because the residuary estate is one ; it does not consist of different parts : it must therefore vest at one and the same time, and the only time at which it can vest is the date of the testator's death." [1]

In this case it will be observed that one of the residuary legatees in whom the residue vested *a morte testatoris* enjoyed the liferent, on the expiry of which alone could it be determined that the capital fell into residue. There is, however, no inconsistency in a liferenter being also the fiar of the estate liferented.[2]

A general residuary bequest, although expressed in terms which postpone vesting, carries the intermediate income, if

---

[1] " A residuary bequest is not equivalent to a gift-over of the general and special legacies, and it does not in the ordinary case suspend the vesting of the general and special legacies until the date of payment "— *per* Lord Skerrington in *Yule's Trs.* v. *Deans*, 1919 S. C. 570, at 574. See also *Wright's Trs.* v. *Wright* (1896), 4 S. L. T , 74 (O. H., Lord Parson), and Lord Kinloch's opinion in *Carter* v. *M'Intosh* (1862), 24 D. 925.

[2] *Maxwell* v. *Wyllie* (1837), 15 S. 1005 ; 12 Fac. 928 ; *Haldane's Trs.* v. *Murphy* (1881), 9 R. 269 (the opinions of the minority were approved in *Gregory's Trs.* v. *Alison* (1889), 16 R. (H. L.) 10 ; 14 App. Cas. 124).

not otherwise disposed of ; in such case the income accumulates as part of the residue.[1]

The word " residue " may, however, be so used by a testator as to show that it refers to the balance of a particular fund [2] or that certain portions of the estate devoted to other purposes are excluded therefrom.[3]

In *Gunn's Trs.* v. *Macfarlane* [4] and *Samson* v. *Raynor*,[5] it was ruled that a bequest of the " free residue " of the estate meant, in the ordinary case, the estate remaining after deduction, *inter alia*, of the amount of the *legitim* claimed by the testator's children.

Lapse of residue.

In general residuary bequests the presumption against intestacy applies with especial force, because the result of the lapse of a residuary bequest is to throw the subjects into intestate succession.[6] But if a bequest be made to parties (not forming a class) in distinct portions, or with words of severance attached, the share of one of these predeceasing the period of vesting will not accresce to the others, but will lapse.[7]

Heirs excluded only by a disposition of the estate.

II. Intestacy.—In order to defeat the claims of the heirs *ab intestato*, it is necessary that the estate be given away by the will, and in no case are the heirs excluded save in so far as the provisions of the will have the effect of disposing

[1] *Turnbull* v. *Cowan* (1848), 6 Bell 222 at 234 ; *Sturgis* v. *Meiklam's Trs., ante.* There are numerous instances of this in the cases on the Thellusson Act.

[2] See *Millar* v. *Morrison* (1894), 21 R. 921.

[3] *Reid's Trs.* v. *Bucher*, 1929 S. C. 615 ; *Lawrence* v. *Stewart*, 1924 S. C. 934 ; *Wingate* v. *Wingate's Trs.,* 1921 S. C. 857, *per* Lord Cullen ; see Ld. Pres. Dunedin's opinion in *Smith* v. *Glasgow Royal Infirmary*, 1909 S. C. 1231.

[4] (1900), 37 S. L. R. 499.

[5] 1928 S. C. 899.

[6] *Pearman* v. *Pearman* (1864), 33 Beav. 394.

[7] *Lawrence* v. *Stewart*, 1924 S. C. 934; *Wingate* v. *Wingate's Trs.*, 1921 S. C.

857. See Chapter VII. p. 157, and *Flett's Trs.* v. *Elphinstone* (1900) 38 S. L. R. 564, where there was a direction that the residue was to be divided into three shares, and on the failure of the parties called to any portion (so the provision was construed) that portion was to " revert and fall to be administered as part of the residue of my estate," the parties appointed to take one share failed, and it was argued that the result of the destination-over was that, as the testator had left no direction save that which had failed, the share fell into intestacy ; but the Lord Ordinary (Kincairney) rejected this contention. See *In re Palmer* [1893], 3 Ch. 369 ; *In re Wand* [1907], 1 Ch. 391 ; *In re Powell* [1918], 1 Ch. 407.

of the estate.[1] It is usual to exclude these heirs by inserting a clause disposing of the whole residue of the testator's
estate ; but if the residuary bequest fail, either partially or
wholly, or if there is no such bequest and the legacies given
in the will lapse, the right of the heirs emerges.

The heirs *ab intestato* are ascertainable at the testator's
death, and the provisions of the will are merely burdens on
their right. Accordingly, if a legacy is given conditionally,
and the condition fails, then (unless the subject is otherwise
disposed of) the failure has no other effect than that of
relieving the testator's legal successors of the contingent
burden on their succession.

The leading case of *Lord* v. *Colvin* [2] affords authority
on all these points. In that case the testator directed his
trustees to divide the residue of his estate between his two
sons, A. and B., and their lawful children ; and in the event
of their dying without issue under the age of twenty-five, to
make over the said residue to the children of C. A. and B.
survived the testator, and died without children and under
age ; C. survived them, and also died without issue. No
right in the residue having vested in the parties called by
the will, the question was, whether the estate fell to A., the
heir of the testator as at his death, or to the heir existing at
the death of C., when it was ascertained that the gift had
lapsed. It was held that A. had taken as heir on the
testator's death, subject to defeasance in the event of the
testamentary bequests subsequently coming into operation. The following exposition of the law occurs in Lord
Curriehill's opinion : " No doubt the testamentary provision
did affect the legal right of the heir in two different ways—
first, by exposing it to the risk of any of the contingencies
eventually happening ; and, secondly, to the postponement
of the term of payment or performance until it should be
ascertained whether or not any of these contingencies should
eventually happen. But the legal right which vested in the
legal heir by law, irrespective of the settlement, was not
prevented from so vesting in him by being merely subjected
to such risks and to such postponement of the term of

Vesting of intestate estate.

---

[1] *Per* Lord Curriehill in *Lord* v. *Colvin* (1865), 3 M. 1083 ; Ld. Pres.
Inglis in *Cowan* v. *Cowan* (1887), 14 R. 670.

[2] (1865), 3 M. 1083.

payment. The effect of these provisions on the legal right of the heir was not to prevent or destroy its existence, but merely to subject it to certain conditions, from which it has now been relieved." After pointing out that the provision as to the attainment of age prevented vesting in the legatees, his Lordship added : " Hence the risk to which the right which vested in the legal heir by law was subjected by this provision was merely this, that in an emergency which was entirely fortuitous, a right to other parties to claim the fund might eventually come into existence. In the meantime, as no ownership of the fund even began to exist in these persons in virtue of this provision, it could not displace the ownership thereof which the law vested in the legal heir on the truster's death ; and although that heir's right was subjected to the risk of the contingency of the conditional legatees attaining the specified age, that condition was of the class denominated resolutive." [1]

It will be observed that in this case the heir was one of the parties favoured under the will. And so, where a gift of residue was made to the testator's children equally, and the share of one child lapsed into intestacy (under the rule of *Paxton's Trs.* v. *Cowie* [2]), it was held that the whole children (including the child whose share had lapsed) took the share as the testator's heirs *ab intestato*.[3]

By the law of intestate succession, the estate vests absolutely in the nearest heir at the time of the intestate's death. In *Grant* v. *Grant's Trs.*,[4] after a father had served heir to his son another child was born to the father. The Court held that the doctrine of vesting subject to defeasance was inapplicable in the case of intestate succession, and that, therefore, the father's right was not affected by the emergence of a nearer heir.

Effect of directions for conversion.

Further, when a testator in his will instructs his trustees to convert the whole or part of his estate, or gives directions

---

[1] *Lord* v. *Colvin* was followed in *Young's Trs.* v. *Young* (1901), 3 F. 616. See also *Hutton's Trs.* v. *Coates* (1868), 6 S. L. R. 146 ; *Hamilton's Trs.* v. *Boyes* (1898), 25 R. 899 (affd. on another point (1899), 1 F. (H. L.) 79) ; *Gregory's Trs.* v. *Alison* (1889), 16 R. (H. L.) 10 ; 14 App. Cas. 125.

[2] *Ante*, Chapter VII., p. 157.
[3] *Wilson's Trs.* v. *Wilson's Trs.* (1894), 22 R. 62.
[4] (1859), 22 D. 53 ; Stair, iii. 5. 50 Ersk., iii. 8. 76 ; Bank., iii. 5. 55-57 ; Bell's Prins. § 1642.

which involve conversion, and the testamentary dispositions with reference to which the directions are given fail, the rights of the testator's heirs are not affected by these directions. The conversion is held to have been directed solely for the purposes of the will ; and the heirs are determined according to the actual character of the subject at the testator's death.[1] If, for example, the subject is heritable, the right of the heir-at-law is not displaced by the circumstance that the trustees under the settlement are directed to sell that subject.

In one case,[2] where the Thellusson Act put a stop to the accumulation of interest and rents, it was held that the heirs entitled to these by virtue of the statute were to be ascertained periodically at the terms at which the interest or rents accrued. This decision was contrary to that in *Lord* v. *Colvin*,[3] at least as regards the proceeds of the moveable estate, and while it has been followed in the case of heritage it has been overruled in so far as it decides that the heirs *in mobilibus* are to be selected as the interest falls in.[4] Accordingly, rents which pass into intestate succession belong to the heir-at-law for the time being at the terms at which they accrue, while the interest of money or moveable property belongs to those who are the testator's heirs *in mobilibus* at the time of his death.[5] The income derived from the accumulation of the rents of heritable property is also regarded as moveable, and falls to these heirs.[6]

Ascertainment of heirs in regard to periodical payments.

Formerly, in the case of intestate moveable succession, no right vested in the heirs *in mobilibus* unless they obtained confirmation or got possession of the subjects, but the necessity of confirmation for this purpose was abolished by the Act 4 Geo. IV. c. 98, and the succession now vests at the intestate's death.[7] In regard to heritable property

Confirmation no longer necessary for vesting.

---

[1] *Cowan* v. *Cowan, supra ; Moon's Trs.* v. *Moon* (1899), 2 F. 201 ; *M'Conochie's Trs.* v. *M'Conochie*, 1912 S. C. 653.

[2] *Campbell's Trs.* v. *Campbell* (1891), 18 R. 992. See also *Moon's Trs.* v. *Moon, supra, per* Lord Trayner.

[3] (1860), 23 D. 111.

[4] *Logan's Trs.* v. *Logan* (1896), 23 R. 848 ; *Moon's Trs.* v. *Moon, supra.*

[5] *Logan's Trs.* v. *Logan, supra ;*

Wilson's Trs. v. *Glasgow Royal Infirmary*, 1917 S. C. 527, *per* Lord Skerrington. *Robertson's Trs.* v. *Robertson's Trs.*, 1933 S C. 639, *per* Lord Sands.

[6] *Watson's Trs.* v. *Brown*, 1923 S. C. 228, and cases in Note 5.

[7] See *Mann* v. *Thomas* (1830), 8 S. 468 ; 5 Fac. 376 ; *Frith* v. *Buchanan* (1837), 15 S. 729 ; 12 Fac. 683.

it is provided by sec. 9 of the Conveyancing Act of 1874, that " a personal right to every estate in land descendible to heirs shall, without service or other procedure, vest, or be held to have vested, in the heir entitled to succeed thereto, by his survivance of the person to whom he is entitled to succeed." [1]

Vesting of legal rights.   Questions of vesting seldom arise with reference to the legal rights of children or spouses. Viewed either as debts or as rights of succession, they become due at the death of **Legitim.** the parent or spouse. Legitim, for instance, vests at the parent's death.[2] This is implied in the argument in favour of immediate vesting derived in several cases from a declaration that the legacy is given in lieu of legitim.[3] When confirmation was required in order to vest the succession of a person dying intestate, it was established that it was not necessary in regard to legitim, and that the right transmitted although it had not been established by that means in the person of the child.[4] And, contrary to the opinions expressed in one case,[5] the weight of authority is in favour of the view that if a child dies without making an election between his legal rights and the bequests made to him in his father's will, the right of election passes to his representatives, and may be competently exercised by them in right of the child.[6] The amount of legitim is measured at the parent's death, and while the child is entitled to interest from the moment of the parent's death,[7] he has no claim to participate in the profits accruing on the share of the estate due to him by way of legitim while it remains in the hands of the trustees and before the time at which he elects to take it.[8]

Jus relictæ.   So also *jus relictæ* vests on the death of the husband,

[1] See *M'Adam* v. *M'Adam* (1879), 6 R. 1256.

[2] See dicta in *Fisher* v. *Dixon* (1843), 2 Bell's Apps. 63 ; 2 D. 1121 ; and *Macdougal* v. *Wilson* (1858), 20 D. 658.

[3] *Ante*, p. 22.

[4] Stair, iii. 8. 50 ; Ersk., iii. 9. 30 ; Bell's Com. i. 137 ; *Jervey* v. *Watt*, 1762, M. 8170 ; *Sibbald* v. *Procurator-Fiscal of St. Andrews*, 1623, M. 8176 ; *Yeaman* v. *Yeaman*, 1686, M. 8176 and 5484 ; *Russel* v. *Brown*, 1876, M. 8177.

[5] *Stewart's Trs.* v. *Stewart* (1851), 14 D. 298.

[6] *M'Murray* v. *M'Murray's Trs.* (1852), 14 D. 1048 ; *Lowson* v. *Young* (1854), 16 D. 1098.

[7] *Bishop's Trs.* v. *Bishop* (1894), 21 R. 728.

[8] *M'Murray* v. *M'Murray's Trs.*, *supra*.

and confirmation was at no time required for this purpose.[1] The widow's claim is against the husband's representatives, and she is entitled to the interest (if there be any) which her portion of the estate may earn between the date of his death and the time of payment.[2] Her right to elect to claim *jus relictæ* in place of the provisions made for her in her husband's will, if not exercised by her, transmits to her representatives.[3] By the Act of 1881,[4] it is provided that the husband's *jus relicti* is subject to the same rules as the wife's *jus relictæ*.

By virtue of her right of terce, a widow is entitled to Terce. one-third of the rents of her husband's heritable estate from the date of his death. This was so, although her service was delayed.[5] In *M'Cleish* v. *Rennie*,[6] it was decided that service by the widow was necessary to render her claim to arrears of rent transmissible to her representative, but the authority of this decision was impugned,[7] and in *Pringle's Exrs.*[8] the question was noticed as being undecided. By Sec. 21 of the Conveyancing (Scotland) Act, 1924,[9] serving has been abolished and an action of declarator substituted.

Courtesy vests immediately upon the wife's death, and Courtesy. no service has ever been required.[10]

---

[1] Stair, iii. 8. 50 ; Bank., iii. 8. 40 ; Ersk., iii. 9. 30 ; Bell's Prins. § 1591.

[2] *M'Intyre* v. *M'Intyre's Trs.* (1865), 3 M. 1074.

[3] *MacGregor's Ex.* v. *MacGregor's Trs.*, 1935 S. C. 13.

[4] Married Women's Property Act, 1881, 44 & 45 Vic. c. 21.

[5] *Semple* v. *Crawford*, 1624, M. 15837 ; *Tenants of Earlhouses* v. *Hepburn*, 1627, M. 15838 ; *Carlyle* v. *Carlyle*, 1725, M. 15851. More's Notes to Stair, ccxvii.

[6] (1826), 1 Fac. 402 ; cf. *M'Aulay* v. *Watson*, 1636, M. 3112. Stair, ii. 6. 15 ; Ersk. ii. 9. 55.

[7] More's Notes, *ibid.* ; Bell's Prins. § 1602 ; cf. *Creditors of Strachan* v. *Baldwin*, 1736, Elchies, " Deathbed," No. 7.

[8] (1870), 8 M. 622.

[9] 14 & 15 Geo. V. c. 27.

[10] Stair, ii. 6. 19 ; Ersk., ii. 9. 52.

CHAPTER XVII.

THE *CONDITIO SI INSTITUTUS SINE LIBERIS DECESSERIT.*

UNDER certain circumstances the law recognises " an equitable exception from the rules of strict construction," [1] in virtue of which there is imported into legacies by legal implication a provision that, if the legatee die without taking a vested interest, his children shall have the legacy. The effect of this provision may be to prevent the legacy falling into residue or intestate succession, or even to defeat a gift-over expressed in the will—*e.g.* a gift-over to survivors.[2]

This provision is usually termed the *conditio si institutus sine liberis decesserit.* It was in part derived from the civil law,[3] although it has not in our law been confined to those circumstances in which it was recognised in that system ; in part, also, it was supported in the early cases on the ground of its being " agreeable to natural equity," [4] or on the strength of the conjecture (founded on the *pietas paterna*) that the testator's intention is thereby carried out.[5]

Deeds in which the *conditio* is admitted. The *conditio* is applied not only in testaments but also in marriage contracts,[6] and other deeds disposing *mortis causa*

[1] *Wallace* v. *Wallaces* (1807), M. " Clause," App. 6.

[2] *Mags. of Montrose* v. *Robertson,* (1738), M. 6398.

[3] Cf. L. J.-C. Patton's opinion in *Douglas's Exrs.* (1869), 7 M. 504 ; and Lord Westbury's opinion in *Young* v. *Robertson* (1862), 4 Macq. 337 ; Dig. 35. 1. 102.

[4] Quoted from *Mags. of Montrose, supra.*

[5] Lord Brougham in *Dixon* v. *Dixon* (1841), 2 Robs. Apps. 1 ; Lord Glenlee in *Hamilton* v. *Hamilton* (1838), 16 S. 478 ; 13 Fac. 397 ; Ld. Pres. M'Neill

and Lord Deas in *Grant's Trs.* v. *Grant* (1862), 24 D. 1211 ; Lord Ardmillan in *M'Call* v. *Dennistoun* (1871), 10 M. 281 ; Lord Neaves in *M'Gown's Trs.* v. *Robertson* (1869), 8 M. 356 ; and Lords Hermand and Succoth in *Neilson* v. *Baillie,* 4th June 1822, F. C. 1 S 458.

[6] *Hughes* v. *Edwardes* (1892), 19 R. (H. L.) 33 ; *Robertson* v. *Houston* (1858), 20 D. 989 ; *Wood* v. *Aitchison* (1789), M. 13043 ; *Rattray* v. *Blair* (1790), Hume 526. This was doubted by L. J.-C. Moncreiff in *Angus' Trs.* v. *Angus* (1880), 17 S. L. R. 536.

of the disponer's property.[1] It does not apply to bequests of specific articles (such as plate, pictures, or furniture) ;[2] it is settled, also, that it is not admissible in *inter vivos* dispositions of special portions of the disponer's property,[3] and the opinion has been expressed that it does not apply to any *inter vivos* deed.[4]

For long after its introduction the *conditio* was confined to the case of gifts to direct descendants of the testator— a limitation which obviously was only consistent with the view that it depended on the *pietas paterna*.[5]

Parties favoured by the conditio.

The earliest case in which the doctrine was extended to relations in the collateral line was *M'Kenzie* v. *Holte's Legatees*,[6] where it was admitted in favour of the families of two sisters and a niece of the testatrix's husband. This extension was sanctioned in *Wallace* v. *Wallaces*,[7] where the person whose children were brought in under the *conditio* was a grand-nephew ; and in *Christie* v. *Paterson*[8] there was a further extension so as to include a bequest to the testator's cousins.

But *Christie* v. *Paterson* was frequently commented on unfavourably in subsequent cases,[9] and was finally overruled in *Hall* v. *Hall*,[10] a case which came before the Whole Court. The testator in this case made her will in favour of her brothers and sisters uterine. Four of these predeceased her, and one of them was survived by a child. It was held that this child was not entitled to share in the gift ; and it was authoritatively laid down in the opinion of the Court, on a review of all the authorities, that the *conditio* has place only in bequests to the testator's direct descendants or to

[1] *Halliday* (1869), 8 M. 112.

[2] *Wauchope* (*Brown's Trs.*) (1882), 10 R. 441 ; *M'Alpine* (1882), 10 R. 837.

[3] *Crichton's Trs.* v. *Howat's Tutor* (1890), 18 R. 260.

[4] In *Halliday* and *Crichton's Trs.* v. *Howat's Tutor, supra.*

[5] *Binning* (1767), M. 13047 ; *Wood* v. *Aitchison* (1789), M. 13043 ; *Rattray* v. *Blair* (1790), Hume's Dec., 526 ; *Cuthbertson* v. *Young* (1781), M. 4279 ; *Roughheads* v. *Rannie* (1794), M. 6403 ; *Fleming* v. *Martin* (1798), M. 8111 ; *Neilson* v. *Baillie*, 4th June 1822, F. C.

Cf. Lord Kinloch's opinion in *M'Call* v. *Dennistoun* (1871), 10 M. 281.

[6] (1781), M. 6602.

[7] (1807, M.), " Clause," App. 6.

[8] 5th July 1822, F. C. and 1 S. 543.

[9] *Rhind's Trs.* v. *Leith* (1866), 5 M. 104 ; *Blair's Exrs.* v. *Taylor* (1876), 3 R. 362 ; *Hall* v. *Hall* (1891), 18 R. 690. Cf. also opinions in *Neilson* v. *Baillie, supra.*

[10] *Supra.* In *Marquis* v. *Prentiss* (1896), 23 R. 595, the *conditio* was excluded because the gift was made by a stranger, and because it was not of the nature of a provision.

his nephews or nieces. It was also stated that no extension of this principle of construction would be allowed.

But within the range of its application the *conditio* is liberally admitted.[1] Thus it is operative in the case of bequests not only to children, but to grandchildren [2] and great-grandchildren,[3] and probably in all instances in which the institute is a direct descendant, however remote, of the testator.[4] Further, it has been held to qualify provisions to grand-nephews,[5] and to children of the testator's brothers and sisters of the half-blood, whether consanguinean or uterine.[6] But it is not admitted where the institutes are illegitimate children of the testator,[7] or, it would appear, where they are related to the testator only by affinity.[8] Nor is it applicable to bequests to " heirs " or " executors " of the testator, although these should happen to be his children or his nephews and nieces.[9]

The parent must be instituted. It is, of course, essential that the parent should be instituted. Therefore, if the parent of the children invoking the *conditio* was dead at the date of the will, the *conditio* cannot apply. Thus, in *Rhind's Trs.* v. *Leith*,[10] the testator left a legacy of money to an aunt, and in the event of her dying before the term of payment leaving children, then to such children equally among them. The aunt predeceased the truster, leaving three children. Grandchildren (the issue of a child who was dead at the date of the will) were also in existence. A question arising whether these grandchildren were entitled in virtue of the *conditio*, it was held that they took no share. In giving judgement, Lord Cowan said : " There must be a legatee instituted in the first instance, otherwise there can be no conditional institution,

---

[1] *Waddell's Trs.* v. *Waddell* (1896), 24 R. 189.

[2] *Mowbray* v. *Scougall* (1834), 12 S. 910 ; 9 Fac. 481 ; affd. on another point 2 S. & M'L. 305.

[3] *Grant* v. *Brooke* (1882), 10 R. 92 ; *Irvine* v. *Irvine* (1873), 11 M. 892.

[4] Lord Shand in *Grant* v. *Brooke*, *supra*.

[5] *Irvine* v. *Irvine*, *supra* ; *Gillespie* v. *Mercer* (1876), 3 R. 561 ; *Cattanach* v. *Thom's Exrs.* (1858), 20 D. 1206.

[6] *Thomson's Trs.* v. *Robb* (1851), 13 D. 1326 ; *Nicol* v. *Nicol's Exrs.* (1876) 3 R. 374.

[7] *Farquharson* v. *Kelly* (1900), 2 F. 863 ; referring to *Earl of Lauderdale* v. *Royle's Exrs.* (1830), 8 S. 771 ; 5 Fac. 603 ; and *Martin's Trs.* v. *Milliken* (1864), 3 M. 326.

[8] See the opinions in *Alexander's Trs.* v. *Paterson*, 1928 S. C. 371.

[9] *Cockburn's Trs.* v. *Dundas* (1864), 2 M. 1185 ; *Black* v. *Valentine* (1844), 6 D. 689.

[10] (1866), 5 M. 104.

either under the express terms of the will or under the implied condition. In all the cases which have occurred there were parties called capable, at the date of the deed, of taking the legacy or provision, on whose failure, antecedent to the vesting or the opening of the succession, the conditional institution was held to come into operation, and the substitution provided for by the deed (if there was such) held to be evacuated. But in such circumstances as those in which this competition occurs, there being no institute, it is a misuse of terms to hold the *conditio sine liberis* to have any application." This rule holds whether the testator is or is not *in loco parentis* to the persons called.[1]

Moreover, as the effect of the *conditio* is to place the child in the room of the parent, it cannot be extended so as to give the child that which the parent could never have taken. In *M'Dougal's Tr.* v. *Heinemann*[2] the testator bequeathed the residue of his estate to his sister and her husband in liferent and to their children who should be in life at the death of the survivor in fee. He also directed that certain farm leases should be made over to such of her sons as his sister should appoint, and that the child succeeding to these leases should be debarred from participating in any other portion of the estate. The leases were appointed to a son, who died before the survivor of his parents leaving children. These children having claimed that under the *conditio* they were entitled to a share of the residue, it was held that, as their father had elected to take the leases, his name was written out of the class of residuary legatees ; he was, therefore, no longer an institute in whose place his children could take.

So also, if the settlement prescribes that vesting in the institute shall not take place until an appointed time, his issue, in the event of his predecease, will not under the *conditio* be entitled to claim right to the bequest at an

---

[1] *Wishart* v. *Grant* (1763), M. 2310 ; *Sturrock* v. *Binny* (1843), 6 D. 117 ; —in which cases, as Lord Cowan observes, the truster was *in loco parentis. Rhind's Trs.* v. *Leith* was followed in *Morrison's Trs.* v. *Macdonalds* (1890), 18 R. 181 ; *Low's Trs.* v. *Whitworth* (1892), 19 R. 431 ; *Barr* v. *Campbell,* 1925 S. C. 317 ; and *Travers's Trs.* v. *Macintyre,* 1934 S. C. 520 ; and was referred to in *M'Dougal's Tr.* v. *Heinemann,* 1918 S. C. (H. L.) 6. The point was left undecided in the case of *Thomson* v. *Cumberland,* 16th Nov. 1814, F. C.

[2] 1918 S. C. (H. L.), 6.

earlier time. In *Dixon's Trs.* v. *Duneher* [1] the funds in a marriage contract were settled on the children of the marriage, but so that they should not vest till the death of both of the spouses. The only child predeceased his mother leaving issue. In a special case brought during the latter's lifetime, it was held that no right had then vested in the issue under the *conditio* as they could not " have any higher right than their father, if now alive, would have had."

Bequest with survivorship clause.

But the fact that the bequest is in favour of a class and the survivors, or of such of the class as may be alive at a certain time, is not fatal to the admission of the *conditio* in the event of one or more of the class predeceasing the time to which the condition of survivance relates. There are cases which point to the opposite conclusion,[2] but the weight of authority supports this proposition. In *Grant* v. *Brooke*,[3] Lord President Inglis said : " The question is whether the words ' to such of their children as may be in life at the death of the survivor ' necessarily limit the disposal of the fee to those children who survived the liferenter, or whether a share of it is to be given to the representatives of those children who predeceased—that is to say, whether the *conditio si sine liberis* applies or not. It is in vain to go over again the authorities on the point, for I think it is now thoroughly settled that words such as we have here do not exclude the application of the *conditio si sine liberis*, and I am therefore of opinion that it must be applied." This statement was regarded as settling the law in *Greig's Trs.* v. *Simpson*.[4]

Bequest to conditional institute.

A further point was also decided in the last-mentioned case. In *Carter's Trs.* v. *Carter*,[5] it was doubted whether

[1] 1918 S. C. 90.

[2] *M'Call* v. *Dennistoun* (1871) 10 M. 281 ; *Crichton's Trs.* v. *Howat's Tutor* (1890), 18 R. 260.

[3] (1882), 10 R. 92. The earlier cases to the same effect are *Gauld's Trs.* v. *Duncan* (1877), 4 R. 691 ; *Aitken's Trs.* v. *Wright* (1871), 10 M. 275 ; *Robertson* v. *Houston* (1858), 20 D. 989 ; *Cattanach* v. *Thom's Exrs.* (1858), 20 D. 1206 ; *Thomson's Trs.* v. *Robb.* (1851), 13 D. 1326 ; *Booths* v. *Black* (1831), 9 S. 406 ; 6 Fac. 292 ; affd. 6 W. & S. 175 ; *Neilson* v. *Baillie*

4th June 1822, F. C. ; 1 S. 427 ; and *Wallace* v. *Wallaces* (1807), M. " Clause," App. No. 6. One of the arguments put forward against the *conditio* in *Dixon* v. *Dixon* (1841), 2 Rob.'s Apps. 1, was that there was no destination over which it could qualify.

[4] 1918 S. C. 321 ; and see also *Campbell's Trs.* v. *Dick*, 1915 S. C. 100, *per* Lord Cullen. Cf. *Travers's Trs.* v. *Macintyre*, 1934 S. C. 520.

[5] (1892), 19 R. 408.

issue could be admitted to the benefit of the *conditio* where the parent was called in the settlement as a conditional institute and not as the legatee favoured in the first instance ; but this doubt was set at rest in *Greig's Trs.* v. *Simpson.*[1] There the trustees were enjoined to pay a share of the residue to the testator's sister " whom failing to her lawful children surviving at my death." The sister and one of her children predeceased the testator, leaving issue. It was contended that, as the parent of the issue was favoured only in the event of the failure of the institute (the testator's sister), there was no room for the application of the *conditio*, but this contention was rejected and the issue admitted to the share the parent would have taken had he survived.

But, inasmuch as the doctrine of the *conditio* is founded on the presumption that the testator has overlooked the possibility of the legatee's predeceasing the time of vesting leaving issue, its admission is excluded where the terms of the will afford evidence that there has been no such oversight on the part of the testator. " This doctrine, which we have borrowed from the Roman law, proceeds entirely on the presumption that the testator, having overlooked or forgotten the contingency of the institute having children, has left children unprovided, if they come into existence. But this presumption may be defeated by opposite presumptions or evidence ; and there can be no stronger evidence to that effect than a clause in the settlement by which the testator does make a provision for the issue of predeceasing legatees, because it incontestably shows that he had them in view when he made the substitution." [2] A striking illustration of this is afforded by *Paterson* v. *Paterson*.[3] The testatrix directed that upon the death of A., to whom a liferent was given, legacies should be paid to two nephews and the residue to one of them. It was declared that none of the benefits provided in the will should vest until they became payable. There was also a clause calling the issue of the

Exclusion of conditio by terms of will.

---

[1] *Supra.* See also *Campbell's Trs.* v. *Dick, supra* ; *Mair's Trs.* v. *Mair,* 1936 S. C. 731.

[2] *Greig* v. *Malcolm* (1835), 13 S. 607 ; 10 Fac. 395, *per* Lord Corehouse. The question in this case was as to the right of issue under the *conditio* to take an accrescing share. See *post,* p. 368. The above passage was approved in *Carter* v. *Carter* (1892), 19 R. 408.

[3] 1935 S. C. (H.L.) 7 ; approving *M'Nab* v. *Brown's Trs.,* 1926 S. C. 387.

nephews in the event of their predeceasing A. The nephews survived A., but died before the testatrix, leaving children. It was held that the testatrix having made explicit provision for the issue in the event of the parent's death before A. (which had not occurred), the *conditio* could not be applied in .the circumstances which had actually occurred. The principle was thus summed up by Lord Tomlin : " Where, as here, there is in one contingency an express conditional institution of issue to the funds in question, there can be no room for a presumed conditional institution in other contingencies for which no express provision is made."

So also, if issue are mentioned in the case of certain legatees and not in the case of others, this affords an argument against the *conditio*. Thus, in *Berwick's Exr*.[1] part of the estate settled by the spouses in a marriage contract was to go to the husband's relatives ; of this portion " his sister A. shall have two-fifths, and his brothers B. and C. *and their children* the other three-fifths." A. predeceased the testators, leaving a child. Did this child take ? It was held not, because, while children were called in the other two gifts, they were not in A.'s case, and this fact was held to indicate a difference of intention in the mind of the testator.

If, however, the bequests are not of the same nature, this distinction, as affording a possible reason for the introduction of children of the legatee in the one case and not in the other, may displace the inference that the predecease has not been overlooked. Thus, in *Dixon* v. *Dixon*,[2] for instance, the testator left legacies of sums of money to his two younger sons and his eldest daughter, adding in each instance the words : " and to the heirs of his (or her) body." He also left legacies to two other daughters, and gave the residue to his eldest son ; but in these gifts heirs or children were not mentioned. The eldest son died before the testator, survived by a child. The case was brought to determine whether this child was entitled to the residue in the place of his father. The main argument against his claim was found in the difference of the styles of the gifts, but the argument was rejected, largely on the ground that, as the gifts were not of the same nature (the one being residue and the others

[1] (1885), 12 R. 565.   [2] (1841), 2 Rob's App. 1.

legacies of money), the presumption that the truster had not overlooked the possibility of issue did not arise with the same force as in other cases. In the case of the special burdens on the estate, it was not unnatural for the testator to provide for their continuance in favour of children, whereas in disposing of the general estate there would not be the same necessity for calling heirs.[1] Lord Brougham, however, added that it did not " appear that such a difference, though certainly a very strong circumstance, can be held generally and absolutely as sufficient to exclude the application of the rule, even where the provisions to which the diversity applies are exactly of the same nature."

This decision was discussed in *Alexander's Trs.* v. *Paterson*.[2] The settlement in this case, which was a universal one, was of rather an elaborate nature, but it is sufficient to say that by the tenth purpose bequests were made to groups of nephews and nieces of the testator and his wife, including one of £1,200 to each of two children of a deceased brother of the testator. One of these children was Alfred Alexander. These legacies did not vest till the first term occurring six months after the testator's death. By the last purpose the residue was to be divided as soon as convenient after his death among a number of legatees with a gift-over to the issue of predeceasers whom failing to the survivors. One of these residuary legatees was Alfred Alexander. He died within six months of the testator's death, leaving a child, and this raised the question whether the legacy of £1,200 was payable to this child. The main difficulty in allowing this claim was that issue were called in the residuary bequest, but not in the tenth purpose. On a consideration of the whole terms of the settlement it was ultimately decided that this circumstance did not suffice to outweigh the other features of the deed which were favourable to the *conditio* and the child's right was sustained. Adverting to the difference in the terms of the legacies and of the residue, Lord Constable said : " It seems to me that any assumption based upon the diverse form in which two gifts are expressed in favour of the same person must depend a good deal upon the character of the respective gifts. In this case the residue was divided among eight

[1] *Per* Lord Ordinary (Jeffrey). [2] 1928 S. C. 371.

selected persons, including collaterals of the testator ; the period of vesting prescribed was different from the period prescribed under the tenth purpose ; and, most important of all, the gift of residue contained a clause of survivorship so as to preclude the possibility of intestacy. The contingency of a residuary legatee predeceasing leaving issue was naturally introduced as a qualification of the destination to survivors. It appears to me that the existence of an express conditional institution of issue in a gift of that character yields no inference that, because a previous provision in favour of one of the residuary legatees contained no such express institution, it must have been designedly omitted, and that, therefore, the implied *conditio* is excluded." His Lordship went on to point out that, while *Dixon* v. *Dixon* was not precisely in point, for the bequests there were in favour of different persons, the ground of judgement was the difference in the character of these bequests.[1] Again, in *Wilkie* v. *Jackson*[2] (which may be contrasted with *Berwick's Exr.*[3]) where the testator disponed his estate to his eldest son, burdening it with the payment of provisions to " each of A., B., and C., my sons, *their heirs or assignees*, the sum of £200 sterling, and to each of D. E. and F., my two daughters, the sum of £100," it was held that the inference arising in this case was overcome by a declaration that the gifts were to be in lieu of legitim ; and in *Mair's Trs.* v. *Mair*,[4] where a share of residue was bequeathed to the testator's brother whom failing to his " children " and the other shares to his nieces and the survivors of them and the " issue " of predeceasers, the use of these different terms was deemed insufficent to rule out the *conditio*.

Effect of separate bequest to issue.

Another circumstance which tends to displace the assumption on which the *conditio* is based, viz., that the testator overlooked the contingency of the legatees' predecease leaving issue, is that an independent provision is made in the will for the issue. Thus, in *Douglas's Exrs.*[5] a legacy of £12,000 was bequeathed to the testator's daughter. She predeceased him, and in a codicil made after

---

[1] See also Lord Fleming's opinion in *Travers's Trs.* v. *Macintyre*, 1934 S. C. 520.

[2] (1836), 14 S. 1121.

[3] (1885), 12 R. 565.

[4] 1936 S. C. 731.

[5] (1869), 7 M. 504.

her death, he bequeathed to her son the sum of £10,000. This was held to be a strong element against the application of the *conditio*. It was extremely improbable that the truster intended the legacies to be cumulative ; on the contrary, the fair inference was that he meant to substitute the £10,000 for the gift which had lapsed.

But in order to satisfy the conditions of this exception, it is necessary that the gift to the children be substantial and not merely nominal ; or " if it is unsubstantial, it must be given with such explanations as show that it was not intended that under any circumstances the individual in question was to take more." [1] In the case from which these words are quoted, the testatrix left to one daughter a specific bequest of silver, etc., and directed that the residue should be divided among her (the testatrix's) children. The daughter predeceased the testatrix, and in a codicil made after the daughter's death the testatrix gave over the subject of the specific legacy to other persons. The daughter had left children. It was held that these children took their mother's share of residue ; for the fact that the special subjects had been given to others was not sufficient to show that the testatrix had intentionally ignored the daughter's children.

So far the path has been marked out with reasonable clearness in the decisions, but beyond this point it is difficult to find very definite guidance for solving the problems attending the *conditio*. The nearest approach to a formulation of the conditions required for its application is to be found in the following passage from the opinion of Lord Justice-Clerk Moncreiff in *Blair's Exrs.* v. *Taylor* [2] : " The application of the *conditio si sine liberis* has been made the subject of decision under a great variety of circumstances. The *conditio* has been held to apply where the settlement is universal, where the beneficiaries are a class, and the provision is of the nature of a family settlement, and where the testator, if not a parent, is at all events *in loco parentis* to the beneficiaries. Where all these elements concur, the *conditio* will be applied. The effect given to these elements depends on two principles, first, that the *delectus personæ* implied in a *nominatim* bequest is excluded when the provision is

Essentials for admission of the conditio.

---

[1] *Per* Lord M'Laren in *Forrester's Trs.* v. *Forrester* (1894), 21 R. 971.

[2] (1876), 3 R. 362.

to a class ; and, secondly, that when the provision is of the nature of a family provision, and where the granter is *in loco parentis* to the beneficiaries, there is a presumption that the granter prefers the issue of a predeceasing beneficiary to any substitute named in the deed. On the other hand, it has been held that where the subject is a special legacy, where the legatees are called *nominatim* and not as a class, and where the testator is not *in loco parentis*, neither a parent literally nor in the position of a parent, the *conditio* will not apply, upon this manifest principle that a bequest to A., whom failing to B., without mention of A.'s heirs, is presumed *ex figura verborum* to go to B. in the event of A.'s death before the testator." Of the conditions noted in this passage the most important would seem to be that the testator must have placed himself *in loco parentis* by the terms of his will, and that the bequest is not inspired by personal favour.[1] These conditions are closely related, and it is not possible to preserve a sharp line of distinction between them.

Provisions in loco parentis.   Unfortunately neither of them is susceptible of exact definition. The most authoritative exposition of the meaning of the first of these is that given by Lord President Inglis in *Bogie's Trs.* v. *Christie* :[2] " Certainly it is quite settled by a long series of decisions that the *conditio* is, as a general rule, applicable to cases of settlements made by an uncle or aunt on nephews or nieces. It is said, however, that that rule is subject to this *proviso*, that the uncle or aunt must have placed him or herself *in loco parentis* to the children, and I assume that that proposition to a certain extent is a qualification of the rule. But it is necessary to consider what is meant by placing themselves *in loco parentis*. It does not mean that the uncle has during his life occupied such a position, or treated his nephews and nieces with that kindness which a parent would show to his children ; what is meant is, that in his settlement he has placed himself in a position like that of a parent towards the legatees—that is to say, that he has made a settlement in their favour similar to what a parent might have been presumed to make." [3]

---

[1] *Keith's Trs.* v. *Keith* (1908), 16 S. L. T. 390 (Lord Dundas).
[2] (1882), 9 R. 453.
[3] See also the remarks in *Berwick's Exr.* (1885), 12 R. 565.

In other words, the testator must have "intended to make a family settlement." [1] In an Outer House case,[2] Lord Low, referring to the doctrine that the truster must have placed himself *in loco parentis*, said : " I take it that the meaning of that doctrine is that the settlement must be of such a character that the inference is that the ruling consideration in the testator's mind was that of relationship, which he regarded as imposing upon him an obligation to make some provision for his nephews and nieces, similar to the obligation which rests upon a father to provide for his children." Whether this condition is satisfied can be determined only with reference to the terms in which the bequest is made, and in this matter little aid is to be obtained from the previous decisions of the Court. The statement that the testator must have placed himself *in loco parentis* to the legatees leaves the application of the *conditio* dependent on the judgement which may be formed as to the motive and purpose in the testator's mind, without affording any guidance as to the means by which that judgement is to be formed. But much of the difficulty which otherwise would have attended this question has been removed by the exposition of the meaning and effect of this expression in *Waddell's Trs.* v. *Waddell*.[3] In that case Lord M'Laren, after noticing that, according to Lord President Inglis's statement in *Bogie's Trs.* v. *Christie*, it is not necessary that all the nephews and nieces should be treated alike, or even that all should be called, observed : " It is easy to see that where so understood the phrase ' *in loco parentis* ' ceases to be a limitation, and expresses only the reason of the

---

[1] *Hall* v. *Hall* (1891), 18 R. 690.

[2] *Johnstone's Exrs.* v. *Johnstone* (1902), 10 S. L. T., 42. The phrase *in loco parentis* is used in the law of England in a different connexion (namely, as to the question whether a legacy is adeemed by subsequent advances), and the rules as to evidence of the fact are different, but the definitions adopted in English Law may be referred to. In *Bennet* v. *Bennet* (1879), 10 Ch. D. 474, Jessel, M.R., says : " So that a person *in loco parentis* means a person taking upon himself the duty of a father to a child

to make a provision for that child." In " Williams on Executors " (12th Ed.), vol. ii., p. 869, it is said that " The proper definition of a person *in loco parentis* to a child is, a person who means to put himself in the situation of the lawful father of the child with reference to the father's office and duty of making a provision for the child."

[3] (1896), 24 R. 189. Cf. Lord Ormidale's opinion in *Gauld's Trs.* v. *Duncan* (1877), 4 R. 691 : " It is sufficient that there is nothing to exclude the condition which the law presumes."

extension of the *conditio* to nephews and nieces. I confess that this consequence does not alarm me. I think it is much better that, the relationship being defined, the principle of implied conditional institution should be liberally applied, than that its application should be determined according to the impression which a judge may form as to the assumption by a testator of a character which probably never entered his mind at all. . . . I cannot help thinking that the true rule, and the only workable rule, is that in the case of a testator who has no children of his own, the benefit of the *conditio* will be given to the issue of his legatees, being nephews or nieces, or their descendants, unless it appear from the will itself that the nature of the bequest was personal favour to the legatee rather than relationship." [1]   Lord Kinnear concurred, " chiefly on the ground that I find nothing in the testament to show that the testator was moved by any other considerations in selecting his nephews and nieces as the objects of his bounty than that of their relationship to him." Of Lord M'Laren's statement it has been said that " the rule so stated really affirms a presumption that the *conditio* applies unless there is something in the will to displace it ; it avoids the difficulty, illustrated by past decisions which are not easy to reconcile, resulting from an attempt to find indications that the testator placed himself *in loco parentis* to the beneficiaries." [2]

Gifts *ex delectu personarum*.

The second condition, that the bequest must not be made *ex delectu personarum*, still remains somewhat indefinite. It is easy to appreciate that, if the motive of the bequest is personal regard for the legatee, there is no reason why it should receive effect when his personal enjoyment of it has ceased to be possible. But it is not so easy in all cases to

---

[1] This passage has been referred to with approval in subsequent cases. See *Alexander's Trs.* v. *Paterson*, 1928 S. C. 371 ; *Travers's Trs.* v. *Macintyre* 1934 S. C. 520 ; *Mair's Trs.* v. *Mair*, 1936 S. C. 731. See also *Johnstone's Exrs.* v. *Johnstone* (1902), 10 S. L. T. 42 (Lord Low) and *Hamilton* v. *Hamilton's Trs.* (1902), 10 S. L. T. 463 (Lord Kincairney).

[2] *Per* Lord Constable in *Alexander's Trs.* v. *Paterson, supra.* In *Farquharson* v. *Kelly* (1900), 2 F. 863, Ld. Pres. Kinross says : " The application of the *conditio* has received a large extension in the case of the children of nephews and nieces, to whom a testator has placed himself *in loco parentis*, and it now appears to be the law that he will be held to have placed himself in that position if he calls the nephews and nieces as a related class, and, so far as appears, not from individual predilection."

ascertain what the motive inspiring the testator was. Relationship does not exclude personal favour ; and where relationship exists, as is always the case when the *conditio* comes in question, a testator himself might often have difficulty in detecting whether relationship or personal favour was his predominant motive. This question falls to be determined on a conspectus of the whole of the provisions of the settlement as read in the light of the facts as to the relationship of the legatees to the testator. In not a few of the cases which have occurred it will be found that the decision has been reached only after weighing certain features of the deed favourable to the *conditio* against others which were unfavourable ; and it is not possible to single out any one circumstance as in itself conclusively determining whether the bequest is or is not made from personal favour.

But it may be said that the strongest indication that the bequest is made in respect of relationship is where the legatees are called under a class description expressive of the relationship between them and the testator, as *e.g.* to his children, or his nephews and nieces, or the children of a brother or sister. In this connexion it may be noted that the circumstance (*a*) that some of the children or nephews and nieces are not included in the bequest,[1] or (*b*) that there are called along with the children or nephews and nieces others to whom the *conditio* does not apply is not necessarily fatal to the *conditio*.[2] In *Bogie's Trs.* v. *Christie*,[3] the testator instructed his trustees to divide his whole estate " between the children of my late brother A. and the children of my late sister B." ; and, although there was a family of a deceased brother which was not called in the will, the *conditio* was applied. The result was the same also in *M'Gown's Trs.* v. *Robertson*,[4] where the testator bequeathed his estate to the families of his nephews and nieces, calling, in the case of one family, only the sons to the exclusion of the daughters. If the bequest is made to the children in

---

[1] *Waddell's Trs.* v. *Waddell* (1896), 24 R. 189, *per* Lord M'Laren ; *Alexander's Trs.* v. *Paterson*, 1928 S. C. 371 ; *Keith's Trs.* v. *Keith* (1908), 16 S. L. T. 390 (Lord Dundas).

[2] *Allan* v. *Thomson's Trs.* (1893), 20 R. 733 ; *Alexander's Trs.* v. *Paterson, supra.*

[3] (1882), 9 R. 453.

[4] (1869), 8 M. 356.

lieu of legitim, this has been deemed favourable to the *conditio*.[1]

On the other hand, if the bequest is made to the legatees *nominatim*, there is difficulty in admitting the *conditio*.[2] If a fund is bequeathed to a number of named individuals, who, in fact, form the whole of a class, this circumstance is probably not of great importance ; for, although the effect of naming the legatees is to exclude members of the class who may subsequently be born,[3] the insertion of the names may be regarded as due merely to a desire to facilitate " the working out of the trust." [4] But, if the bequest takes the form of a gift of a specific sum to the several legatees, and more particular if the sums are of varying amounts— as distinguished from the bequest of a fund to them collectively—this, in the general case, would point to personal favour as influencing the bequests.[5] The *conditio*, it has been said, applies only to gifts in the nature of provisions, not to simple legacies.[6] Thus, legacies stated by the testatrix to be left to the legatees " as momentoes of me," [7] and a legacy to a daughter " for her own uses " [8] were held to be personal to the legatees. In *Allan's Trs.* v. *Thomson*,[9] stress was laid on the fact that children of a niece took under the *conditio* a share of the residue bequeathed to her as excluding its application to a pecuniary bequest made to her in the will.[10]

<table>
<tr><td>Under conditio
children take
only parent's
original share.</td><td>When the conditio applies there is this limitation on the right of those who are admitted under it, viz., that they</td></tr>
</table>

---

[1] *Wilkie* v. *Jackson* (1836), 14 S. 1121 ; L. J.-C. Patton's opinion in *Douglas's Exrs.* (1869), 7 M. 504.

[2] In *Blair's Exrs.* v. *Taylor* (1876), 20 R. 733, L. J.-C. Moncreiff observed that the Court in *Hamilton* v. *Hamilton* (1838), 16 S. 478, 13 Fac. 397, considered that the fact that the legatees were named was sufficient to exclude the *conditio* ; but, although this was certainly an element in the case, the reports show that the decision proceeded also on other features of the deed.

[3] See *Gillespie* v. *Mercer* (1876), 3 R. 561.

[4] *Allan* v. *Thomson's Trs.* (1893), 20 R. 733, *per* L. J.-C. Macdonald. See also *Bowman* v. *Richter* (1900), 2 F. 624 ; and Lord M'Laren's opinion in *Forrester's Trs.* v. *Forrester* (1894), 21 R. 971 ; *Keith's Trs.* v. *Keith* (1908), 16 S. L. T. 390 (Lord Dundas).

[5] *M'Call* v. *Dennistoun* (1871), 10 M. 281 ; *Hamilton* v. *Hamilton* (1838), 16 S. 478 ; 13 Fac. 397 ; *Gillespie* v. *Mercer* (1876), 3 R. 561. Contrast *Bryce's Trs.* (1878), 5 R. 722.

[6] *Douglas's Exrs.* (1869), 7 M. 504.

[7] *Allan* v. *Thomson's Trs.* (1893), 20 R. 733. See also 1908 S. C. 483.

[8] *Douglas's Exrs., supra.*

[9] 1908 S. C. 483.

[10] *Supra*, p. 362.

are preferred only to the institute's original share, and not to any share that would have accresced to him or her had he or she survived the time of vesting. Suppose, for instance, that a father makes a bequest to his children—six in number, say—in simple terms, and one of these children predeceases the father leaving issue, and that thereafter another predeceases him without having had issue, then the issue of the predeceaser will take their parent's original sixth portion, but will not share in the portion of the other predeceaser, which will pass to the surviving children of the testator, or as the case may be. In some of the earlier cases it was held that where the gift was made to a class to be ascertained at a future date, the issue of predeceasing members would take equal shares with the surviving members,[1] but this distinction no longer holds. As the law now stands, the right of those taking in virtue of the *conditio* in no case extends beyond the parent's original share.[2] In *Neville* v. *Shepherd* [3] the rule was stated in terms approved in later cases. " It is settled as matter of legal implication, as distinguished from construction, that a child under the *conditio* never takes more than what is described as the parent's original share,— that is, the share which the parent would take supposing every one in the destination to survive the period of payment. . . . The reason is this, that the right of children under the *conditio* is an equitable extension of the will, and

[1] *Rattray* v *Blair* (1790), Hume's Decs. 526; *Thomson* v. *Scougall* (1835), 2 S. & M'L. 305. See *Halliday* (1869), 8 M. 112; but the terms of the special case appear to have precluded the consideration of this question In *Taylor* ((1884), 21 S. L. R. 298; 11 R. 423) the gift was to the testator's sons, to the children of a son (predeceased), and to the testator's daughters, in liferent and their issue in fee, with a destination-over, on failure of any of the legatees, to " the surviving residuary beneficiaries " ; one of the children of the (predeceased) son died leaving issue, and thereafter a daughter died childless ; and it was held (following *Roughead* v. *Rannie*, 1794, M. 6403) that the issue of the son's child were entitled to participate in the share of

the daughter. This decision appears to be inconsistent with the law settled in the cases cited in the next note.

[2] *Beveridge's Trs.* v. *Beveridge*, 1930 S. C. 578, at 582 ; *Crosbie's Trs.* v. *Crosbie*, 1927 S. C. 159 ; *Craik's Trs.* v. *Anderson*, 1932 S. C. 61 ; *Farquharson* v. *Kelly* (1900), 2 F. 863 ; *Bowman* v. *Richter* (1900), 2 F. 624 ; *Neville* v. *Shepherd* (1895), 23 R. 351 ; *Cumming's Trs.* v. *White* (1893), 20 R. 454 ; *Henderson* v. *Hendersons* (1890), 17 R. 293 ; (*ante*, p. 104) ; *Aitken's Trs.* v. *Wright* (1871), 10 M. 275 ; *Graham's Tr.* v. *Grahams* (1868), 6 M. 820. See also *Young* v. *Robertson* (1862), 4 Macq. 337. Lord Cowan's opinion in *Walker* v. *Park* (1859), 21 D. 286.

[3] *Supra.*

cannot reasonably be extended beyond this, that what the truster thought a reasonable provision for one to whom he was in *loco parentis* shall pass to that person's children. The extent of what is considered a reasonable provision is fixed by the provision which the parent has actually made on the assumption that all his children survive."

The effect of the *conditio* is, it would appear, to introduce the children according to the legal rules of succession : if the subject be heritable, the heir-at-law takes ; if moveable, the heirs *in mobilibus* are entitled. This is the effect of the decision in *Grant's Trs.* v. *Grant*.[1] In that case the testatrix directed her trustees to convey a specific heritable estate and the residue to her third son—the two elder sons being insane ; her daughters were not called. The son predeceasing the time of vesting, it was held that in virtue of the *conditio* his eldest son took the heritable estate, and that his other son took the residue. This result may, however, be displaced by evidence of a contrary intention on the part of the testator. In *Nairn's Trs.* v. *Melville*,[2] the Court, while recognising the authority of *Grant's Trs.*, held that the terms of the deed led to a different result. In this case trustees were directed to hold the estate (which was entirely heritable) for the truster's children in liferent, and on the death of all of them it was to be divided among " the child or children . . . then surviving, *per stirpes*," of the truster's children. One liferentrix had a son, who predeceased the last of the liferenters, leaving several children. The *conditio* was assumed to be applicable ; and it was found that under it all the children of the predeceasing grandchild were entitled, largely on the ground that it was clear that the gift to the grandchildren included in each case the whole family, and that this intention must be carried out in the case of those taking by virtue of the *conditio*.

Lastly, the principle of implied conditional institution operates in favour of more remote descendants of the institute as well as of children of the institute. In *Irvine* v. *Irvine*,[3] for example, the testator's nephew to whom the

---

[1] (1862), 24 D. 1211, overruling Lord Neaves in *Earl of Airlie* v. *Ogilvy* (1857), 29 S. J. 169.

[2] (1877), 5 R. 128, In this case it is questioned whether *Grant's Trs.* was a case on the *conditio*.

[3] (1873), 11 M. 892 ; *Campbell's Trs.* v. *Dick*, 1915 S. C. 100, *per* Lord Mackenzie, at 108.

bequest was made, in the event which occurred, died before the period of vesting, leaving a son and two grandchildren, the children of a predeceasing son and daughter. All of these being alive at the date of the vesting of the legacy, it was held that the subject of the bequest was divisible into three parts, and that each of the grandchildren was entitled to one of these in the room and place of their parent.

CHAPTER XVIII.

THE INTEREST OF THE BENEFICIARY: WHETHER A LIFERENT OR A FEE IS GIVEN.

Gift of interest, with no limit as to its duration.

I. Whether the Words of Gift carry a Liferent or a Fee.—There is a rule in English Law that a gift of the interest or produce of a fund, without any limit as to continuance, will, in the absence of words disposing of the fee, be construed as equivalent to a gift of the principal.[1] But there is no such rule in Scots Law ;[2] and the extent of the gift is in each case to be determined on the terms used in the will.[3] Where the gift is of the rents of an heritable property, it is more difficult to hold that the fee is carried than in the case of a gift of the interest of a moveable subject.[4] Thus, in *Mackenzie's Trs.* v. *Mackenzie,*[5] where the testator instructed that the rent of his houses should be divided among certain relatives, and made no further provision as to the property, it was held, in a question between these parties and the heir-at-law, that the *corpus* was un-

---

[1] Williams on Executors (12th Ed.), vol. ii., 768.

[2] *Sanderson's Exr.* v. *Kerr* (1860), 23 D. 227, *per* Lord Cowan ; *Sim* v. *Duncan* (1900), 2 F. 434 ; *Lethem* v. *Evans* 1918, 1 S. L. T. 27 (Lord Hunter). See also *Henderson's Trs.* (1892), 29 S. L. R. 356 ; *Crawford's Trs.* v. *Working Boys' Home* (1901), 8 S. L. T. 371 (Lord Kyllachy).

[3] *Sim* v. *Duncan, supra.*

[4] *Vide* Lord Moncreiff's opinion in *Mackenzie's Trs.* v. *Mackenzie* (1899), 2 F. 330. In *Henderson's Trs.* v. *Hendersons* (1876), 3 R. 320, a direction to hold and apply the rents of a subject was held (on the terms of the deed) to carry the fee.

[5] *Supra.*

disposed of and fell to the latter. Similarly, where a testatrix expressed the bequest in these terms : " I want my four daughters to draw the rents and divide them equally between them," it was held that these words were insufficient, under section 20 of the Consolidation Act of 1868, to carry the fee away from the heir-at-law.[1]

If, however, there is added to the gift of interest a direction or power to trustees to apply the principal for behoof of the legatee, this element may raise the gift into that of a fee.[2] Thus, in *Lawson's Trs.* v. *Lawson*,[3] the truster directed his trustees either to invest two-thirds of his estate " and pay the proceeds thereof to my said sisters equally, . . . or, if my said trustees should think it more advisable, I authorise them or him to purchase with the said two-thirds . . . an annuity payable to my said two sisters equally during all the days and years of their lives." There was no other provision as to the two-thirds. It was held that these words carried the fee, because the direction as to the annuity indicated that the truster contemplated the application of the principal as well as of the interest for behoof of the legatees.

For the same reason, a direction to trustees to " hold " a share of an estate " for behoof of the said A. and his family as follows, . . . for payment of the interest of the said share to the said A. to the extent of one-half thereof, and the interest of the other half " to his children, with a direction to the trustees to expend the capital for behoof of A. or his children if they stood in need of it, and in such manner as the trustees thought fit, was held to give the fee of one half of the share to A. and the fee of the other half to his children.[4]

But, on the other hand, words referring to the gift as limited to the lifetime of the legatee are adverse to the idea of the gift being a gift of the fee. Thus a gift in these terms : " I . . . will and dispose of all my . . . belongings in favour of my daughters . . . during their lifetime " was considered insufficient to carry the fee, although there was no further disposal of the estate. The words " during their lifetime " made it impossible to construe the clause as

Words limiting the gift to the legatee's lifetime.

[1] *Sim* v. *Duncan, supra.*
[2] *Sanderson's Exrs.* v. *Kerr, supra.*
[3] (1890), 17 R. 1167.
[4] *Gillies' Trs.* v. *Hodge* (1900), 3 F. 238.

equivalent to an absolute gift.[1] So also in *Duncan* v. *Edinburgh Royal Infirmary*,[2] where the testatrix left and bequeathed all she possessed to her brother " during his lifetime " with (as the Court construed the bequest) a gift of the fee to his issue, whom failing to two infirmaries, it was held, largely because of the words quoted, that his right was no more than a liferent.

Provision for disposal of the subject on legatee's death.

On the other hand, the mere fact that a disposition is made of the estate after the death of a legatee will not suffice to restrict his interest to a liferent, if there are no other features of the deed pointing to this restriction. In *O'Reilly* v. *Baroness Sempill*,[3] the testatrix by a codicil instructed her trustees to make over the residue of her estate to A. and her heirs and assignees. By a later codicil the testatrix, on the narrative that there was no prospect of A.'s having issue, disponed and bequeathed the residue to B. " as her (A.'s) successor " to succeed her therein. It was held both in the Court of Session and in the House of Lords, that A. was fiar in the property and that B. was merely a

---

[1] *Spink's Exrs.* v. *Simpson* (1894), 21 R. 551. In *Patrick* v. *Fowler* (1900), 2 F. 690, where the testator gave the " interest " of his property to his two sisters, and provided that it should be paid on their death to other parties, it was held that the fee was not disposed of under the will ; and in *Anderson* v. *Thomson* (1877) 4 R. 1101, a direction to trustees to distribute the residue of the estate among persons named " annually " was held to be a gift in fee, the word " annually " not being sufficient to abate the force of the other words of gift. A gift of the " proceeds " of an estate may mean either the realised value thereof (a gift in fee) or the interest arising from it (a gift of the liferent) ; if the deed directs that the proceeds are to be paid annually or from time to time, a presumption arises that only the interest is given (*Henderson's Trs.* (1892), 29 S. L. R. 356).

[2] 1936 S. C. 811.

[3] (1855), 2 Macq. 288 ; *M'Dowall* v. *M'Gill* (1847), 9 D. 1284 ; *Lyon* v.

Lyon (1888), 15 R. 394 ; *Rae's Trs.* v. *Rae* (1893), 20 R. 826 ; *Mitchell* v. *General Assembly of the Church of Scotland* (1895), 2 S. L. T. 629 (Lord Stormonth-Darling) ; *Davis* v. *Davis* (1898), 6 S. L. T. 24 (Lord Kincairney); *Young's Trs.* v. *Young* (1899), 7 S. L. T. 266 (Lord Kyllachy). Contrast *Sinclair* v. *Sinclair's Exrs.* (1901), 8 S. L. T. 485 (Lord Kyllachy). The words may, however, be such as to constitute a precatory trust, as to which see *Wilson* v. *Lindsay* (1878), 5 R. 539 ; *Barclay's Exr.* v. *Macleod* (1880), 7 R. 477 ; *Johnston* (1880), 18 S. L. R. 60 ; *Reddie's Trs.* v. *Lindsay* (1890), 17 R. 558 ; *Macpherson* v. *Macpherson's Curator Bonis* (1894), 21 R. 386 ; *Bannatyne's Trs.* v. *Dunlop* (1894), 1 S. L. T. 484 (Lord Moncreiff) ; *Urquhart's Exrs.* v. *Abbott* (1899), 1 F. 1149 ; *Cram* v. *Cumming* (1899), 37 S. L. R. 115 ; *Smart* v. *Smart*, 1926 S. C. 392 ; *Comiskey* v. *Bowring-Hanbury* [1905], A. C. 84 ; Lewin on Trusts (13th Ed.), 92 *et seq.*

substitute, whose *spes successionis* was liable to be defeated by A.'s disposing of the subject. The fact that the testatrix spoke of B.'s succeeding A. made it clear that A.'s right was not reduced, because the idea of succession implies that there has been another antecedently in the same right. Again, in *Alexander* v. *Alexander*,[1] the testator directed his trustees that his whole property should be divided among his children. He provided with regard to a portion of his daughter's share that it should be lodged " on an heritable bond, or in the public funds, that she may receive the interest of it during all the days of her life, and her children shall be her heirs " ; and as to the share of one of his sons, he directed that it should be lodged in the same way, " that there may be something for his family in case of his death." Both the son and the daughter were held to be vested in the fee of their shares. So also in *Reid.* v. *Dobie*,[2] a bequest of her estate by the testatrix to her husband and " after him " to her sister was held to confer on the husband a right of fee.

The extent of the beneficiary's right—whether a fee or a liferent—under a direction to trustees to " hold " or to " invest " or to " hold and apply " a fund for his behoof has been frequently discussed in cases involving the doctrine of repugnancy[3] or the principle of construction adopted in *Lindsay's Trs.* v. *Lindsay*[4] ; and the decisions noted in the earlier chapters dealing with these matters may be referred to.

The effect of such directions is largely dependent on the context in which they appear ; but there is a recognised rule of construction, viz., that " where in testamentary writings a provision is once regularly created, it shall not be held to be taken away except by clear words importing or inferring a revocation." [5] Thus, a declaration (following an instruction to trustees to pay or apply the subject to or for behoof of the legatee) that the testator intends that the

[1] (1849), 12 D. 345 and 348.
[2] 1921 S. C. 662. See also *Ironside's Exr.* v. *Ironside's Exr.*, 1933 S. C. 116; contrast *Carmichael's Exrs.* v. *Carmichael*, 1909 S. C. 1387, where on the terms of the will it was held that the legatee had no more than a liferent.
[3] *Ante*, p. 336.
[4] *Ante*, p. 146.
[5] *Scott* v. *Sceales* (1865), 3 M. 1130 ; *Grant* v. *Dyer* (1813), 2 Dow 73, at 86 ; *Chapman* v. *Macbean* (1860), 22 D. 745.

provision shall be secured, in so far as practicable or convenient, for the legatee's benefit and that of her children exclusive of the *jus mariti* of her husband,[1] and a provision in a codicil that the beneficiaries shall have no power during their lives to deal with the subjects given them in the will save as to the interest thereof, but shall have power to dispose of them by will,[2] have been considered insufficient to reduce to a liferent the right of fee previously conferred on them.

In cases where it is doubtful whether a right of fee or merely a liferent is conferred, a declaration that the legatee shall possess certain specified and limited powers has been deemed favourable to the construction of the bequest as giving merely a liferent, because if the testator had intended to give a fee the enumeration of these limited powers would have been unnecessary.[3]

II. Rights Intermediate between Fee and Liferent.— As the result of certain comparatively recent decisions there has come to be recognised a somewhat anomalous species of right or interest intermediate between a liferent and a fee.[4] The nature and conditions of this right are expounded in *Denholm's Trs.* v. *Denholm's Trs.*[5] By a mutual settlement a wife gave to her husband her whole estate " with full power " to him " to consume such parts or portions of the capital during his lifetime as he may find or think necessary, and also power to him to realise, sell, and dispose of my said estates . . . as he may think proper and in general to

---

[1] *Scott's Trs.* v. *Stack* (1865), 3 M. 950 ; *Newall's Tr.* v. *Inglis's Trs.* (1898), 25 R. 1176.

[2] *Clouston's Trs.* v. *Bulloch* (1889), 16 R. 937.

[3] See *Miller Richard's Trs.* v. *Miller Richard* (1903), 5 F. 909 ; *Peden's Trs.* v. *Peden* (1903), 5 F. 1014 ; *Anderson's Trs.* v. *Anderson* (1904), 7 F. 224 ; *Downie's Trs.* v. *Cullen* (1882), 9 R. 749 ; *Ogilvie's Trs.* (1870), 8 M. 427 ; and Ld. Pres. Hope's opinion in *Miller* v. *Miller* (1833), 12 S. 31 ; *Nicol's Trs.* v. *Farquhar*, 1918 S. C. 358, *per* Lord Salvesen.

[4] In *Forsyth* v. *Forsyth* (1905), 12 S. L. T. 778, Lord Pearson held that under the terms of a bequest, the beneficiary's interest " was more than a liferent and less than a fee."

[5] 1907 S. C. 61 ; 1908 S. C. 255. Contrast *Barr's Trs.* v. *Barr's Trs.* (1891), 18 R. 541, where a bequest to a beneficiary " during her lifetime," with similar powers, was held to give her a liferent with power to use and (possibly) dispose of the sum bequeathed in her lifetime ; and *Mickel's J. F.* v. *Oliphant* (1892), 20 R. 172, where the beneficiary was held to be fiar. See also *Corrance's Trs.* v. *Glen* (1903), 5 F. 777 ; and *Burnett's Trs.* v. *Burnett*, 1909 S. C. 223 ; and p. 243 *ante.*

deal and intromit therewith as freely as I could have done myself." She appointed her husband to be her executor, and on his death she assigned for certain trust purposes " my said estate or such portion as may be unconsumed by my said husband." In the only opinion delivered in the Inner House (Lord Stormonth-Darling's) it was laid down that the effect of all these clauses was " to cut down the absolute right of fee originally conferred on the husband, not to a liferent (because a liferent would have been inconsistent with the powers which she wished him to have), but to a right limited to sale, administration, and consumption during his lifetime. Such being, in my opinion, the measure of the husband's right, the wife was free to dispose of any portion of her estate remaining unconsumed at his death by giving it to trustees, as she did." This decision was with some reluctance followed in *Heavyside* v. *Smith*.[1] The testator in this case by his *mortis causâ* settlement conveyed directly to a stepdaughter his whole estate, and, in the event (which occurred) of her brother surviving her, " the revenue of the residue of my estate that may be remaining over at her death " was to fall to him in liferent and at his death to the testator's heirs whomsoever in fee. It will be observed that in this case there was not, as there was in *Denholm's Trs.*, a specification of any powers to be enjoyed by the stepdaughter ; but there was this similarity that the estate given over on her death was not that bequeathed to her, but so much as remained of it at her death.[2] The Court considered itself to be bound by the earlier decision, but the opinions indicate that, had the question been open, it would have been disposed to adopt the view of English Law that the disposition after the death of the stepdaughter was ineffectual either as being repugnant to the bequest to her or on the ground of the uncertainty of its terms.[3] It has been said that in neither of these cases was there any initial gift of fee ; [4] and their effect has been summed up thus :

[1] 1929 S. C. 68.

[2] In this respect differing from *Ironside's Exr.* v. *Ironside's Exr.*, 1933 S. C. 116.

[3] For the English Law, see Jarman on Wills (7th Ed.), pp. 437 and 1168.

[4] *Per* Ld. Pres. Clyde in *Ironside's Exr.* v. *Ironside's Exr.*, *supra*. But see

Denholm's Trs., 1907 S. C., *per* Lord Dundas, at 63, Lord Stormonth-Darling, at 64, and 1908 S. C., Lord Dundas, at 259, and Lord Stormonth-Darling, at 265 ; and *Heavyside* v. *Smith*, *per* Lord Ormidale, at 73.

" The donee was held to be in the position of a trustee, with power to use the trust-estate for his own benefit (if required) ; and, if not so required, the estate at his death was to revert to the testator's trustees for the purposes of his settlement." [1]

III. Gifts in Liferent Ex Figura Verborum construed as Gifts of the Fee.—In *Cumstie* v. *Cumstie's Trs.*,[2] Lord President Inglis pointed out that there were two cases in which nominal liferents were construed as gifts of the fee :—

1. Gifts to a beneficiary in liferent with an absolute *jus disponendi* superadded.

2. Gifts to a parent in liferent and to children *nascituri* in fee.

General Principle.

(1) Liferent, with Jus Disponendi superadded. — The absolute and unfettered power of disposal of a subject is the " peculiar and highest badge of property." [3]   The grant of a power of this nature raises, therefore, the implication that the grantee was intended to take in fee, the gift of the essential attribute of the right inferring the gift of the right itself.   " If an estate or a sum of money be given to an individual who is *sui juris*, without words of limitation or a declaration of the extent of his ownership,[4] but with words indicative of the intention of the testator that he should have the absolute *jus disponendi*, then, in any case, those words are to be taken as indicating an intention that he should be the absolute owner.   Thus, if I give an estate to A. B. to do therewith as he pleases, to give to such persons as he shall think fit, and to deal with it at his will and pleasure, all those expressions are nothing more than a form of denoting absolute ownership, and the intention to give absolute ownership." [5]

This statement of the law is confined to the case where there are no words limiting the beneficiary's interest ; but,

---

[1] *Per* Ld. Pres. Clyde in *Ironside's Exr.* v. *Ironside's Exr.*, 1933 S. C. 116. Cf. *Massy* v. *Scott's Trs.* and other decisions, *ante*, p. 328.

[2] (1876), 3 R. 921.

[3] *Per* Ld. Pres. Inglis in *Alves* v. *Alves* (1861), 23 D. 712 ; 33 S. J. 354. " The proper distinction betwixt fiar and liferenter is the complete right of

property and power of disposal in the former "—Lord Glenlee in *Fisher* v. *Dixon* (1831), 10 S. 55 ; 7 Fac. 47 (affd. 6 W. & S. 431).

[4] *Vide* p. 386, *post*.

[5] *Per* Westbury, L. C., in *Pursell* v. *Elder* (1865), 3 M. (H. L.) 59 ; *post*, p. 384.

even where there are such words, as, for example (to take the most common case), if that interest is described as a liferent, then if the testator proceeds to confer on the life-renter an absolute *jus disponendi*, " it may not be an unfair inference that that person is the full proprietor of the estate, because it is difficult to see what other right a proprietor can have than the full right of enjoyment and the full right of disposal." [1] It is a question of the extent of the powers granted and of the interest bestowed under the deed, for no deed which confers anything short of the full right of the enjoyment and the absolute *jus disponendi* will give the complete right of property.

This principle is illustrated by the exceptions to it, for although acknowledged in all the cases, it appears to have been applied only in *Rattray's Trs.* v. *Rattray*.[2] In that case the testator instructed his trustees to pay an annual allow-ance to his widow, and on her death to realise the estate (if they deemed this expedient) and to divide the residue into three shares. On the division of the residue a share was to be set aside for each of his daughter and his two grandchildren, and there was to be paid " to them or for their behoof during their respective lives the annual income or revenue of said shares," and at their respective deaths their shares were to be paid *to their respective heirs or assignees*. There was also a declaration that the shares should not vest before the death of the testator's widow, and a destination-over as to the daughter's share, referring to the widow's death. The three legatees survived the widow, and there-after the daughter died, having disposed of her share by will. In a special case brought to determine the rights of the parties in the estate, the Court, reasoning from the use of the word " assignees " that a general power of assign-ment or disposal was granted by the will, found that the residuary legatees were fiars. No right of fee was vested in the daughter prior to the widow's death, because of the destination-over ; but, as the daughter had survived that

Liferent with powers super-added con-strued as a fee.

<hr>

[1] *Per* L. J.-C. Inglis in *Alves* v. *Alves* (1861), 23 D. 712. Ld. Pres. Clyde in *Murray's Trs.* v. *MacGregor's Trs.*, 1931 S. C. 516.

[2] (1899), 1 F. 510 ; *Peden's Tr.* v.

Peden (1903), 5 F. 1014, *per* Lord Moncreiff ; see also *Quested* v. *Mitchell* (1855), 24 L. J. Ch. 722. Contrast *Douglas's Trs.* (1902), 5 F. 69, *post*.

event, her will was effectual to carry her share. In this case it will be noticed that, under any other construction, the fee would have been undisposed of under the will.

The doctrine is subject to the following limitations :—

(1) The right of a party who is called to the liferent is not enlarged by the grant of powers, however ample, if there are other parties called in the event of default of the exercise of the powers. A gift of the subject in the event of the non-exercise of the power excludes the construction of the liferent as equivalent to a fee. This is very explicitly stated in *Morris* v. *Tennant*.[1] In that case a liferent of half of the estate was given to each of two daughters, and the fee to their issue ; and the deed provided that, in the event of neither leaving issue, " full power and faculty is hereby committed to my said daughters respectively to settle, destine, and convey the fee . . . to such person or persons, and in such way and manner, as they may think fit " ; and there was a gift-over to three parties *nominatim* failing the exercise of these powers. The question raised in the case was whether, there being no issue of either daughter, a will made by the survivor was struck at by the law of deathbed, as being a disposition by a proprietor, or whether, as being merely the exercise of a power, it was saved from the operation of that law. The House of Lords (affirming the decision of the First Division) sustained the will, on the ground that the daughters were merely liferenters with powers, and not fiars. In his opinion, Lord St Leonards states that even the most extended powers will not make the donee of the powers fiar if there be a provision in favour of others in the event of the powers not being exercised.

This decision was followed in *Murray's Trs.* v. *MacGregor's Trs.*[2] In that case the truster directed his trustees to hold a share of the residue of his estate in trust for such persons and such purposes as his daughter should " from time to time during her life by deed revocable or irrevocable or by will or codicil appoint " and until, and in default of, appointment upon trust to pay the income to her during

---

[1] (1855), 27 S. J. 546 ; 18 D. (H. L.) 42 ; *Rattray's Trs.* v. *Rattray, supra ; Rollo* v. *Rollo* (1843), 5 D. 446 ; *Tait's Trs.* v. *Neill* (1903), 6 F. 138 ; *Forrest's Trs.* v. *Reid* (1904), 7 F. 142, *per* Lord M'Laren ; Farwell on Powers (3rd Ed.), p. 72.
[2] 1931 S. C. 516.

her life with a destination of the share to certain trustees acting under a separate indenture. It was held that the daughter's right was not one of fee, the Lord President observing : " If the conferment of a power of disposal— however unqualified—upon the donee of the liferent is coupled with a gift of the fee to someone else, it is only natural that (in so far as the power of disposal is not exercised) the express destination of the fee should prevail over an implication which is no longer a necessary one."

In *Alves* v. *Alves*,[1] a residuary clause was (with other elements) founded on as supporting the view that liferenters who were also donees of a power took no higher interest than a liferent.

(2) Again, in order that a right of liferent and a power of disposal, taken together, may amount to a fee, both must be given in unqualified terms. " As the law stands at present upon authority . . . the Court will not declare a fee unless there is both an unlimited liferent and an absolute power of disposal, as opposed to a mere testamentary power of disposal." [2] Thus, in *Douglas's Trs.*[3] the liferenter and donee of the power was held to be merely a liferenter, because the gift of liferent was made in qualified terms. By the will, in that case, trustees were instructed to pay the interest of a sum of money to the testator's daughter, for her maintenance and support during her lifetime, declaring that in the event of her marriage the interest was not to be liable to the claims of her husband or his creditors, and that the capital was to go on her death (if unmarried) to residue, and (if married) *to her heirs or assignees*. The daughter married, and thereafter claimed the fee. It was held that she was merely a liferentrix. It was unnecessary to decide as to the extent of the powers granted,[4] because, in any case, the qualified terms in which the liferent was conferred effectually limited the daughter's interest.

So also in *Ewing's Trs.* v. *Ewing*,[5] although the most

The liferent and the power of disposal must be unqualified to confer a fee.

---

[1] (1861), 23 D. 712 ; Lord Rutherfurd Clark in *Lawson's Trs.* v. *Lawson* (1890), 17 R. 1167.

[2] *Per* Ld. Pres. Dunedin in *Mackenzie's Trs.* v. *Kilmarnock's Trs.*, 1909 S. C. 472 ; *Ewing's Trs.* v. *Ewing*, 1909 S. C. 409.

[3] (1902), 5 F. 69.

[4] Lord Adam was of opinion that the power of disposal was testamentary ; Lord M'Laren thought otherwise.

[5] 1909 S. C. 409.

ample powers of disposal were given to the liferentrix, her right was not thereby converted into a fee owing to the fact that she had no more than an alimentary liferent.

And the power of disposal must be absolute. Thus a liferent with a power to dispose by testament or *mortis causa* deed is not a fee,[1] and the donee cannot by making an appointment in favour of himself convert his right of liferent into a right of fee.[2]

Where the liferenter has the power to dispose of the property by will or *mortis causa* deed, this amounts to nothing more than a power to nominate those who are to enjoy the bounty of the person who has entrusted the liferenter with the power.[3] Such powers fall short of the powers inherent in a gift of fee. Even where the power is given in terms which do not explicitly limit its exercise to testamentary writings, if it be clear from the context or from the nature of the subject that the testator has intended the power to be exercised only by will or *mortis causa* deed, there will be no fee in the liferenter.[4]

---

[1] *In re Weddell*, 1849, Scots Exchequer Reports No. 9; *Alves v. Alves, infra*; *Peden's Tr. v. Peden* (1903), 5 F. 1014; *Miller Richard's Trs. v. Miller Richard* (1903), 5 F. 909; *Mackenzie's Trs. v. Kilmarnock's Trs.*, 1909 S. C. 472. Cf. *Hyslop v. Maxwell's Trs.* (1834), 12 S. 413; 9 Fac. 246.

[2] *Tait's Trs. v. Neill* (1903), 6 F. 138.

[3] *In re Weddell, supra.*

[4] With reference to the question as to the extent of the power conferred on the liferenter, the following points may be noted: In *Douglas's Trs.* (1902), 5 F. 69, Lord M'Laren indicates that the fact that the fund is payable to the appointees only on the liferenter's death does not, *per se*, show that the power is testamentary (see also Farwell on Powers (3rd Ed.), p. 69, but contrast *Reid v. Reid's Trs., post*). As previously noted, the use of the term "assignees" imports an unqualified power of disposal (*Rattray's Trs. v. Rattray, supra*) and in *Bowie's Trs. v. Paterson* (1889) 16 R.

983 will be found an instance of an assignation incorporating an exercise of a power; a power to "legate and bequeath" is testamentary (*Peden's Tr. v. Peden* (1903), 5 F. 1014) and a power to "devise . . . by deed or writing under her hand" was held not to be an *inter vivos* power (*Tait's Trs. v. Neill* (1903) 6 F. 138). In *Buchanan's Trs. v. Whyte* (1890) 17 R. (H. L.) 53, it is shown that a deed in exercise of a power may be *mortis causa*, but not testamentary, and, therefore, capable of vesting a right in the appointee, though he may predecease the donee of the power. (See also the opinion of L. J.-C. Inglis in *Alves v. Alves* (1861), 23 D. 712.) In England it has been held that, if a tenant for life has power to appoint a fund at her death, the mere fact that she is restrained from anticipating her life interest is no ground for holding that the power is exercisable only by will—*In re Waddington*, 1897, W. N. 6 (Romer, J.); Farwell on Powers (3rd Ed.), p. 197.

Thus, in *Alves* v. *Alves*,[1] trustees were directed to hold the residue and to pay the revenue to the truster's widow, and on her death to divide the capital into three parts. Of these one third was to be paid to such person as the widow should direct " by any testamentary or other writing under her hand." The widow did not exercise the power. It was found that this third had not vested in her, but fell into residue. The expression " other writing " was interpreted to mean any *mortis causa* deed, because this was indicated by the facts : (1) that the writing could not take effect till her death, when alone the trustees were directed to pay ; and (2) that the fund (being residue) was to be distributed on the widow's death, and, therefore, the amounts of the respective shares could not be ascertained until the time appointed for distribution arrived.

Similarly, in *Reid* v. *Reid's Trs.*,[2] where the testator made a direct bequest (without the intervention of a trust) of his whole estate to his sister, " for her sole and separate use in liferent, and at her own option as to destination in the event of her death," it was held that the power was testamentary, and that the legatee was a liferenter.

Again, where the power is to dispose of the subject by *inter vivos* deeds or acts alone, the liferenter's interest is not enlarged. The liferenter who is the donee of such a power can make the subject his property by exercising the power,[3] but in so far as the power is not exercised, the subject will not be carried by his will. In *Miller's Trs.* v. *Findlay*,[4] a power was given to a liferentrix " *during her life* to sell, burden, or otherwise dispose onerously or gratuitously." It was held that the subject was not carried by the liferenter's will.

And a provision authorising a liferentrix to encroach upon the capital does not convert her right into a fee. Thus in *Sprot* v. *Pennycook*,[5] a liferentrix was given " liberty to appropriate out of the stock . . . such sum or sums, from time to time, as she may find needful for her own use, over and above the free income, or as she desires to have for her

---

[1] (1861), 23 D. 712.   [4] (1896), 24 R. 114.

[2] (1899), 1 F. 969.   [5] (1855), 17 D. 840.

[3] *Howe's Trs.* v. *Howe's Jud. Factor* (1903), 5 F. 1099.

own purposes and disposal, without limitation or restriction as to the amount of such sum or sums." A *mortis causa* disposition of the subject by the liferenter was held to be *ultra vires*. The extent of the powers conferred on the liferenter by such clauses appears to depend entirely on the manner in which they are expressed in the will. But even when the liferentrix has the power of appropriating the whole subject for her requirements or comfort, that does not entitle her to dispose of it by will ; she may make the whole her own by using it, but it is not within her power to give away what has not been required by her in her lifetime.[1]

A power to borrow is not a general power, and does not raise the liferent to a fee.[2]

Power of appointment given to a married woman. Again, where a liferent is given to a married woman and the fee to her issue, and a power of disposal is given to the liferentrix failing issue, the liferent is not regarded as a fee.[3] In the leading case of *Pursell* v. *Elder*,[4] the truster made a gift of the interest of a sum of money to his niece. He declared that it was " destined to her use and for the benefit of her offspring " ; that it was to be exclusive of the *jus mariti*, and was for the purpose of securing her in the necessaries of life ; and that " at her death the principal sum " should " devolve upon her children," whom failing on the testator's heirs. There was a residuary clause in the will. By a codicil the gift-over to the heirs was revoked, and the truster committed to the liferentrix's " discretion alone, as she may hereafter see cause, *the sole and ultimate disposal of* " the sum. It was held, on the death of the liferentrix without children, that the fee had not vested in her, but fell into residue. Lord Westbury noticed the case in which a grant of absolute powers might be equivalent to a fee,[5] and added : " But if a gift is made to a *femme couvert*, and provision is made for her children, and then these words are annexed to the gift, that in the event of her

---

[1] Contrast *Reddie's Trs.* v. *Lindsay* (1890), 17 R. 558 with dicta in *Thomson* v. *Smith* (1849), 12 D. 276. See also *Barr's Trs.* v. *Barr's Trs.* (1891), 18 R. 541 ; and *M'Kinlay's Trs.* (1898), 5 S. L. T. 253 (Lord Pearson) ; *Young's Trs.* v. *Young* (1899), 7 S. L. T. 266 (Lord Kyllachy).

[2] *Boustead* v. *Gardner* (1879), 7 R. 139 (case of a reserved liferent).

[3] See *Rattray's Trs.* v. *Rattray* (1899), 1 F. 510.

[4] (1865), 3 M. (H. L.) 59.

[5] *Supra*, p. 378.

having no children the property is committed to her discretion alone, as she may thereafter think fit to deal with it, those are words which, having regard to the reference to her discretion, and to the cause for the exercise of that discretion, and to the fact that they are annexed to a gift made to a *femme couvert* who is not *sui juris*, must, I think, in conformity with every principle, and, so far as I know, in conformity with every authority, be held to amount only to an indication of intention that the *femme couvert* shall have a power of appointment or of disposition, and not to be indicative of an intention that the *femme couvert* shall become the absolute owner." [1]

Again, the fact that there is no disposal of the subject in the event of the non-exercise of the power, and that in that event it will fall into intestacy, is not sufficient to lead to the conclusion that the donee was intended to take in fee. [2]

The question is raised by the case of *Howe's Trs.* v. *Howe's Judicial Factor*, [3] whether an unqualified gift of a liferent, with an absolute *jus disponendi* superadded, vests the property in the party to whom these are given, or whether an exercise of the power of disposal is required. In that case the testator gave his estate to his wife in liferent, and to his children in fee, whom failing to his heirs whomsoever. He proceeded to empower his widow, " in case she may desire the same for her own personal comfort, or for the maintenance and education of such child or children of the marriage, or the promotion of their prospects in life, to use and apply for these purposes " the whole or part of the capital : also, " in case of the failure of·children, to test upon or execute conveyances *inter vivos* or settlements *mortis causa* . . . so as to sopite the destination to " the husband's heirs ; and failing exercise of the power, the estate was to go to these heirs. [4] There was no issue of the marriage. The wife survived the husband, and died without exercising

Whether an exercise of the power is required to vest the fee.

---

[1] In *Mackenzie's Trs.* v. *Kilmarnock's Trs.*, 1909 S. C. 472, Lord M'Laren observed : " According to the judgement of the House of Lords in *Pursell* v. *Elder*, a protected life interest in a married woman can never be expanded into a fee, even where a plenary power of disposal is given along with it."

[2] *Reid* v. *Reid's Trs.* (1899), 1 F. 969.

[3] (1903), 5 F. 1099.

[4] This destination-over would appear to exclude the contention that the liferentrix was fiar, *supra*, p. 380.

the power. In a question between the husband's heirs and the factor on the widow's estate, it was held that the widow had only a right of liferent, and that the destination to the husband's heirs was operative. Lord Trayner said : " A liferent coupled with an absolute right of disposal is regarded as a fee in the general case, but not in every case, and it has been determined that where the exercise of the power of disposal is necessary in order to create a right of fee, no such right is created as long as the power remains unexercised. On this point I adopt the language of Lord M'Laren upon Wills (§ 2020 *seq.*), and I am therefore of opinion that while Mrs Howe, by exercising the power conferred upon her, might have turned her right into one of fee, she not having done so, her right at the time of her death was one of liferent and nothing more."

The proposition, that the exercise if the *jus disponendi* may be required to lodge the fee in the nominal liferenter, appears to rest solely upon the authority of this case. It cannot be said, however, that this question was presented for decision in the previous cases, for in all of these (with one exception) the powers granted fell short of the absolute power of disposal ; and in the exceptional case (*Rattray's Trs.* v. *Rattray* [1]) the power was in any case exercised. In English Law a gift to A. indefinitely, and without words expressing his interest, with a general power of disposition superadded, vests the absolute property in A. without appointment ; [2] but in the case of a gift to A. *for life*, with a power of disposal added, " unless the power is exercised, it does not pass to A. or those who take from him by descent, as it would if vested in him absolutely." [3] This distinction was apparently present to the mind of Lord Westbury in stating the law in the passage already quoted from his opinion in *Pursell* v. *Elder*,[4] for he speaks of a gift to an

[1] *Supra*, p. 379. In cases such as *Sprot* v. *Pennycook, supra,* the exercise of the power is required, the reason being that the exercise is the only measure of the extent of the (limited) power granted.

[2] *Bradly* v. *Westcott* (1807), 13 Ves. 445 ; *Langham* v. *Nenny* (1797), 3 Ves. 467 ; *In re Maxwell's Will* (1857), 24 Beav. 246 ; Sugden on Powers, chapter iv,, sec. 1. 9 11 ; *Ex parte Gilchrist* (1886), 17 Q. B. D. 521. (Fry's, L.J., opinion.)

[3] Per Romilly, M. R., in *In re Maxwell's Will, supra* ; *Scott* v. *Josselyn* (1859), 26 Beav. 174 ; *Reith* v. *Seymour* (1828), 4 Russ. 263 ; *In re Van Hagan* (1880), 16 Ch. D. 18 ; Farwell on Powers (3rd Ed.), pp. 62 and 74.

[4] *Ante,* p. 378.

individual " without words of limitation or a declaration of the extent of his ownership."

Hitherto the cases considered have been those where a liferent was conferred by the grantor or testator on a beneficiary. In the case of a reserved liferent, the retention of a power of disposal may probably more easily be construed as equivalent to a reservation of the right of property in the subject ; [1] and, if the power reserved is one of absolute disposal, the grantor or testator remains fiar. In *Baillie* v. *Clark*,[2] for example, a father took a conveyance to himself in liferent and to his son *nominatim* in fee, reserving to himself full power to burden or dispose of the lands at his pleasure. According to the words of the destination, taken by themselves, the fee was in the son ; but the powers reserved were those of a fiar, and because of this reservation it was held that the fee remained with the father.

Reserved powers of disposal.

(2) **Gift to a Party in Liferent and to his Issue *Nascituris* in Fee.** — In the celebrated case of *Frog's Creditors* v. *His Children*,[3] it was established as a settled rule of construction that where a conveyance was made to one in liferent and to his issue unnamed or unborn in fee, the fee was in the parent, and the children had only a hope of succession. In that case a heritable subject was directly conveyed to A. in liferent and to the heirs lawfully to be procreated of his body in fee, and failing of him by decease without heirs of his body, to other parties in liferent and their issue in fee, which all failing, to the disponer's " nearest lawful heirs whatsoever " ; and it was held, in a question

The rule of Frog's Creditors.

---

[1] *Earl of Dunfermline* v. *Earl of Callander* (1676), M. 2941 ; *Cuming* v. *Ld. Adv.* (1756), M. 4268 and 15854 ; 3 Ross's L. C. (Land Rights) 712 ; *Davidson* v. *Davidson* (1687), M. 3255 ; *Dickson* v. *Dickson* (1780), M. 4269 ; 3 Ross's L. C. (Land Rights) 715 ; *Anderson* v. *Young & Trotter* (1784), M. 4128. Cf. opinions in *Morris* v. *Tenant* (1855), 27 S. J. 546 ; 18 D. (H. L.) 42.

[2] 23rd Feb. 1809, F. C ; 3 Ross, L. C. 713. This case is referred to in *Scott* v. *Maxwell* (1854), 26 S. J. 535 ; 17 D. (H. L.) 15.

[3] (1735), M. 4262 ; 3 Ross's Leading Cases (Land Rights), 602 ; *Dewar* v. *M'Kinnon* (1825), 3 Ross's L. C. 607 ; 1 W. & S. 161 (fee to heir-male of a marriage) ; *Lillie* v. *Riddell* (1741), M. 4267 ; *Douglas* v. *Ainslie* (1761), M. 4269 ; *Campbell of Ederline* v. *M'Neil* (1766), M. 4287 (fee to heirs-male of liferenter) ; *Williamson* v. *Cochran* (1828), 6 S. 1035 ; 3 Fac. 1060 ; *Lindsay* v. *Dott* (1807), M. " Fiar," App. 1 (" Children procreated or to be procreated ").

between A's. creditors and his children, that A. was the
fiar. This rule of construction, under which a nominal
liferent was raised to a fee, was rendered necessary, it was
thought, by the requirement of the feudal law that a fee
should not be left *in pendente*. In subsequent cases this
" purely arbitrary rule " [1] was condemned as violating the
clearly expressed intention of the maker of the deed. It
could not be over-ruled, but the Court set itself so far as
possible to limit its application.[2] Sixty years after the date
of *Frog's Creditors*, a deep inroad on the rule was made by
the decision in *Newlands* v. *Newland's Creditors* [3] to the effect
that it was inapplicable where the liferent was qualified by
the word " allenarly." In such cases the difficulty as to
the pendency of the fee was overcome by holding that a
fiduciary fee was lodged in the parent for behoof of the
children.[4] It is clear that if this solution had occurred to
the judges who decided *Frog's Creditors*, it might equally
well have been adopted in that case ; for the addition of
the word " allenarly " makes no substantial difference in
the expression of the testator's or grantor's intention.[5] The
effect of the decision in *Newlands* was, it has been said, that
" a new subtlety was evoked to redress the balance disturbed
by the regretted enforcement of the former subtlety." [6] But
the " new subtlety " commended itself inasmuch as it preserved the grantor's intended disposition from frustration
under the rule established in the earlier decision ; and the
example thus set was followed in the course of the later
cases, in all of which a like anxiety to narrow, so far as
possible, the scope of that rule is apparent. Finally in
1921, when the Trusts (Scotland) Act [7] was passed, the
opportunity was taken of clearing up this branch of the
law. Section 8 of that Act (put shortly) provides that a
liferent shall not be deemed to be a fee by reason only of

---

[1] *Per* Lord M'Laren in *Gifford's Trs.*
v. *Gifford* (1903), 5 F. 723.

[2] *Gifford's Trs.* v. *Gifford, supra* ;
Ld. Pres. Inglis in *Cumstie* v. *Cumstie's
Trs.* (1876), 3 R. 921 ; *Brash's Trs.* v.
Phillipson, 1916 S. C. 271 ; *Mearns*
v. *Charles*, 1926 S. L. T. 119 (Lord
Moncrieff).

[3] (1794), M. 4289 ; 3 Ross's L. C.
(Land Rights) 634.

[4] For the meaning and effect of a
fiduciary, see p. 392 *post*.

[5] *Per* Lord Loughborough, L. C.,
in *Newlands* v. *Newlands' Creditors,
supra* ; *Lockhart's Trs.* v. *Lockhart*,
1921 S. C. 761.

[6] *Per* Lord Ardmillan in *Cumstie* v.
Cumstie's Trs., supra.

[7] 11 & 12 Geo. V. c. 58.

the absence of the word " allenarly," and that in all cases that word is to be read into the deed. By the second subsection the liferenter is enabled to apply to the Court for powers, and the Court is also empowered to appoint trustees to hold the subjects. The section applies in cases where the liferent opens after the date of the passing of the Act.

The effect of this legislation is apparently that in cases where, under the rule of *Newlands* case, a fiduciary fee would be lodged in the liferenter owing to the use of the word " allenarly," a like result is to obtain, although that word does not appear in the deed. The decision in *Frog's Creditors* by which the nominal liferent was converted into a fee has thus become of little more than historical interest. But as the rule of that case enters so deeply into the decisions in the past regarding gifts in liferent and fee, and as, moreover, it is possible that cases may arise as to liferents taking effect before the date of the statute or conferred by English trust deeds,[1] it has been thought well to retain the following note of the decisions as to the application of the rule.

The decision in *Frog's* case related to a heritable subject, but it was early established that it applied also in the case of moveable property.[2] Nor was its application confined to deeds in the shape of a direct conveyance ; it was applicable to testamentary deeds and even, in certain cases, to trust settlements.[3] But it is doubtful whether there was any place for it in conveyances or destinations by one spouse in favour of the other, or in matrimonial deeds under which property was settled on children of the marriage in fee.[4]

Where the disposition or bequest was in favour of a parent in liferent and a named child in fee, the word " liferent " received its natural interpretation, there being no difficulty in such cases as to the lodgement of the fee.[5]

---

[1] In *Cripps's Trs.* v. *Cripps*, 1926 S. C. 188, it was held that the Act did not apply to an English trust-deed, although it related to heritage in Scotland.

[2] *Ralston* v. *Hamilton* (1862), 4 Macq. 397 ; *Mure* v. *Mure*, 1786, M.

4288 ; *Macintosh* v. *Gordon* (1845), 4 Bell's App. ; 3 Ross's L. C. 617.

[3] See *post*, p. 398.

[4] *MacKellar* v. *Marquis* (1840), 3 D. 172 ; 3 Ross's L. C. 741 ; *Lockhart's Trs.* v. *Lockhart*, 1921 S. C. 761.

[5] *M'Intosh* v. *M'Intosh*, 28th Jan. 1812, F. C. ; 3 Ross's L. C. 708.

In a gift to A. in liferent and his children *natis nominatim* and to children *nascituris*, the fee vests in the children named, for behoof of themselves and for those who may be subsequently born ; [1] and in *Martin's Trs.* v. *Milliken*,[2] where a named individual was called to the fee along with the children, the fee was held to vest in him, subject to defeasance as children came into existence. But, if the terms of the deed were such as to fall within the rule of *Frog's Creditors*, the circumstance that members of the class to whom the fee was in terms given were in existence at the time when the deed was made or came into operation was not sufficient to confine the parent to a liferent, because the rights of the parties fell to be determined by the provisions of the will, and not by extrinsic circumstances.[3]

Nor, apparently, was the principle excluded by the fact that the deed provided for the disposal of the fee in the event of failure of issue : [4] thus, in *Mackintosh* v. *Gordon*,[5] where a sum of money was provided to a natural daughter in liferent on her marriage with A., and to the issue to be procreated of the marriage in fee, whom failing to A., the daughter was held to be a fiar.

Applied only to dispositions to parent and child. The rule applied only to gifts to parents and children, and not to cases where the parties were not so related. This opinion was expressed by Lord President Inglis in *Cumstie* v. *Cumstie's Trs.*,[6] where the parties called to the fee were described as " heirs whomsoever " of the liferenter. In *Ramsay* v. *Beveridge*,[7] where the residue of an estate was directly conveyed to two brothers and a sister in liferent, and to the issue of the sister in fee, it was observed, in the opinion of the Lord Justice-Clerk (Hope), that the fee could

---

[1] *Dykes and Boyd* v. *Boyd*, 3rd June 1813, F. C. ; *Macgowan* v. *Robb* (1864), 2 M. 943 ; *ante*, pp. 196 and 273.

[2] (1864), 3 M. 326.

[3] *Ferguson's Trs.* v. *Hamilton* (1860), 22 D. 1442 ; affd. 4 Macq. 397 ; 24 D. (H. L.) 34 ; *M'Clymont's Exrs.* v. *Osborne* (1895). 22 R. 411 ; *Beveridges* v. *Beveridge's Trs.* (1878), 5 R. 1116 ; *Lindsay* v. *Dott* (1807), M. " Fiar," App. No. 1.

[4] *Vide* Lord Moncreiff's opinion in *Gifford's Trs.* v. *Gifford, supra* ; Lord Watson in *Studd* v. *Cook* (1883), 10 R. (H. L.) 53.

[5] (1845), 4 Bell's App. 105, 3 Ross's L. C., p. 607 ; *Allardice* v. *Allardice* (1795) Bell's Folio Cases, 3 Ross, L. C. 655 ; *Mearns* v. *Charles*, 1926 S. L. T. 118 (Lord Moncrieff).

[6] (1876), 3 R. 921.

[7] (1854), 16 D. 764.

not be in the brothers, and that there would be difficulty even in holding the sister to be a fiar, seeing that her liferent and her children's right of fee did not coincide in extent.

Again, it was well settled that the rule of *Frog's Creditors* was excluded not only where the liferent was qualified by the words " allenarly," [1] or " only," or " merely," [2] but also where similar expressions of an intention to limit the parent's estate were used in the destination ; [3] and a description of the liferent as " alimentary " was held to have the same effect. [4] On the other hand, the force of the word " allenarly " might be overcome by a context indicating that the testator intended the parent to have more than a liferent (as, for example, if a power of disposal was given [5]) ; but in that case the liferent was raised to a fee, not in obedience to the principle of construction here considered, but because of the testator's expressions of intention.

Again, although no taxative words appeared in the deed, the rule of *Frog's Creditors* was not, it was laid down, " an inflexible rule, but must yield to reasonable presumption that the maker of the deed intended otherwise." [6] Thus, in *Maule*,[7] although the liferent was not described as " allenarly " in the words of disposition, the party was limited to a liferent because in other parts of the deed his

Effect of the word " allenarly " or context.

---

[1] *Newlands* v. *Newlands' Creditors* (1794), M. 4289 ; 3 Ross's Leading Cases (Land Rights), p. 634 ; *Allardice* v. *Allardice* (1795), Bell's Fol. Cas. 156 ; 3 Ross's L. C. 655.

[2] *Vide* Lord Ardmillan's opinion in *Cumstie* v. *Cumstie's Trs.* (1876), 3 R. 921 ; *Beveridges* v. *Beveridge's Trs.* (1878), 5 R. 1116 ; *Campbell* v. *Campbell* (1843), 5 D. 1083.

[3] *Per* L. J.-C. Moncreiff in *Beveridges* v. *Beveridge's Trs., supra ; Miller* v. *Miller* (1833), 12 S. 31 ; *Young* v. *Watson* (1835), 14 S. 85 ; 11 Fac. 64.

[4] *Gerran* (1781), M. 4402 ; *Douglas* v. *Sharpe* (1811), Hume's Decs., p. 173 ; *Dawson* (1877), 4 R. 597 ; Ivory's Note to Ersk., iii. 8. 36. Contrast *Hutton's Trs.* v. *Hutton*

(1847), 9 D. 639 ; and *Kennedy* v. *Allan* (1825), 3 S. 554.

[5] Ld. Pres. Inglis in *Cumstie* v. *Cumstie's Trs., supra.* Cf. opinions in this case as to the influence of " allenarly " in cases of *reserved* liferents.

[6] *Per* Lord Watson in *Studd* v. *Cook* (1883), 10 R. (H. L.) 53. See also *Lockhart's Trs.* v. *Lockhart*, 1921 S. C. 761 ; *Ramsay* v. *Beveridge, supra ; Gifford's Trs.* v. *Gifford* (1903), 5 F. 723 (*post*, p. 401)) ; *Napier* v. *Scott* (1827), 2 W. & S. 550 ; *Watson* v. *Watson* (1854), 16 D. 803 ; *Rait* v. *Arbuthnott* (1892), 19 R. 687.

[7] (1876), 3 R. 831. Cf. also *Livingstone* v. *Waddell's Trs.* (1899), 1 F. 831.

rights and powers were defined by way of contrast with those of a proprietor in fee.

Vesting in children where parent is fiduciary fiar.

Where the fiduciary fee is lodged in the liferenter, he holds the subject in trust for the persons called to the fee ; [1] but it is only technically a trust, and his powers are simply those of a liferenter.[2] In the case of a gift to A. in liferent allenarly and his children *nascituris* in fee, the substantial fee vests in the children as they are born,[3] unless the terms in which they are called are inconsistent with vesting before the termination of the liferent, as, for example, where they are described as heirs of the body,[4] or where the gift is limited to the survivors.[5]

Application of doctrine of fiduciary fee.

The doctrine of the fiduciary fee was originally applied in the case of destinations to a parent in liferent and his children *nascituri* in fee ; and for long it remained uncertain whether it was applicable to dispositions in favour of others than children of the liferenter. As the fiduciary fee was a device invented in order to give effect to the grantor's intention, and as it has no other effect than to constitute the liferenter a bare trustee, it might be thought to be available in all cases where the expressed intention of the grantor was liable to be defeated by the principle forbidding that the fee should be *in pendente*. But this extension of the doctrine of the fiduciary fee has never been sanctioned. In *Elmslie* v. *Fraser*,[6] Lord Fullerton said : " Is this doctrine to be carried beyond the case of a fiduciary fee for behoof

---

[1] " The father in such a case is merely a trustee for his son."—Ld. J.-C. Braxfield in *Preston* v. *Welwood*, (1791), Bell's Oct. Cases, 198.

[2] *Harvey* v. *Donald*, 26th May 1815, F. C. (noticed in *Martin's Trs.* v. *Milliken* (1864), 3 M. 326) ; Lord Ardmillan in *Cumstie* v. *Cumstie's Trs.* (1876), 3 R. 921. Cf. also Lord Fullerton's opinion in *Elmslie* v. *Fraser, infra*; Fraser on Husband and Wife, p. 1453.

[3] *Beattie's Trs.* v. *Cooper's Trs.* (1862), 24 D. 519 ; *Robertson* (1869), 7 M. 1114 (*ante*, p. 216) ; *Douglas* v. *Thomson* (1870), 8 M. 374 ; *Maule* (1876), 3 R. 831, *per* Ld. Pres. Inglis, at 836.

[4] *Ferguson* v. *Ferguson* (1875), 2 R. 627 ; *Black* v. *Mason* (1881), 8 R. 497.

[5] *Snell* v. *White* (1872), 10 M. 745. In this case the disposition was to A. in liferentallenarly and to her daughter and children *nascituris* " and the survivors " in fee, and " failing the said child or children " to others. The children as they were born acquired a beneficial interest, subject to defeasance in favour of those children who survived A. Two children were alive at A.'s death (others having predeceased) ; these took the whole subject. The gift-over was construed as a conditional institution, which was defeated by the existence of children at A.'s death.

[6] (1850), 12 D. 724 ; 3 Ross, L. C. 679.

of the children of the liferenter himself ? We can conceive a disposition to A. in liferent allenarly and to the children *nascituri* of B. in fee. No doubt the fee is vested in A. so as to take it out of the grantor ; but can it be said that A., who has no connexion with the children of B., is to be looked on as a trustee for them ? That is a very delicate question."

The question was not decided in this case and it did not arise for decision till 1876. In *Cumstie* v. *Cumstie's Trs.*,[1] the destination in the deed before the Court was to A. in liferent allenarly and his " heirs whomsoever " in fee. It was decided that there might be a fiduciary fee where the destination was to the heirs of the liferenter.

In subsequent cases the question of a further extension of the doctrine has been more than once canvassed. Thus, in *Allen* v. *Flint*,[2] a heritable property was conveyed to the disponer's children in liferent allenarly and to their issue in fee, equally among them. On a construction of this bequest, it was held that the granter's grandchildren took the subject *per stirpes*. Each child was therefore the fiduciary fiar for his own family. But in examining the argument submitted in favour of a distribution *per capita*, Lord President Inglis pointed out that that construction would create a serious difficulty as to the fiduciary fee. The rights of the children could only be secured by the fiction of a fiduciary fee, and, therefore, under the proposed construction, it would be necessary to hold that the liferenters were fiduciary fiars for the children of them all as one class jointly interested in the bequest. This, however, his Lordship observed, would be a great anomaly.

So also, in *Logan's Trs.* v. *Ellis*,[3] trustees were directed to divide the residue of the truster's estate among his children and to lay out and invest the shares, taking the writings in favour of his daughters, to the extent of their interests, in liferent and their children in fee, whom failing to the unmarried daughters for their liferent use allenarly,

---

[1] *Supra.* Lord Deas dissented, holding that the liferenter was restricted merely as between him and his children ; and that as against remoter heirs he took the fee.

[2] (1886), 13 R. 975.

[3] (1890), 17 R. 425. But contrast *Allardice* v. *Allardice, post.* p. 397.

whom failing to the married daughters in liferent and their issue in fee, etc. The Court rejected as inadmissible the proposition that each daughter could be held a fiduciary fiar not only for her issue, but for a series of other liferenters and fiars.

Again, in the case of *Tristram* v. *M'Haffies*,[1] a disposition was made directly in favour of the disponer's two sons, William and Alexander, " equally between them, and failing either of them without lawful issue, to the survivor of them, the lawful issue of the predeceaser always coming in place of their parent, in liferent . . . allenarly, and to their lawful children equally among them, share and share alike, in fee." Both William and Alexander survived their father. William died leaving issue, and thereafter Alexander died without issue. It was held that each had held the fiduciary fee of a half-share for behoof of his children, and that on Alexander's death his portion fell into intestacy. The Court rejected the argument that the substantial fee of the whole had vested in William's children, and that a fiduciary fee was held for their behoof by Alexander as well as by their father. Lord M'Laren observed : " It is not necessary to affirm that under no circumstances can a liferenter be also a fiduciary fiar for grantees other than his own issue. But it was pointed out by the late Lord President in the case of *Allen* v. *Flint*, that there are serious theoretical difficulties in admitting a construction which would make each liferenter a fiduciary fiar for his own children in conjunction with the children of the other liferenter. In the present case the supposed construction, for example, would make William M'Haffie fiduciary fiar for Alexander's children, as well as his own children. On William's death, Alexander had no children, but it was possible that children might be born to him. How is it possible that their interests should be safeguarded, seeing that the fiduciary fee in William's half-share comes to an end with William's life ? The difficulty—I may say the impossibility—of explicating such a destination is a very strong argument against the supposition that such rights were intended to be created, and in favour of the supposition that each liferenter was a fiduciary fiar for his own children only to the effect that the children should take collectively the

---

[1] (1894), 22 R. 121. Cf. *Turner* v. *Gaw* (1894), 21 R. 563.

fee of the one-half share which was liferented by the parent."
Lord Kinnear dissented, holding that, in the circumstances
of the case, Alexander was fiduciary fiar for William's
children. It was admitted in the opinions, that had the
childless brother died first the survivor would have taken a
liferent and a fiduciary fee of the whole. But when the
survivor died without issue, his share was not taken by the
descendants of the predeceaser, but lapsed into intestacy.

The question was again raised in *Colville's Trs.* v. *Marin-
den.*[1] Miss Margaret Blackburn, by disposition and settlement, disponed a bond and disposition in security to her
grandnieces, nine in number, and the survivors of them in
liferent while they remained unmarried, and on the marriage
or death of all of these to the heir of entail in possession of
certain estates in fee. Of this destination the Lord President
(Dunedin) observed : " I think Miss Margaret Blackburn
attempted an impossibility in conveyancing. She, being in
right of the bond and disposition in security, disponed that
bond and disposition in security in favour of a certain
number of unmarried liferentrices who were alive. That, of
course, was quite good. But then she proceeded to dispose
of the fee to a person unknown, who might or might not be
in existence—namely, the person who at the expiry of these
liferents would possess the character of heir of entail under
a certain entail—and she did that by means of a direct
conveyance without the interposition of a trust. As I say,
I think that is a conveyancing impossibility. We are all
familiar with the case of *Frog's Creditors*, and it has again
and again been said that the principle of *Frog's Creditors*
would not be extended. *Frog's Creditors* decided that a
disposition to a parent in liferent and children in fee will
be construed as a fee in the parent, and in the subsequent
case of *Newlands* there is introduced a fiduciary fee in the
parent where the liferent is a liferent allenarly. There was
a difference of judicial opinion, with very high authorities
on both sides, in *Cumstie's Trs.*, but I will be content to
take the result of what was arrived at in *Cumstie's Trs.*,
namely that you could have a fiduciary fee for heirs whomsoever ; but I have never yet heard—and I do not think that
we ought to extend the doctrine—of the doctrine of a

[1] 1908 S. C. 911.

fiduciary fee for somebody who is neither a child nor an heir in any sense of the person in whom the fiduciary fee is created. Accordingly I think that what Miss Blackburn wanted to do, if it could be done effectually, could only have been done by the interposition of a trust."

This authoritative dictum has been brought under the consideration of the Court in the cases of *Devlin* v. *Lowrie* [1] and *Cripps's Trs.* v. *Cripps*,[2] In the former a heritable subject was disponed to two sisters " in conjunct fee and liferent for their alimentary liferent use allenarly and the heirs of the survivor." It was decided after the death of one of the liferenters that the survivor was fiar *fiduciarie* for her heirs. In the argument attention was directed to the position of the fee while both liferenters were in life ; but the Court, stressing the words in Lord Dunedin's dictum, " heirs in any sense of the person in whom the fiduciary fee is created," were of opinion that the fiduciary fee then resided in the liferentrices conjunctly. This was held to involve no extension of the doctrine of the fiduciary fee.[3]

In the later case it was indicated that there was no incongruity in a liferenter being regarded as fiduciary fiar for behoof not only of the institutes, his own children, but also of those persons who were called under an elaborate destination in the event of failure of such children.

Successive Liferents. A further point occurred in this case. Under the destination the lands were destined to the testator's widow in liferent in the event, which happened, of her survivance, and " subject thereto " to his eldest son in liferent. The interposition of the widow's right was considered to be no obstacle to the vesting of a fiduciary fee in the son. Lord Ormidale thought that under the phraseology of the deed the son's liferent right vested, though not beneficially, *a morte testatoris* ; while the Lord Justice-Clerk (Alness), with whom Lord Anderson concurred, saw " no reason why a liferenter in *posse*, equally with a liferenter in *esse*, should not be a fiduciary fiar." This theory would seem to involve a considerable extension of the doctrine of the fiduciary fee,

---

[1] 1922 S. C. 255.
[2] 1926 S. C. 188.
[3] The Court founded on the decisions in *Watterstone* v. *Rentons*

(1801) M. 4297 ; *Rollo* v. *Ramsay* (1832), 11 S. 132 ; *Bryson* v. *Munro's Trs.* (1893), 20 R. 986.

and it would appear also to be not altogether consistent with other decisions.

In *Allardice* v. *Allardice*,[1] the disposition was in favour of the grantor's eldest son in liferent allenarly and to the heirs of his body by any future marriage in fee, which failing to his second son in liferent allenarly and the heirs of his body in fee, which failing to the grantor's own nearest heirs and assignees in fee. It was argued that the eldest son could not be fiduciary fiar for his brother and his children, but this argument did not weigh with the Court. The Lord Justice-Clerk (Braxfield) observed : " I own I did not see a question in this case. The only difference betwixt it and *Newlands* is that there is here a succession of liferenters, but there is nothing in that."

Again, in *Campbell* v. *Duncan*[2] the question arose in regard to a disposition in favour of the grantor's daughter (Mrs Duncan) and her son and the survivor of them in liferent allenarly in the order mentioned and to the heirs of the body of the son with a further destination. It was held here that the fiduciary fee was in the daughter, and on her death in her son. " No case," said the Lord Ordinary (Skerrington), " was cited where a postponed liferenter duly infeft, but whose possession was contingent on survivance, was held to be a fiduciary fiar in preference to a liferenter infeft and in possession. A legal fiction ought not to be extended beyond what is absolutely necessary, and in such cases simplicity is preferable to logical consistency. I hold that Mrs Duncan, so long as she was liferentrix, was also the fiduciary fiar, but that on her death both rights came to an end, and that a fiduciary fee was thenceforth vested in the person of the defender as the liferenter in succession."

The theory of a fiduciary fee in the liferenter was accepted, as has been seen, as affording a means of escape from *Frog's Creditors*. But where in the deed conferring the liferent a continuing trust was set up, no difficulty could arise as to

Rule of Frog's Creditors excluded where a trust is constituted.

---

[1] (1795), Bell's Folio Cases, 156 ; 3 Ross L. C. 655. This case may be open to the explanation that as the first liferenter's issue were the primary institutes, and as issue might at any time during his life come into existence, he was fiduciary fiar for behoof of such issue ; but see Lord Eskgrove's opinion.

[2] (1913), 1 S. L. T. 260

the situation of the fee. The appointment of trustees to hold the funds or estate removed all difficulty as to the pendency of the fee, the trustees supplying the place of the non-existent fiars. Thus, where a father bound himself to invest a sum in land or heritable securities, taking the titles in the names of trustees for behoof of A. in liferent and the heirs of the marriage in fee, it was held that A. was merely a liferenter.[1]

But it was necessary that it should appear that the testator intended that the trust management should be continued during the subsistence of the liferent.

Hence, if the trustees were merely directed to make payment or to denude of a subject, as the trust, in regard to the subject, terminated at the time appointed for payment, the difficulty of thereafter finding a lodgement for the fee admitted the rule of *Frog's Creditors*. For example, in *Ralston* v. *Hamilton*,[2] the testator appointed trustees, and directed that certain sums should be paid to the beneficiaries at the first term occurring after twelve months from his death. One of these sums was given in these terms : " To A. in liferent and his children, equally among them, in fee, £20,000." It was held that, immediate payment being directed, A. was the absolute fiar. A similar decision had been pronounced in the earlier case of *Hutton's Trs.* v. *Hutton*.[3] In that case the testator appointed his trustees to hold for A. in liferent, and on his death to *pay* the share liferented by him to four parties named in liferent and their issue respectively in fee, declaring that the shares of females were to be exclusive of the claims of their husbands or creditors. It was held that on A.'s death the four parties acquired the substantial fee.

Distinction between executory and executed trusts.

In this connexion the distinction between executory and executed trusts was of importance. An executory trust has

---

[1] *Seton* v. *Seton's Creditors*, 1793, M. 4219 ; 3 Ross's L. C. 685. In *Gifford's Trs.* v. *Gifford* (1903), 5 F. 723, Lord Stormonth-Darling observed, in regard to this case, that " the direction to hold, at all events till the birth of an heir, was inferred from the circumstance of the deed being a marriage contract."

[2] (1862), 4 Macq. 397.

[3] (1847), 9 D. 639. See also *Beveridges* v. *Beveridge's Trs.* (1878), 5 R. 1116 ; and *Fraser* (1901), 8 S. L. T. 466 (Lord Kincairney) ; *Mearns* v. *Charles*, 1926 S. L. T. 118 (Lord Moncrieff) ; *Dalrymple's Trs.* v. *Watson*, 1932 S. L. T. 480 (Lord Moncrieff).

been defined [1] as meaning " not simply a trust under which an act has to be done, which applies to every case, but one in which there is something to be performed which is not defined by the original settlor ; where he has expressed an intention in general words which is to be carried out in a complete and legal form by the persons who are entrusted with the estate." This distinction has been frequently noticed in questions arising upon the construction of directions given to trustees as to making an entail of the testator's estates, and as to the manner in which the trustees are to perform this duty. The distinction was, however, also adverted to in *Mitchell's Trs.* v. *Smith*,[2] where the truster, after instructing his trustees to retain his estate for behoof of his children, stated that it was his wish that the shares of his daughters should be settled on them in liferent and their issue in fee. The Court held that it was the duty of the trustees in settling the shares to carry out the truster's wish, and secure the rights of the issue by inserting in any deed of settlement the word " allenarly," or by providing that the shares should be held by trustees.

In the two following cases a direction to make payment was deemed not to be displaced by a subordinate direction that the subject was to be *invested* for behoof of the beneficiaries. In *Macintosh* v. *Gordon*,[3] the deed under consideration was a bond of provision in which a parent obliged himself to pay a sum to his natural daughter in liferent and to the children to be procreated of her marriage in fee. The bond provided that, in the event of the sum being paid up at any time, it should be reinvested at the sight of certain parties. It was argued that this provision rendered the rule of *Frog's Creditors* inadmissible, as it amounted to the creation of a trust ; but the Court rejected the argument, on the ground that the legal character of the parties' rights under the leading clause was not altered by this direction, seeing that the re-investment was to be made in the same terms as those of the original bond. Accordingly, the

Subordinate direction to invest does not exclude the rule.

---

[1] Per Lord St Leonards in *Graham* v. *Stewart* (1855), 2 Macq. 295. See *Sandys* v. *Bain's Trs.* (1897), 25 R. 261, and cases there cited ; Lewin on Trusts (13th Ed.), 77.

[2] (1880), 7 R. 1086 ; *Brash's Trs.* v. *Philipson*, 1916 S. C. 271.

[3] (1845), 4 Bell's App. 105 ; 3 Ross's L. C. 617.

daughter was held to have been fiar. Again, in *M'Clymont's Exrs.* v. *Osborne*,[1] the testator nominated trustees, and directed them, with regard to the residue, " to pay over the same as under . . . one-third of said residue to be invested in " debentures or shares " in name of A., she to receive the interest or dividends from same during her lifetime for the maintenance . . . of her children, and at her death the principal to be divided equally among her children." Here, also, it was held that a fee was conferred on A.

But no technical language is required in order to create a trust, and the Court will yield readily to any indication in the deed that the maker of the deed really intended the subject to be retained.

Continuing
trust implied
from provisions
of the deed. Thus, in *Mein* v. *Taylor*,[2] the granter of the deed conveyed his estate to four parties under the burdens therein mentioned, and declared that " the said subjects should be held by them in liferent and belong to their children in fee." He instructed the disponees to divide the subjects, and directed that certain shares should be held by one of them (A.) in liferent, " and *at his decease* the fee and property thereof " should be divided among his children ; and the disponees or the survivors of them were to see that the shares of A.'s daughters were secured for them in liferent and their issue in fee. There was no mention of a trust in the deed ; but the Court held that the terms of the conveyance clearly implied a trust ; and further, that the directions as to division on A.'s death showed that the trust was to be maintained till that event. A., accordingly, was held to be a mere liferenter.

And so, also, in *Ross* v. *King*,[3] where the direction was in these terms : " It is my will and I hereby direct that my said trustees shall hold . . . in trust for my said son A. in liferent and his lawful issue in fee, whom failing " for a succession of persons in liferent and their issue in fee : " and I ordain my trustees to convey my property accordingly." It was held (as against the assignee of the first liferenter) that the leading instruction to hold controlled the

---

[1] (1895), 22 R. 411. See also *Alexander* v. *Alexander* (1849), 12 D. 345. Cf. *Ewan* v. *Watt* (1828), 6 S. 1125 ; 3 Fac. 1135.

[2] (1830), 4 W. & S. 22.
[3] (1847), 9 D. 1327.

direction to convey, and provided for the continuance of the trust, and that no fee was carried to the nominal liferenter.

Again, the case of *Gifford's Trs.* v. *Gifford* [1] presents a further example of a direction in a deed intermediate in character between the two categories of cases already noticed, for there was no direction to the trustees either to pay or to hold. The testator directed his trustees to hold certain sums for behoof of his son A. and his nephews and nieces in liferent allenarly and of their issue in fee ; to purchase and entail certain lands on A. ; to expend of the remaining residue a specified sum for certain purposes ; and if any surplus remained over and above that sum, " it shall belong one half to my son, the said A., in liferent, and to his issue other than the heirs of entail, in fee, whom failing to my unmarried nieces equally in fee ; and the other half shall belong equally among my unmarried nieces." The question was whether the half of the surplus belonged to A. in liferent or in fee. It was held that A. was merely a liferenter. The opinions in the case are founded largely on the general presumption in favour of the natural interpretation being given to terms occurring in wills ; and the decision appears to be an authority for the proposition that in a trust settlement the rule of *Frog's* case is applicable only where there is an express direction to the trustees to terminate the trust, or to do an act which involves the termination of the trust, in regard to the share given to children *nascituris* in fee. The construction in Lord Gifford's case was aided by the circumstance that the maintenance of the trust management was required and provided in regard to the general purposes of the deed, and that the subject of the gift was the surplus remaining after the fulfilment of these purposes.

Hitherto the rule of *Frog's Creditors* has been discussed with reference to cases in which the rights of the parent and the children are created solely by the disposition in their favour. But where a parent who has a title to lands dispones these to himself in liferent allenarly and to his issue *nascituris* in fee, the question is somewhat different ; for, in order that he shall be divested, it is necessary that

The granter may have fee in virtue of pre-existing title.

[1] (1903), 5 F. 723

infeftment shall be taken in the fee. Thus, in *Falconer* v. *Wright*,[1] a party by his marriage contract conveyed certain lands to which he was heir-apparent, to himself " in liferent for his liferent use allenarly, and the children and bairns of the marriage " in fee. He made up titles, and was infeft " for his liferent use allenarly," but no mention of the fee was made in the instrument of sasine. In a competition between his creditors and his children, it was held that the father was fiar. The *ratio decidendi* was that apart from the disposition he was absolute fiar, and that, as the infeftment following upon the marriage was not an infeftment in the fee, the estate remained unaltered upon the former investiture. Had the father taken infeftment for himself in liferent allenarly and for the children in fee in terms of the marriage contract, his right would have been reduced to a fiduciary fee, and the children would have been vested in the beneficial fee ; but, as it was, while the children were entitled to rank with his creditors in virtue of the personal obligation in the contract, they had no real right in the subjects.

[1] (1824), 2 S. 633 ; 3 S. 455 ; 3 Ross's L. C. 662 ; *Dundas* v. *Dundas* (1823), 2 S. 145 ; *Houlditch* v. *Spald-* *ing* (1847), 9 D. 1204 ; *Stewart* v. *Rae* (1883), 10 R. 463 ; *Thomson* v. *Blair* (1900), 8 S. L. T. 234 (Lord Kyllachy).

INDEX